The Mueller
Investigation and Beyond

The Mueller Investigation and Beyond

Ellen S. Podgor
GARY R. TROMBLEY FAMILY WHITE COLLAR CRIME RESEARCH PROFESSOR
PROFESSOR OF LAW
STETSON UNIVERSITY COLLEGE OF LAW

Katrice Bridges Copeland
PROFESSOR OF LAW
PENN STATE LAW

Michael R. Dimino, Sr.
PROFESSOR OF LAW
WIDENER UNIVERSITY COMMONWEALTH LAW SCHOOL

Ruthann Robson
UNIVERSITY DISTINGUISHED PROFESSOR & PROFESSOR OF LAW
CUNY SCHOOL OF LAW

Louis J. Virelli, III
PROFESSOR OF LAW
STETSON UNIVERSITY COLLEGE OF LAW

Andrew M. Wright
PARTNER, K&L GATES

Ellen C. Yaroshefsky
HOWARD LICHTENSTEIN DISTINGUISHED PROFESSOR OF LEGAL ETHICS AND
EXECUTIVE DIRECTOR OF THE MONROE H. FREEDMAN INSTITUTE FOR THE
STUDY OF LEGAL ETHICS
HOFSTRA UNIVERSITY SCHOOL OF LAW

CAROLINA ACADEMIC PRESS
Durham, North Carolina

Library of Congress Cataloging-in-Publication Data

Names: Podgor, Ellen S., 1952- author.
Title: The Mueller investigation and beyond / Ellen S. Podgor, Katrice
  Bridges Copeland, Michael R. Dimino, Sr., Ruthann Robson, Louis J.
  Virelli, III, Andrew M. Wright, Ellen C. Yaroshefsky.
Description: Durham : Carolina Academic Press, 2019.
Identifiers: LCCN 2019036996 | ISBN 9781531016753 (paperback) | ISBN
  9781531016760 (ebook)
Subjects: LCSH: Presidents--United States--Election--2016. | Propaganda,
  Russian--United States. | Hacking--Russia (Federation) |
  Elections--Corrupt practices--United States. | Political
  campaigns--Corrupt practices--United States. | Trump, Donald, 1946- |
  Mueller, Robert S., III, 1944-
Classification: LCC KF4910 .P63 2019 | DDC 342.73/07--dc23
LC record available at https://lccn.loc.gov/2019036996

eISBN 978-1-5310-1676-0

Carolina Academic Press
700 Kent Street
Durham, North Carolina 27701
Telephone (919) 489-7486
Fax (919) 493-5668
www.cap-press.com

Printed in the United States of America

To Cheryl
Ellen S. Podgor

To Lincoln A. Copeland
Katrice Bridges Copeland

To Jennifer (Dimino)
Michael R. Dimino

For all the Stormys, Summers, and Jane Does
Ruthann Robson

To Meg, Gavin, and Ella
Louis J. Virelli, III

To Caprice Roberts and Garrett Robert Wright
Andrew M. Wright

To Eric Poulos for his unwavering support
Ellen C. Yaroshefsky

Summary of Contents

Contents

Preface

It is impossible to provide in a single legal casebook a comprehensive review and analysis of the Mueller Report and the legal issues arising during the investigation. There are also ongoing matters that make this discussion tentative in many areas. Thus, this book provides discussion of select areas that can assist students with a capstone understanding of different aspects of law. Looking at this investigation allows law students the opportunity to place into a single context many of the concepts they have previously learned in undergraduate or law school.

Chapter One provides a general overview of the appointment and purpose of having a special counsel in this instance. It also covers Special Counsel Robert Mueller's submission of his Report and the statements made by Attorney General Barr upon release of the unredacted portions of the Report. This chapter provides the contextual setting for the later chapters in the book.

Chapter Two looks at the appointment of Special Counsel Robert Mueller and the controversaries raised following his appointment. It examines cases where a special counsel appointment has been reviewed in courts. Both administrative law and constitutional law are the focus of this chapter.

Chapter Three recognizes that Special Counsel's investigation operates parallel to congressional, criminal, and counterintelligence investigations. The role of attorney-client privilege, immunity and compelled testimony are examined here. This chapter includes historical context for examination of these legislative, evidence, criminal law, and administrative issues.

Chapter Four focuses on ethics issues that arose during the Mueller Investigation. It provides a historical setting looking at the Nixon recordings and Watergate, while also examining the law regarding tape recording and the ethical constraints on lawyer secret recordings. It considers public commentary by lawyers who serve as media pundits, and also those who are counsel on a case. This chapter provides examination of professional responsibility issues.

Chapter Five looks at an issue that arose during this investigation, namely, the role of the attorney-client privilege with respect to Michael Cohen, former Trump Organization Executive Vice President and Special Counsel to Donald J. Trump. Considered here is whether Michael Cohen was acting as an attorney providing legal advice or whether his role was one to provide business advice. In conjunction with this review is whether the crime-fraud exception applied to these circumstances. The chapter concludes with a discussion of how to protect the attorney-client privilege when an attorney receives a search warrant. This chapter provides examination of evidence issues.

Chapter Six considers two issues of election law related to the Trump Campaign's behavior surrounding the 2016 election. First, it asks whether, if Trump Campaign officials agreed to receive damaging information about Secretary Hillary Clinton from foreign persons, the Campaign officials violated the federal ban on "accept[ing] or receiv[ing]" a "thing of value" from a foreign national. Second, the chapter addresses whether the payment of hush money to two of Trump's alleged mistresses (and the Campaign's failure to report the payments to the FEC) would constitute illegal contributions to the campaign if the payments were an attempt to prevent the public from learning damaging information about the candidate. This chapter offers an examination of election law issues.

Chapter Seven looks at Obstruction of Justice, the focus of Volume Two of the Mueller Report. It dissects the applicable federal obstruction statutes and considers this with the Mueller Report's legal framework. It then looks at the executive summaries that match the law with the alleged conduct. It concludes by examining statutory and constitutional defenses that were considered during the Mueller Investigation. This chapter offers an examination of criminal law, federal criminal law, and white-collar crime issues.

Chapter Eight, the final chapter in the book, looks beyond the Mueller Report to issues referenced in the report but not a focus of the investigation into Russian interference with the election. It looks at civil lawsuits regarding alleged sexual misconduct by the President. It considers the variety of civil lawsuits, the statute of limitations of these actions, the role of Presidential Immunity, and the doctrine of defamation. This chapter offers an examination of constitutional law, presidential power, civil procedure, and the First Amendment.

Throughout the book there are instances in both cases and other materials where the authors of the chapter edited the material. When there are materials that are edited, the authors typically will use * * * to show that material from the original has been removed. It should also be noted that the authors may have removed footnotes and case citations throughout the materials. The citations or urls are often provided so that students interested in seeing the full cases or other items can go to view this material.

We acknowledge Professor Bradley A. Smith, the Josiah H. Blackmore II/Shirley M. Nault Professor of Law at Capital University Law School for allowing us to reprint a part of his article, *Michael Cohen Pled Guilty to Something That Is Not a Crime*, from the NAT'L REV., Dec. 12, 2018, in Chapter Six of the book.

We thank Cheryl Segal who provided last-minute editorial assistance. The authors also thank the participants in the Southeast Association of Law Schools (SEALS) discussion group on the Mueller Investigation, and specifically Professor Lori Ringhand for her comments regarding Chapter Six, pertaining to Election Law. Thanks also go to research assistant Alexis M. Arnemann (Stetson). In addition, the authors thank Stetson University College of Law's faculty support and specifically Shannon Edgar.

Ellen S. Podgor
Katrice Bridges Copeland
Michael R. Dimino, Sr.
Ruthann Robson
Louis J. Virelli, III
Andrew M. Wright
Ellen C. Yaroshefsky

August 2019

The Mueller
Investigation and Beyond

Chapter One

Introduction

I. Generally

A. Appointment

On May 17, 2017, Acting Attorney General Rod Rosenstein issued Order 3915-2017 for the appointment of a special counsel to investigate Russian interference with the 2016 Presidential election.[1] That Order states:

Appointment of Special Counsel to Investigate Russian Interference with the 2016 Presidential Election and Related Matters

By virtue of the authority vested in me as Acting Attorney General, including 28 U.S.C. §§ 509, 510, and 515, in order to discharge my responsibility to provide supervision and management of the Department of Justice, and to ensure a full and thorough investigation of the Russian government's efforts to interfere in the 2016 presidential election, I hereby order as follows:

(a) Robert S. Mueller III is appointed to serve as Special Counsel for the United States Department of Justice.

(b) The Special Counsel is authorized to conduct the investigation confirmed by then-FBI Director James B. Comey in testimony before the House Permanent Select Committee on Intelligence on March 20, 2017, including:

   (i) any links and/or coordination between the Russian government and individuals associated with the campaign of President Donald Trump; and

---

1. *See Special Counsel Investigations: History, Authority, Appointment and Removal*, Congressional Research Service (Updated March 13, 2019), *available at* https://fas.org/sgp/crs/misc/R44857.pdf (discussing the history of Appointments prior to and after the expiration of the Ethics in Government Act); *see also* Chap. 2 for a discussion of the Mueller's appointment as special counsel.

(ii) any matters that arose or may arise directly from the investigation; and

(iii) any other matters within the scope of 28 C.F.R. §600.4(a).

(c) If the Special Counsel believes it is necessary and appropriate, the Special Counsel is authorized to prosecute federal crimes arising from the investigation of these matters.

(d) Sections 600.4 through 600.10 of Title 28 of the Code of Federal Regulations are applicable to the Special Counsel.

B. Special Counsel Robert Mueller

The individual selected to serve as Special Counsel was Robert Swan Mueller III. Mueller was the "second longest-serving FBI director in the history of the agency,"[2] having served from 2001 to 2013. He received his undergraduate degree from Princeton University, his master's in international relations from New York University, and his J.D. from Virginia Law School. Between his master's degree and attendance at law school he served as a Marine Corp officer in Vietnam, receiving distinctions including the Bronze Star, two Navy Commendation Medals, and the Purple Heart.[3]

In addition to his experience as FBI director, Mueller had prior experience working at several large law firms, and served in several different government prosecution positions including being an Assistant United States Attorney, as Chief of the Criminal Division in the U.S. Attorney's Office for the District of Northern California, and later as the Acting United States Attorney for the District of Massachusetts.[4] He also had served as acting deputy attorney general during George W. Bush's administration.[5]

C. The Special Counsel Investigation

Robert Mueller served as Special Counsel from May 17, 2017, until the close of the Special Counsel's office on May 29, 2019. Mueller's team included at its height nineteen attorneys, of which fourteen "were on detail from the Justice Department."[6] The costs of the investigation are detailed in four Statement of Expenditures provided

---

2. Dareh Gregorian, *Who is Robert Mueller, The Man Behind the Report on Trump?*, NBCNews, *available at* https://www.nbcnews.com/politics/justice-department/who-robert-mueller-man-behind-report-trump-n974296.

3. *See Biography of Robert Mueller, available at* https://www.biography.com/political-figure/robert-mueller.

4. *Id.*

5. *Id.*

6. Olivia Beavers & Morgan Chalfant, *Key Numbers to Know for Mueller's Testimony*, The Hill, July 22, 2019, *available at* //thehill.com/homenews/administration/453941-key-numbers-to-know-for-muellers-testimony; *see also* Noah Weiland, Emil Cochrane & Troy Griggs, *Robert Mueller and His Prosecutors: Who They Are and What They've Done*, Jan. 25, 2019, *available at* https://www.nytimes.com/interactive/2018/11/30/us/mueller-investigation-team-prosecutors.html.

on the Special Counsel's website with the Department of Justice.[7] Although the Special Counsel investigation ended on May 29, 2019, there are continuing ongoing investigations by federal prosecutors.[8]

During this investigation his team "issued over 2,800 subpoenas," "interviewed approximately 500 witnesses as part of its investigation," and had "80 witnesses testif[y] before the grand jury."[9] There were "nearly 50 orders authorizing the use of pen registers"[10] and "the investigators obtained more than 230 communications records orders through a federal statute."[11]

To date, five people have been sentenced to prison, one individual convicted at trial, seven individuals have plead guilty, thirty-seven people and/or entities have been charged.[12] In total there have been 199 overall criminal counts presented in charging documents.[13] The following is a listing from the Department of Justice—Special Counsel's website (https://www.justice.gov/sco) of the individuals and entities court documents where there have been convictions at trial or guilty pleas.

U.S. v. Michael Cohen (1:18-cr-850, Southern District of New York) — Michael Cohen of New York, New York, pleaded guilty on Nov. 29, 2018, to making false statements to the U.S. Congress in violation of 18 U.S.C. 1001 (a)(2). Cohen was sentenced on December 12, 2018, to serve two months in prison and pay a $50,000 fine. (Plea Agreement) (Criminal Information)

U.S. v. Paul J. Manafort, Jr. (1:17-cr-201, District of Columbia) — Paul J. Manafort, Jr., of Alexandria, Va., pleaded guilty on September 14, 2018, to a superseding criminal information filed today in the District of Columbia, which includes conspiracy against the United States (conspiracy to commit

---

7. Statement of Expenditures, Department of Justice—Special Counsel's Office, *available at* https://www.justice.gov/sco/statements-expenditures. It should also be noted that as a result of the investigation moneys were recovered from individuals. In the House Judiciary Committee Testimony Transcript (Part 1), Rep. Jerry Nadler noted that "[i]n the Paul Manafort case alone, you recovered as much as $42 million so that the cost of your investigation to the taxpayers approaches zero." *See Oversight of the Report on the Investigation into Russian Interference in the 2016 Presidential Election: Former Special Counsel Robert S. Mueller, III,* House Judiciary Committee Testimony (Part 1), Rep. Jerry Nadler, *available at* https://judiciary.house.gov/legislation/hearings/oversight-report-investigation-russian-interference-2016-presidential-election (July 24, 2019).

8. For example, former Roger Stone aide, Andrew Miller, testified before a federal grand jury on May 31, 2019. *See* CNN, *Special Counsel Investigation, available at* https://www.cnn.com/interactive/2017/politics/russia-investigations/#/investigations/specialCounsel/all; *See also* "Former Trump Associate Roger Stone" is set for trial in November 2019. *See* Danielle Wallace, *Roger Stone Loses Bid to Get Indictment Scrapped: 'No One But Himself to Blame,'* Fox News, Aug. 2, 2019, *available at* https://www.foxnews.com/politics/roger-stone-loses-bid-to-get-indictment-scrapped-no-one-to-blame-but-himself.

9. *See* Olivia Beavers & Morgan Chalfant, *supra* note 6.

10. *Id.*

11. *Id.*

12. *See* Charges and Pleas, CNN Politics, (last updated 3-8-19), *available at* https://www.cnn.com/interactive/2017/politics/russia-investigations/#/charges. (showing CNN interactive breakdown of number of individuals charged and convicted from Special Counsel Mueller's investigation).

13. *Id.*

money laundering, tax fraud, failing to file Foreign Bank Account Reports and Violating the Foreign Agents Registration Act, and lying and misrepresenting to the Department of Justice) and conspiracy to obstruct justice (witness tampering). On March 13, 2019, Manafort was sentenced to serve 73 months in prison, with 30 months to run concurrent with his sentence in the Eastern District of Virginia. (Superseding Criminal Information, Exhibits, Plea Agreement, Statement of the Offense)

U.S. v. Richard W. Gates III (1:17-cr-201, District of Columbia) — Richard W. Gates III of Richmond, Va., pleaded guilty on Feb. 23, 2018, to a superseding criminal information that includes: count one of the indictment, which charges conspiracy against the United States, in violation of 18 U.S.C. 371 (which includes conspiracy to violate 26 U.S.C. 7206(1), 31 U.S.C. 5312 and 5322(b), and 22 U.S.C. 612, 618(a)(1), and 618(a)(2)), and a charge of making false statements to the Special Counsel's Office and FBI agents, in violation of 18 U.S.C. 1001. (Superseding Criminal Information, Plea Agreement, Statement of the Offense)

U.S. v. Paul J. Manafort, Jr., and Richard W. Gates III (1:18-cr-83, Eastern District of Virginia) — Paul J. Manafort, Jr., of Alexandria, Va., and Richard W. Gates III, of Richmond, Va., were indicted by a federal grand jury on Feb. 22, 2018, in the Eastern District of Virginia. The indictment contains 32 counts: 16 counts related to false individual income tax returns, seven counts of failure to file reports of foreign bank and financial accounts, five counts of bank fraud conspiracy, and four counts of bank fraud. On March 1, 2018, the court granted a motion to dismiss without prejudice the charges against Gates, following his guilty plea in a related case in the District of Columbia (1:17-cr-201). On Aug. 21, 2018, a federal jury found Manafort guilty on eight counts: counts 1–5, subscribing to a false individual income tax return for tax years 2010–2014; count 12, failure to file reports of foreign bank and financial accounts for year 2012; count 25, bank fraud; and count 27, bank fraud. The court declared a mistrial on 10 counts (counts 11, 13–14, 24, 26, 28–32). As part of his plea agreement on Sept. 14, 2018, Manafort admitted his guilt of the remaining counts against him in this case. On March 7, 2019, Manafort was sentenced to 47 months in prison and ordered to pay a $50,000 fine. (Indictment)

U.S. v. Alex van der Zwaan (1:18-cr-31, District of Columbia) — Alex van der Zwaan, of London, pleaded guilty on Feb. 20, 2018, to making false statements to FBI agents, in violation of 18 U.S.C. 1001. Van der Zwaan was sentenced on April 3, 2018, to serve 30 days in prison and pay a $20,000 fine. (Criminal Information, Plea Agreement, Statement of the Offense)

U.S. v. Richard Pinedo, et al. (1:18-cr-24, District of Columbia) — Richard Pinedo, of Santa Paula, Calif., pleaded guilty on Feb. 12, 2018, to identity fraud, in violation of 18 U.S.C. 1028. On Oct. 10, 2018, Pinedo was sentenced to serve six months in prison, followed by six months of home confinement, and ordered to complete 100 hours of community service. (Criminal Information, Plea Agreement, Statement of the Offense)

***U.S. v. Michael T. Flynn* (1:17-cr-232, District of Columbia)** — Lieutenant General Michael T. Flynn (Ret.), of Alexandria, Va., pleaded guilty on Dec. 1, 2017, to making false statements to FBI agents, in violation of 18 U.S.C. 1001. (Criminal Information, Plea Agreement, Statement of the Offense)

***U.S. v. George Papadopoulos* (1:17-cr-182, District of Columbia)** — George Papadopoulos, of Chicago, Illinois, pleaded guilty on Oct. 5, 2017, to making false statements to FBI agents, in violation of 18 U.S.C. 1001. The case was unsealed on Oct. 30, 2017. On Sept. 7, 2018, Papadopoulos was sentenced to serve 14 days in prison, pay a $9,500 fine, and complete 200 hours of community service. (Criminal Information, Plea Agreement, Statement of the Offense)

The Department of Justice — Special Counsel's website also includes Indictments against individuals and entities with pending cases. This includes the Indictment against *U.S. v. Internet Research Agency, et al.* The Special Counsel's website states that "[a] federal grand jury in the District of Columbia returned an indictment on Feb. 16, 2018, against 13 Russian nationals and three Russian entities accused of violating U.S. criminal laws in order to interfere with U.S. elections and political processes. The indictment charges all of the defendants with conspiracy to defraud the United States, three defendants with conspiracy to commit wire fraud and bank fraud, and five defendants with aggravated identity theft."[14] This indictment provides graphic details of the alleged Russian interference in the election.[15]

D. The Mueller Report

On March 22, 2019, prior to leaving the position of Special Counsel, Mueller provided his report to Attorney General William Barr. This 448-page Report, with a number of appendices, is commonly referred to as the Mueller Report. The following is the Introduction to this report:

Mueller Report — Introduction to Volume I

This report is submitted to the Attorney General pursuant to 28 C.F.R. §600.8(c), which states that, "[a]t the conclusion of the Special Counsel's work, he ... shall provide the Attorney General a confidential report explaining the prosecution or declination decisions [the Special Counsel] reached."

---

14. *See* U.S. Department of Justice — Special Counsel's Office, *available at* https://www.justice.gov/sco.

15. *Id.* at https://www.justice.gov/file/1035477/download.

The Russian government interfered in the 2016 presidential election in sweeping and systematic fashion. Evidence of Russian government operations began to surface in mid-2016. In June, the Democratic National Committee and its cyber response team publicly announced that Russian hackers had compromised its computer network. Releases of hacked materials—hacks that public reporting soon attributed to the Russian government—began that same month. Additional releases followed in July through the organization WikiLeaks, with further releases in October and November.

In late July 2016, soon after WikiLeaks's first release of stolen documents, a foreign government contacted the FBI about a May 2016 encounter with Trump Campaign foreign policy advisor George Papadopoulos. Papadopoulos had suggested to a representative of that foreign government that the Trump Campaign had received indications from the Russian government that it could assist the Campaign through the anonymous release of information damaging to Democratic presidential candidate Hillary Clinton. That information prompted the FBI on July 31, 2016, to open an investigation into whether individuals associated with the Trump Campaign were coordinating with the Russian government in its interference activities.

That fall, two federal agencies jointly announced that the Russian government "directed recent compromises of e-mails from US persons and institutions, including US political organizations," and, "[t]hese thefts and disclosures are intended to interfere with the US election process." After the election, in late December 2016, the United States imposed sanctions on Russia for having interfered in the election. By early 2017, several congressional committees were examining Russia's interference in the election.

Within the Executive Branch, these investigatory efforts ultimately led to the May 2017 appointment of Special Counsel Robert S. Mueller, III. The order appointing the Special Counsel authorized him to investigate "the Russian government's efforts to interfere in the 2016 presidential election," including any links or coordination between the Russian government and individuals associated with the Trump Campaign.

As set forth in detail in this report, the Special Counsel's investigation established that Russia interfered in the 2016 presidential election principally through two operations. First, a Russian entity carried out a social media campaign that favored presidential candidate Donald J. Trump and disparaged presidential candidate Hillary Clinton. Second, a Russian intelligence service conducted computer-intrusion operations against entities, employees, and volunteers working on the Clinton Campaign and then released stolen documents. The investigation also identified numerous links between the Russian government and the Trump Campaign. Although the investigation established that the Russian government perceived it would benefit from a Trump presidency and worked to secure that outcome, and that the Campaign expected it would benefit electorally from information stolen and released through Russian efforts, the investigation did not establish that members of the Trump Campaign conspired or coordinated with the Russian government in its election interference activities. * * *

The report describes actions and events that the Special Counsel's Office found to be supported by the evidence collected in our investigation. In some instances, the report points out the absence of evidence or conflicts in the evidence about a particular fact or event. In other instances, when substantial, credible evidence enabled the Office to reach a conclusion with confidence, the report states that the investigation established that certain actions or events occurred. A statement that the investigation did not establish particular facts does not mean there was no evidence of those facts.

In evaluating whether evidence about collective action of multiple individuals constituted a crime, we applied the framework of conspiracy law, not the concept of "collusion." In so doing, the Office recognized that the word "collud[e]" was used in communications with the Acting Attorney General confirming certain aspects of the investigation's scope and that the term has frequently been invoked in public reporting about the investigation. But collusion is not a specific offense or theory of liability found in the United States Code, nor is it a term of art in federal criminal law. For those reasons, the Office's focus in analyzing questions of joint criminal liability was on conspiracy as defined in federal law. In connection with that analysis, we addressed the factual question whether members of the Trump Campaign "coordinat[ed]" — a term that appears in the appointment order — with Russian election interference activities. Like collusion, "coordination" does not have a settled definition in federal criminal law. We understood coordination to require an agreement — tacit or express — between the Trump Campaign and the Russian government on election interference. That requires more than the two parties taking actions that were informed by or responsive to the other's actions or interests. We applied the term coordination in that sense when stating in the report that the investigation did not establish that the Trump Campaign coordinated with the Russian government in its election interference activities. * * *

The report on our investigation consists of two volumes:

Volume I describes the factual results of the Special Counsel's investigation of Russia's interference in the 2016 presidential election and its interactions with the Trump Campaign. Section I describes the scope of the investigation. Sections II and III describe the principal ways Russia interfered in the 2016 presidential election. Section IV describes links between the Russian government and individuals associated with the Trump Campaign. Section V sets forth the Special Counsel's charging decisions.

Volume II addresses the President's actions towards the FBI's investigation into Russia's interference in the 2016 presidential election and related matters, and his actions towards the Special Counsel's investigation. Volume II separately states its framework and the considerations that guided that investigation.

II. Response to the Mueller Report

A. Attorney General William P. Barr's letter of March 24, 2019

Dear Chairman Graham, Chairman Nadler, Ranking Member Feinstein, and Ranking Member Collins:

As a supplement to the notification provided on Friday, March 22, 2019, I am writing today to advise you of the principal conclusions reached by Special Counsel Robert S. Mueller Ill and to inform you about the status of my initial review of the report he has prepared.

The Special Counsel's Report

On Friday, the Special Counsel submitted to me a "confidential report explaining the prosecution or declination decisions" he has reached, as required by 28 C.F.R. 600.8(c). This report is entitled "Report on the Investigation into Russian Interference in the 2016 Presidential Election." Although my review is ongoing, I believe that it is in the public interest to describe the report and to summarize the principal conclusions reached by the Special Counsel and the results of his investigation.

The report explains that the Special Counsel and his staff thoroughly investigated allegations that members of the presidential campaign of Donald J. Trump, and others associated with it, conspired with the Russian government in its efforts to interfere in the 2016 U.S. presidential election, or sought to obstruct the related federal investigations. In the report, the Special Counsel noted that, in completing his investigation, he employed 19 lawyers who were assisted by a team of approximately 40 FBI agents, intelligence analysts, forensic accountants, and other professional staff. The Special Counsel issued more than 2,800 subpoenas, executed nearly 500 search warrants, obtained more than 230 orders for communication records, issued almost 50 orders authorizing use of pen registers, made 13 requests to foreign governments for evidence, and interviewed approximately 500 witnesses.

The Special Counsel obtained a number of indictments and convictions of individuals and entities in connection with his investigation, all of which have been publicly disclosed. During the course of his investigation, the Special Counsel also referred several matters to other offices for further action. The report does not recommend any further indictments, nor did the Special Counsel obtain any sealed indictments that have yet to be made public. Below, I summarize the principal conclusions set out in the Special Counsel's report.

<u>Russian Interference in the 2016 U.S. Presidential Election.</u> The Special Counsel's report is divided into two parts. The first describes the results of the Special Counsel's investigation into Russia's interference in the 2016 U.S. presidential election. The report outlines the Russian effort to influence the election and documents crimes committed by persons associated with the Russian government in connection with those efforts. The report further explains that a primary consideration for the Special Counsel's investigation was whether any Americans including individuals associated

with the Trump campaign—joined the Russian conspiracies to influence the election, which would be a federal crime. The Special Counsel's investigation did not find that the Trump campaign or anyone associated with it conspired or coordinated with Russia in its efforts to influence the 2016 U.S. presidential election. As the report states: "[T]he investigation did not establish that members of the Trump Campaign conspired or coordinated with the Russian government in its election interference activities."[1]

The Special Counsel's investigation determined that there were two main Russian efforts to influence the 2016 election. The first involved attempts by a Russian organization, the Internet Research Agency (IRA), to conduct disinformation and social media operations in the United States designed to sow social discord, eventually with the aim of interfering with the election. As noted above, the Special Counsel did not find that any U.S. person or Trump campaign official or associate conspired or knowingly coordinated with the IRA in its efforts, although the Special Counsel brought criminal charges against a number of Russian nationals and entities in connection with these activities.

The second element involved the Russian government's efforts to conduct computer hacking operations designed to gather and disseminate information to influence the election. The Special Counsel found that Russian government actors successfully hacked into computers and obtained emails from persons affiliated with the Clinton campaign and Democratic Party organizations, and publicly disseminated those materials through various intermediaries, including WikiLeaks. Based on these activities, the Special Counsel brought criminal charges against a number of Russian military officers for conspiring to hack into computers in the United States for purposes of influencing the election. But as noted above, the Special Counsel did not find that the Trump campaign, or anyone associated with it, conspired or coordinated with the Russian government in these efforts, despite multiple offers from Russian-affiliated individuals to assist the Trump campaign.

Obstruction of Justice. The report's second part addresses a number of actions by the President—most of which have been the subject of public reporting—that the Special Counsel investigated as potentially raising obstruction-of-justice concerns. After making a "thorough factual investigation" into these matters, the Special Counsel considered whether to evaluate the conduct under Department standards governing prosecution and declination decisions but ultimately determined not to make a traditional prosecutorial judgment. The Special Counsel therefore did not draw a conclusion—one way or the other—as to whether the examined conduct constituted obstruction. Instead, for each of the relevant actions investigated, the report sets out evidence on both sides of the question and leaves unresolved what the Special Counsel views as "difficult issues" of law and fact concerning whether the President's actions

---

1. In assessing potential conspiracy charges, the Special Counsel also considered whether members of the Trump campaign "coordinated" with Russian election interference activities. The Special Counsel defined "coordination" as an "agreement—tacit or express—between the Trump Campaign and the Russian government on election interference."

and intent could be viewed as obstruction. The Special Counsel states that "while this report does not conclude that the President committed a crime, it also does not exonerate him."

The Special Counsel's decision to describe the facts of his obstruction investigation without reaching any legal conclusions leaves it to the Attorney General to determine whether the conduct described in the report constitutes a crime. Over the course of the investigation, the Special Counsel's office engaged in discussions with certain Department officials regarding many of the legal and factual matters at issue in the Special Counsel's obstruction investigation. After reviewing the Special Counsel's final report on these issues; consulting with Department officials, including the Office of Legal Counsel; and applying the principles of federal prosecution that guide our charging decisions, Deputy Attorney General Rod Rosenstein and I have concluded that the evidence developed during the Special Counsel's investigation is not sufficient to establish that the President committed an obstruction-of-justice offense. Our determination was made without regard to, and is not based on, the constitutional considerations that surround the indictment and criminal prosecution of a sitting president.[2]

In making this determination, we noted that the Special Counsel recognized that "the evidence does not establish that the President was involved in an underlying crime related to Russian election interference," and that, while not determinative, the absence of such evidence bears upon the President's intent with respect to obstruction. Generally speaking, to obtain and sustain an obstruction conviction, the government would need to prove beyond a reasonable doubt that a person, acting with corrupt intent, engaged in obstructive conduct with a sufficient nexus to a pending or contemplated proceeding. In cataloguing the President's actions, many of which took place in public view, the report identifies no actions that, in our judgment, constitute obstructive conduct, had a nexus to a pending or contemplated proceeding, and were done with corrupt intent, each of which, under the Department's principles of federal prosecution guiding charging decisions, would need to be proven beyond a reasonable doubt to establish an obstruction-of-justice offense.

Status of the Department's Review

The relevant regulations contemplate that the Special Counsel's report will be a "confidential report" to the Attorney General. *See* Office of Special Counsel, 64 Fed. Reg. 37,038, 37,040–41 (July 9, 1999). As I have previously stated, however, I am mindful of the public interest in this matter. For that reason, my goal and intent is to release as much of the Special Counsel's report as I can consistent with applicable law, regulations, and Departmental policies.

Based on my discussions with the Special Counsel and my initial review, it is apparent that the report contains material that is or could be subject to Federal Rule of Criminal Procedure 6(e), which imposes restrictions on the use and disclosure of

---

2. *See A Sitting President's Amenability to Indictment and Criminal Prosecution*, 24 Op. O.L.C. 222 (2000).

information relating to "matter[s] occurring before [a] grand jury." Fed. R. Crim. P. 6(e)(2)(B). Rule 6(e) generally limits disclosure of certain grand jury information in a criminal investigation and prosecution. *Id.* Disclosure of 6(e) material beyond the strict limits set forth in the rule is a crime in certain circumstances. *See, e.g.,* 18 U.S.C. §401(3). This restriction protects the integrity of grand jury proceedings and ensures that the unique and invaluable investigative powers of a grand jury are used strictly for their intended criminal justice function.

Given these restrictions, the schedule for processing the report depends in part on how quickly the Department can identify the 6(e) material that by law cannot be made public. I have requested the assistance of the Special Counsel in identifying all 6(e) information contained in the report as quickly as possible. Separately, I also must identify any information that could impact other ongoing matters, including those that the Special Counsel has referred to other offices. As soon as that process is complete, I will be in a position to move forward expeditiously in determining what can be released in light of applicable law, regulations, and Departmental policies.

As I observed in my initial notification, the Special Counsel regulations provide that "the Attorney General may determine that public release of" notifications to your respective Committees "would be in the public interest." 28 C.F.R. 600.9(c). I have so determined, and I will disclose this letter to the public after delivering it to you. * * *

B. Attorney General Barr's Remarks on April 18, 2019

Attorney General William P. Barr Delivers
Remarks on the Release of the Report on the Investigation into
Russian Interference in the 2016 Presidential Election

Washington, DC — Thursday, April 18, 2019

Good Morning. Thank you all for being here today.

On March 22, 2019, Special Counsel Robert Mueller concluded his investigation of matters related to Russian attempts to interfere in the 2016 presidential election and submitted his confidential report to me pursuant to Department of Justice regulations.

As I said during my Senate confirmation hearing and since, I am committed to ensuring the greatest possible degree of transparency concerning the Special Counsel's investigation, consistent with the law.

At 11:00 this morning, I will transmit copies of a public version of the Special Counsel's report to the Chairmen and Ranking Members of the House and Senate Judiciary Committees. The Department of Justice will also make the report available to the American public by posting it on the Department's website after it has been delivered to Congress.

I would like to offer a few comments today on the report.

But before I do that, I want to thank Deputy Attorney General Rod Rosenstein for joining me here today and for his assistance and counsel throughout this process.

Rod has served the Department of Justice for many years with dedication and distinction, and it has been a great privilege and pleasure to work with him since my confirmation. He had well-deserved plans to step back from public service that I interrupted by asking him to help in my transition. Rod has been an invaluable partner, and I am grateful that he was willing to help me and has been able to see the Special Counsel's investigation to its conclusion. Thank you, Rod.

I would also like to thank Special Counsel Mueller for his service and the thoroughness of his investigation, particularly his work exposing the nature of Russia's attempts to interfere in our electoral process.

As you know, one of the primary purposes of the Special Counsel's investigation was to determine whether members of the presidential campaign of Donald J. Trump, or any individuals associated with that campaign, conspired or coordinated with the Russian government to interfere in the 2016 election. Volume I of the Special Counsel's report describes the results of that investigation. As you will see, the Special Counsel's report states that his "investigation did not establish that members of the Trump Campaign conspired or coordinated with the Russian government in its election interference activities."

I am sure that all Americans share my concerns about the efforts of the Russian government to interfere in our presidential election. As the Special Counsel's report makes clear, the Russian government sought to interfere in our election. But thanks to the Special Counsel's thorough investigation, we now know that the Russian operatives who perpetrated these schemes did not have the cooperation of President Trump or the Trump campaign—or the knowing assistance of any other Americans for that matter. That is something that all Americans can and should be grateful to have confirmed.

The Special Counsel's report outlines two main efforts by the Russian government to influence the 2016 election:

First, the report details efforts by the Internet Research Agency, a Russian company with close ties to the Russian government, to sow social discord among American voters through disinformation and social media operations. Following a thorough investigation of this disinformation campaign, the Special Counsel brought charges in federal court against several Russian nationals and entities for their respective roles in this scheme. Those charges remain pending, and the individual defendants remain at large.

But the Special Counsel found no evidence that any Americans—including anyone associated with the Trump campaign—conspired or coordinated with the Russian government or the IRA in carrying out this illegal scheme. Indeed, as the report states, "[t]he investigation did not identify evidence that any U.S. persons knowingly or intentionally coordinated with the IRA's interference operation." Put another way, the Special Counsel found no "collusion" by any Americans in the IRA's illegal activity.

Second, the report details efforts by Russian military officials associated with the GRU to hack into computers and steal documents and emails from individuals affiliated with the Democratic Party and the presidential campaign of Hillary Rodham Clinton for the purpose of eventually publicizing those emails. Obtaining such unauthorized access into computers is a federal crime. Following a thorough investigation of these hacking operations, the Special Counsel brought charges in federal court against several Russian military officers for their respective roles in these illegal hacking activities. Those charges are still pending and the defendants remain at large.

But again, the Special Counsel's report did not find any evidence that members of the Trump campaign or anyone associated with the campaign conspired or coordinated with the Russian government in its hacking operations. In other words, there was no evidence of Trump campaign "collusion" with the Russian government's hacking.

The Special Counsel's investigation also examined Russian efforts to publish stolen emails and documents on the internet. The Special Counsel found that, after the GRU disseminated some of the stolen materials through its own controlled entities, DCLeaks and Guccifer 2.0, the GRU transferred some of the stolen materials to Wikileaks for publication. Wikileaks then made a series of document dumps. The Special Counsel also investigated whether any member or affiliate of the Trump campaign encouraged or otherwise played a role in these dissemination efforts. Under applicable law, publication of these types of materials would not be criminal unless the publisher also participated in the underlying hacking conspiracy. Here too, the Special Counsel's report did not find that any person associated with the Trump campaign illegally participated in the dissemination of the materials.

Finally, the Special Counsel investigated a number of "links" or "contacts" between Trump Campaign officials and individuals connected with the Russian government during the 2016 presidential campaign. After reviewing those contacts, the Special Counsel did not find any conspiracy to violate U.S. law involving Russia-linked persons and any persons associated with the Trump campaign.

So that is the bottom line. After nearly two years of investigation, thousands of subpoenas, and hundreds of warrants and witness interviews, the Special Counsel confirmed that the Russian government sponsored efforts to illegally interfere with the 2016 presidential election but did not find that the Trump campaign or other Americans colluded in those schemes.

After finding no underlying collusion with Russia, the Special Counsel's report goes on to consider whether certain actions of the President could amount to obstruction of the Special Counsel's investigation. As I addressed in my March 24th letter, the Special Counsel did not make a traditional prosecutorial judgment regarding this allegation. Instead, the report recounts ten episodes involving the President and discusses potential legal theories for connecting these actions to elements of an obstruction offense.

After carefully reviewing the facts and legal theories outlined in the report, and in consultation with the Office of Legal Counsel and other Department lawyers, the Deputy Attorney General and I concluded that the evidence developed by the Special

Counsel is not sufficient to establish that the President committed an obstruction-of-justice offense.

Although the Deputy Attorney General and I disagreed with some of the Special Counsel's legal theories and felt that some of the episodes examined did not amount to obstruction as a matter of law, we did not rely solely on that in making our decision. Instead, we accepted the Special Counsel's legal framework for purposes of our analysis and evaluated the evidence as presented by the Special Counsel in reaching our conclusion.

In assessing the President's actions discussed in the report, it is important to bear in mind the context. President Trump faced an unprecedented situation. As he entered into office, and sought to perform his responsibilities as President, federal agents and prosecutors were scrutinizing his conduct before and after taking office, and the conduct of some of his associates. At the same time, there was relentless speculation in the news media about the President's personal culpability. Yet, as he said from the beginning, there was in fact no collusion. And as the Special Counsel's report acknowledges, there is substantial evidence to show that the President was frustrated and angered by a sincere belief that the investigation was undermining his presidency, propelled by his political opponents, and fueled by illegal leaks. Nonetheless, the White House fully cooperated with the Special Counsel's investigation, providing unfettered access to campaign and White House documents, directing senior aides to testify freely, and asserting no privilege claims. And at the same time, the President took no act that in fact deprived the Special Counsel of the documents and witnesses necessary to complete his investigation. Apart from whether the acts were obstructive, this evidence of noncorrupt motives weighs heavily against any allegation that the President had a corrupt intent to obstruct the investigation.

Now, before I take questions, I want to address a few aspects of the process for producing the public report that I am releasing today. As I said several times, the report contains limited redactions relating to four categories of information. To ensure as much transparency as possible, these redactions have been clearly labelled and color-coded so that readers can tell which redactions correspond to which categories.

As you will see, most of the redactions were compelled by the need to prevent harm to ongoing matters and to comply with court orders prohibiting the public disclosure of information bearing upon ongoing investigations and criminal cases, such as the IRA case and the Roger Stone case.

These redactions were applied by Department of Justice attorneys working closely together with attorneys from the Special Counsel's Office, as well as with the intelligence community, and prosecutors who are handling ongoing cases. The redactions are their work product.

Consistent with long-standing Executive Branch practice, the decision whether to assert Executive privilege over any portion of the report rested with the President of the United States. Because the White House voluntarily cooperated with the Special Counsel's investigation, significant portions of the report contain material over which the President could have asserted privilege. And he would have been well within his rights to do so. Following my March 29th letter, the Office of the White House Counsel requested the opportunity to review the redacted version of the report in order to advise the President on the potential invocation of privilege, which is consistent with long-standing practice. Following that review, the President confirmed that, in the interests of transparency and full disclosure to the American people, he would not assert privilege over the Special Counsel's report. Accordingly, the public report I am releasing today contains redactions only for the four categories that I previously outlined, and no material has been redacted based on executive privilege.

In addition, earlier this week, the President's personal counsel requested and were given the opportunity to read a final version of the redacted report before it was publicly released. That request was consistent with the practice followed under the Ethics in Government Act, which permitted individuals named in a report prepared by an Independent Counsel the opportunity to read the report before publication. The President's personal lawyers were not permitted to make, and did not request, any redactions.

In addition to making the redacted report public, we are also committed to working with Congress to accommodate their legitimate oversight interests with respect to the Special Counsel's investigation. We have been consulting with Chairman Graham and Chairman Nadler throughout this process, and we will continue to do so.

Given the limited nature of the redactions, I believe that the publicly released report will allow every American to understand the results of the Special Counsel's investigation. Nevertheless, in an effort to accommodate congressional requests, we will make available to a bipartisan group of leaders from several Congressional committees a version of the report with all redactions removed except those relating to grand-jury information. Thus, these members of Congress will be able to see all of the redacted material for themselves—with the limited exception of that which, by law, cannot be shared.

I believe that this accommodation, together with my upcoming testimony before the Senate and House Judiciary Committees, will satisfy any need Congress has for information regarding the Special Counsel's investigation.

Once again, I would like to thank you all for being here today. I now have a few minutes for questions. * * *

C. Special Counsel Robert Mueller's Statement on March 29, 2019

Special Counsel Robert S. Mueller III Makes Statement on
Investigation into Russian Interference in the 2016 Presidential Election

Washington, DC—Wednesday, May 29, 2019

Two years ago, the Acting Attorney General asked me to serve as Special Counsel, and he created the Special Counsel's Office.

The appointment order directed the office to investigate Russian interference in the 2016 presidential election. This included investigating any links or coordination between the Russian government and individuals associated with the Trump campaign.

I have not spoken publicly during our investigation. I am speaking today because our investigation is complete. The Attorney General has made the report on our investigation largely public. And we are formally closing the Special Counsel's Office. As well, I am resigning from the Department of Justice and returning to private life.

I'll make a few remarks about the results of our work. But beyond these few remarks, it is important that the office's written work speak for itself.

Let me begin where the appointment order begins: and that is interference in the 2016 presidential election.

As alleged by the grand jury in an indictment, Russian intelligence officers who were part of the Russian military launched a concerted attack on our political system.

The indictment alleges that they used sophisticated cyber techniques to hack into computers and networks used by the Clinton campaign. They stole private information, and then released that information through fake online identities and through the organization WikiLeaks. The releases were designed and timed to interfere with our election and to damage a presidential candidate.

And at the same time, as the grand jury alleged in a separate indictment, a private Russian entity engaged in a social media operation where Russian citizens posed as Americans in order to interfere in the election.

These indictments contain allegations. And we are not commenting on the guilt or innocence of any specific defendant. Every defendant is presumed innocent unless and until proven guilty in court.

The indictments allege, and the other activities in our report describe, efforts to interfere in our political system. They needed to be investigated and understood. That is among the reasons why the Department of Justice established our office.

That is also a reason we investigated efforts to obstruct the investigation. The matters we investigated were of paramount importance. It was critical for us to obtain full and accurate information from every person we questioned. When a subject of an investigation obstructs that investigation or lies to investigators, it strikes at the core of the government's effort to find the truth and hold wrongdoers accountable.

Let me say a word about the report. The report has two parts addressing the two main issues we were asked to investigate.

The first volume of the report details numerous efforts emanating from Russia to influence the election. This volume includes a discussion of the Trump campaign's response to this activity, as well as our conclusion that there was insufficient evidence to charge a broader conspiracy.

And in the second volume, the report describes the results and analysis of our obstruction of justice investigation involving the President.

The order appointing me Special Counsel authorized us to investigate actions that could obstruct the investigation. We conducted that investigation and we kept the office of the Acting Attorney General apprised of the progress of our work.

As set forth in our report, after that investigation, if we had confidence that the President clearly did not commit a crime, we would have said that.

We did not, however, make a determination as to whether the President did commit a crime. The introduction to volume two of our report explains that decision.

It explains that under long-standing Department policy, a President cannot be charged with a federal crime while he is in office. That is unconstitutional. Even if the charge is kept under seal and hidden from public view—that too is prohibited.

The Special Counsel's Office is part of the Department of Justice and, by regulation, it was bound by that Department policy. Charging the President with a crime was therefore not an option we could consider.

The Department's written opinion explaining the policy against charging a President makes several important points that further informed our handling of the obstruction investigation. Those points are summarized in our report. And I will describe two of them:

First, the opinion explicitly permits the investigation of a sitting President because it is important to preserve evidence while memories are fresh and documents are available. Among other things, that evidence could be used if there were co-conspirators who could now be charged.

And second, the opinion says that the Constitution requires a process other than the criminal justice system to formally accuse a sitting President of wrongdoing.

And beyond Department policy, we were guided by principles of fairness. It would be unfair to potentially accuse somebody of a crime when there can be no court resolution of an actual charge.

So that was the Justice Department policy and those were the principles under which we operated. From them we concluded that we would not reach a determination—one way or the other—about whether the President committed a crime. That is the office's final position and we will not comment on any other conclusions or hypotheticals about the President.

We conducted an independent criminal investigation and reported the results to the Attorney General—as required by Department regulations.

The Attorney General then concluded that it was appropriate to provide our report to Congress and the American people.

At one point in time I requested that certain portions of the report be released. The Attorney General preferred to make the entire report public all at once. We appreciate that the Attorney General made the report largely public. I do not question the Attorney General's good faith in that decision.

I hope and expect this to be the only time that I will speak about this matter. I am making that decision myself—no one has told me whether I can or should testify or speak further about this matter.

There has been discussion about an appearance before Congress. Any testimony from this office would not go beyond our report. It contains our findings and analysis, and the reasons for the decisions we made. We chose those words carefully, and the work speaks for itself.

The report is my testimony. I would not provide information beyond that which is already public in any appearance before Congress.

In addition, access to our underlying work product is being decided in a process that does not involve our office.

So beyond what I have said here today and what is contained in our written work, I do not believe it is appropriate for me to speak further about the investigation or to comment on the actions of the Justice Department or Congress.

It is for that reason that I will not take questions here today.

Before I step away, I want to thank the attorneys, the FBI agents, the analysts, and the professional staff who helped us conduct this investigation in a fair and independent manner. These individuals, who spent nearly two years with the Special Counsel's Office, were of the highest integrity.

I will close by reiterating the central allegation of our indictments—that there were multiple, systematic efforts to interfere in our election.

That allegation deserves the attention of every American.

Thank you.

Notes & Questions

1. **Comments of Attorney General Barr and Special Counsel Mueller.** Are the comments of each of these individuals consistent? Are they stressing different aspects of this investigation in their statements? *See* Charlie Savage, *How Barr's Excerpts Compare to the Mueller Report's Findings*, N.Y. Times, Apr. 20, 2019, *available at* https://www.nytimes.com/2019/04/19/us/politics/mueller-report-william-barr-excerpts.html.

2. **Prosecutorial Statements.** Should Special Counsel Mueller have made comments to the public prior to the conclusion of the investigation? Consider Model Rules of Professional, Rule 3.8(f) which states:

The prosecutor in a criminal case shall:

(f) except for statements that are necessary to inform the public of the nature and extent of the prosecutor's action and that serve a legitimate law enforcement purpose, refrain from making extrajudicial comments that have a substantial likelihood of heightening public condemnation of the accused and exercise reasonable care to prevent investigators, law enforcement personnel, employees or other persons assisting or associated with the prosecutor in a criminal case from making an extrajudicial statement that the prosecutor would be prohibited from making under Rule 3.6 or this Rule.

3. **Congressional Testimony.** On July 24, 2019, Special Counsel Mueller testified before the House Judiciary Committee (https://www.youtube.com/watch?v=6b_EuI JhgOk) and also the House Select Committee on Intelligence (https://www.you tube.com/watch?v=ru_106qkUhk&feature=youtu.be). Should he have been called to testify before Congress?

Chapter Two

Constitutional Appointments

I. Generally

The constitutional term for hiring high-ranking government officials is appointment, after the language in Article II of the Constitution. Section 2 of Article II reads, in pertinent part:

> The President shall ... nominate, and by and with the Advice and Consent of the Senate, shall appoint Ambassadors, other public Ministers and Consuls, Judges of the supreme Court, and all other Officers of the United States ...: but the Congress may by Law vest the Appointment of such inferior Officers, as they think proper, in the President alone, in the Courts of Law, or in the Heads of Departments.

At first glance, it may not seem obvious why a relatively short document like the Constitution would focus so much attention on the way that unelected members of government are hired. In reality, however, the appointments process is a key feature of the concept of separation of powers that our constitutional democracy is founded on.

Consider this: The Founders created a system of government where the laws are made by Congress, a group of elected individuals with many diverse interests and priorities. Those laws are executed—enforced—by a single person, the president of the United States, in whom Article II vests all of the federal government's "executive power." Executing all of the Nation's laws is of course too big a job for one person, so Congress created federal departments (agencies) to help the president fulfill his constitutional duties. The most well-known agencies are generally those that make up the president's "cabinet"; they are almost always headed by leaders who hold the title of "Secretary" and are the president's closest advisors and aides in enforcing the laws.

Agency leaders—"Officers of the United States" in the words of Article II—necessarily occupy positions of significant power. This was even true during the revolutionary period when the size and ambition of the federal government were far less than they are today (think of Alexander Hamilton as Treasury Secretary and Thomas Jefferson as Secretary of State). It stands to reason, then, that the choice of who to entrust with that power is a critical one that can have serious consequences for the efficacy and integrity of government.

Now that we know how important the choice of officers can be, who should we entrust with that decision? As with many features of constitutional law, the answer is that the power is separated, or shared. In general, and according to Article II, all "Officers of the United States" (along with all ambassadors, Supreme Court justices, etc.) may be appointed by the combined efforts of the president and Senate, through its advice and consent function.

You have likely seen this process play out on television. The president chooses a new Secretary of State, Supreme Court justice, etc., and the lucky nominee is forced to spend hours—if not days—in front of a committee of Senators asking the nominee questions about his or her qualifications, plans for the job, policy views, etc. This grilling is part of the Senate's advice and consent process; once the committee members are finished questioning the president's nominee, they vote on his or her acceptability. If the committee supports the nominee, then the full Senate votes. A nominee who receives a majority of the votes in the Senate has received its consent and can be appointed by the president to fill the position to which they were nominated.

But why split up the responsibility among two branches of government? It unquestionably makes it more difficult to get officers appointed, which in turn slows down the functioning of the agencies or institutions they are chosen to lead. The benefits are at least three-fold. First, it is important for the president to be able to choose his officers, especially in the executive branch. Those officers will, after all, be working directly, and solely, for the president. By winning election, the president is chosen by the people to execute the laws in the way he thinks most benefits the Nation; it is important that the president and the individuals working most closely with him to achieve that mission are on the same page. Second, including the Senate in the process helps ensure that the nominee is qualified and competent, rather than simply the beneficiary of presidential patronage. The Senate confirmation process provides a group other than the president an opportunity to scrutinize the nominee's qualifications and viewpoints on relevant issues, and often does so publicly. This benefit starts to fade if the president and Senate are so closely aligned politically that the confirmation process is effectively a rubber stamp of the president's choice, but even then forcing the Senate to go through the process publicly can create separate and powerful political pressure to more carefully scrutinize presidential nominees. Finally, limiting confirmation to one house of Congress—the Senate but not the House of Representatives—makes the process more manageable and less likely to lead to deadlock. The Senate is a smaller group that was designed to be more deliberative and stable than the House (Senators serve for longer terms, six years, than Representatives' two), thereby making it a more efficient choice without sacrificing any competence or expertise.

These features of the appointment process make it an example of constitutional checks and balances—a phrase you are no doubt familiar with but that you may not have spent as much time thinking about before law school. "Checks and balances" is not written anywhere in the Constitution (nor is its converse, "separation of powers"), but it is hard at work in what is referred to as "constitutional structure," the interactions between different constitutional clauses and actors that are just as critical to achieving the system of government envisioned by the Framers as the text itself. By forcing the president and (at least one house of) Congress to work together, the appointments process creates a structure whereby the president is able to choose his closest advisors and colleagues, but the Senate can provide a check against particularly unwise or inappropriate choices.

The system works quite well in most instances. It becomes particularly strained, however, in the (rare) case that is the subject of this course. When the time comes to investigate and potentially prosecute high-ranking members of the executive branch, including the president himself, the normal checks and balances of the appointments process make less sense. First of all, investigation and prosecution are core executive functions, meaning they are traditionally the exclusive responsibility of the president and people who work for him. So a special counsel will inevitably be a member of the executive branch. This alone is not necessarily problematic, until we think more carefully about the purpose of the special counsel. It is vital that a special counsel has sufficient authority to hold the president accountable in the event he has broken the law. This level of power can only realistically be vested in someone with enough authority to qualify as an "Officer of the United States" subject to the appointments process in Article II. But how can we let the president choose his own special counsel? Assuming the investigation is warranted, the special counsel <u>must</u> be independent of the people he or she is investigating. If the special counsel is hand-picked by the president, or can be fired (removed) by the president whenever he likes, that independence is lost or, at best, severely compromised.

But what about the Senate? Can't it check the president to prevent the appointment of a special counsel that is biased toward the president? Not really. Even if we were to rely on the Senate to confirm as special counsel only people that it felt confident would act independently, the president is not required to nominate anyone that would meet that description. Article II has been interpreted to leave the nomination process entirely within the president's discretion. In other words, the Constitution allows the president to choose anyone he likes as a nominee to high office, regardless of their qualifications or abilities, and does not give any other branch—not the legislature or the courts—the power to limit that choice. The check on the president's broad nomination power, of course, is Senate confirmation. The Senate could continually reject nominees for a position like special counsel that it found unacceptable, thereby preventing the president from abusing his discretion in choosing a nominee, but that would only delay the investigation and allow the president to escape scrutiny through inaction, rather than via a sympathetic special counsel. Either way, the traditional appointments process becomes fraught when the officer at issue is a special counsel—like Robert Mueller—empowered to investigate the president and other high-ranking executive officials and to "prosecute federal crimes arising from the investigation of these matters."

So what are we to do? How can we hold the president accountable while staying within the appointments process designed—and mandated—by Article II? This is precisely the issue in the ongoing dispute in the lower federal courts over the appointment of Special Counsel Robert Mueller to head an investigation into Russian interference in the 2016 presidential election. The remainder of this chapter will address some of the issues surrounding the appointment of the special counsel. It begins by briefly describing the hiring of Robert Mueller and the mechanics and current law of constitutional appointments. It provides excerpts of recent cases relating to the Mueller appointment, in the process reviewing the Court's most prominent treatment of the appointment of individuals empowered to investigate and potentially prosecute high ranking members of the executive branch, *Morrison v. Olson*, 487 U.S. 654 (1988). More specifically, the case excerpts address two critical issues in the constitutionality of the Mueller appointment: (1) why the special counsel is not properly deemed an "employee" whose appointment would be entirely outside of the Appointments Clause, and (2) why his appointment meets the requirements for an "inferior Officer" appointed by a "Head[] of Department[]" under Article II.

II. The Mueller Appointment

Robert Mueller was appointed by Acting Attorney General (AAG) Rod Rosenstein on May 17, 2019 to investigate "(i) any links and/or coordination between the Russian government and individuals associated with the campaign of President Donald Trump; and (ii) any matters that arose or may arise directly from the investigation; and (iii) any other matters within the scope of 28 C.F.R. §600.4(a)."[1] Rod Rosenstein, Acting Attorney General, *Order No. 3915-2017: Appointment of Special Counsel to Investigate Russian Interference With the 2016 Presidential Election and Related Matters* (May 17, 2017). The AAG was left to make the appointment decision because Attorney General Jeff Sessions recused himself from the matter due to his involvement with the Trump

---

1. Section 600.4(a) describes the original and additional jurisdiction as follows:

(a) Original jurisdiction. The jurisdiction of a Special Counsel shall be established by the Attorney General. The Special Counsel will be provided with a specific factual statement of the matter to be investigated. The jurisdiction of a Special Counsel shall also include the authority to investigate and prosecute federal crimes committed in the course of, and with intent to interfere with, the Special Counsel's investigation, such as perjury, obstruction of justice, destruction of evidence, and intimidation of witnesses; and to conduct appeals arising out of the matter being investigated and/or prosecuted.

(b) Additional jurisdiction. If in the course of his or her investigation the Special Counsel concludes that additional jurisdiction beyond that specified in his or her original jurisdiction is necessary in order to fully investigate and resolve the matters assigned, or to investigate new matters that come to light in the course of his or her investigation, he or she shall consult with the Attorney General, who will determine whether to include the additional matters within the Special Counsel's jurisdiction or assign them elsewhere.

(c) Civil and administrative jurisdiction. If in the course of his or her investigation the Special Counsel determines that administrative remedies, civil sanctions or other governmental action outside the criminal justice system might be appropriate, he or she shall consult with the Attorney General with respect to the appropriate component to take any necessary action. A Special Counsel shall not have civil or administrative authority unless specifically granted such jurisdiction by the Attorney General.

Campaign during the time period relevant to the investigation. Mark Landler and Eric Lichtblau, *Jeff Sessions Recuses Himself From Russia Inquiry*, N.Y. TIMES, Mar. 2, 2017, https://www.nytimes.com/2017/03/02/us/politics/jeff-sessions-russia-trump-investigation-democrats.html.

Special Counsel Mueller was appointed pursuant to a DOJ regulation authorizing the Attorney General to appoint a special counsel when "he or she determines a criminal investigation ... is warranted" and concludes that assigning that investigation to existing DOJ officials would "present a conflict of interest" such that "it would be in the public interest to appoint an outside Special Counsel to assume responsibility for the matter." 28 C.F.R. §600.1. Additional regulations explain that the special counsel's jurisdiction is set and controlled by the Attorney General; the special counsel must "comply with the rules, regulations, procedures, practices and policies of the Department of Justice;" and the Attorney General may only discipline or remove a special counsel for "misconduct, dereliction of duty, incapacity, conflict of interest, and for other good cause, including violation of Departmental policies." 28 C.F.R. §§600.4; 600.7(a), (d).

The DOJ regulations governing appointment of a special counsel, and relied on by AAG Rosenstein to appoint Robert Mueller, were developed as the successor to the Ethics in Government Act (EGA), 5 U.S.C. §§591–99 (expired). The EGA vested the appointment of an independent counsel with power to investigate high-ranking executive officials in a three-judge court upon referral by the Attorney General. The constitutionality of the EGA was upheld by the Supreme Court in *Morrison v. Olson*, *supra*. Although *Morrison* is distinct because it involves a statute—the EGA—that Congress has allowed to expire, it remains the most analogous Supreme Court precedent for the constitutionality of a special counsel.

III. The Mechanics of Constitutional Appointments and the Special Counsel

The Appointments Clause of Article II contains the blueprint for appointments. It is admirable (and arguably unusual) for its clarity. It explains precisely what the appointments process entails for each type of nominee and the role for each government actor(s) involved in that process.

In graphic form, this is what the Appointments Clause requires:

Position to Be Filled	Appointment Process
Principal Officer	President with the advice and consent of the Senate
Inferior Officer	President with the advice and consent of the Senate OR Congress vests appointment in (1) President alone, (2) Courts of Law, or (3) Heads of Departments
Employee	Appointments Clause does not apply

As can be seen in the above chart, there are at least three features of the Appointments Clause that raise interpretive questions relevant to the special counsel: who is an *officer*, who is an *inferior officer*, and who is a *head of a department*? The next section will address the first of these issues and the following section tackles the latter two.

A. The Definition of an "Officer"

The president's power to nominate, and with the advice and consent of the Senate appoint, applies to an explicitly defined group of people, including ambassadors, judges, and for present purposes, "Officers of the United States." That does not tell us, however, which positions qualify as "Officers" subject to the requirements of the Appointments Clause. Government actors that do not qualify as officers under Article II are generally categorized as "employees" and do not have to meet the Appointments Clause requirements to be hired or fired.

The Supreme Court recently addressed the distinctions between officers and employees in the context of the appointment of administrative law judges (ALJs) for the Securities and Exchange Commission (SEC), the independent agency responsible for regulating American securities markets. For decades, ALJs, who preside over evidentiary hearings traditionally called "formal adjudications" in administrative law,[2] were considered employees whose hiring did not require compliance with the Appointments Clause. This was largely because all aspects of ALJ decisions — including conclusions of both law <u>and</u> fact — are subject to review *do novo* by the heads of the agency, in this case the SEC Commissioners. Since ALJ decisions were not themselves final, the argument goes, ALJs were employees, not officers. As a result, ALJs could be hired outside of the process described in Article II. And they were. SEC ALJs were appointed by the Chief ALJ for the agency, who was clearly not the president, and was widely understood to be neither a "Court of Law" nor a "Head[] of Department[]". In *Lucia*, excerpted below, the Supreme Court revisited whether ALJs, despite not being able to issue final decisions, were nonetheless powerful enough in their own right to merit officer status, and thus fall under the Appointments Clause.

Lucia v. Securities and Exchange Commission
138 S.Ct. 2044 (2018)

Justice KAGAN delivered the opinion of the Court.

The Appointments Clause of the Constitution lays out the permissible methods of appointing "Officers of the United States," a class of government officials distinct from mere employees. Art. II, § 2, cl. 2. This case requires us to decide whether administrative law judges (ALJs) of the Securities and Exchange Commission (SEC or

---

2. More specifically, they preside over proceedings governed by sections 554, 556, and 557 of the Administrative Procedure Act, 5 U.S.C. § 501 *et seq.*

Commission) qualify as such "Officers." In keeping with *Freytag v. Commissioner*, 501 U.S. 868 (1991), we hold that they do.

I

The SEC has statutory authority to enforce the nation's securities laws. One way it can do so is by instituting an administrative proceeding against an alleged wrongdoer. By law, the Commission may itself preside over such a proceeding. See 17 C.F.R. § 201.110 (2017). But the Commission also may, and typically does, delegate that task to an ALJ. * * *

An ALJ assigned to hear an SEC enforcement action has extensive powers — the "authority to do all things necessary and appropriate to discharge his or her duties" and ensure a "fair and orderly" adversarial proceeding. §§ 201.111, 200.14(a). Those powers "include, but are not limited to," supervising discovery; issuing, revoking, or modifying subpoenas; deciding motions; ruling on the admissibility of evidence; administering oaths; hearing and examining witnesses; generally "[r]egulating the course of" the proceeding and the "conduct of the parties and their counsel"; and imposing sanctions for "[c]ontemptuous conduct" or violations of procedural requirements. * * * As that list suggests, an SEC ALJ exercises authority "comparable to" that of a federal district judge conducting a bench trial. * * *

After a hearing ends, the ALJ issues an "initial decision." § 201.360(a)(1). That decision must set out "findings and conclusions" about all "material issues of fact [and] law"; it also must include the "appropriate order, sanction, relief, or denial thereof." § 201.360(b). The Commission can then review the ALJ's decision, either upon request or sua sponte. See § 201.360(d)(1). But if it opts against review, the Commission "issue[s] an order that the [ALJ's] decision has become final." § 201.360(d)(2). At that point, the initial decision is "deemed the action of the Commission." § 78d-1(c).

This case began when the SEC instituted an administrative proceeding against petitioner Raymond Lucia and his investment company. Lucia marketed a retirement savings strategy called "Buckets of Money." In the SEC's view, Lucia used misleading slideshow presentations to deceive prospective clients. The SEC charged Lucia under the Investment Advisers Act, § 80b-1 et seq., and assigned ALJ Cameron Elliot to adjudicate the case. After nine days of testimony and argument, Judge Elliot issued an initial decision concluding that Lucia had violated the Act and imposing sanctions, including civil penalties of $300,000 and a lifetime bar from the investment industry. In his decision, Judge Elliot made factual findings about only one of the four ways the SEC thought Lucia's slideshow misled investors. The Commission thus remanded for factfinding on the other three claims, explaining that an ALJ's "personal experience with the witnesses" places him "in the best position to make findings of fact" and "resolve any conflicts in the evidence." * * * Judge Elliot then made additional findings of deception and issued a revised initial decision, with the same sanctions. * * *

On appeal to the SEC, Lucia argued that the administrative proceeding was invalid because Judge Elliot had not been constitutionally appointed. According to Lucia, the Commission's ALJs are "Officers of the United States" and thus subject to the Appointments Clause. Under that Clause, Lucia noted, only the President, "Courts of Law," or "Heads of Departments" can appoint "Officers." See Art. II, §2, cl. 2. And none of those actors had made Judge Elliot an ALJ. To be sure, the Commission itself counts as a "Head[ ] of Department[ ]." * * * But the Commission had left the task of appointing ALJs, including Judge Elliot, to SEC staff members. * * * As a result, Lucia contended, Judge Elliot lacked constitutional authority to do his job.

The Commission rejected Lucia's argument. It held that the SEC's ALJs are not "Officers of the United States." Instead, they are "mere employees"—officials with lesser responsibilities who fall outside the Appointments Clause's ambit. * * * The Commission reasoned that its ALJs do not "exercise significant authority independent of [its own] supervision." * * *Because that is so (said the SEC), they need no special, high-level appointment. * * *

Lucia's claim fared no better in the Court of Appeals for the D.C. Circuit. A panel of that court seconded the Commission's view that SEC ALJs are employees rather than officers, and so are not subject to the Appointments Clause. * * * Lucia then petitioned for rehearing en banc. The Court of Appeals granted that request and heard argument in the case. But the ten members of the en banc court divided evenly, resulting in a per curiam order denying Lucia's claim. * * * That decision conflicted with one from the Court of Appeals for the Tenth Circuit. *See Bandimere v. SEC*, 844 F.3d 1168, 1179 (2016).

Lucia asked us to resolve the split by deciding whether the Commission's ALJs are "Officers of the United States within the meaning of the Appointments Clause." * * * Up to that point, the Federal Government (as represented by the Department of Justice) had defended the Commission's position that SEC ALJs are employees, not officers. But in responding to Lucia's petition, the Government switched sides. * * * So when we granted the petition * * * we also appointed an amicus curiae to defend the judgment below. * * * We now reverse.

II

The sole question here is whether the Commission's ALJs are "Officers of the United States" or simply employees of the Federal Government. The Appointments Clause prescribes the exclusive means of appointing "Officers." Only the President, a court of law, or a head of department can do so. See Art. II, §2, cl. 2.3 And as all parties agree, none of those actors appointed Judge Elliot before he heard Lucia's case; instead, SEC staff members gave him an ALJ slot. * * * So if the Commission's ALJs are constitutional officers, Lucia raises a valid Appointments Clause claim. The only way to defeat his position is to show that those ALJs are not officers at all, but instead non-officer employees—part of the broad swath of "lesser functionaries" in the Government's workforce. * * * For if that is true, the Appointments Clause cares not a whit about who named them. * * *

Two decisions set out this Court's basic framework for distinguishing between officers and employees. [*United States v.*] *Germaine*[, 99 U.S. 508 (1879)] held that "civil surgeons" (doctors hired to perform various physical exams) were mere employees because their duties were "occasional or temporary" rather than "continuing and permanent." * * * Stressing "ideas of tenure [and] duration," the Court there made clear that an individual must occupy a "continuing" position established by law to qualify as an officer. * * * *Buckley* [*v. Valeo*, 424 U.S. 1, 132 (1976),] then set out another requirement, central to this case. It determined that members of a federal commission were officers only after finding that they "exercis[ed] significant authority pursuant to the laws of the United States." * * * The inquiry thus focused on the extent of power an individual wields in carrying out his assigned functions.

Both the amicus and the Government urge us to elaborate on *Buckley*'s "significant authority" test, but another of our precedents makes that project unnecessary. * * * [I]n *Freytag v. Commissioner*, 501 U.S. 868 (1991), we applied the unadorned "significant authority" test to adjudicative officials who are near-carbon copies of the Commission's ALJs. As we now explain, our analysis there (sans any more detailed legal criteria) necessarily decides this case.

The officials at issue in *Freytag* were the "special trial judges" (STJs) of the United States Tax Court. The authority of those judges depended on the significance of the tax dispute before them. In "comparatively narrow and minor matters," they could both hear and definitively resolve a case for the Tax Court. * * * In more major matters, they could preside over the hearing, but could not issue the final decision; instead, they were to "prepare proposed findings and an opinion" for a regular Tax Court judge to consider. * * * The proceeding challenged in *Freytag* was a major one, involving $1.5 billion in alleged tax deficiencies. * * * After conducting a 14-week trial, the STJ drafted a proposed decision in favor of the Government. A regular judge then adopted the STJ's work as the opinion of the Tax Court. * * * The losing parties argued on appeal that the STJ was not constitutionally appointed.

This Court held that the Tax Court's STJs are officers, not mere employees. Citing *Germaine*, the Court first found that STJs hold a continuing office established by law. * * * They serve on an ongoing, rather than a "temporary [or] episodic[,] basis"; and their "duties, salary, and means of appointment" are all specified in the Tax Code. * * * The Court then considered, as *Buckley* demands, the "significance" of the "authority" STJs wield. * * * In addressing that issue, the Government had argued that STJs are employees, rather than officers, in all cases (like the one at issue) in which they could not "enter a final decision." * * * But the Court thought the Government's focus on finality "ignore[d] the significance of the duties and discretion that [STJs] possess." * * * Describing the responsibilities involved in presiding over adversarial hearings, the Court said: STJs "take testimony, conduct trials, rule on the admissibility of evidence, and have the power to enforce compliance with discovery orders." * * * And the Court observed that "[i]n the course of carrying out these important functions, the [STJs] exercise significant discretion." * * * That fact meant they were officers, even when their decisions were not final. * * *

Freytag says everything necessary to decide this case. To begin, the Commission's ALJs, like the Tax Court's STJs, hold a continuing office established by law. * * * Indeed, everyone here — Lucia, the Government, and the amicus — agrees on that point. * * * Far from serving temporarily or episodically, SEC ALJs "receive[ ] a career appointment." 5 C.F.R. § 930.204(a) (2018). And that appointment is to a position created by statute, down to its "duties, salary, and means of appointment." * * *

Still more, the Commission's ALJs exercise the same "significant discretion" when carrying out the same "important functions" as STJs do. * * * Both sets of officials have all the authority needed to ensure fair and orderly adversarial hearings — indeed, nearly all the tools of federal trial judges. * * * Consider in order the four specific (if overlapping) powers *Freytag* mentioned. First, the Commission's ALJs (like the Tax Court's STJs) "take testimony." * * * More precisely, they "[r]eceiv[e] evidence" and "[e]xamine witnesses" at hearings, and may also take pre-hearing depositions. * * * Second, the ALJs (like STJs) "conduct trials." * * * As detailed earlier, they administer oaths, rule on motions, and generally "regulat[e] the course of" a hearing, as well as the conduct of parties and counsel. * * * Third, the ALJs (like STJs) "rule on the admissibility of evidence." * * * They thus critically shape the administrative record (as they also do when issuing document subpoenas). * * * And fourth, the ALJs (like STJs) "have the power to enforce compliance with discovery orders." * * * In particular, they may punish all "[c]ontemptuous conduct," including violations of those orders, by means as severe as excluding the offender from the hearing. * * * So point for point — straight from *Freytag*'s list — the Commission's ALJs have equivalent duties and powers as STJs in conducting adversarial inquiries.

And at the close of those proceedings, ALJs issue decisions much like that in *Freytag* — except with potentially more independent effect. As the *Freytag* Court recounted, STJs "prepare proposed findings and an opinion" adjudicating charges and assessing tax liabilities. * * * Similarly, the Commission's ALJs issue decisions containing factual findings, legal conclusions, and appropriate remedies. * * * And what happens next reveals that the ALJ can play the more autonomous role. In a major case like *Freytag*, a regular Tax Court judge must always review an STJ's opinion. And that opinion counts for nothing unless the regular judge adopts it as his own. * * * By contrast, the SEC can decide against reviewing an ALJ decision at all. And when the SEC declines review (and issues an order saying so), the ALJ's decision itself "becomes final" and is "deemed the action of the Commission." * * * That last-word capacity makes this an a fortiori case: If the Tax Court's STJs are officers, as *Freytag* held, then the Commission's ALJs must be too.

The amicus offers up two distinctions to support the opposite conclusion. His main argument relates to "the power to enforce compliance with discovery orders" — the fourth of *Freytag*'s listed functions. * * * The Tax Court's STJs, he states, had that power "because they had authority to punish contempt" (including discovery violations) through fines or imprisonment. * * * By contrast, he observes, the Commission's ALJs have less capacious power to sanction misconduct. The amicus's secondary distinction involves how the Tax Court and Commission, respectively, review the factfinding of STJs and ALJs. The Tax Court's rules state that an STJ's findings of fact "shall be presumed" correct. Tax Court Rule 183(d). In comparison, the amicus notes, the SEC's regulations include no such deferential standard. * * *

But those distinctions make no difference for officer status. To start with the amicus's primary point, *Freytag* referenced only the general "power to enforce compliance with discovery orders," not any particular method of doing so. * * * True enough, the power to toss malefactors in jail is an especially muscular means of enforcement — the nuclear option of compliance tools. But just as armies can often enforce their will through conventional weapons, so too can administrative judges. As noted earlier, the Commission's ALJs can respond to discovery violations and other contemptuous conduct by excluding the wrongdoer (whether party or lawyer) from the proceedings — a powerful disincentive to resist a court order. * * * Similarly, if the offender is an attorney, the ALJ can "[s]ummarily suspend" him from representing his client — not something the typical lawyer wants to invite. * * * And finally, a judge who will, in the end, issue an opinion complete with factual findings, legal conclusions, and sanctions has substantial informal power to ensure the parties stay in line. Contrary to the amicus's view, all that is enough to satisfy *Freytag*'s fourth item (even supposing, which we do not decide, that each of those items is necessary for someone conducting adversarial hearings to count as an officer).

And the amicus's standard-of-review distinction fares just as badly. The *Freytag* Court never suggested that the deference given to STJs' factual findings mattered to its Appointments Clause analysis. Indeed, the relevant part of *Freytag* did not so much as mention the subject (even though it came up at oral argument, * * *). And anyway, the Commission often accords a similar deference to its ALJs, even if not by regulation. The Commission has repeatedly stated, as it did below, that its ALJs are in the "best position to make findings of fact" and "resolve any conflicts in the evidence." * * * And when factfinding derives from credibility judgments, as it frequently does, acceptance is near-automatic. Recognizing ALJs' "personal experience with the witnesses," the Commission adopts their "credibility finding[s] absent overwhelming evidence to the contrary." * * * That practice erases the constitutional line the amicus proposes to draw. * * *

[The Court discussed the appropriate remedy]

We accordingly reverse the judgment of the Court of Appeals and remand the case for further proceedings consistent with this opinion. * * *

Justice THOMAS, with whom Justice GORSUCH joins, concurring.

I agree with the Court that this case is indistinguishable from *Freytag v. Commissioner*, 501 U.S. 868 (1991). If the special trial judges in *Freytag* were "Officers of the United States," Art. II, §2, cl. 2, then so are the administrative law judges of the Securities and Exchange Commission. Moving forward, however, this Court will not be able to decide every Appointments Clause case by comparing it to *Freytag*. And, as the Court acknowledges, our precedents in this area do not provide much guidance. * * * While precedents like *Freytag* discuss what is sufficient to make someone an officer of the United States, our precedents have never clearly defined what is necessary.

I would resolve that question based on the original public meaning of "Officers of the United States." To the Founders, this term encompassed all federal civil officials " 'with responsibility for an ongoing statutory duty.' " * * *

* * * The Founders likely understood the term "Officers of the United States" to encompass all federal civil officials who perform an ongoing, statutory duty—no matter how important or significant the duty. * * * "Officers of the United States" was probably not a term of art that the Constitution used to signify some special type of official. Based on how the Founders used it and similar terms, the phrase "of the United States" was merely a synonym for "federal," and the word "Office[r]" carried its ordinary meaning. * * * The ordinary meaning of "officer" was anyone who performed a continuous public duty. * * * For federal officers, that duty is "established by Law"—that is, by statute. Art. II, § 2, cl. 2. The Founders considered individuals to be officers even if they performed only ministerial statutory duties—including recordkeepers, clerks, and tidewaiters (individuals who watched goods land at a customhouse). * * * Early congressional practice reflected this understanding. With exceptions not relevant here, Congress required all federal officials with ongoing statutory duties to be appointed in compliance with the Appointments Clause. * * *

Applying the original meaning here, the administrative law judges of the Securities and Exchange Commission easily qualify as "Officers of the United States." These judges exercise many of the agency's statutory duties, including issuing initial decisions in adversarial proceedings. * * * As explained, the importance or significance of these statutory duties is irrelevant. All that matters is that the judges are continuously responsible for performing them.

In short, the administrative law judges of the Securities Exchange Commission are "Officers of the United States" under the original meaning of the Appointments Clause. They have " 'responsibility for an ongoing statutory duty,' " which is sufficient to resolve this case. * * * Because the Court reaches the same conclusion by correctly applying *Freytag*, I join its opinion.

Justice BREYER, with whom Justice GINSBURG and Justice SOTOMAYOR join as to Part III, concurring in the judgment in part and dissenting in part.

I agree with the Court that the Securities and Exchange Commission did not properly appoint the Administrative Law Judge who presided over petitioner Lucia's hearing. But I disagree with the majority in respect to two matters. First, I would rest our conclusion upon statutory, not constitutional, grounds. * * * Second, I disagree with the Court in respect to the proper remedy. * * *

I

* * * I do not believe that the Administrative Procedure Act permits the Commission to delegate its power to appoint its administrative law judges to its staff. We have held that, for purposes of the Constitution's Appointments Clause, the Commission itself is a " 'Hea[d]' " of a " 'Departmen[t].' " * * * Thus, reading the statute as referring to the Commission itself, and not to its staff, avoids a difficult constitutional question, namely, the very question that the Court answers today: whether the Commission's

administrative law judges are constitutional "inferior Officers" whose appointment Congress may vest only in the President, the "Courts of Law," or the "Heads of Departments." * * *

I have found no other statutory provision that would permit the Commission to delegate the power to appoint its administrative law judges to its staff. The statute establishing and governing the Commission does allow the Commission to "delegate, by published order or rule, any of its functions to a division of the Commission, an individual Commissioner, an administrative law judge, or an employee or employee board." 15 U.S.C. §78d-1(a). But this provision requires a "published order or rule," and the Commission here published no relevant delegating order or rule. Rather, Lucia discovered the Commission's appointment system for administrative law judges only when the Commission's enforcement division staff filed an affidavit in this case describing that staff-based system. * * * Regardless, the same constitutional-avoidance reasons that should inform our construction of the Administrative Procedure Act should also lead us to interpret the Commission's general delegation authority as excluding the power to delegate to staff the authority to appoint its administrative law judges, so as to avoid the constitutional question the Court reaches in this case. * * *

The analysis may differ for other agencies that employ administrative law judges. Each agency's governing statute is different, and some, unlike the Commission's, may allow the delegation of duties without a published order or rule. * * * Similarly, other agencies' administrative law judges perform distinct functions, and their means of appointment may therefore not raise the constitutional questions that inform my reading of the relevant statutes here.

The upshot, in my view, is that for statutory, not constitutional, reasons, the Commission did not lawfully appoint the Administrative Law Judge here at issue. And this Court should decide no more than that. * * *

II

* * *

III

Separately, I also disagree with the majority's conclusion that the proper remedy in this case requires a hearing before a different administrative law judge. * * * For these reasons, I concur in the judgment in part and, with respect, I dissent in part.

Justice SOTOMAYOR, with whom Justice GINSBURG joins, dissenting.

The Court today and scholars acknowledge that this Court's Appointments Clause jurisprudence offers little guidance on who qualifies as an "Officer of the United States." * * *

To provide guidance to Congress and the Executive Branch, I would hold that one requisite component of "significant authority" is the ability to make final, binding decisions on behalf of the Government. Accordingly, a person who merely advises and provides recommendations to an officer would not herself qualify as an officer. * * *

Nevertheless, I would hold that Commission ALJs are not officers because they lack final decisionmaking authority. As the Commission explained below, the Commission retains "'plenary authority over the course of [its] administrative proceedings and the rulings of [its] law judges.'" * * * As a final matter, although I would conclude that Commission ALJs are not officers, I share Justice BREYER's concerns regarding the Court's choice of remedy, and so I join Part III of his opinion. * * *

Notes and Questions

1. *Defining Officers.* How did the court decide that ALJs were officers despite not having final decisionmaking authority as a matter of law? Shouldn't the lack of final decisionmaking authority have been enough to resolve the issue on its own? If not, will it be difficult for courts to apply the rationale in *Lucia* going forward? Think about whether you agree with the Court's rationale and if it is workable.

2. *Mueller as Officer.* The officer-employee distinction is straightforward with respect to the Mueller appointment because the parties agree that the special counsel is at minimum an "Officer of the United States." But do the circumstances of his appointment bear that out? Does he occupy a "continuing position established by law"? Should that be the most important feature of the analysis? Why or why not?

B. Principal Versus Inferior Officers and "Heads of Departments"

The second and third interpretive issues under the Appointments Clause relate to the fact that the appointments process is potentially different for different "classes" of officer. Referring back to the chart at the start of this subsection, it is clear that the president may appoint officers with Senate consent. This would appear to apply to <u>all</u> officers, regardless of whether they qualify as inferior officers under Article II, and indeed this is how the Clause has been interpreted and applied.

Inferior officers, however, may be appointed by an alternative process, to be determined by Congress. In order to establish, then, whether an officer has been properly appointed under the Constitution, we may first have to decide whether they are a principal or inferior officer. If they are an inferior officer, Congress has more options. Congress may create an alternative appointment scheme for an inferior officer by choosing among the three options given to it by Article II: it may "vest" the appointment of inferior officers in "the President alone [without Senate approval], the Courts of Law, or Heads of Departments." This raises the issue of how to define the various entities that Congress may empower to appoint inferior officers. "The President alone" is not ambiguous, but the definitions of "Courts of Law" and "Heads of Departments" have been the subject of prior (and recent) Supreme Court decisions.

The Supreme Court dealt with the distinction between principal and inferior officers in a case closely analogous to Special Counsel Mueller's. *Morrison v. Olson* involved a challenge to Title VII of the EGA, which authorized the appointment of an independent counsel to "investigate and, if appropriate, prosecute certain high-ranking Government officials for violations of federal criminal laws." The challenge arose in response to a request by Independent Counsel Alexia Morrison to enforce a subpoena against high-ranking executive branch officials. Under the EGA, the independent counsel "may be removed from office, other than by impeachment and conviction, only * * * for good cause." *Morrison*, 487 U.S. at 660–63.

In a 7–1 decision, the Court upheld the constitutionality of the independent counsel's appointment. It concluded that, despite her significant independence and power, Independent Counsel Morrison was an inferior officer under Article II such that her appointment by a "Court[] of Law," the Special Division of the District of Columbia Circuit, was constitutional.

The Court explained that Independent Counsel Morrison was best thought of as an inferior officer because:

> First, appellant is subject to removal by a higher Executive Branch official. Although appellant may not be "subordinate" to the Attorney General (and the President) insofar as she possesses a degree of independent discretion * * * the fact that she can be removed by the Attorney General indicates that she is to some degree "inferior" in rank and authority. Second, appellant is empowered by the Act to perform only certain, limited duties. * * * Admittedly, the Act delegates to appellant "full power and independent authority to exercise all investigative and prosecutorial functions and powers of the Department of Justice," but this grant of authority does not include any authority to formulate policy for the Government * * *

> Third, appellant's office is limited in jurisdiction. * * * Finally, appellant's office is limited in tenure. * * * [A]n independent counsel is appointed essentially to accomplish a single task, * * * In our view, these factors relating to the "ideas of tenure, duration ... and duties" of the independent counsel, are sufficient to establish that appellant is an "inferior" officer in the constitutional sense.

Id. at 671–72. The principal-inferior officer distinction addressed in *Morrison* and the question of whether the AAG can be a "Head[] of Department[]" for appointments purposes were both raised in legal challenges to the appointment of Special Counsel Mueller. The following cases address each of these issues and highlight some of the challenges faced by courts trying to balance the need for special counsel independence with the requirements of the Appointments Clause.

United States v. Concord Management & Consulting LLC

317 F.Supp. 3d 598 (D.C. Cir. 2018)

MEMORANDUM OPINION

DABNEY L. FRIEDRICH, United States District Judge

Concord Management and Consulting LLC moves to dismiss the indictment on the ground that Special Counsel Robert Mueller was appointed unlawfully by Acting Attorney General Rod Rosenstein. * * * The Court will deny Concord's motion. The

Special Counsel's appointment complies with the Constitution's Appointments Clause because (1) the Special Counsel is an "inferior Officer"; and (2) Congress "by Law vest[ed]" the Acting Attorney General with the power to make the appointment. * * *

First, the Special Counsel is an inferior officer because he is directed and supervised by the Acting Attorney General. Although the Special Counsel regulations may not permit the Acting Attorney General to countermand certain decisions made by the Special Counsel, the Special Counsel remains subject to the Acting Attorney General's plenary supervision: the Acting Attorney General has the discretionary power to rescind or revise the regulations; moreover, the Acting Attorney General effectively has the power to remove the Special Counsel at will, either via the regulations or by rescinding or revising the regulations. Second, Congress vested the Acting Attorney General with the power to appoint the Special Counsel. Even though no statute explicitly authorizes the Acting Attorney General to make the appointment, Supreme Court and D.C. Circuit precedent make clear that the Acting Attorney General has the necessary statutory authority.

Concord's secondary arguments also fail. The appointment does not violate core separation-of-powers principles. Nor has the Special Counsel exceeded his authority under the appointment order by investigating and prosecuting Concord. Accordingly, and for the reasons stated below, the Court will deny Concord's motion to dismiss the indictment.

I. BACKGROUND

A. The Office of the Special Counsel

During the Watergate era, special prosecutors were appointed through executive-branch regulations. In 1978, Congress enacted the Ethics in Government Act, which allowed for the appointment of a special prosecutor later renamed the "independent counsel." *See* Pub. L. No. 95-521, §601(a) (1978); *see also* Ethics in Government Act Amendments of 1982, Pub. L. No. 97-409, §2 (1983). Under the Act, if the Attorney General determined that certain investigations or prosecutions were warranted, the Attorney General applied to a special three-judge court, which then selected and appointed an independent counsel. Pub. L. No. 95-521, §601(a). In the face of a constitutional challenge, the independent counsel provisions of the Ethics in Government Act were upheld in *Morrison v. Olson*, 487 U.S. 654 (1988). The provisions expired in 1999, and Congress declined to renew them. Then-Attorney General Janet Reno testified before the Senate, "The Independent Counsel Act is structurally flawed and * * * those flaws cannot be corrected within our constitutional framework. * * * [T]he independent counsel is vested with the full gamut of prosecutorial powers, but with little of its accountability. He has not been confirmed by the Senate. * * * Accountability is no small matter. It goes to the very heart of our constitutional scheme." The Future of the Independent Counsel Act: Hearing Before the S. Comm. on Governmental Affairs, 106th Cong. (March 17, 1999) (statement of Janet Reno, Att'y Gen. of the United States).

As the independent counsel provisions of the Ethics in Government Act expired in 1999, the Attorney General promulgated the Office of the Special Counsel regulations to "replace" the Act. *See* Office of Special Counsel, 64 Fed. Reg. 37,038, 37,038 (July 9, 1999) (published at 28 C.F.R. §§ 600.1–600.10). Under the regulations, the Attorney General "appoint[s] a Special Counsel when he or she determines that criminal investigation of a person or matter is warranted and—

(a) That investigation or prosecution of that person or matter by a United States Attorney's Office or litigating Division of the Department of Justice would present a conflict of interest for the Department or other extraordinary circumstances; and

(b) That under the circumstances, it would be in the public interest to appoint an outside Special Counsel to assume responsibility for the matter."

* * * The regulations govern the Special Counsel's jurisdiction, powers, and duties. They "seek to strike a balance between independence and accountability in certain sensitive investigations." * * * According to the regulations' preamble, the Special Counsel is "free to structure the investigation as he or she wishes and to exercise independent prosecutorial discretion to decide whether charges should be brought, within the context of the established procedures of the Department." * * * "Nevertheless, it is intended that ultimate responsibility for the matter and how it is handled continue[s] to rest with the Attorney General (or the Acting Attorney General if the Attorney General is personally recused in the matter)." * * *

B. Appointment of Special Counsel Robert Mueller

[The court discusses the appointment of special counsel Mueller].

C. *United States v. Internet Research Agency, et al.*

[O]n February 16, 2018, the grand jury returned an eight-count indictment against thirteen individuals and three corporate entities: Internet Research Agency LLC, Concord Management and Consulting LLC, and Concord Catering. * * * Under 18 U.S.C. § 371, the indictment charges that the defendants conspired to defraud the United States by impeding the lawful functions of the Federal Election Commission, the Department of Justice, and the Department of State. * * * Also, under 18 U.S.C. §§ 1343 and 1344, the indictment charges that the Internet Research Agency and two individual defendants conspired to commit wire and bank fraud. * * * And under 18 U.S.C. § 1028A, the indictment charges that the Internet Research Agency and four individual defendants committed aggravated identity theft. * * *

* * * At the ensuing initial appearance and arraignment on May 9, defense counsel stated that Concord was not properly served under Rule 4, but nonetheless, Concord authorized defense counsel to enter a voluntary appearance, subject Concord to the Court's jurisdiction, and plead not guilty, which defense counsel did. * * *

* * * [O]n June 25, Concord filed a motion to dismiss the indictment "based on the Special Counsel's unlawful appointment and lack of authority." * * * Concord's motion argues that (1) the appointment of the Special Counsel violates the Appointments Clause of the Constitution; (2) the regulations governing the Special Counsel violate core separation-of-powers principles; and (3) even if the regulations are valid

and binding, the order appointing the Special Counsel is inconsistent with the regulations and does not authorize the prosecution of Concord. * * *

D. Related Cases

[The court discusses the opinions in cases involving Paul Manafort and a grand jury case involving a witness ordered to appear before the grand jury].

II. LEGAL STANDARDS

Under Rule 12(b)(1) of the Federal Rules of Criminal Procedure, a party "may raise by pretrial motion any defense, objection, or request that the court can determine without a trial on the merits." * * * Relevant here, a defendant may raise a "defect in the indictment" by challenging the constitutionality of the Special Counsel's appointment and his authority to bring an indictment. Fed. R. Crim. P. 12(b)(3); * * * "When considering a motion to dismiss an indictment, a court assumes the truth of [the indictment's] factual allegations." * * *

III. THE APPOINTMENTS CLAUSE

* * * Concord argues that the appointment of the Special Counsel violates the Appointments Clause in two ways. First, the Special Counsel is not an inferior officer. * * * Second, even if the Special Counsel is an inferior officer, Congress has not "by Law vested" his appointment in the Acting Attorney General. * * *

A. The Special Counsel as an "inferior Officer"

Consistent with the Appointments Clause, the Acting Attorney General may not appoint a Special Counsel outside of the nomination-and-confirmation process unless the Special Counsel is an "inferior Officer." U.S. Const. art. II, § 2, cl. 2. "Generally speaking, the term 'inferior officer' connotes a relationship with some higher ranking officer or officers below the President." *Edmond* [*v. United States*, 520 U.S. 651, 662 (1997)]. That is, "[w]hether one is an 'inferior' officer depends on whether he has a superior." * * * "It is not enough that other officers may be identified who formally maintain a higher rank, or possess responsibilities of a greater magnitude." * * * Rather, "'inferior officers are officers whose work is directed and supervised at some level' by other officers appointed by the President with the Senate's consent." * * *

For evaluating direction and supervision, *Edmond* "emphasized three factors": whether an officer is (1) "subject to the substantial supervision and oversight of" another executive officer who is a principal officer or is "subordinate" to a principal officer, (2) subject to "revers[al]" by "another executive branch entity" so that the officer has "no power to render a final decision on behalf of the United States unless permitted to do so by other Executive Officers," and (3) "removable ... without cause." * * * Of these factors, the third—the removal power—is likely "the most important to a Court's determination of principal-inferior status." * * *

Statutes and regulations provide the framework for evaluating the direction and supervision of the Special Counsel. * * * The Special Counsel regulations matter because they have the "force of law" so long as "extant." * * * Thus they bind the Department of Justice and the Acting Attorney General. * * * The Special Counsel's principal argument is that, despite the constraints imposed by the regulations, the Acting Attorney General retains control of the Special Counsel. Therefore, the Court does not begin its analysis by "looking solely to statutes." * * * Instead, the Court first examines the Acting Attorney General's ability to direct and supervise the Special Counsel under the presently binding statutes and regulations. Next, the Court evaluates (if necessary) whether the analysis is affected by the regulations' potential for revocation or revision. For if the Acting Attorney General is able to "rescind the regulations at will," the regulations—no matter how constraining they purport to be—"do not meaningfully restrict" the Acting Attorney General's plenary supervisory power. * * *

1. Direction and Supervision of the Special Counsel

The relevant statutes give the Acting Attorney General "virtually plenary authority" to direct and supervise a Special Counsel. * * * That authority, however, is circumscribed by the Special Counsel regulations in several ways.

a. Supervision, Oversight, and Final Decisionmaking Power

As to the first and second factors emphasized by *Edmond*, the Acting Attorney General establishes the parameters of the Special Counsel's investigation at its outset, and Department of Justice policies frame the investigation as it proceeds. The investigation only comes into existence by the action of the Acting Attorney General, 28 C.F.R. §600.1, and the Acting Attorney General defines the scope of the Special Counsel's "jurisdiction." * * * The Special Counsel may request "additional jurisdiction," but only the Acting Attorney General can grant the request. * * * Also, throughout the investigation, the Special Counsel "shall consult with appropriate offices within the Department for guidance with respect to established practices, policies and procedures." * * * This consultation requirement affords the Acting Attorney General the opportunity to exert his supervisory powers, which will be discussed further below.

In addition to consulting with the appropriate offices, the Office of the Special Counsel must adhere to the Department of Justice's ethical standards, and the Special Counsel "shall comply with" the Department of the Justice's "rules, regulations, procedures, practices and policies." *Id.* §600.7(a), (c). One governing policy is the U.S. Attorneys' Manual, but other than that, it is unclear what "procedures, practices and polices" shape the Special Counsel's actions. Further complicating things, the Special Counsel represents that certain policies do not bind it. Specifically, the Criminal Division's Public Integrity Section published a manual in late 2017 that "addresses how the Department handles all federal election offenses...."; the manual indicates that §371 conspiracies based on violations of the Federal Election Campaign Act must prove "willfulness," but the Special Counsel relies on a different policy—the Department's "litigating position" embodied in Supreme Court and First Circuit briefs filed in 2016 or 2017—to establish that the Special Counsel need not have charged willfulness in this case. * * * [W]ithout more certainty about the governing polices, it is difficult to draw strong conclusions about how §600.7(a) contributes to the Acting Attorney General's supervisory ability.

Also, the Special Counsel must provide information about his actions to the Acting Attorney General. This matters because, without information upon which to act, the Acting Attorney General would be unequipped to direct and supervise the Special Counsel. The Special Counsel "shall notify" the Acting Attorney General "of events in the course of the investigation in conformity with the Departmental guidelines with respect to Urgent Reports," 28 C.F.R. §600.8(b), which are "major developments in significant investigations and litigation," "law enforcement emergencies," and "events affecting the Department that are likely to generate national media or Congressional attention," USAM §§1-13.100. Such major developments "*may* include" the initiation of investigations, filing of criminal charges, arrests, pleas, trials, verdicts, settlements, and sentencings, but the Special Counsel regulations and Department of Justice policies do not appear to *require* notification of all such developments. USAM §1-13.120 * * * Even so, the Acting Attorney General "may request that the Special Counsel provide an explanation for *any* investigative or prosecutorial step." 28 C.F.R. §600.7(b) (emphasis added). Therefore, the Acting Attorney General has access to as much information as he requests to direct and supervise an investigation.

Information-sharing alone, however, does not guarantee adequate supervision. The Acting Attorney General must also retain the authority to direct the Special Counsel and countermand certain decisions. * * *

Does the Acting Attorney General possess the power to supervise and reverse the Special Counsel? The key regulatory provision reads:

> The Special Counsel shall not be subject to the day-to-day supervision of any official of the Department. However, the Attorney General may request that the Special Counsel provide an explanation for any investigative or prosecutorial step, and may after review conclude that the action is so inappropriate or unwarranted under established Departmental practices that it should not be pursued. In conducting that review, the Attorney General will give great weight to the views of the Special Counsel. If the Attorney General concludes that a proposed action by a Special Counsel should not be pursued, the Attorney General shall notify Congress as specified in §600.9(a)(3).

28 C.F.R. §600.7(b). Thus, the Acting Attorney General has the power to "conclude"—after giving "great weight to the views of the Special Counsel"—that an action "is so inappropriate or unwarranted under established Departmental practices that it *should* not be pursued." *Id.* (emphasis added). But the power to come to this conclusion is not always the power to mandate or countermand the Special Counsel's actions, for a number of reasons.

First, "should" is generally "precatory, not mandatory." * * * Although the use of "should" instead of "shall" is not "automatically determinative," * * * the same subprovision requires that, if the Acting Attorney General concludes that a proposed action should not be pursued," certain actions must follow—in particular, the Acting Attorney General "shall notify Congress." 28 C.F.R. §600.7(b). Pointedly missing is any requirement that the Special Counsel "shall" comply with the conclusion. * * *

Further context does not turn "should" into a mandatory term. The Special Counsel argues that "should" is sufficiently ambiguous that its meaning ought to be ascertained from the "the context of the regulation" and the Attorney General's "intent," such as is embodied in the regulations' background section. * * * The background section states that "the intent of the regulations is to ensure that ultimate responsibility" for how a Special Counsel investigation "is handled will continue to rest with the Attorney General." * * * But the background section also makes very strong statements about the Special Counsel's independence. For example, the immediately preceding sentence says the Special Counsel "would be free to structure the investigation as he or she wishes and to exercise independent prosecutorial discretion to decide whether charges should be brought." * * * The background therefore cuts both ways, providing little reason to think that "should" means "shall." * * *

Regardless, even crediting the Special Counsel's argument that "should" can be read as a mandatory "shall," some Special Counsel decisions remain insulated from review or countermand under §600.7(b). At most, the Acting Attorney General is able to countermand actions that—after giving "great weight to the views of the Special Counsel"—are "so inappropriate or unwarranted under established Departmental practices." 28 C.F.R. §600.7(b). As noted, it is unclear from the provision what "established Departmental practices" shape the Special Counsel's actions. And troublingly, the importance of the decision and the Acting Attorney General's desired course of action are not considerations specified in the text. The provision prevents the Acting Attorney General from countermanding a decision with which he disagrees, no matter how vehemently, so long as the decision does not rise to the level of "so inappropriate or unwarranted under established Departmental practices." * * * As a result, the Special Counsel regulations prevent the Acting Attorney General from directing a course of action based on legitimate reasons other than established Departmental practices. Such legitimate reasons might include, for example, resource limitations, Department-wide strategy and policy considerations, and the exercise of prosecutorial discretion.

The Special Counsel represents that, under Departmental practices and policies, the Acting Attorney General gets the last say on certain major or serious decisions, even if the decisions are otherwise within the bounds of the Special Counsel's discretion. If so, that enhances the Acting Attorney General's ability to countermand under §600.7(b), but it is unclear how much. * * * At the very least, some Special Counsel decisions remain insulated from review or countermand.

b. Removal

Turning to the third and likely most important *Edmond* factor, the Special Counsel argues that his removability subjects him to the direction and supervision of the Acting Attorney General. * * * If available to the Acting Attorney General, "[t]he power to remove officers at will and without cause is a powerful tool for control of an inferior." * * * Here, "[t]he Special Counsel may be disciplined or removed from office only by the personal action of the Attorney General," and "[t]he Attorney General may remove a Special Counsel for misconduct, dereliction of duty, incapacity, conflict of interest, or for other good cause, including violation of Departmental policies." 28 C.F.R. § 600.7(d).

These grounds for removal may impose only a minimal restriction on the Acting Attorney General because "misconduct," "dereliction of duty," and especially "other good cause" are susceptible to broad readings. They might permit removal, for example, if the Special Counsel refused to follow an order from the Acting Attorney General, even if the order involved decisions that would otherwise be within the scope of the Special Counsel's discretion. * * *

"Good cause" in particular is an "open-textured expression" that defies easy definition. * * * If "other good cause" in the 1999 Special Counsel regulations tracks or "reaches[es] farther" than this interpretation of "inefficiency," then the removal provision imposes only minimal restrictions on the Acting Attorney General. * * *

Indeed, the Office of the Special Counsel understands "good cause" in just this way. At the motion hearing, the Special Counsel represented, without limitation, that "good cause" would exist if the Special Counsel did not follow any order from the Acting Attorney General. * * * Supporting this understanding, the removal provision specifies that "good cause" "include[es] violation of Departmental policies," and the Special Counsel understands such policies to include that the Acting Attorney General gets the last say on certain decisions. 28 C.F.R. § 600.7(d); * * * If the Special Counsel is correct that "good cause" essentially includes "failure to accept supervision," then the for-cause removal provision imposes only a minimal restriction on the Acting Attorney General's power to remove the Special Counsel, and the Appointments Clause problem dissipates. * * *

There is reason to think, however, that the Special Counsel regulations afford the Special Counsel more substantial protection against removal, and thus risk rendering him a principal officer. * * * As discussed above, the regulations — at most — only require the Special Counsel to follow the Acting Attorney General's countermand orders for actions deemed "so inappropriate or unwarranted under established Departmental practices." 28 C.F.R. § 600.7(b); * * * With regard to actions that do not rise to that level, the regulations do not clearly require the Special Counsel to follow orders, so it is difficult to see how "good cause" would arise from the Special Counsel's refusal to follow orders. Under such circumstances, the Special Counsel could rightly resist removal on the ground that he was proceeding in full compliance with the regulations, while the Acting Attorney General would not have a similarly steady leg to stand. After all, the Acting Attorney General would be seeking to remove the Special Counsel for not following orders that the Special Counsel was under no duty to follow.

In the event that the for-cause removal standard in the Special Counsel regulations confers substantial protection against removal, the Appointments Clause problem re-emerges. The Special Counsel argues that for-cause removal does not make him a principal officer because "when [C]ongress ... vests the appointment of inferior officers in the heads of departments, it may limit and restrict the power of removal as it deems best for the public interest." * * * The cases cited by the Special Counsel, however, do not persuade the Court. It is unlikely that the broad and dated language of *Perkins* survived *Edmond*, which demands that inferior officers be subordinate to superiors and does not contemplate allowing unremovable officers if "for the public interest." 116 U.S. at 485; 520 U.S. at 662–63. Also, *Perkins* involved a low-ranking naval cadet who was likely well-supervised by the military chain of command, irrespective of any limits on his removal, and the cadet sought only damages, not reinstatement or other protection from removal. * * * The Special Counsel also invokes *Morrison v. Olson* to demonstrate that he is an inferior officer. There, the Supreme Court found the independent counsel to be an inferior officer even though she was removable only for good cause. * * * *Morrison*, however, "relied heavily" on factors other than removal, as discussed below. * * * Thus, "while the presence of a 'good cause' restriction in *Morrison* did not prevent a finding of inferior officer status, [*Morrison*] clearly did not hold that such a restriction on removal was generally consistent with the status of inferior officer." * * * Therefore, the Special Counsel's for-cause removal protection, if substantial, "supports a finding" that the Special Counsel is a principal officer. * * *

In sum, the regulations as written may prevent the Acting Attorney General from countermanding certain actions taken by the Special Counsel. Even so, if the Special Counsel — as he contends — is only minimally protected from removal, then the Special Counsel remains subject to significant direction and supervision by the Acting Attorney General and is thus an inferior officer.

On the other hand, if the for-cause removal provision affords the Special Counsel substantial protection from removal, then in certain circumstances the Acting Attorney General might be unable to countermand the Special Counsel *and* unable to remove the Special Counsel. If such constraints bind the Acting Attorney General against his wishes, the Special Counsel is not truly inferior.

2. Rescission or Revision of the Special Counsel Regulations

Regardless whether the Special Counsel regulations enable the Acting Attorney General to direct and supervise the Special Counsel, the regulations do not bind the Acting Attorney General against his wishes. Rather, the regulations persist only so long as the Acting Attorney General allows them to remain in effect. As in *Sealed Case*, "[s]ubject to generally applicable procedural requirements," the Department of Justice "may rescind this regulation at any time, thereby abolishing the Office of [Special] Counsel." *In re Sealed Case*, 829 F.2d 50, 56 (D.C. Cir. 1987); *see also* [*United States v.*] *Nixon*, 418 U.S. [683, 696 (1974)] (noting that "the regulation defining the Special Prosecutor's authority" binds the executive branch so long as it "remains in force," but "it is theoretically possible for the Attorney General to amend or revoke the regulation defining the Special Prosecutor's authority"); * * *

The regulations' revocability is "[t]he crucial difference" between the Special Counsel regulations and a statute that seeks to bind the executive branch from without, and it is this difference that ensures the Special Counsel is an inferior officer. * * * That is, to the extent that the regulations threaten to impair the Acting Attorney

General's ability to direct and supervise the Special Counsel, the Department of Justice may simply rescind or revise the regulations at any time. This ability to rescind or revise the regulations as needed means that the Special Counsel is subject to the Acting Attorney General's plenary supervision. It also makes the Special Counsel effectively removable at will: if the for-cause provision stands in the way, the Acting Attorney General need only rescind or revise the regulation in order to remove the Special Counsel. *See id.* at 65 (Williams, J., concurring) (explaining that special prosecutor Lawrence Walsh was an inferior officer due to "the Attorney General's complete legal freedom to dispose of [him] by revocation of the Regulations"); * * *

The D.C. Circuit added one caveat in *Sealed Case*. The decision to rescind the Special Counsel regulations would be "[s]ubject to generally applicable procedural requirements." *In re Sealed Case*, 829 F.2d at 56. Conceivably, procedural rulemaking requirements—such as notice-and-comment or the 30-day delay rule—could impose burdens such that the executive branch would not truly be free to rescind the regulations at will. *See* 5 U.S.C. § 553. Such requirements, however, do not apply to "matter[s] relating to agency management or personnel," *id.* § 553(a)(2); notice-and-comment is not required for "rules of agency organization, procedure, or practice," *id.* § 553(b)(A); and the 30-day delay rule does not apply to "interpretative rules and statements of policy" or when the agency finds "good cause," *id.* § 553(d). Indeed, when promulgated in 1999, the Special Counsel regulations relied on these exceptions to avoid the usual procedural requirements. * * * A decision to rescind or revise the Special Counsel regulations likewise fits comfortably within the exceptions, so procedural requirements would not hamper the decision.

In addition, the Acting Attorney General retains a free hand to rescind the regulations because such a decision likely would be unreviewable. Under the Administrative Procedure Act, judicial review is not available for actions "committed to agency discretion by law." 5 U.S.C. § 701(a)(2). Under this standard, "review is not to be had if the statute is drawn so that a court would have no meaningful standard against which to judge the agency's exercise of discretion." * * * Thus, in determining whether a particular action is "committed to agency discretion by law," courts ask whether "statutes are drawn in such broad terms that in a given case there is no law to apply." * * * Here, "[t]he sources of authority invoked by the Attorney General speak in the broadest imaginable terms," so "the search for any 'law to apply' is singularly unproductive." * * * Therefore, the Administrative Procedure Act would not provide for judicial review of a decision to rescind or revise the regulations, and in the absence of any other viable claim, the decision would be unreviewable.

In the absence of procedural requirements or judicial review to hamstring his discretion, the Acting Attorney General retains the power to rescind or revise the Special Counsel regulations at will, and any purported limits on the power to remove or countermand persist only with the acquiescence of the Acting Attorney General. As a result, the Special Counsel is effectively removable at will, subject to the Acting Attorney General's plenary supervision, and thus an inferior officer.

3. *Morrison v. Olson*

Even if the Special Counsel is an inferior officer under *Edmond*, Concord argues in the alternative that the Special Counsel remains a principal officer under *Morrison v. Olson*. * * * Although *Morrison* has been called into doubt by seemingly all quarters, there is no need to consider *Morrison*'s continuing vitality because the result is no different under *Morrison*.

Morrison did not set forth a definitive test for differentiating between inferior and principal officers, but it identified four relevant factors: whether the officer is (1) "subject to removal by a higher Executive Branch official," (2) "empowered ... to perform only certain, limited duties," (3) "limited in jurisdiction," and (4) "limited in tenure." * * * Of these factors, only the jurisdictional inquiry arguably weighs against inferiority here. Independent Counsel Alexia Morrison's "office" was "limited in jurisdiction" because the Ethics in Government Act was "restricted in applicability to certain federal officials suspected of certain serious federal crimes" and because "an independent counsel can only act within the scope of the jurisdiction that has been granted" by the appointing authority. * * * That jurisdictional grant was quite narrow: Morrison was directed to investigate "whether the testimony of [Assistant Attorney General Theodore] Olson and his revision of such testimony on March 10, 1983 [before a House Subcommittee] violated either 18 U.S.C. § 1505 or § 1001, or any other provision of federal law," and she "ha[d] jurisdiction to investigate [and prosecute] any other allegation of evidence of violation of any Federal criminal law by Theodore Olson developed during investigations, by the Independent Counsel, referred to above, and connected with or arising out of that investigation...." * * * In contrast, the Special Counsel possesses a broad jurisdiction to investigate "any links and/or coordination between the Russian government and individuals associated with the campaign of President Donald Trump" and "any matters that arose directly from the investigation." * * * The Special Counsel may also "prosecute federal crimes arising from the investigation of these matters." * * * This jurisdictional framework is arguably broader than Morrison's, which cuts against inferiority.

The other three factors, however, point in the opposite direction. Like the Independent Counsel, the Special Counsel is "empowered ... to perform only certain, limited duties," in the sense that his "role is restricted primarily to investigation and, if appropriate, prosecution for certain federal crimes." * * * Also, the Special Counsel is "limited in tenure." * * * *Morrison* did not view this factor as requiring a time limit, but rather considered an officer's tenure limited if the officer "is appointed essentially to accomplish a single task, and when that task is over the office is terminated," which describes the Special Counsel's tenure. * * * Finally, the Special Counsel is far more removable than the Independent Counsel was. The Independent Counsel was removable "only for good cause," which the Supreme Court did not define but understood to afford some degree of protection. * * * The Special Counsel, as discussed above, is effectively removable at will. * * * Under *Morrison*, therefore, the Special Counsel is an inferior officer. * * *

B. The Statutory Authority to Appoint the Special Counsel

Qualifying as an inferior officer, however, is not enough to satisfy the Appointments Clause. Congress must also "by Law vest" the authority to appoint the inferior officer in a "Head of Department" — here, the Acting Attorney General. * * * The Special Counsel contends that multiple statutory provisions establish the Acting Attorney General's appointment authority, and the Special Counsel primarily relies on 28 U.S.C. § 533(1) and 28 U.S.C. § 515(b). * * * Concord argues that no provision gets the job done. * * * On a blank slate, this might be a difficult question because the statutory provisions "do not explicitly authorize" the Acting Attorney General to appoint a Special Counsel. * * * Even so, Supreme Court and D.C. Circuit precedent foreclose Concord's argument.

1. 28 U.S.C. § 533(1)

The text of § 533(1) offers the most promising hook for the Acting Attorney General's authority to appoint a Special Counsel. It states: "The Attorney General may appoint officials — (1) to detect and prosecute crimes against the United States." 28 U.S.C. § 533(1). Concord, however, raises strong arguments that § 533 does not confer the authority at issue here. First, the provision refers to "officials," not "officers." Although the two words share the same root and overlapping definitions, * * * they are not necessarily synonyms. An "official" is someone "invested with an office," but "esp. a subordinate one." * * * This definition may connote the subservience and lesser authority associated with a mere employee, functionary, or agent. In contrast, an "officer" holds the more substantial responsibility of an "office of trust, authority, or command," not simply that of an "office." * * * Also, in the specific context of appointments by department heads, "officer" is a distinct and well-established legal term. * * * When vesting appointment authority in department heads, other provisions specifically confer the power to appoint "officers," not "officials." * * * These provisions show that, had Congress meant to confer "officer"-appointing power via § 533 or any other provision, "it easily could have done so." * * *

In addition, the use of "officials" in § 533 is notable because provisions in the same chapter refer to "officers." * * * Further context also supports a circumscribed reading of § 533. Section 533(1) is located alongside three other provisions authorizing the appointment of FBI-centric officials. * * * Section 533's placement suggests interpreting the provision within the narrower context of its surrounding provisions governing the FBI and its investigations, not as a broad grant of authority for the Attorney General to appoint inferior officers generally and a Special Counsel in particular.

2. 28 U.S.C. § 515(b)

Likewise, § 515(b) does not explicitly authorize the Acting Attorney General to appoint a Special Counsel. * * * On its face, § 515 does not explicitly empower the Acting Attorney General to appoint or retain anyone. Instead, § 515(a) empowers "any attorney specially appointed by the Attorney General under law" to do certain things — namely, conduct legal proceedings. *Id.* § 515(a). And § 515(b) imposes a requirement that "[e]ach attorney specially retained under authority of the Department of Justice shall be commissioned" and "shall take the oath." *Id.* § 515(b). But neither appears to vest the Acting Attorney General with the power to appoint or retain such attorneys. * * *

Furthermore, § 515 refers to attorneys who are specially appointed by the Attorney General "under law" and specially retained "under Authority of the Department of Justice." These clauses become surplusage if § 515 provides standalone appointment power, for in that case the statute could have referred to attorneys "specially appointed under this section" or simply attorneys "specially appointed." To avoid rendering these[] clauses in § 515 superfluous, Concord counsels that they should be read to require some other law or authority—outside of § 515—to authorize the Acting Attorney General to make the special appointment. * * *

3. 5 U.S.C. § 301 and 28 U.S.C. §§ 509 and 510

As additional sources of appointment authority, the Special Counsel points to three other statutory provisions that are no more explicit: §§ 509, 510, and 301. Section 509 vests in the Attorney General the "functions of other officers of the Department" and the "functions of agencies and employees of the Department of Justice," while § 510 permits the Attorney General to "authorize[e] the performance by any other officer, employee, or agency of the Department of Justice of any function of the Attorney General." 28 U.S.C. §§ 509, 510. But the Attorney General's general power to delegate duties to an existing officer is not the same as the power to appoint the officer in the first place.

Under the even broader § 301—the "housekeeping statute"—department heads "may prescribe regulations for the government of his department, the conduct of its employees, [and] the distribution and performance of its business." 5 U.S.C. § 301. This power to "keep house," however, is not the same as the power to "build the house" by appointing officers. Otherwise, § 301 would threaten to swallow up the statutory appointment schemes enacted for various agencies, including the Department of Justice. * * * In sum, the individual provisions relied upon by the Special Counsel "do not explicitly authorize" the Acting Attorney General to appoint him. * * *

4. *Nixon* and *Sealed Case*

Even though the statutes "do not explicitly authorize" the Acting Attorney General to appoint the Special Counsel, *Nixon* and *Sealed Case* establish that the statutory provisions "accommodate the delegation at issue." *In re Sealed Case*, 829 F.2d at 55. Both cases involved similar officers: special prosecutors appointed via Department of Justice regulations. In both, the Supreme Court and the D.C. Circuit stated that Congress empowered the Attorney General to appoint the officers, albeit without analyzing specifically how any individual provision or combination of provisions accomplished this. Discussing Leon Jaworski's appointment in *Nixon*, the Supreme Court explained:

> Congress has vested in the Attorney General the power to conduct the criminal litigation of the United States Government. 28 U.S.C. § 516. It has also vested in him the power to appoint subordinate officers to assist him in the

discharge of his duties. 28 U.S.C. §§ 509, 510, 515, 533. Acting pursuant to those statutes, the Attorney General has delegated the authority to represent the United States in these particular matters to a Special Prosecutor with unique authority and tenure.

Nixon, 418 U.S. at 694, 94 S.Ct. 3090. Similarly, *Sealed Case* addressed Lawrence Walsh's appointment under Department of Justice regulations to investigate the Iran/Contra affair, particularly then-Lieutenant Colonel Oliver North and any associates. *See In re Sealed Case*, 829 F.2d at 51–54. Noting that *Nixon* "presupposed the validity" of an "indistinguishable" regulation appointing a special prosecutor, the D.C. Circuit stated:

> We have no difficulty concluding that the Attorney General possessed the statutory authority to create the Office of Independent Counsel: Iran/Contra and to convey to it the "investigative and prosecutorial functions and powers" described in 28 C.F.R. § 600.1(a) of the regulation. The statutory provisions relied upon by the Attorney General in promulgating the regulation are 5 U.S.C. § 301 and 28 U.S.C. §§ 509, 510, and 515. While these provisions do not explicitly authorize the Attorney General to create an Office of Independent Counsel virtually free of ongoing supervision, we read them as accommodating the delegation at issue here.

* * *

Concord dismisses these statements as mere dicta on an issue that was not presented to, nor analyzed by, the higher courts. But these statements are not dicta. They are necessary steps toward the higher courts' ultimate conclusions, so they are authoritative here. * * *

Moreover, in *Sealed Case*, Oliver North and Lawrence Walsh *did* present the issue to the D.C. Circuit, at least at a high level of generality. * * * Finally, even if the statements were dicta, they would still carry significant weight. * * *

As a result, *Nixon* and *Sealed Case* resolve the issue. "The statutory provisions relied upon by the [Acting] Attorney General in promulgating the regulations ... do not explicitly authorize the [Acting] Attorney General to create an Office of [Special] Counsel," but they "accommodat[e] the delegation at issue here." * * * That is, Congress "vested in [the Acting Attorney General] the power to appoint subordinate officers to assist him in the discharge of his duties," including "a Special Prosecutor with unique authority and tenure" such as the Special Counsel. * * *

IV. THE SEPARATION OF POWERS

Next, Concord briefly contends that the Special Counsel position violates core separation-of-powers principles in two ways. The arguments resemble Concord's Appointments Clause challenge, just at a higher level of generality, and they fail for much the same reasons.

Concord first argues that if the Special Counsel regulations are not binding on the Special Counsel, then "there is no limitation at all on the scope of an investigation and prosecution," and "the byproduct is a powerful prosecutor, unguided, uncon-strained, unfettered, and, indeed, foreign to this Nation's three-branch constitutional order." * * * To the contrary, in the absence of the regulations, the Special Counsel would be subject to the Acting Attorney General's plenary control by statute. * * * Because executive power would remain wholly within the executive branch, no sep-aration-of-powers problem would arise.

Second, Concord argues that Congress did not authorize the Attorney General to promulgate the Special Counsel regulations, which are thus "ultra vires" and lead to an "un-cabined federal prosecutorial authority." * * * The Attorney General, how-ever, has ample authority to issue regulations that govern the Department of Justice. * * * This case does not present an encroachment by one branch against another. Executive power, particularly the core executive power of prosecution, remains vested exclusively in the executive and subject to the executive's control. * * * As constituted, the Special Counsel position does not violate core separation-of-powers principles.

V. THE APPOINTMENT ORDER

Finally, Concord argues that the Special Counsel's appointment order violates the Special Counsel regulations and the appointment order does not authorize the pros-ecution of Concord. * * *

A. Consistency with the Special Counsel Regulations

The appointment order, according to Concord, violates § 600.1 and § 600.4 of the Special Counsel regulations. * * * Concord's challenge fails at the outset, however, because the Special Counsel regulations do not create judicially enforceable rights. As Judge Berman-Jackson and Judge Ellis explained at length, "the Special Counsel Regulations are internal 'rules of agency organization, procedure, or practice,' and not substantive rules that affect the rights and obligations of individuals outside the Department." [*United States v.*] *Manafort*, 312 F.Supp.3d [60,] 76 [(D.C. Cir. 2018)]. Because "internal agency regulations that were not required by the Constitution or a statute are not enforceable by the defendant in a criminal prosecution," the Special Counsel regulations "do not afford defendant grounds to move to dismiss the indict-ment." * * *

Even if Concord could bring a challenge, the appointment order does not violate the Special Counsel regulations. According to Concord, the Special Counsel appoint-ment order violates § 600.1 because the appointment order does not establish the need for a criminal investigation of Concord, a conflict of interest as to Concord, or extraordinary circumstances as to Concord. * * * But § 600.1 is not defendant-specific. Rather, it permits the Acting Attorney General to appoint a Special Counsel upon a determination that a "criminal investigation of a ... *matter* is warranted," an "inves-tigation or prosecution of that ... *matter* by a United States Attorney's Office or lit-igating Division of the Department of Justice would present a conflict of interest for the Department or other extraordinary circumstances," and "it would be in the public interest to appoint an outside Special Counsel to assume responsibility for the *matter*."

* * * Therefore, the appointment order's omission of defendant-specific determinations does not conflict with §600.1.

The appointment order is also consistent with §600.4, which states:

> The jurisdiction of a Special Counsel shall be established by the Attorney General. The Special Counsel will be provided with a specific factual statement of the matter to be investigated. The jurisdiction of a Special Counsel shall also include the authority to investigate and prosecute federal crimes committed in the course of, and with intent to interfere with, the Special Counsel's investigation....

28 C.F.R. §600.4. Concord argues that the appointment order violates §600.4 by giving the Special Counsel jurisdiction to investigate "any matters that arose or may arise directly from" the FBI's counter-intelligence investigation. * * * As explained by Judge Berman-Jackson, however, §600.4 does not impose a limit on the Acting Attorney General's power to delegate authority to the Special Counsel "as he sees fit." *Manafort*, 312 F.Supp.3d 60 * * *. Therefore, the appointment order is on solid ground when it confers jurisdiction over "matters that arose or may arise directly from" the investigation.

B. Authority to Prosecute Concord

Concord also contends that the Special Counsel exceeded his authority under the appointment order by investigating and prosecuting Concord. * * * Concord faults the indictment for lacking allegations regarding the Russian government, President Trump's campaign, links or coordination between Concord and the Russian government or President Trump's campaign, or interference by Concord with the Special Counsel's investigation. * * * The appointment order, however, does not limit the Special Counsel to investigating individuals and entities that are part of the Russian government. Rather, the Special Counsel may investigate the Russian government's interference "efforts," which involved non-governmental third parties. * * * Concord's alleged actions are therefore within the scope of the Special Counsel's investigation. Because the investigation of Concord was authorized, so was the prosecution. * * * Therefore, by investigating and prosecuting Concord, the Special Counsel did not exceed his authority.

CONCLUSION

For the foregoing reasons, the Court denies Concord's Motion to Dismiss the Indictment Based on the Special Counsel's Appointment and Authority. * * *

In re Grand Jury Investigation
916 F.3d 1047 (D.C. Cir. 2019)

Opinion for the court filed by Circuit Judge Rogers.

Andrew Miller appeals an order holding him in contempt for failing to comply with grand jury subpoenas served on him by Special Counsel Robert S. Mueller, III. He contends the Special Counsel's appointment is unlawful under the Appointments

Clause of the Constitution, and therefore the contempt order should be reversed. We affirm.

* * * On appeal, Miller challenges the authority of Special Counsel Mueller on the grounds that his appointment is unlawful under the Appointments Clause because: (1) the Special Counsel is a principal officer who was not appointed by the President with the advice and consent of the Senate; (2) Congress did not "by law" authorize the Special Counsel's appointment; and (3) the Special Counsel was not appointed by a "Head of Department" because the Attorney General's recusal from the subject matter of the Special Counsel's investigation did not make the Deputy Attorney General the Acting Attorney General. This court's review is *de novo.* * * *

As interpreted by the Supreme Court, the Appointments Clause distinguishes between "principal officers," who must be nominated by the President with advice and consent of the Senate, and "inferior officers," who may be appointed by the President alone, or by heads of departments, or by the judiciary, as Congress allows. *Morrison v. Olson*, 487 U.S. 654, 670–71, (1988) (quoting *Buckley v. Valeo*, 424 U.S. 1, 132 (1976)). Thus, if Special Counsel Mueller is a principal officer, his appointment was in violation of the Appointments Clause because he was not appointed by the President with advice and consent of the Senate. Binding precedent instructs that Special Counsel Mueller is an inferior officer under the Appointments Clause.

An inferior officer is one "whose work is directed and supervised at some level by others who were appointed by Presidential nomination with the advice and consent of the Senate." *Edmond v. United States*, 520 U.S. 651, 663 (1997). In *Edmond*, the Supreme Court applied three factors to determine whether an officer was inferior: degree of oversight, final decision-making authority, and removability. According to Miller, those considerations point to Special Counsel Mueller being a principal, rather than inferior, officer because the Office of Special Counsel regulations impose various limitations on the Attorney General's ability to exercise effective oversight of the Special Counsel. But as foreshadowed in this court's opinion in *In re Sealed Case*, 829 F.2d 50 (D.C. Cir. 1987), a supervisor's ability to rescind provisions assuring an officer's independence can render that officer inferior. There, this court recognized that an independent counsel was an inferior officer because his office was created pursuant to a regulation and "the Attorney General may rescind this regulation at any time, thereby abolishing the Office of Independent Counsel." * * *

The Attorney General, an officer appointed by the President with the advice and consent of the Senate, has authority to rescind at any time the Office of Special Counsel regulations or otherwise render them inapplicable to the Special Counsel. Unlike the independent counsel in *Morrison*, whose independence and tenure protection were secured by Title VI of the Ethics in Government Act, Special Counsel Mueller is subject to greater executive oversight because the limitations on the Attorney General's oversight and removal powers are in regulations that the Attorney General can revise or repeal, * * * ; absent such limitations, the Attorney General would retain plenary supervisory authority of the Special Counsel under 28 U.S.C. § 509. Furthermore, even if at the time of the appointment of Special Counsel Mueller only the Attorney General could rescind the regulations, the Acting Attorney General could essentially accomplish the same thing with specific regard to Special Counsel Mueller by amending his Appointment Order of May 17, 2017, to eliminate the Order's good cause limitations on the Special Counsel's removal (on which Miller focuses particular attention).

In either event, Special Counsel Mueller effectively serves at the pleasure of an Executive Branch officer who was appointed with the advice and consent of the Senate. *See* 28 U.S.C. §§ 509, 515(a), 516; * * * The control thereby maintained means the Special Counsel is an inferior officer. * * * Miller's contention that Special Counsel Mueller is a principal officer under the Appointments Clause thus fails. * * *

The question whether Congress has "by law" vested appointment of Special Counsel Mueller in the Attorney General has already been decided by the Supreme Court. In *United States v. Nixon*, 418 U.S. 683, 694 (1974), the Court stated: "[Congress] has also vested in [the Attorney General] the power to appoint subordinate officers to assist him in the discharge of his duties. 28 U.S.C. §§ 509, 510, 515, 533." In acting pursuant to those statutes, the Court held, the Attorney General validly delegated authority to a special prosecutor to investigate offenses arising out of the 1972 presidential election and allegations involving President Richard M. Nixon. * * *

Miller contends, unpersuasively, that the quoted sentence in *Nixon* * * * is dictum because the issue whether the Attorney General had statutory authority to appoint a special prosecutor was not directly presented and the Supreme Court did not analyze the text of the specific statutes. It is true that a statement not necessary to a court's holding is dictum. * * * But Miller misreads *Nixon*, for the Supreme Court was presented with the question whether a justiciable controversy existed. When the Special Prosecutor issued a subpoena to the President to produce certain recordings and documents, the President moved to quash the subpoena, asserting a claim of executive privilege, * * * and maintained the claim was nonjusticiable because it was "intraexecutive" in character * * *. The Supreme Court held there was a justiciable controversy because the regulations issued by the Attorney General gave the Special Prosecutor authority to contest the President's invocation of executive privilege during the investigation. * * * In this analysis, the Attorney General's statutory authority to issue the regulations was a necessary antecedent to determining whether the regulations were valid, and, therefore, was necessary to the decision that a justiciable controversy existed. The Supreme Court's quoted statement regarding the Attorney General's power to appoint subordinate officers is, therefore, not dictum. Moreover, under this court's precedent, "carefully considered language of the Supreme Court, even if technically dictum, generally must be treated as authoritative." * * *

Furthermore, in *Sealed Case* this court recognized that the statutory scheme creating the Department vests authority in the Attorney General to appoint inferior officers to investigate and to prosecute matters with a level of independence. There, the Attorney General appointed an independent counsel and promulgated regulations to create an office to investigate whether Lieutenant Colonel Oliver L. North and other officials violated federal criminal law in connection with the shipment or sale of military arms to Iran and the transfer or diversion of funds connected to any sales (referred to as the Iran/Contra matter). The Attorney General also authorized the independent counsel to prosecute any violations of federal criminal laws uncovered during investigation of the Iran/Contra matter. * * * North refused to comply with a grand jury subpoena, arguing that the independent counsel's appointment was invalid. * * * This court disagreed:

> We have no difficulty concluding that the Attorney General possessed the statutory authority to create the Office of Independent Counsel: Iran/Contra and to convey to it the 'investigative and prosecutorial functions and powers' described in ... the regulation.... While [5 U.S.C. § 301 and 28 U.S.C. §§ 509, 510, and 515] do not explicitly authorize the Attorney General to create an Office of Independent Counsel virtually free of ongoing supervision, we read them as accommodating the delegation at issue here.

The issue before the court was whether the independent counsel was authorized to investigate and to prosecute officials in regard to the Iran/Contra matter. As such, the Attorney General's authority to appoint an independent counsel was antecedent to deciding whether the Attorney General validly delegated authority to the independent counsel. The court's quoted statements regarding the Attorney General's statutory authority to appoint an independent counsel are, therefore, not dicta as Miller suggests.

To the extent Miller incorporates arguments of Amicus Curiae Concord Management, he maintains that in *Sealed Case* this court held only that the Attorney General had authority to delegate powers to an already appointed position inside the Department, not authority to appoint a new special counsel outside of the Department. The court expressly noted that the statutory scheme authorized the Attorney General to delegate powers to "others within the Department of Justice." * * * Miller is correct that in that case, the independent counsel had two parallel appointments: one from the Attorney General to the Office of Independent Counsel: Iran/Contra and an earlier one from a Special Division under the Ethics in Government Act, 28 U.S.C. § 593(b). But this court explicitly declined to address whether the independent counsel's initial appointment under the Act was valid, thereby avoiding the need to consider any constitutional questions raised by the Act. * * * Therefore, this court assumed that the independent counsel did not already hold a position inside the Department when it held that the Attorney General's appointment of him to the Office of Independent Counsel: Iran/Contra was valid. That analysis applies equally to the facts of the instant case.

Because binding precedent establishes that Congress has "by law" vested authority in the Attorney General to appoint the Special Counsel as an inferior officer, this court has no need to go further to identify the specific sources of this authority. * * * Miller's cursory references to a "clear statement" argument he presented to the district court are insufficient to preserve that issue for appeal and it is forfeited. * * *

The statutory and regulatory scheme demonstrate, contrary to Miller's contention, that at the time of Special Counsel Mueller's appointment, Acting Attorney General Rosenstein was the "Head of Department" under the Appointments Clause as to the matter on which the Attorney General was recused. The Attorney General is the head of the Department of Justice, 28 U.S.C. §503, and an Acting Attorney General becomes the head of the Department when acting in that capacity because an acting officer is vested with the same authority that could be exercised by the officer for whom he acts, * * *

Miller's view that the Attorney General's recusal did not make the Deputy Attorney General the "Acting" Attorney General, and, therefore, the Deputy Attorney General lacked authority to appoint Special Counsel Mueller as an inferior officer, ignores the statutory scheme. Section 508(a) of Title 28 provides: "In case of a vacancy in the office of Attorney General, or of his absence or disability, the Deputy Attorney General may exercise all the duties of that office." The word "disability" means the "inability to do something" or "lack of legal qualification to do a thing." *Webster's Third New International Dictionary* 642 (1981). Congress is presumed to use words to have their ordinary meaning absent indication to the contrary. * * *

Miller would qualify Congress's meaning as limited to a "wholesale absence or disability, not a recusal to act on a single issue." * * * His interpretation is contrary to the structure Congress created for the Department whereby the Deputy Attorney General can carry on when the Attorney General is unable to act on a matter. A statute and Department regulation disqualify any officer or Department employee from participating in an investigation or prosecution that may involve "a personal, financial, or political conflict of interest, or the appearance thereof." * * * Department regulation 28 C.F.R. §45.2(a) bars involvement where there is a conflict of interest, and then-Attorney General Sessions invoked that regulation as to the investigation of Russia's interference in the 2016 presidential campaign. * * * At the time of the Special Counsel's appointment then, the Attorney General had a "disability" because he lacked legal qualification to participate in any matters related to that conflict. * * * Under Miller's view, there could be no Attorney General, acting or otherwise, to be in charge of the matter.

Our understanding of Congress's use of the word "disability" in Section 508 accords with courts' interpretations of Rule 25(a) of the Federal Rules of Criminal Procedure. Rule 25(a) provides that if a judge cannot proceed to preside at a trial due to "death, sickness, or other disability," another judge may complete the trial. Courts have interpreted "disability" to include recusal. * * * In challenging the validity of the analogy on the basis that all federal judges have been appointed by the President with the advice and consent of the Senate, 28 U.S.C. §133, Miller overlooks that by statute so is the Deputy Attorney General, 28 U.S.C. §504. * * * Therefore, the Attorney General's single-issue recusal is a "disability" that created a vacancy that the Deputy Attorney General was eligible to fill. * * *

Still Miller maintains that Section 508 does not make the Deputy Attorney General an "acting" officer but only authorizes the Deputy Attorney General to perform the duties of the Attorney General's office and the Attorney General remains the "Head of Department" for Appointments Clause purposes. Congress has authorized the Deputy Attorney General to perform "all the duties of th[e] office" in case of a vacancy, 28 U.S.C. §508(a), such that the Deputy becomes the "Acting" Attorney General. As to the recused matter, the Acting Attorney General has authority to appoint inferior officers because that is part of the authority that could be exercised by the Attorney General. Miller's position that the Deputy Attorney General only becomes the "Acting" Attorney General if the Federal Vacancies Reform Act, 5 U.S.C. §3345, is triggered—and that the Act is triggered, he maintains, only upon a complete inability to perform the functions and duties of the Attorney General's office—overlooks that the Act explicitly provides it is not the exclusive means to designate an "acting" official. * * * Miller does not explain why 28 U.S.C. §508 is not such a statute that temporarily authorizes an officer to temporarily perform the duties of the Attorney General. * * * Therefore, Special Counsel Mueller was properly appointed by a head of Department, who at the time was the Acting Attorney General.

Because the Special Counsel is an inferior officer, and the Deputy Attorney General became the head of the Department by virtue of becoming the Acting Attorney General as a result of a vacancy created by the disability of the Attorney General through recusal on the matter, we hold that Miller's challenge to the appointment of the Special Counsel fails. Accordingly, we affirm the order finding Miller in civil contempt.

Notes and Questions

1. *Shifting Precedent?* Compare the court's reasoning in *Concord Management* to the above excerpt from *Morrison*. Why did the *Concord Management* court not simply rely on *Morrison* to hold that Special Counsel Mueller is an inferior officer? Is the EGA's for cause removal provision really evidence that the independent counsel is inferior to the Attorney General? What did the court in *Concord Management* think?

2. *Delegation of Authority.* In the case of the special counsel, there was no dispute as to whether the applicable DOJ regulations vested his appointment in a "Head[]" of Department[]"—the Attorney General (AG) is clearly the head of the DOJ. 28 U.S.C. §503. The issue was whether the fact that the AG's recusal, which left the special counsel appointment to the AAG, rather than the AG himself, rendered the appointment unconstitutional because it was no longer effectuated by the head of a department. How did the courts in *Concord Management* and *In re Grand Jury Investigation* handle this unique and interesting situation? Which authorities did they look to and how did they interpret them to reach their conclusion?

3. *Problems with Delegation.* Why were the courts so concerned about whether a specific delegation to appoint the special counsel existed from the AG to the AAG? Consider the text of the Appointments Clause, in particular the requirement that Congress "vest" the appointment of inferior officers in a department head.

4. *(More) Problems with Delegation.* Why does the Appointments Clause limit itself to department *heads*? If Congress tells the AG that she can appoint an inferior officer, for example, why should we care that the AG asked one of her subordinates (i.e., not the agency head) to complete the task? Ask yourself what the advantages are to having an agency head—someone who themselves was appointed, and can likely be fired, directly by the president—making important decisions about who should be an inferior officer? If the agency head is more closely aligned with the president than say, an agency employee (e.g., a career bureaucrat), do the voters retain more influence over the appointment? Put another way, if your job depends on winning an election, will you pay more attention to public opinion when making your decisions? What are the advantages of having our leaders think about the public's perception of their choices before they make them? The draw-backs? The answer lies in the same separation of powers principles that began this chapter.

Chapter Three

The Mueller Investigation and Congress: Legal Complexities of Parallel Inquiries

I. Introduction

Congress has an array of policy and oversight interests in the Russian active measures to disrupt American democratic processes. By the time Deputy Attorney General Rod Rosenstein appointed former FBI Director and Deputy Attorney General Robert Mueller as Special Counsel, a number of congressional committees had commenced some sort of investigative activity. Moreover, Mueller's appointment—and the reasons for it—presented one of the quintessential high-profile, politically charged investigations that is bound to attract congressional interest.

Parallel and overlapping congressional, criminal, and counterintelligence investigations raise their own set of thorny legal issues. They create opportunities for cooperation and generate tension. They react to one another in dynamic and unpredictable ways. Congressional investigations can generate process crimes like perjury, obstruction of justice, and witness tampering. And criminal investigations often serve as the basis for Congress to initiate an inquiry.

Prosecutors' jobs can be complicated by congressional investigation. Multiple appearances by the same witness can become a problem for prosecutors if information the prosecutors rely on for conviction gets undermined by impeachment evidence developed in a congressional appearance. Or, if Congress grants immunity to a witness in one of its hearings, it can render a subsequent prosecution of that witness for conduct related to the immunized testimony nearly impossible. Further, conflicts arise when Congress seeks materials from the Department of Justice about criminal investigations.

For its part, Congress can find its access to information impeded due to issues related to parallel criminal investigations. It is on the receiving end of Department of Justice objections to production of investigative files, grand jury material, and legal analysis sought by congressional committees. One traditional concern for Congress is that witnesses who may be targets, subjects, or witnesses in a criminal investigation are less likely to cooperate with a congressional investigation. Under those circumstances, they are more likely to consider assertion of Fifth Amendment rights against self-incrimination.

Witnesses in overlapping investigations have to manage additional risks associated with multiple witness appearances, waiver of privileges, and reputational or business harms. Lawyers traditionally do not want their clients to give multiple appearances before investigating bodies because of the risk that inconsistent statements could create false statements liability. There are some eighteen criminal statutes that cover behavior of those ensnared by congressional investigation, so the stakes are always high with any contact with government. The political—and at times politicized—nature of congressional investigations exacerbates that concern. Members of Congress may have partisan incentives to hunt for transcript discrepancies, and they do so without the limitations on extrajudicial statements under which prosecutors operate.

Mueller's investigation into Russian government's active efforts to interfere in the U.S. presidential election operated in an environment of intense parallel congressional activity from its inception. The Mueller Report describes the environment preceding his appointment:

> Between mid-January 2017 and early February 2017, three congressional committees—the House Permanent Select Committee on Intelligence (HPSCI), the Senate Select Committee on Intelligence (SSCI), and the Senate Judiciary Committee (SJC)—announced that they would conduct inquiries, or had already been conducting inquiries, into Russian interference in the election. Then-FBI Director James Comey later confirmed to Congress the existence of the FBI's investigation into Russian interference that had begun before the election. On March 20, 2017, in open-session testimony before HPSCI, Comey stated:
>
>> I have been authorized by the Department of Justice to confirm that the FBI, as part of our counterintelligence mission, is investigating the Russian government's efforts to interfere in the 2016 presidential election, and that includes investigating the nature of any links between individuals associated with the Trump campaign and the Russian government and whether there was any coordination between the campaign and Russia's efforts* * * As with any counterintelligence investigation, this will also include an assessment of whether any crimes were committed.
>
> The investigation continued under then-Director Comey for the next seven weeks until May 9, 2017, when President Trump fired Comey as FBI Director. * * *[1]

Note that the Mueller Report quotes Comey's congressional testimony. Later passages in the Mueller Report rely on congressional testimony by Jared Kushner, Donald Trump, Jr., and others.

---

1. Mueller Report, Vol. I, p. 8.

Throughout his tenure, the Special Counsel received repeated requests and referrals from Congress. In the aftermath of the release of a redacted version of the Mueller Report, the tussle over redacted material and underlying evidence has resulted in a full-blown constitutional standoff between Congress and the Executive.

Mueller also used the power of his office to vindicate congressional investigative interests. The Mueller Report notes "the Office concluded that the Principles of Federal Prosecution supported charging certain individuals connected to the Campaign with making false statements or otherwise obstructing this investigation or parallel congressional investigations."[2] Most notably, the Special Counsel prosecuted President Trump's former lawyer and self-described "fixer" Michael Cohen for lying to Congress about the status of Trump Organization efforts to build a hotel in Moscow.

This chapter examines some of the legal questions the Mueller investigations generated by looking at historical examples raising similar issues. Section II addresses the question of whether production of communications traditionally covered by attorney-client privilege to Congress pursuant to a subpoena constitutes waiver for purposes of parallel criminal or civil litigation. In Section III, we revisit a famous Iran-Contra scandal to shed light on the challenges presented to prosecutions of witnesses who have been granted use immunity in order to compel their testimony before Congress. Finally, Section IV presents the starkly divergent legal views held by Congress and the Executive with respect to access to law enforcement files and grand jury information when Congress is investigating.

II. Congressional Investigations, Attorney-Client Privilege, and Waiver in Parallel Proceedings

Lawyers are guardians of attorney-client confidences and other evidentiary privileges designed to promote candor in relationships between marital spouses, doctors and their patients, worshipers and their religious clergy. Parallel legal proceedings always present a risk that disclosure of privileged information in, say, a civil action will thereby waive protection from disclosure in a criminal investigation. Therefore, lawyers assiduously try to protect privileged information from disclosure across all manner of litigation and investigations. (*See* Chap. 5, discussing the attorney-client privilege as it relates to Michael Cohen.)

But Congress does not deem itself legally bound to privileges recognized by the common law and Federal Rules of Evidence. According to the Congressional Research Service, "it is the congressional committee alone that determines whether to accept a claim of attorney-client privilege."[3] Work product protections are even more prob-

---

2. Mueller Report, Vol. I, p. 174.

3. Alissa M. Dolan et al., Cong. Research Serv., RL30240, *Congressional Oversight Manual* 48 (2014). *See also* James Hamilton & Randall Mark Levine, *The Applicability of the Attorney-Client Priv-*

lematic because not only does Congress reject a legal limit to its ability to obtain work product, at least two federal courts have held that work product prepared in anticipation of congressional investigations fails to meet the "in anticipation of litigation" prong of the test.[4]

As such, Congress has had success at compelling production of attorney-client communications and attorney work product that would traditionally be protected from disclosure in judicial proceedings. Those significant disclosure risks presented by a congressional investigation become even more acute in parallel criminal investigations or civil litigation. So, what effect does production of privileged materials to Congress have on waiver? Can subsequent litigants or law enforcement entities successfully claim that production to Congress allows for open season on those otherwise privileged documents?

Iron Workers Local Union No. 17 Ins. Fund v. Philip Morris, Inc.

35 F. Supp. 2d 582 (N.D. Ohio 1999)

OPINION AND ORDER

GWIN, District Judge.

On December 28, 1998, Plaintiff Funds moved this Court for an order declaring that defendants had previously waived their claim of privilege with regard to certain documents produced in other actions or before Congress. In response, defendants claim that no waiver has occurred and that such documents remain privileged. With their opposition, the defendants ask this Court to keep highly probative evidence from the fact-finder when the evidence is already available to all who would merely look.

Because the moving tobacco defendants fail to sustain their burden of showing that they had not waived the privilege for tactical advantage in providing materials to the U.S. House of Representatives, and because the defendants fail to sustain their burden of showing that they had not waived the privilege for tactical advantage in settling the Minnesota state court litigation, this Court denies the defendants' motion.

I. Background of this action

The plaintiffs are certain trusts organized to provide health-related benefits to workers and their families. The representative plaintiffs are six jointly-administered, multi-employer health and welfare trust funds in the State of Ohio. The plaintiffs make claim on behalf of themselves and a class of approximately 100 other similarly-

---

ilege before Congress, available at http://www.martindale.com/government/article_Bingham-McCutchen-LLP_834882.htm (Nov. 6, 2009) (quoting then-House Oversight Committee Chairman Rep. Edolphus Towns (D-N.Y.): "Congress has the right to refuse … an assertion of the attorney-client privilege.").

4. *See, e.g., In re* Grand Jury Subpoena Duces Tecum, 112 F.3d 910, 924 (8th Cir. 1997) (declining to provide work product protection to White House documents prepared in anticipation of congressional investigations); P. & B. Marina, Ltd., 136 F.R.D. 50, 58–59 (E.D.N.Y. 1991) (holding lobbyist letter to client not protected work product).

situated health and welfare trusts, all in Ohio. Both the named plaintiffs and the members of the certified class are nonprofit, tax-exempt trusts organized under the Employee Retirement Income Security Act ("ERISA"), 29 U.S.C. §§ 1100.01 *et seq.*, and the Taft-Hartley Act, 29 U.S.C. § 186(c) (5).

On May 20, 1997, Plaintiff Funds brought this action against tobacco-related entities. The plaintiffs allege that since about 1953, the defendants illegally shifted the large health care costs of smoking onto plaintiffs, class members, and other health care payers. Plaintiff Funds seek to recover costs incurred because of the defendants' alleged wrongful conduct. The Funds characterize their damages as economic losses arising from the "diminishment and expenditure of Fund assets" paid to provide medical treatment for tobacco-related illnesses.

To date, three (3) counts remain for adjudication. In Count I of the Amended Complaint, plaintiffs make claim under the Federal Racketeer Influenced and Corrupt Organizations Act of 1970, also known as RICO. 18 U.S.C. § 1961 *et seq.* * * *

The Court has set this case for jury trial on February 22, 1999.

II. Discussion of confidentiality claim

A. Introduction

Plaintiff Funds move this Court for an order declaring that certain documents are not privileged. The documents involved include documents produced ... to the U.S. House of Representatives, Committee on Commerce. In requesting an order that these documents are not privileged, plaintiffs say the defendants have waived any privilege that might otherwise attend such documents.

In Congressional inquiries, defendants in this action produced ... documents over which they had initially asserted a privilege or protection. * * * [T]he United States House of Representatives Committee on Commerce has released certain document produced to it. These documents were placed on the Committee's Internet website.

B. Background of release

By 1997 * * * Congress and the executive branch negotiated a so-called "national settlement" with cigarette manufacturers and their trade associations. These negotiations envisioned payments by the cigarette manufacturers and passage of federal legislation that would grant defendants certain limitations and protections respecting their liability in smoking and health lawsuits. * * *

Congress began review of a possible nationwide tobacco settlement. In the Fall of 1997, the House Committee on Commerce began consideration of a national settlement of tobacco litigation. On November 13, 1997, Congressman Thomas Bliley of Virginia, the Chairman of the Commerce Committee, wrote to certain defendants in this action. Chairman Bliley requested the defendants to produce 864 documents identified in [as privileged in parallel state litigation]. With this request, Chairman Bliley said the Commerce Committee was considering legislation that, if enacted, "would provide the tobacco industry with limited immunity from lawsuits."

On December 4, 1997, Chairman Bliley issued subpoenas to each of the defendants, commanding the production of the documents by noon the following day, December 5, 1997. Defendant Philip Morris complied with the subpoena and produced the documents on December 5, 1997. In producing the documents, Defendant Philip Morris was not directly ordered to produce the records at a Commerce Committee hearing, nor did the Committee ever vote to enforce the subpoena.

On February 10, 1998, the master in the [civil litigation in Minnesota] made a further recommendation suggesting defendants be ordered to produce another 39,000. These 39,000 documents had been withheld from production on privilege grounds.

After this further recommendation, Chairman Bliley again issued subpoenas to the cigarette defendants on February 19, 1995. In these subpoenas, Chairman Bliley demanded production of the additional documents identified in the special master's February 10, 1998 recommendation. The subpoena required production of the documents by March 12, 1998. In his letter demanding production, Chairman Bliley thanked the tobacco companies for "cooperation with the efforts of the Committee on Commerce to inform our Members and the American public on issues central to the proposed tobacco settlement."

After receiving Chairman Bliley's February 19, 1995 letter, the cigarette manufacturers engaged in discussions with Chairman Bliley (and/or his staff). * * *

On April 6, 1998, the date that the United States Supreme Court declined to stay production of the documents before the Minnesota court, Chairman Bliley wrote the Minnesota tobacco defendants. He wrote:

> The claim of privilege for the documents requested in the subpoenas will not be recognized. Further, unless the documents in question are produced immediately, I intend to proceed with a contempt resolution for enforcement of the subpoenas by the House of Representatives.
>
> After consulting with the Committee's Ranking Member, Mr. Dingell, we have agreed to conduct a confidential review of the documents produced pursuant to the February 19, 1998 subpoenas to determine their suitability for release.
>
> I urge your clients to remedy their current non-compliance status by immediately producing the subpoenaed documents.

On the same day, the defendants produced approximately 37,000 documents on CD-ROM with privilege logs, searchable indices, and a glossary of names (items not called for by the subpoenas, but clearly of great assistance to anyone seeking to review this massive production). With the documents, each of the tobacco defendants submitted its own cover letter accompanying the production. * * * In these cover letters, the Minnesota tobacco defendants claimed that they produced the documents only to avoid contempt citation. For instance, in its response letter to Chairman Bliley, Defendant R.J. Reynolds again complained about the Minnesota procedure. RJR's two-page letter included the following:

While your letter of April 6, 1998 states that the Committee will not recognize the claim of privilege for the documents requested, R.J. Reynolds does not waive any claims of privilege it may have concerning these documents and are [sic] producing them, not voluntarily, but solely under the threat of contempt of Congress for non-compliance with the subpoena.

Other tobacco defendants made like responses.

In producing the documents to Congress, the tobacco defendants sought no ruling by the Commerce Committee that the document production was required despite the defendants' privilege claims.

On April 22, 1998, the Commerce Committee made public nearly all of the documents that had been produced. The Commerce Committee posted them on the Internet. All of the documents produced in compliance with the February 19, 1998 subpoena are now publicly available on the Internet. * * *

III. Discussion

Plaintiff Funds move this Court for an order declaring that the defendants have waived their claim of privilege over certain documents produced either in previous litigation or before Congress. * * * The Funds also say the defendants waived any claim of privilege when they voluntarily produced the documents to the House Committee on Commerce. The plaintiffs lastly say the privilege was lost by defendants' public statements and widespread disclosure of these documents.

Before deciding whether the defendants have waived the any claim or attorney-client or work-product privilege, the Court briefly discusses the law and policy attendant to privilege.

A. The Privilege

Rule 501 of the Federal Rules of Evidence provides that "the privilege of a witness … shall be governed by the principles of the common law as they may be interpreted by the courts of the United States in the light of reason and experience." See *Wolfle v. United States*, 291 U.S. 7, 12, (1934) (establishing common-law standard). The Rule is to be "construed … to the end that the truth may be ascertained and proceedings justly determined." *Fed.R.Evid. 102*. In light of its truthseeking role, the Court is "disinclined to exercise [its Rule 501] authority expansively." *University of Pennsylvania v. EEOC*, 493 U.S. 182, 189 (1990). To the contrary, "courts have historically been cautious about privileges." *United States v. Nixon*, 418 U.S. 683, 710 n.18 (1974).

A strict construction of privileges is appropriate because "privileges obstruct the search for truth," *Branzburg v. Hayes*, 408 U.S. 665, 690 n. 29, (1972), and "contravene the fundamental principle that the 'public * * * has a right to every [person's] evidence.'" *University of Pennsylvania*, 493 U.S. at 189 (quotation omitted).

Privileges "are not lightly created," *Nixon*, 418 U.S. at 710 and "must be strictly construed." *University of Pennsylvania*, 493 U.S. at 189 (quotation omitted). A privilege applies only where it is "necessary to achieve its purpose," *Fisher v. United States*, 425

U.S. 391, 403 (1976), and "promotes sufficiently important interests to outweigh the need for probative evidence." *Jaffee v. Redmond*, 518 U.S. 1, 9–10 (1996) (quotation omitted).

Because privileges obstruct the search for truth, federal courts should be wary to find privilege except when the same is clearly shown. For these reasons, courts recognize privileges and defined their scope only to the extent established by the common law, and only to the extent that they serve a "public good transcending the normally predominant principle of utilizing all rational means for ascertaining the truth." *Id.* at 9 (quotation omitted). * * *

Because privileges keep relevant evidence from the fact-finder, the party making claim of an attorney-client privilege bears the burden of proving that the privilege is applicable. The privilege claimant must show not only that the privilege exists, but must also show that the privilege has not been waived.

The privilege is ordinarily strictly construed. Judge Carr of this Court described the narrow application of the attorney-client privilege in *United States v. Skeddle*, 989 F. Supp. 890 (N.D. Ohio 1997). He wrote:

> The attorney-client privilege is "the oldest of the privileges for confidential communications known to the common law," *Upjohn Co. v. United States*, 449 U.S. 383, 389 (1981), but "[t]he privilege cannot stand in the face of countervailing law or strong public policy and should be strictly confined within the narrowest possible limits underlying its purpose." *United States v. Goldberger & Dubin, P.C.*, 935 F.2d 501, 504 (2nd Cir. 1991). Thus, "while [s]ociety has every interest in assuring that legal advice is sought about how contemplated business transactions can be made to conform to the law ... [it], however, has no interest in facilitating the commission of contemplated but not yet committed crimes, torts, or frauds." Epstein, The Attorney-Client Privilege and the Work-Product Doctrine 251 (3rd ed.1997).

Skeddle, 989 F. Supp. at 900 (parallel citations omitted).

The existence of the privilege and the applicability of any exception to the privilege is a question of fact for the judge. The burden of establishing the existence of the privilege rests with the party asserting the privilege. *In re Grand Jury Investigation No. 83-2-35*, 723 F.2d 447, 454 (6th Cir.1983) * * * Thus, a party seeking privilege has the burden to show that (1) the communications were received from a client during the course of the client's search for legal advice from the attorney in his or her capacity as such; (2) the communications were made in confidence; and (3) the privilege as to these communications has not been waived. * * *

C. The production to Chairman Bliley

Plaintiff Funds * * * argue that the defendants waived any right to claim attorney-client or work-product privilege when it voluntarily released the subject documents to the House Committee on Commerce. Here, the plaintiffs contend that the defendants failed to sufficiently challenge Chairman Bliley's subpoenas.

As described above, on April 6, 1998, the tobacco defendants produced to Chairman Bliley all the documents earlier produced in the Minnesota litigation. The defendants made this production without citation for contempt and without receiving a ruling from the Chair at a hearing of the Commerce Committee. Plaintiffs suggest that the defendants' failure in this regard constitutes a waiver of the privilege. The Court agrees.

The standards employed in determining whether a party has sufficiently taken steps to contest a legislative subpoena are high. Generally, a party seeking to preserve a claimed privilege, despite Congressional subpoena, must challenge such a subpoena by standing in contempt of Congress. In *Sanders v. McClellan*, 463 F.2d 894 (D.C. Cir. 1972), the District of Columbia Court of Appeals identified certain steps to be followed when making such a challenge. The court stated:

> A witness may address his claims to the Subcommittee, which may sustain objections. Were the Subcommittee to insist, however, upon some response beyond the witness' conception of his obligation, and he refused to comply, no punitive action could be taken against him unless the full Committee obtained from the Senate as a whole a citation of the witness for contempt, the citation had been referred to the United States Attorney, and an indictment returned or information filed. Should prosecution occur, the witness' claims could then be raised before the trial court.

Id. at 899 (citations omitted).

In short, a party must do more than merely object to Congress' ruling. Instead, a party must risk standing in contempt of Congress. *See Sanders, supra; United States v. Bryan,* 339 U.S. 323, 333 (1950). It is fair for a court to require the witness show "that some serious effort was made to convince the Chair/and or the committee itself to recognize the privilege claims being asserted." *Commonwealth of Massachusetts,* 1998 LEXIS 438, *30.[5]

In the instant case, several factors indicate that the … tobacco defendants did not exhaust all remedies available for maintaining a claim of privilege before Chairman Bliley's committee * * * [T]he record shows no real effort by defendants to challenge the order of Chairman Bliley or to seek support for such a challenge from the Commerce Committee itself. The * * * tobacco defendants did not record any *specific* argument to Chairman Bliley or to the Committee as a whole against the production of these documents. The record here shows no effort by the tobacco defendants to meet with Chairman Bliley or other members of the Committee. The record shows

---

5. *See also* Hutcheson v. United States, 369 U.S. 599 (1962) ("[I]t is not until the question is asked that the interrogator [Congress] can know whether it will be answered or will be met with some constitutional objection."); Westinghouse Elec. Corp. v. Republic of Philippines, 951 F.2d 1414, 1427 n.14 (3rd Cir.1991) (requiring more than a motion to quash in order to protect against waiver of privilege); United States v. Tobin, 195 F. Supp. 588, 589 (D.D.C.1961) ("[H]aving failed to give the [Congressional] committee the opportunity to deal with the [privilege] issue, [defendant] may not properly assert it here.").

no filing of a legal memorandum setting forth the bases for the privilege with the committee or statement to the committee of the factual bases for the privileges. Also, the record shows no submission of a privilege log.

Further, the record shows no request by the tobacco defendant for a hearing on their objections. See *United States v. Bryan*, 339 U.S. 323, 332–33 (1950) ("[W]e agree that respondent could rightfully have demanded attendance of a quorum of the Committee and declined to testify or to produce documents so long as a quorum was not present.... In the first place, if respondent had legitimate reasons for failing to produce the records of the association, a decent respect for the House of Representatives, by whose authority the subpoenas issued, would have required that she state her reasons for noncompliance upon the return of the writ.").

At the time the defendants produced documents to the House Committee on Commerce, the defendants were soliciting Congress and the Commerce Committee for favorable treatment in the pending global tobacco settlement. The defendants asked Congressional support for a June 1997 legislative settlement of tobacco litigation. The settlement proposal was then pending before the Bliley committee. A few weeks before receiving the subpoenas, the defendants had told the Bliley committee that it could expect their full cooperation. Plaintiffs show evidence that defendants faced choosing between thwarting the request of Congress at a time the defendants sought Congressional support for legislation these tobacco defendant wanted. * * *

As a general matter, the defendants' disclosures to Congress took place under circumstances in which the tobacco defendants were solicitous of engendering good will with Congress. The defendants had reason to satisfy Chairman Bliley's request for documents. Chairman Bliley supervised legislation, then pending, that would limit the liability of these defendants in smoking and health litigation. Congress would not likely allow this legislation to go forward without letting Congress see the defendants' documents that had been found subject to the crime-fraud exception in the Minnesota proceedings. The tobacco defendants had good reason to disclose the documents and to argue that the Minnesota litigation wrongly found a crime or fraud. * * *

For these reasons, the Court finds that the defendants waived any claim of privilege when it disclosed and released certain documents to Chairman Bliley and the House Committee on Commerce. As related, the record gives no evidence that these defendants sufficiently exhausted or discussed with Congress the merits of their privilege claims. See *Commonwealth of Massachusetts*, 1998 LEXIS 438 at *37.

* * *

IV. Conclusion

For the reasons outlined above, the Court finds * * * that the defendants waived the privilege when they released documents to Chairman Bliley and the Committee on Commerce. Accordingly, the Court grants that part of Plaintiff Funds' motion to declare privilege/protections assertions over certain documents to be waived. However, the Court denies that part of the plaintiffs' motion which seeks the production of additional documents due to "subject matter waiver."

IT IS SO ORDERED.

Notes

1. *Walking the Contempt Plank.* According to the *Iron Workers* court: "In short, a party must do more than merely object to Congress' ruling. Instead, a party must risk standing in contempt of Congress." What incentive does this ruling create for private parties to cooperate with congressional document requests or subpoenas? The opinion seems to state that the only way to preserve attorney-client privilege over documents produced to Congress is to refuse compliance and seek judicial protection as a defense to a congressional finding of contempt. Even if done for purely legal privilege preservation reasons, noncompliance itself would erode goodwill with Congress and cause broader reputational harm.

2. *Split Court Authorities.* The *Iron Workers* court adopted language from a state court ruling. *See Commonwealth of Massachusetts v. Phillip Morris, et al.*, 1998 LEXIS 438 (Mass. Super. Ct. July 30, 1998) (holding that the companies had failed to sufficiently resist the committee's subpoenas). However, other courts have held the privilege was not waived for documents produced to Congress or other investigative government bodies pursuant to a subpoena or statutory requirement. *See, e.g., FTC v. Owens-Corning Fiberglass Corp.*, 626 F.2d 966, 970 (D.C. Cir. 1980) (release of information to a congressional committee is not deemed to be disclosure to the general public); *Exxon Corp. v. FTC*, 589 F.2d 582 (D.C. Cir. 1978); *Rockwell International Corp. v. U.S. Department of Justice*, 235 F.3d 598, 604 (D.C. Cir. 2001) (compliance with a statutory obligation to provide Congress with information did not waive its FOIA exemption protection); *Murphy v. Department of the Army*, 613 F.2d 1151, 1155–59 (D.C. Cir. 1979); *Florida House of Representatives v. Department of Commerce*, 961 F.2d 941, 946 (11th Cir. 1992); *United States v. Zolin*, 809 F.2d 1411, 1415 (9th Cir. 1987), aff'd in part, vacated in part, 491 U.S. 554 (1989) ("When disclosure is involuntary, we will find the privilege preserved if the privilege holder has made efforts 'reasonably designed' to protect and preserve the privilege.").

3. *Problem.* You are the general counsel of an energy company that has a subpoena from a committee conducting a congressional investigation. The subject matter of the congressional inquiry is also the subject of a federal grand jury investigation. Many of the documents responsive to the committee's subpoena relate to an internal investigation you conducted and would likely be subject to attorney-client privilege in a court proceeding. You have already advised your client that corporations do not have an act-of-production Fifth Amendment privilege against self-incrimination that could defeat the subpoena. Given the *Iron Horse* ruling and uncertainty coming from a split of authorities, what advice would you give the company to maximize the chances of protecting privileged materials from waiver in the criminal investigation or parallel civil litigation?

III. The Fifth Amendment, Immunity Grants, and Compelled Testimony

One of the problematic issues in parallel congressional and criminal investigations is the Fifth Amendment privilege against self-incrimination, which provides that "[n]o person ... shall be compelled in any criminal case to be a witness against himself." Because there can be criminal risks to providing congressional testimony, the Fifth Amendment can be asserted in front of Congress despite the "criminal case" language in the constitutional text.[5]

If a witness invokes the Fifth Amendment as a shield from an obligation to testify, the government entity—whether a federal prosecutor like Mueller or an investigating committee of Congress—may overcome it by granting immunity from prosecution for that testimony.[6]

Numerous witnesses in the Mueller investigation asserted their Fifth Amendment rights.[7] Similarly, several witnesses invoked the Fifth Amendment before congressional committees investigating related Russian election interference issues. For example, on Self-Incrimination Clause grounds, former National Security Adviser Michael Flynn refused to comply with a Senate Select Committee on Intelligence subpoena for documents and testimony.[8] He requested that the Senate committee grant him immunity, prompting President Trump to tweet that "Mike Flynn should ask for immunity in that this is a witch hunt (excuse for big election loss), by media & Dems, of historic proportion!"[9] The committee denied Flynn's request. Flynn subsequently pleaded guilty to a count of felony false statements under 18 U.S.C. § 1001.[10]

But what if Congress had decided to grant Flynn's request? As the next case arising out of the Iran-Contra scandal of the 1980s illustrates, a prior congressional grant

---

5. *See* Quinn v. United States, 349 U.S. 155, 161 (1955) (holding that the Fifth Amendment's Self-Incrimination Clause limits congressional investigative power to compel testimony).

6. *See* Kastigar v. United States, 406 U.S. 441, 448 (1972). *See also* MORTON ROSENBERG, CONG. RESEARCH SERV., 95–464, INVESTIGATIVE OVERSIGHT: AN INTRODUCTION TO THE LAW, PRACTICE AND PROCEDURE OF CONGRESSIONAL INQUIRY 7 (1995) ("When a witness before a committee asserts his constitutional privilege, the committee may obtain a court order which compels him to testify and grants him immunity against the use of his testimony and information derived from that testimony in a subsequent prosecution."); 18 U.S.C. § 6005 (2012) (outlining the procedure for Congress to obtain such a court order).

7. *See* Mueller Report, Vol. 1, p. 10 ("Some individuals invoked their Fifth Amendment right against compelled self-incrimination and were not, in the Office's judgment, appropriate candidates for grants of immunity.").

8. *See* Letter from Robert Kelner, Covington & Burling LLP, counsel for Michael Flynn, to Sens. Richard Burr and Mark R. Warner (May 22, 2017).

9. Tweet of Donald J. Trump (@realDonaldTrump), Mar. 31, 2017.

10. *See* United States v. Flynn, Case 1:17-cr-00232-RC, D.D.C. Dec. 1, 2017 (Statement of the Offense).

of use immunity to a witness can become an effective bar to a subsequent criminal prosecution.

United States v. North

910 F.2d 843 (D.C. Cir. 1990)

PER CURIAM:

INTRODUCTION

In November of 1986, a Lebanese newspaper reported that the United States had secretly sold weapons to Iran. Two months later, Congress established two committees charged with investigating the sales of arms to Iran, the diversion of proceeds therefrom to rebels (or "Contras") fighting in Nicaragua, and the attempted cover-up of these activities (controversial events popularly known as "the Iran/Contra Affair"). In July of 1987, Lieutenant Colonel Oliver L. North, a former member of the National Security Council ("NSC") staff, testified before the Iran/Contra congressional committees. North asserted his Fifth Amendment right not to testify before the committees, but the government compelled his testimony by a grant of use immunity pursuant to 18 U.S.C. § 6002. North testified for six days. His testimony was carried live on national television and radio, replayed on news shows, and analyzed in the public media.

Contemporaneously with the congressional investigation, and pursuant to the Independent Counsel statute, 28 U.S.C. §§ 591–599, the Special Division of this Court, see 28 U.S.C. § 49, appointed Lawrence E. Walsh as Independent Counsel ("IC") and charged him with the investigation and prosecution of any criminal wrongdoing by government officials in the Iran/Contra events. As a result of the efforts of the IC, North was indicted and tried on twelve counts arising from his role in the Iran/Contra Affair. After extensive pretrial proceedings and a twelve-week trial, North was convicted in May of 1989 on three counts: aiding and abetting an endeavor to obstruct Congress in violation of 18 U.S.C. §§ 1505 and 2 ("Count 6"); destroying, altering, or removing official NSC documents in violation of 18 U.S.C. § 2071 ("Count 9"); and accepting an illegal gratuity, consisting of a security system for his home, in violation of 18 U.S.C. § 201(c) (1) (B) ("Count 10"). North now appeals his convictions on these counts.

SUMMARY

Because of the length and complexity of our disposition of North's appeal, we summarize our holdings.

(1) The District Court erred in failing to hold a full hearing as required by *Kastigar v. United States*, 406 U.S. 441 (1972), to ensure that the IC made no use of North's immunized congressional testimony. North's convictions on all three counts are therefore vacated and remanded to the District Court for a *Kastigar* proceeding consistent with this opinion.

* * *

> No person ... shall be compelled in any criminal case to
> be a witness against himself....

U.S. Const. amend. V.

North argues that his Fifth Amendment right against self-incrimination was violated, asserting that the District Court failed to require the IC to establish independent sources for the testimony of witnesses before the grand jury and at trial and to demonstrate that witnesses did not in any way use North's compelled testimony. North further argues that his Fifth Amendment right was violated by the District Court's failure to determine whether or not the IC made "nonevidentiary" use of the immunized testimony.

North's argument depends on the long-recognized principle that a predicate to liberal constitutional government is the freedom of a citizen from government compulsion to testify against himself:

> And any compulsory discovery by extorting the party's oath, or compelling the production of his private books and papers, to convict him of crime, or to forfeit his property, is contrary to the principles of free government. It is abhorrent to the instincts of an Englishman; it is abhorrent to the instincts of an American. It may suit the purposes of despotic power; but it cannot abide the pure atmosphere of political liberty and personal freedom.

Boyd v. United States, 116 U.S. 616, 631–32 (1886). This rule has been established in England at least since 1641. See 8 Wigmore, Evidence Sec. 2250 at 284 & n. 69 (McNaughton rev. ed. 1961). * * *

Because the privilege against self-incrimination "reflects many of our fundamental values and most noble aspirations," *Murphy v. Waterfront Comm'n*, 378 U.S. 52, 55 (1964), and because it is "the essential mainstay of our adversary system," the Constitution requires "that the government seeking to punish an individual produce the evidence against him by its own independent labors, rather than by the cruel, simple expedient of compelling it from his own mouth." *Miranda v. Arizona*, 384 U.S. 436, 460 (1966).

The prohibition against compelled testimony is not absolute, however. Under the rule of *Kastigar v. United States*, 406 U.S. 441 (1972), a grant of use immunity under 18 U.S.C. § 6002 enables the government to compel a witness's self-incriminating testimony. This is so because the statute prohibits the government both from using the immunized testimony itself and also from using any evidence derived directly or indirectly therefrom. Stated conversely, use immunity conferred under the statute is "coextensive with the scope of the privilege against self-incrimination, and therefore is sufficient to compel testimony over a claim of the privilege.... [Use immunity] prohibits the prosecutorial authorities from using the compelled testimony in any respect...." *Kastigar*, 406 U.S. at 453 (emphasis in original). * * *

When the government proceeds to prosecute a previously immunized witness, it has "the heavy burden of proving that all of the evidence it proposes to use was derived from legitimate independent sources." *Kastigar*, 406 U.S. at 461–62. The Court characterized the government's affirmative burden as "heavy." Most courts following *Kastigar* have imposed a "preponderance of the evidence" evidentiary burden on the government. *See White Collar Crime: Fifth Survey of Law-Immunity*, 26 AM. CRIM. L. REV. 1169, 1179 & n.62 (1989) (hereafter "Immunity"). * * *

A trial court must normally hold a hearing (a "*Kastigar* hearing") for the purpose of allowing the government to demonstrate that it obtained all of the evidence it proposes to use from sources independent of the compelled testimony. *See, e.g., United States v. Rinaldi*, 808 F.2d 1579, 1584 (D.C. Cir. 1987). * * * As this Court pointed out in *United States v. De Diego*, 511 F.2d 818, 823–24 (D.C. Cir. 1975), a trial court may hold a *Kastigar* hearing pre-trial, post-trial, mid-trial (as evidence is offered), or it may employ some combination of these methods. A pre-trial hearing is the most common choice.

Whenever the hearing is held, the failure of the government to meet its burden can have most drastic consequences. One commentator has stated that "[i]f the tainted evidence was presented to the grand jury, the indictment will be dismissed; when tainted evidence is introduced at trial, the defendant is entitled to a new trial. [Defendants] are afforded similar protections against nonevidentiary uses of immunized testimony." *Immunity* at 1179 (footnotes omitted). * * *

A district court holding a *Kastigar* hearing "must make specific findings on the independent nature of this proposed [allegedly tainted] evidence." *Rinaldi*, 808 F.2d at 1584. Because the burden is upon the government, the appellate court "may not infer findings favorable to it on these questions." * * * A district court's determination that the government has carried its burden of showing independent sources is a factual finding that is subject to review under the "clearly erroneous" standard. * * *

Before North's trial, the District Court held a "preliminary" *Kastigar* inquiry and issued an order based thereon which it subsequently adopted as final (with certain changes) without benefit of further proceedings or hearings. * * *

After reviewing the relevant factual and statutory background, the District Court made four findings concerning the government's alleged use of immunized testimony before the grand jury. *Kastigar Memo*, 698 F. Supp. at 314–15. First, "[d]efendants' immunized testimony was not submitted to the grand jury in any form." Second, "[t]he grand jurors were effectively warned not to read about or look at or listen to this immunized testimony and it played no part in the grand jury's unanimous decision to indict." Third, "[t]he grand jury transcript and exhibits reflect solid proof and ample probable cause to indict on each and every count." Fourth, "[n]one of the testimony or exhibits presented to the grand jury became known to the prosecuting attorneys on Independent Counsel's staff or to him personally either from the immunized testimony itself or from leads derived from the testimony, directly or indirectly." *Id.*

In reaching these conclusions, the District Court noted that the "Independent Counsel's legitimate independent leads to every significant witness were carefully documented."; that the grand jury heard many witnesses before the immunity order issued; that North's testimony was undertaken and concluded while the grand jury was in recess; and that the "grand jurors were specifically, repeatedly and effectively instructed to avoid exposure to any immunized testimony." The District Court provided examples of various warnings given to grand jurors, and to grand jury witnesses. The District Court also noted that Associate Independent Counsel were "apparently careful to avoid broad, rambling questions," and that "written materials from Independent Counsel demonstrat[ed] that all the prosecutor's substantive witnesses were known to him before the first immunity grant" (citations omitted).

Addressing what it referred to as nonevidentiary problems, the District Court noted that "[w]itnesses, probably a considerable number of them, have had their memories refreshed by the immunized testimony," but because of its belief that "there is no way of determining, except possibly by a trial before the trial, whether or not any defendant was placed in a substantially worse position by the possible refreshment of a witness' memory through such exposure," the District Court concluded that "[i]f testimony remains truthful the refreshment itself is not an evidentiary use" (citations omitted).

North's primary *Kastigar* complaint is that the District Court failed to require the IC to demonstrate an independent source for each item of evidence or testimony presented to the grand jury and the petit jury, and that the District Court erred in focusing almost wholly on the IC's leads to witnesses, rather than on the content of the witnesses' testimony. * * * North also protests that his immunized testimony was improperly used to refresh the recollection of witnesses before the grand jury and at trial, that this refreshment caused them to alter their testimony, and that the District Court failed to give this question the careful examination it deserved. In our discussion here, we first consider alleged nonevidentiary use of immunized testimony by the IC. We will then proceed to consider the use of immunized testimony to refresh witnesses' recollections. Finally, we will address the distinction between use of immunized testimony as a lead to procure witnesses and use insofar as it affects the substantive content of witnesses' testimony.

* * * [C]ontrary to the District Court, we conclude that the use of immunized testimony by witnesses to refresh their memories, or otherwise to focus their thoughts, organize their testimony, or alter their prior or contemporaneous statements, constitutes evidentiary use rather than nonevidentiary use. The District Court on remand is to hold the searching type of *Kastigar* hearing described in detail below, concerning North's allegations of refreshment. Finally, because the District Court apparently interpreted *Kastigar* as prohibiting the government only from using immunized testimony as a lead rather than using it at all, we hold that the District Court's truncated *Kastigar* inquiry was insufficient to protect North's Fifth Amendment right to avoid self-incrimination.

The District Court briefly discussed the problem of nonevidentiary use of immunized testimony through witnesses and through the IC's staff. *Kastigar Memo* * * *. The District Court found that witnesses had their memories refreshed with immunized testimony by "hearing the testimony, reading about it, being questioned about aspects of it before the Select Committees and, to some extent, by exposure to it in the course of responding to inquiries within their respective agencies." * * * This exposure was not motivated, the Court found, by a desire "to harm a defendant or help the prosecution." * * *

The District Court was similarly untroubled by allegations of prosecutorial exposure to immunized testimony through a grand juror or a witness: "Defendants in their zeal treat this as if even the tiniest exposure to a witness or grand juror constituted exposure to an incurable disease. Such is clearly not the case. Exposure to a fleeting snippet means nothing." * * * As a matter of "common sense," the District Court determined that a "prosecutor who inadvertently overhears mention of a fact already confirmed by his own independent investigation" cannot be said to have used immunized testimony; similarly, a defendant's "Fifth Amendment rights are not infringed if a witness hears immunized testimony yet testifies solely to facts personally known to the witness." * * *

An initial difficulty is that a precise definition of the term nonevidentiary use is elusive. * * *

Kastigar itself did not expressly discuss the propriety of nonevidentiary use. The Court simply held that immunity from use and derivative use is coextensive with the scope of the privilege against self-incrimination, and therefore is sufficient to compel testimony over a claim of the privilege. While a grant of immunity must afford protection commensurate with that afforded by the privilege, it need not be broader. Transactional immunity, which accords full immunity from prosecution for the offense to which the compelled testimony relates, affords the witness considerably broader protection than does the Fifth Amendment privilege.

Thus, because "[i]mmunity from the use of compelled testimony, as well as evidence derived directly and indirectly therefrom" provides protection coextensive with the Fifth Amendment, the use immunity statute "prohibits the prosecutorial authorities from using the compelled testimony in any respect, and it therefore insures that the testimony cannot lead to the infliction of criminal penalties on the witness." * * *

We cannot agree with the District Court that the use of immunized testimony to refresh the memories of witnesses is a nonevidentiary matter and that therefore refreshment should not be subject to a *Kastigar* hearing because "[n]o court has ever so required, nor did Kastigar suggest anything of the kind." * * * In our view, the use of immunized testimony by witnesses to refresh their memories, or otherwise to focus their thoughts, organize their testimony, or alter their prior or contemporaneous statements, constitutes indirect evidentiary not nonevidentiary use. This observation also applies to witnesses who studied, reviewed, or were exposed to the immunized testimony in order to prepare themselves or others as witnesses.

Strictly speaking, the term direct evidentiary use may describe only attempts by the prosecutors to offer the immunized testimony directly to the grand jury or trial jury, as by offering the testimony as an exhibit. But the testimony of other witnesses is also evidence that is to be considered by the grand jury or the trial jury. When the government puts on witnesses who refresh, supplement, or modify that evidence with compelled testimony, the government uses that testimony to indict and convict.

The fact that the government violates the Fifth Amendment in a circuitous or hap-hazard fashion is cold comfort to the citizen who has been forced to incriminate him-self by threat of imprisonment for contempt. The stern language of *Kastigar* does not become lenient because the compelled testimony is used to form and alter evidence in oblique ways exclusively, or at a slight distance from the chair of the immunized witness. Such a looming constitutional infirmity cannot be dismissed as merely nonev-identiary. This type of use by witnesses is not only evidentiary in any meaningful sense of the term; it is at the core of the criminal proceeding.

In summary, the use of immunized testimony—before the grand jury or at trial—to augment or refresh recollection is an evidentiary use and must be dealt with as such.

Both the trial and the grand jury proceedings involved "a considerable number" of witnesses who had "their memories refreshed by the immunized testimony," * * * a use of compelled testimony that the District Court treated as nonevidentiary. The District Court stated that "[t]here is no way a trier of fact can determine whether the memories of these witnesses would be substantially different if it had not been stim-ulated by a bit of the immunized testimony itself" and that "there is no way of de-termining, except possibly by a trial before the trial, whether or not any defendant was placed in a substantially worse position by the possible refreshment of a witness' memory through such exposure." The District Court found that such taint occurs in the "natural course of events" because "[m]emory is a mysterious thing that can be stirred by a shaggy dog or a broken promise" (citations omitted).

This observation, while likely true, is not dispositive of the searching inquiry *Kasti-gar* requires. The fact that a sizable number of grand jury witnesses, trial witnesses, and their aides apparently immersed themselves in North's immunized testimony leads us to doubt whether what is in question here is simply "stimulation" of memory by "a bit" of compelled testimony. Whether the government's use of compelled tes-timony occurs in the natural course of events or results from an unprecedented aber-ration is irrelevant to a citizen's Fifth Amendment right. *Kastigar* does not prohibit simply "a whole lot of use," or "excessive use," or "primary use" of compelled testimony. It prohibits "any use," direct or indirect. From a prosecutor's standpoint, an unhappy byproduct of the Fifth Amendment is that *Kastigar* may very well require a trial within a trial (or a trial before, during, or after the trial) if such a proceeding is necessary for the court to determine whether or not the government has in any fashion used compelled testimony to indict or convict a defendant.

We readily understand how court and counsel might sigh prior to such an under-taking. Such a *Kastigar* proceeding could consume substantial amounts of time, per-sonnel, and money, only to lead to the conclusion that a defendant—perhaps a guilty defendant—cannot be prosecuted. Yet the very purpose of the Fifth Amendment under these circumstances is to prevent the prosecutor from transmogrifying into the inquisitor, complete with that officer's most pernicious tool—the power of the state to force a person to incriminate himself. As between the clear constitutional command and the convenience of the government, our duty is to enforce the former and discount the latter. * * *

Even before the congressional Iran/Contra committees began taking testimony, the IC recognized this problem in his memorandum to the committees concerning use immunity: "[A]ny grant of use and derivative use immunity would create serious—and perhaps insurmountable—barriers to the prosecution of the immunized witness." *Memorandum of the Independent Counsel Concerning Use Immunity* 1 (Jan. 13, 1987) (Submitted to the Joint Congressional Iran/Contra Committees) (JA at 2502). *See also id.* at 4 (JA at 2505) ("Indeed, the prosecutor must demonstrate that all its evidence is based on entirely legitimate sources, independent of the compelled testimony.... [S]ince *Kastigar*, most lower courts have held that Section 6002 prohibits both evidentiary and nonevidentiary use of compelled testimony.") (emphasis in original); *id.* at 5 (JA at 2506) ("Under these principles, the prosecution must not only prove that all of its evidence was derived from sources independent of the immunized testimony, but also demonstrate that no nonevidentiary or strategic use was made of the immunized testimony or the fruits of the testimony. In practice, these burdens are often very difficult to satisfy."). * * * These observations have indeed proven prescient, and we commend them to the District Court upon remand.

"Identity of Witness" vs. "Content of Testimony"

The refreshment of witnesses' recollections is indicative, but not exhaustive, of the *Kastigar* questions left unanswered on the present record. The District Court's disposition of the "identity-of-witness" issue does not dispose of the "content-of-testimony" *Kastigar* problem: the District Court inquired as to whether the names of witnesses were derived independently of the immunized testimony, but it made no determination of the extent to which the substantive content of the witnesses' testimony may have been shaped, altered, or affected by the immunized testimony.

A central problem in this case is that many grand jury and trial witnesses were thoroughly soaked in North's immunized testimony, but no effort was made to determine what effect, if any, this extensive exposure had on their testimony. Papers filed under seal indicate that officials and attorneys from the Department of Justice, the Central Intelligence Agency, the White House, and the Department of State gathered, studied, and summarized North's immunized testimony in order to prepare themselves or their superiors and colleagues for their testimony before the investigating committees and the grand jury. * * *

The testimony of Robert C. McFarlane, the National Security Advisor to President Reagan, is especially troubling and is indeed emblematic of both the weakness of the IC's position and the necessity of further *Kastigar* inquiry. Although McFarlane completed his grand jury testimony before North gave his immunized testimony, McFarlane was a key government witness at trial. He testified before the investigating committees prior to North's immunized testimony, but then specifically requested and was granted a second appearance after North testified in order to respond to North's testimony. *See Senate Select Comm. on Secret Military Assistance to Iran and the Nicaraguan Opposition & House Select Comm. to Investigate Covert Arms Transactions with Iran, Report of the Congressional Comm. Investigating the Iran/Contra Affair, with Supplemental, Minority and Additional Views*, S.Rep. No. 216, H.R.Rep.

No. 433, 100th Cong., 1st Sess. 687 (1987). In his second appearance on Capitol Hill, McFarlane revised his earlier testimony in light of North's testimony, and directly responded to North's testimony at certain points. See, e.g., id. at 40, 41, 399 and accompanying notes. He also apparently managed to recall items that he had not remembered in his prior testimony. McFarlane subsequently testified at North's trial. Trial Transcript at 3916 et seq. (JA at 1041 et seq.). No effort was made to determine what use — if any — this government witness made of North's testimony in his trial testimony.

The core purpose of the immunity statute, 18 U.S.C. §§ 6001–6005, is to allow the prosecution of an immunized witness while preventing use of his compelled testimony. One forbidden use of the immunized testimony is the identification of a witness, but other uses of a citizen's immunized testimony — as by presenting the testimony of grand jury or trial witnesses that has been derived from or influenced by the immunized testimony — are equally forbidden. * * *

We conclude that the District Court's reliance on warnings to witnesses (to avoid testifying as to anything they had learned from North's immunized testimony) was not sufficient to ensure that North's testimony was not used. * * *

The convictions are vacated and the case is remanded to the District Court. On remand, if the prosecution is to continue, the District Court must hold a full *Kastigar* hearing that will inquire into the content as well as the sources of the grand jury and trial witnesses' testimony. That inquiry must proceed witness-by-witness; if necessary, it will proceed line-by-line and item-by-item. For each grand jury and trial witness, the prosecution must show by a preponderance of the evidence that no use whatsoever was made of any of the immunized testimony either by the witness or by the Office of Independent Counsel in questioning the witness. This burden may be met by establishing that the witness was never exposed to North's immunized testimony, or that the allegedly tainted testimony contains no evidence not "canned" by the prosecution before such exposure occurred. Unless the District Court can make express findings that the government has carried this heavy burden as to the content of all of the testimony of each witness, that testimony cannot survive the *Kastigar* test. We remind the prosecution that the *Kastigar* burden is "heavy" not because of the evidentiary standard, but because of the constitutional standard: the government has to meet its proof only by a preponderance of the evidence, but any failure to meet that standard must result in exclusion of the testimony.

If the District Court finds that the government has failed to carry its burden with respect to any item or part of the testimony of any grand jury or trial witness, it should then consider whether that failure is harmless beyond a reasonable doubt. If the District Court concludes that the government's failure to carry its burden with respect to that particular witness or item is harmless beyond a reasonable doubt, the District Court should memorialize its conclusions and rationales in writing. If the government has in fact introduced trial evidence that fails the *Kastigar* analysis, then the defendant is entitled to a new trial. If the same is true as to grand jury evidence, then the indictment must be dismissed.

Chief Judge WALD authored an opinion dissenting in part, and Circuit Judge SIL-BERMAN wrote an opinion concurring in part and dissenting in part.

Notes

1. *What Happened Next?* After this appellate ruling the Independent Counsel filed for a rehearing and a portion of the opinion related to jury instructions not excerpted here was withdrawn. *See United States v. North*, 920 F.2d 940 (D.C. Cir. 1990). Following a denial of certiorari by the U.S. Supreme Court, the Independent Counsel returned to the trial court for the *Kastigar* hearings deemed necessary by the D.C. Circuit. During two days of hearings, Robert McFarlane testified that his trial testimony was "colored" by North's immunized congressional testimony. At that point, the Independent Counsel agreed to voluntary dismissal of the indictment.[11]

2. *Perjured, Compelled Testimony.* Should the Fifth Amendment privilege against self-incrimination protections applied to *Kastigar* immunity grants recognize a difference between a prosecution for the underlying information giving rise to the grant and a prosecution for false testimony given under the grant itself? It is clear that the Fifth Amendment should preclude use of North's immunized testimony for, say, obstruction of justice related to shredding documents under investigation. But should that immunized testimony be precluded from use in establishing that North committed perjury while under oath and compulsion due to the immunity grant?

3. *Mueller Investigation Problem.* What incentives does this ruling create? Let's say you were a member of Congress considering whether to grant President Trump's former campaign manager Paul Manafort immunity in order to compel his testimony at a time a grand jury was considering whether to indict him?

IV. Executive Privilege: Open Investigations, Investigative Methods, and Grand Jury Secrecy

Executive privilege doctrine rose to the forefront of confrontations between Congress and the Trump administration over access to Special Counsel Mueller's work papers and underlying evidence. That doctrine represents an assertion of presidential authority to preserve Executive Branch confidentiality interests by withholding information from a judicial or congressional proceeding.[12]

Traditionally, the Executive Branch has vigorously sought to protect open investigative files and sensitive law enforcement methods from disclosure. Federal prosecutors often raise concern that disclosure of investigative files to Congress may risk

---

11. *See* Order, United States v. North (D.D.C. Sept. 16, 1991) (dismissing the indictment with prejudice).

12. *See generally* Andrew M. Wright, *Constitutional Conflict and Congressional Oversight*, 98 Marq. L. Rev. 881 (2014) (discussing executive privilege doctrine).

exposure of confidential sources and investigative techniques. Exposure of confidential sources could jeopardize ongoing law enforcement activities, frustrate future recruitment of sources, or, worse, risk the safety of the cooperating source. Likewise, investigative techniques exposed could similarly frustrate an ongoing investigation. For example, if Congress disclosed the existence of a wiretap it would render it useless as call participates moved to other modes of communications.

In addition, rules and statutes backed by criminal penalties reinforce the Department of Justice's longstanding efforts to resist production of grand jury deliberations — including production of evidence that would reveal a grand jury's investigative interest. All of these categories of information have been the subject of executive privilege assertions in administrations of both parties prior to the Mueller investigation.

Law enforcement confidentiality interests create significant tensions when a congressional committee has overlapping investigative interests. For example, Congress may want to see evidence presented to a grand jury. Congress may, of course, seek to interview witnesses in its own right rather than rely on grand jury transcripts. However, Congress may want to see the transcripts to test credibility, and the grand jury may know about witnesses and evidence that Congress does not know about.

These tensions were on full display during the Mueller investigation. In his communications with Congress about the Mueller report, Attorney General Barr emphasized executive branch concerns about disclosures techniques and sources that could compromise ongoing intelligence and law enforcement efforts.[13] Congress then subpoenaed Mueller's unredacted report and investigative files, and President Trump asserted executive privilege.[14] Thereafter, the House passed a resolution authorizing litigation to seek judicial enforcement of the congressional subpoenas.

The following two documents represent the divergent views of Congress and the Executive in connection with pre-Mueller investigations where law enforcement confidentiality interests conflicted with a congressional subpoena.

---

13. *See* Letter from Attorney General Barr to Sen. Lindsey Graham and Rep. Jerrold Nadler (Mar. 29, 2019) (notifying the Senate and House Judiciary Committee chairs that the Department would be redacting grand jury materials, information that could reveal compromising intelligence sources and methods, and "material that could affect other ongoing matters" including those the Special Counsel referred to other offices for continued investigation).

14. Letter from Attorney General William Barr to Rep. Jerrold Nadler (May 8, 2019).

A. Executive Branch Confidentiality Interests in Law Enforcement

In this Reagan-era memorandum prepared by the Department of Justice's Office of Legal Counsel, the Executive Branch makes its case for resisting production of law enforcement investigative materials to Congress:

Congressional Subpoenas of Department of Justice Investigative Files

Congressional subpoenas seeking information from the Department of Justice concerning two closed investigations and one open investigation may be complied with only if the materials sought may be revealed consistent with Rule 6(e) of the Federal Rules of Criminal Procedure, which requires the Department to maintain the secrecy of matters occurring before the grand jury, and with the President's constitutional obligation to executive faithfully the laws of the United States.

If it is determined after review of the requested documents that compliance with the subpoena would jeopardize the ongoing criminal investigation, we would advise the President to assert executive privilege to ensure the continued confidentiality of the documents contained in the open investigative file.

Because of the importance of the process of determining whether documents may be released to Congress consistent with Rule 6(e) and the President's constitutional obligations, Congress must allow Executive Branch officials sufficient time to review the requested documents.

October 17, 1984

Memorandum Opinion for the Deputy Attorney General

On Monday, October 1, 1984, the Subcommittee on Administrative Practice and Procedure of the Committee on the Judiciary of the United States Senate issued to Assistant Attorney General Stephen S. Trott of the Criminal Division a subpoena, signed by Subcommittee Chairman Charles E. Grassley, calling for Mr. Trott to appear before the Subcommittee at 9:30 a.m. on October 4, 1984 and to produce at that time documents pertaining to three investigations of alleged false shipbuilding claims against the Navy by Company A, Company B, and Company C. Specifically, the October 1 subpoena seeks production of the following described documents:

(1) All prosecutors' memoranda concerning the above named companies, including, but not limited to, all recommendations for or against prosecution, all reports and memoranda about the status of the investigations, all reports and memoranda concerning investigative plans, all legal analyses prepared with reference to any of the cases, and any dissenting views by one or more of the attorneys with respect to any of the reports and memoranda indicated above.

(2) The report forwarded earlier this year to the Department of Justice by Elsie Munsell, U.S. Attorney for the Eastern District of Virginia, commenting on the 1983 report of the Office of Policy and Management Analysis, Department of Justice, entitled "Review of Navy Claims Investigations."

(3) All other reports and memoranda of the U.S. Attorney's Office for the Eastern District of Virginia dealing with the subject of Navy shipbuilding claims.

(4) A list of all documents within these three categories of documents.

The subpoena was served on Assistant Attorney General Trott on October 1, 1984, following a joint hearing of the Subcommittee on International Trade, Finance, and Security Economics of the Joint Economic Committee and Senator Grassley's Subcommittee, at which Mr. Trott appeared for two-and-one-half hours. The subpoena itself did not exclude grand jury materials from the document request. In a letter of August 9, 1984, however, Senators Proxmire and Grassley indicated that the Subcommittee was not seeking grand jury materials.

In response to the subpoena, Assistant Attorney General Trott appeared before the Subcommittee on October 4, 1984, and read a statement. In brief, Mr. Trott agreed to make available documents related to the closed Company A and Company C investigations (subject to the need to redact grand jury materials), but objected to the production of documents pertaining to the open Company B investigation. Following the hearing, Assistant Attorney General McConnell met with Chairman Grassley, Assistant Attorney General Trott, and others.

The following day, on October 5, 1984, the Subcommittee issued another subpoena, again signed by Chairman Grassley. This subpoena was issued to the Attorney General "or designated custodian of described documents" and commands him to appear before the Subcommittee at 10:00 a.m. on October 19, 1984, and to produce the following specified documents:

(1) All prosecutors' memoranda concerning [Company B], including, but not limited to, all recommendations for or against prosecution, all reports and memoranda about the status of the investigation, all reports and memoranda concerning investigative plans, all reports and memoranda from the Federal Bureau of Investigation regarding this investigation, and any dissenting views by one or more of the attorneys with respect to any of the reports and memoranda indicated above.

(2) A list of all documents described above.

This request does not include 6(e) material.

* * * We have attempted below to provide you with general guidance to assist you in advising the President concerning the need to reconcile the obligation of the Executive Branch to respond to the subpoenas with its obligation to maintain the secrecy of grand jury materials and to resist improper congressional attempts to interfere with the Executive's conduct of ongoing criminal investigations.

Based upon our understanding of the facts of this dispute and upon a renewed examination of the relevant legal and historical precedents, we believe that a number of the documents covered by the subpoenas relating to all three investigations may be covered by the requirement of Rule 6(e) of the Federal Rules of Criminal Procedure, which requires the Department to maintain the secrecy of "matters occurring before the grand jury." In addition, documents in the files of the Company B investigation, an ongoing criminal investigation, may be shielded from disclosure to Congress by a claim of executive privilege. We are fully cognizant of the President's announcement that "[t]he policy of this Administration is to comply with Congressional requests for information to the fullest extent consistent with the constitutional and statutory obligations of the Executive Branch * * * [E]xecutive privilege will be asserted only in the most compelling circumstances, and only after careful review demonstrates that assertion of the privilege is necessary." Memorandum from President Reagan to the Heads of all Executive Departments and Agencies (Nov. 4, 1982). Nevertheless, we believe that both Rule 6(e) and the probability that certain documents covered by the request will be privileged require that careful consideration be given to the documents and the potential effects of disclosure before documents from the Company B file are made available to the Subcommittee.

For the reasons detailed below, our recommendation at this time, based upon the conclusion of the Criminal Division that disclosure of the Company B investigative documents will substantially interfere with the Department's ongoing criminal investigation in that case, and subject to our own review of the documents, is to advise the President to assert executive privilege to ensure the continued confidentiality of the documents contained in the open investigative file. * * *

I. Background

The events leading up to the issuance of the subpoena are as follows: On February 7, 1984, Vice Chairman Proxmire of the Subcommittee on International Trade, Finance and Security Economics of the Joint Economic Committee wrote to the Attorney General to inquire about the status of a Department of Justice investigation of alleged fraudulent shipbuilding claims filed with the Navy. The Vice Chairman was particularly interested in the Department's anticipated treatment of Mr. D, a former head of a division of Company B, who had offered to provide information to the Department regarding these claims. In that letter, Senator Proxmire asked five specific questions relating to the Department's earlier investigation of the shipbuilding matter, the termination of the investigation in 1981, and any current Department plans to reopen the investigation and to speak with Mr. D. In his response of February 17, 1984, Assistant Attorney General Trott explained that Mr. D was at the time a fugitive from a federal indictment, and that the Department was attempting to secure whatever information it could from Mr. D regarding the shipbuilding matter without compromising that pending prosecution. * * *

On May 9, 1984, Senator Proxmire again wrote to the Attorney General with a list of specific requests for information. Mr. Trott responded in full to some of those questions, but declined to respond to others. In a letter of June 14, 1984, he declined to provide the names of specific career employees who had worked on the earlier investigation without some particular articulated legislative need. In addition, he asserted that it would be improper for him to provide internal Department of Justice legal memoranda on a pending matter because premature public disclosure would prejudice the interests of the investigation. He informed the Subcommittee that deletion of grand jury material was not practical because that material was so extensive that its deletion would render the documents meaningless. In an exchange of letters in late July 1984, Mr. Trott and Senator Proxmire agreed to work together to resolve any outstanding disclosure issues. * * *

At the appointed hour on October 4, 1984, Assistant Attorney General Trott appeared before the Subcommittee and read a prepared statement. That statement explained that the Department of Justice was making available to the Subcommittee all of the subpoenaed material that, in the judgment of Assistant Attorney General Trott and his staff, was not prohibited from release by Rule 6(e) of the Federal Rules of Criminal Procedure, which imposes an obligation to maintain the secrecy of "matters occurring before the grand jury." Documents related to the Company A and Company C investigations were therefore made available after redaction to protect grand jury materials. With respect to this redacted grand jury material, Mr. Trott explained his intention to file a motion in the Eastern District of Virginia no later than October 12, 1984 seeking permission to release the remainder of the subpoenaed material. We have been informed that such a motion was filed and is currently pending before the court.

Assistant Attorney General Trott's statement to the Subcommittee explained that different treatment is required of information relating to the Company B investigation, because that matter is currently the subject of an open criminal investigation that is pending before an active grand jury. Due to the need to protect the integrity of the prosecutorial process, Mr. Trott declined to release the files from the Company B investigation, but offered to make them available on the same basis as the other two cases, "[a]s soon as the [Company B] case is closed." * * *

To summarize, Mr. Trott has made available to the Subcommittee all documents relative to the closed investigations, with redactions made to enable the Department to comply with Rule 6(e)'s prohibition on disclosure of matters occurring before the grand jury. Consistent with a prior representation to the Subcommittee, the Department has filed a motion with the district court on this issue to clarify the application of Rule 6(e) to the specific documents contained in the two closed files. The Department has agreed to provide all documents from the two closed files that are determined not to contain grand jury materials. With respect to the investigation of Company B, Mr. Trott has informed the Subcommittee that the Department is hindered in complying with the subpoena both by Rule 6(e), which presents particular problems because the investigation is currently under the review of a sitting grand jury, and by the Executive's obligation not to compromise an ongoing criminal investigation. On October 9, the Subcommittee was provided a list of the approximately 56 documents in the Company B file.

* * *

II. Impediments to Disclosure

The principal objections to release of certain of the subpoenaed files can be divided into two categories: the attorneys' obligation under Federal Criminal Procedure Rule 6(e) to protect the confidentiality of matters occurring before the grand jury, and the obligation of the Executive Branch not to disclose internal information pertaining to an open investigation. In an effort to resolve the first issue, the Criminal Division has filed a motion with the appropriate district court seeking guidance on the applicability of Rule 6(e) to the subpoenaed files of the two closed cases. Under the rule, disclosure may be made "when so directed by a court preliminarily or in connection with a judicial proceeding." *Douglas Oil Co. v. Petrol Stops Northwest*, 441 U.S. 211, 220 (1979). With respect to the two closed cases, the Department has expressed its intention to release all materials that are not protected by the court's decision regarding the reach of Rule 6(e). The October 1 subpoena thus appears to us to have been substantially complied with, at least with respect to the two closed investigations. The open investigation raises more serious concerns. On the one hand, the October 5 subpoena purports to disavow any intention to request grand jury materials relating to the Company B investigation. On the other hand, the descriptions of requested documents in the attachment to the subpoena depict materials which are, for the most part, quintessentially grand jury materials when requested in the context of an ongoing criminal investigation. For example, "all prosecutors' memoranda," documents revealing "the status of the investigation," and "investigative plans," as specified in the subpoena, are precisely the type of information the courts have required to be withheld in order to protect the integrity of the grand jury process. Thus, the nominal exclusion of 6(e) materials from the subpoena does not correct an apparent failure on the part of the Subcommittee to recognize that files of a case under active consideration by a grand jury may likely be protected in their entirety from disclosure by Rule 6(e). In light of this uncertainty in the intended scope of the subpoena, we explain in more detail the restrictions imposed on the Department by the courts through Rule 6(e).

A. Duty to Protect Grand Jury Secrecy

The secrecy of grand jury activities, which enjoys ancient common law roots, has received consistent and emphatic protection from the Supreme Court over the years. See, e.g., *United States v. Baggot*, 463 U.S. 476 (1983) * * * The doctrine is an outgrowth of the extraordinary powers granted the grand jury. In order to determine when there is probable cause to believe a crime has been committed and to screen charges not warranting prosecution, the operation of the grand jury "generally [is] unrestrained by the technical procedural and evidentiary rules governing the conduct of criminal trials." *United States v. Calandra*, 414 U.S. 338, 343 (1974). Unlike most administrative investigations, the scope of the grand jury's inquiry is not "limited narrowly by questions of propriety or forecasts of the probable result of the investigation, or by doubts whether any particular individual will be found properly subject to an accusation of crime." *Id.* (*quoting Blair v. United States*, 250 U.S. 273, 282 (1919)).

The broad powers enjoyed by the grand jury, as well as its need to pursue investigations effectively, have given rise to a "long-established policy that maintains the secrecy of grand jury proceedings in the federal courts." *United States v. Proctor and Gamble Co.*, 356 U.S. at 681. As explained on several occasions by the Supreme Court, this doctrine serves several distinct purposes: (1) to prevent the escape of persons whose indictment may be contemplated; (2) to ensure freedom to the grand jury in its deliberations; (3) to prevent subornation of perjury or tampering with grand jury witnesses; (4) to encourage the free disclosure of information to the grand jury; and (5) to protect from unfavorable publicity persons who are accused of crimes but are ultimately exonerated. * * * Thus, grand jury secrecy is "'as important for the protection of the innocent as for the pursuit of the guilty.'" *United States v. Sells*, 463 U.S. at 424–25 (*quoting United States v. Johnson*, 319 U.S. 503, 513 (1943)).

This long established policy is currently codified in Rule 6(e) of the Federal Rules of Criminal Procedure. Under this Rule, no attorney for the Department of Justice may disclose "matters occurring before the grand jury" to any other person, unless one of five narrow exceptions is met.* While none of these exceptions covers disclosure of grand jury materials to a committee of Congress in the present circumstances, it is useful to review the courts' treatment of two of these exceptions, which highlight the importance the courts place on shielding matters that fall within Rule 6(e).

The first of these exceptions permits disclosure of "matters occurring before a grand jury," "when so directed by a court preliminary to or in connection with a judicial proceeding." Fed. R. Crim. P. 6(e)(3)(c)(i). Narrowly interpreting the scope of this section, the Supreme Court recently held in *United States v. Baggot*, 463 U.S. at 480, that the section provided an exemption only "when the primary purpose of the disclosure is … to assist in preparation or conduct of a judicial proceeding." Thus, under the Court's decision in *Baggot,* the Internal Revenue Service could not obtain information pertaining to matters occurring before the grand jury for use in a civil tax audit because the audit was not related to "some identifiable litigation." *Id.*

Although committees of Congress have on occasion sought to claim this exception as a basis for enforcement of subpoenas seeking material protected by Rule 6(e), the analysis employed by the Supreme Court in *Baggot,* as well as in several lower court decisions denying such claims, does not sustain such an argument in this case. A congressional committee's oversight responsibilities simply "do not constitute a 'judicial proceeding'" within the meaning of Rule 6(e). *In re Grand Jury Impanelled October 2, 1978,* 5IO F. Supp. 112, 114 (0.0.C. 1981); *see also In re Grand Jury Investigation of Uranium Industry,* 1979-2 Trade Cas. (CCH) Cfi 62,798, at 78,639, 78,643–44

---

*. The exceptions include (1) disclosure to another government attorney for use m the performance of such attorney's duty; (2) disclosure to such government personnel as are deemed necessary to assist an attorney for the government in the performance of his duties; (3) disclosure directed by a court preliminary to or in connection with a judicial proceeding; (4) disclosure by a government attorney to another grand jury, and (5) disclosure at the request of a defendant and approved by a court "upon a showing that grounds may exist for a motion to dismiss the indictment because of matters occurring before the grand jury." Fed. R. Crim. P. 6(e).

(D.D.C. Aug. 16, 1979). Indeed, the Subcommittee apparently concedes that its inquiry is subject to the restrictions of Rule 6(e).

The other exception that has recently been the subject of Supreme Court examination is set forth in Rule 6(e)(3)(A)(i), which permits disclosure to "an attorney for the government for use in the performance of such attorneys' duty." The language of this provision is exceedingly broad, and would ordinarily suggest that attorneys for the government—generally defined in Rule 54(c) of the Federal Rules of Criminal Procedure to cover all authorized attorneys in the Department of Justice—could freely exchange grand jury materials. In *United States v. Sells Engineering*, 463 U.S. at 428, however, the Supreme Court once again interpreted an exception to Rule 6(e) very narrowly, finding that disclosure among Department of Justice attorneys "is limited to use by those attorneys who conduct the criminal matters to which the materials pertain." As a general matter, therefore, Department attorneys who are assisting the grand jury may not disclose such materials to any other attorney in the Department for purposes of civil litigation even though there may be a legitimate use for the materials under this exception and the attorneys work for the same Department.

In reaching this narrow construction of what would otherwise appear to be a rather broad authorizing provision, the Court in *Sells* relied heavily on the need to maintain the secrecy of grand jury proceedings. Among other things, it suggested that expanding the number of persons with access to grand jury materials would "threat[en] … the willingness of witnesses to come forward and to testify fully and carefully." 463 U.S. at 432. "If a witness knows or fears that his testimony before the grand jury will be routinely available for use in governmental civil litigation or administrative action," the Court reasoned, "he well may be less willing to speak for fear that he will get himself into trouble in some other forum." Id. Although the decision in Sells obviously does not bear directly on the question of what materials can be disclosed to a congressional committee in these circumstances, it does serve to highlight the importance the Supreme Court places on the protections of Rule 6(e), even to the point of precluding attorneys within this Department engaged in parallel civil and criminal investigation from exchanging grand jury material subject to Rule 6(e).

Because the materials sought by the Subcommittee relate to three separate grand jury investigations, and do not fall within any of the exceptions to Rule 6(e) secrecy, it is necessary for this Department to review each document to determine whether release of its contents would reveal a "matter occurring before the grand jury." While the meaning of this ambiguous phrase has been the subject of extensive litigation, and some apparently inconsistent judicial decisions, compare, *e.g., Fund for Constitutional Government v. National Archives*, 656 F.2d 856, 870 (D.C. Cir. 1981) with, *e.g., United States v. Weinstein*, 511 F.2d 622,627 n.5 (2d Cir.), *cert. denied*, 422 U.S. 1042 (1975), it is generally recognized that Rule 6(e) prohibits the disclosure of any material that would reveal the strategy or direction of the grand jury investigation, the nature of the evidence produced before the grand jury, the views expressed by members of the grand jury, or anything else about the grand jury's deliberations. See *Fund for Constitutional Government v. National Archives*, 656 F.2d at 869; *United States*

v. Hughes, 429 F.2d 1293, 1294 (10th Cir. 1970). The application of this general standard, however, requires sensitive judgments with respect to all of the documents by
attorneys who are familiar with the particular investigation. Moreover, there exists
some uncertainty as to the application of Rule 6(e) to documents which have been
subpoenaed by or presented to the grand jury, but which are sought for their own
sake rather than to learn what took place before the grand jury. *See United States v.
Interstate Dress Carriers, Inc.*, 280 F.2d 52, 54 (2d Cir. 1960). * * *

In light of the Supreme Court's recent pronouncements in *Sells* and *Baggot*, we
cannot overemphasize the statutory duty of government attorneys to protect grand
jury materials. It is therefore imperative that the Department screen the documents
sought by the Subcommittee's October 5 subpoena and withhold those which are
prohibited from disclosure under Rule 6(e). Because of the uncertainty in determining
whether some documents are protected, and the importance of the issue, steps may
have to be taken to clarify the application of Rule 6(e) to any of the open files about
which there is doubt.

Members of our Office have discussed certain facts relating to the Company B file
with the Deputy Chief of the Fraud Section, Criminal Division, the attorney responsible for supervising the investigation. The Deputy Chief believes that a very high
percentage of the substance of the files, perhaps 98 to 99 percent, relates to matters
occurring before the grand jury. This high percentage is explained by the fact that
the investigators in this case were unable to obtain evidence or cooperation without
the assistance of the grand jury process, so virtually the entire investigation was conducted before the grand jury. The Deputy Chief has stated that redaction of grand
jury materials would not be feasible because little or nothing of substance would remain. Assistant Attorney General Trott has informed the Subcommittee of the im-
practicability of redacting grand jury materials.

* * * Depending upon the decision with respect to other possible bases for protecting these documents from disclosure to the Subcommittee, it may be necessary
or desirable to seek judicial guidance in determining which documents or portions
of documents are protected from disclosure under Rule 6(e). We discuss this option
further below.

B. Duty to Protect the Integrity of Ongoing Investigations

In the case of an ongoing criminal investigation, not only are the concerns of Rule
6(e) heightened because the case is currently before the grand jury, but also further
concerns counsel against compliance with a congressional subpoena. The policy of
the Executive Branch throughout this Nation's history has been generally to decline
to provide committees of Congress with access to, or copies of, open law enforcement
files except in extraordinary circumstances. Attorney General Robert Jackson, subsequently a Justice of the Supreme Court, articulated this position over forty years ago:

It is the position of this Department, restated now with the approval of and at the
direction of the President, that all investigative reports are confidential documents
of the executive department of the Government, to aid in the duty laid upon the

President by the Constitution to "take care that the laws be faithfully executed," and that congressional or public access to them would not be in the public interest.

> Disclosure of the reports could not do otherwise than seriously prejudice law enforcement. Counsel for a defendant or prospective defendant, could have no greater help than to know how much or how little information the Government has, and what witnesses or sources of information it can rely upon. This is exactly what these reports are intended to contain.

40 Op. Att'y Gen. 45, 46 (1941).

Thus the dissemination of law enforcement files would prejudice the cause of effective law enforcement and, because the reasons for the policy of confidentiality are as sound and fundamental to the administration of justice today as they were forty years ago, there would appear to be no reason not to adhere in this instance to the consistent position of previous presidents and attorneys general. Deputy Assistant Attorney General Kauper explained the concerns:

> Over a number of years, a number of reasons have been advanced for the traditional refusal of the Executive to supply Congress with information from open investigative files. Most important, the Executive cannot effectively investigate if Congress is, in a sense, a partner in the investigation. If a congressional committee is fully apprised of all details of an investigation as the investigation proceeds, there is a substantial danger that congressional pressures will influence the course of the investigation.

Memorandum for Edward L. Morgan, Deputy Counsel to the President, from Thomas E. Kauper, Deputy Assistant Attorney General, Office of Legal Counsel, Re: Submission of Open CID Investigation Files 2 (Dec. 19, 1969).

This policy with respect to Executive Branch investigations was first expressed by President Washington and has been reaffirmed by or on behalf of most of our Presidents, including Presidents Jefferson, Jackson, Lincoln, Theodore Roosevelt, Franklin Roosevelt, and Eisenhower. No President, to our knowledge, has departed from this position affirming the confidentiality of law enforcement files.

Other grounds for objecting to the disclosure of law enforcement files include: the potential damage to proper law enforcement which would be caused by the revelation of sensitive techniques, methods or strategy; concern over the safety of confidential informants and the chilling effect on sources of information; sensitivity to the rights of innocent individuals who may be identified in law enforcement files but who may not be guilty of any violation of law; and well-founded fears that the perception of the integrity, impartiality and fairness of the law enforcement process as a whole will be damaged if sensitive material is distributed beyond those persons necessarily involved in the investigation and prosecution process. These concerns are very close to those which underlie Rule 6(e), but they extend to the entire investigative process, not just those problems associated with a grand jury.

Not the least internal concern, of course, is that effective and candid deliberations among the numerous advisers who participate in a case in various roles and at various stages of a prosecution would be rendered impossible if confidential deliberative communications were held open to public scrutiny. *Cf United States v. Nixon*, 418 U.S. 683, 708 (1974). The deliberative memoranda that constitute a significant portion of investigative files are ah intrinsic part of the prosecutorial process. Employees of the Department would be reluctant to express their personal, unofficial views if those views could be obtained by Congress upon request. This concern is particularly acute in the context of an ongoing investigation in which persons called upon to make recommendations regarding prosecution must be assured that their advice will not be subject to immediate review and publicity by a congressional committee.

In addition, potential targets of enforcement actions are entitled to protection from widespread premature disclosure of investigative information. Because the Congress and the Department of Justice are both part of the United States Government which prosecutes a criminal defendant, there is "no difference between prejudicial publicity instigated by the United States through its executive arm and prejudicial publicity instigated by the United States through its legislative arm." *Delaney v. United States*, 199 F.2d 107, 114 (1st Cir. 1952). Pretrial publicity originating in Congress, therefore, can be attributed to the Government as a whole and can require postponement or other modification of the prosecution on due process grounds. *Id.* The discretion of prosecutive officials to conduct their investigations and trials in the manner they deem to be the most efficient and constructive can be infringed by precipitous disclosures which prompt a court to impose remedial procedural obligations upon the Government.

The Department of Justice also has an obligation to ensure that the fairness of the decisionmaking with respect to its prosecutorial function is not compromised by excessive congressional pressures, and that the due process rights of those under investigation are not violated. *See Pillsbury v. Federal Trade Comm'n*, 354 F.2d 952 (5th Cir. 1966). Just as an agency's ability to fulfill its statutory obligation may be impermissibly strained by pressure from the Legislative Branch during the administrative decisionmaking process, *D.C. Federation of Civic Ass'ns v. Volpe*, 459 F.2d 1231, 1246–1247 (D.C. Cir.), cen. denied, 405 U.S. 1030 (1972), excessive interference with the exercise of prosecutorial discretion can substantially prejudice the rights of persons under investigation. Persons who ultimately are not prosecuted may be subjected to prejudicial publicity without being given an opportunity to cleanse themselves of the stain of unfounded allegations. Moreover, the injection of impermissible factors in the decision whether to initiate prosecution offends not only the rights of the accused, but also the professional obligation of government attorneys to the integrity of the judicial process and, ultimately, the obligation of the Executive faithfully to execute the laws.

Article II of the Constitution places the power to enforce the laws squarely in the Executive Branch of Government. The Executive therefore has the exclusive authority to enforce the laws adopted by Congress, and neither the Judicial nor Legislative Branches may directly interfere with the prosecutorial discretion of the Executive by directing the Executive to prosecute particular individuals. *United States v. Nixon*, 418

U.S. 683, 693 (1974); *Confiscation Cases*, 74 U.S. (7 Wall.) 454, 457 (1869). This principle was explained in *Smith v. United States*, 375 F.2d 243 (5th Cir.), *cert. denied*, 389 U.S. 841 (1967), in which the court considered the applicability of the Federal Tort Claims Act to a prosecutorial decision not to arrest or prosecute persons injuring plaintiffs business. The court ruled that the government was immune from suit under the discretionary decision exception of the Act on the ground that the Executive's prosecutorial discretion was rooted in the separation of powers under the Constitution:

> The President of the United States is charged in Article 2, Section 3, of the Constitution with the duty to "take care that the laws be faithfully executed ..." The Attorney General is the President's surrogate in the prosecution of all offenses against the United States.... The discretion of the Attorney General in choosing whether to prosecute or not to prosecute, or to abandon a prosecution already started, is absolute....

This discretion is required in all cases. * * *

We emphasize that this discretion, exercised in even the lowliest and least consequential cases, can affect the policies, duties, and success of a function placed under the control of the Attorney General by our Constitution and statutes.375 F.2d at 246–47. * * *

C. Specific Application to this Investigation

The wisdom and necessity of these general principles, developed over years of judicial, congressional and executive experience, are clearly illustrated by consideration of the specific damaging effects congressional interference has had and may continue to have upon the Company B investigation. The principal trial attorney responsible for the investigation, the Deputy Chief of the Fraud Section of the Criminal Division, prepared a statement which outlines the specific ways in which release of prosecutive or investigative memoranda would interfere with the ongoing investigation of the Electric Boat matter. The following concerns are drawn from that statement.

The key witness in the Company B matter, Mr. D, has already delayed cooperating with the Department because he hoped to benefit from congressional pressure on the Department related to his pending indictment in another matter. Further, certain Members of Congress have declared that they possess substantial evidence relevant to the Company B investigation but have refused Department of Justice requests for access to that evidence.

In addition, employees of Company B, both former and present, are in fear of retribution if their cooperation should be disclosed. The Department may be unable to secure reliable evidence from employees if it cannot guarantee total confidentiality. Further, disclosure of Federal Bureau of Investigation reports will effectively preclude the Bureau's providing assistance in the investigation and deprive the Department of the valuable resources on which it depends. Moreover, the pursuit of parallel investigations of the same matter by a congressional subcommittee and the Department of Justice will confuse matters in the public eye and enable potential targets to continue to play Congress and the Department against one another.

The Department also has serious concerns about the possibility of jeopardizing the indictments that may be secured as a result of the investigation. Department participation in abusive publicity or inadvertent release of grand jury material inextricably bound up with other material, whether willing or in response to a congressional subpoena, could subject an indictment to dismissal. In sum, the serious concerns for the integrity of the investigative and prosecutive process that underlie the legal principles discussed above have vivid application to the current matter.

III. Limitations on Power to Withhold

The policy of confidentiality does not necessarily extend to all material contained in investigative files. Depending upon the nature of the specific files and type of investigation involved, certain of the information contained in such files may be shared with Congress in response to a proper request. Indeed, Assistant Attorney General Trott has informed the Subcommittee that the Department will release all documents in the closed files that are judicially determined not to reveal grand jury material. In the same vein, there may be documents in even the open Company B files that do not implicate any of the constitutional or pragmatic problems identified in our discussion. If that is the case, those documents should be turned over to Congress in response to a proper request. However, each document should be examined in light of the basic principles articulated above.

An additional limitation on the assertion of executive privilege is that the privilege should not be invoked to conceal evidence of wrongdoing or criminality on the part of executive officers. The documents must therefore be reviewed for any evidence of misconduct which would render the assertion of privilege inappropriate. "[I]t should always be remembered that even the most carefully administered department or agency may have made a mistake or failed to discover a wrongdoing committed inside or outside the Government." Study, *Congressional Inquiries Concerning the Decision-making Process and Documents of the Executive Branch: 1953–1960.* The greatest danger attending any assertion of executive privilege has always arisen from the difficulty, perhaps impossibility, of establishing with absolute certainty that no mistake or wrongdoing will subsequently come to light which lends credence to congressional assertions that the privilege has been improperly invoked. We are unaware of any serious allegations of criminal or unethical conduct in this matter, but we nevertheless strongly recommend a document-by-document review of the relevant materials to avoid any possibility of a misapplication of the privilege.

IV. Needs of Congress

The letters from Senator Proxmire and Senator Grassley do not specify the purpose for seeking access to an open investigative file. Although they have cited their intent to review the Department of Justice's management of certain fraud investigations, neither the letters nor the subpoenas articulate a reason for including an ongoing investigation in that review process. In our opinion, the mere statement of review power falls far short of the test established by the United States Court of Appeals for the District of Columbia: "The sufficiency of the Committee's showing must depend solely on whether the subpoenaed evidence is demonstrably critical to the fulfillment of the committee's functions." *Senate Select Committee on Presidential Campaign Activities v. Nixon*, 498 F.2d 725, 731 (D.C. Cir. 1974).

V. Recommendations and Conclusions

The above discussion emphasizes the fact-specific nature of the determinations required to be made before investigative files can be turned over to Congress consistent with federal prosecutors' obligations to the court and to potential defendants, and the constitutional obligation of the Executive to execute the laws. The very core of these determinations necessitates a careful review and deliberation for every document involved. In addition, the complexity of our obligations to preserve the confidentiality of matters occurring before the grand jury involves a careful examination of each document in the Company B file. Because of the importance of protecting this investigation and future Department of Justice investigations, and based upon the conclusion of the Criminal Division concerning the dangers to the ongoing criminal investigation, we believe documents in the open file should not be disclosed to the Subcommittee. * * *

Finally, in the event that there is not adequate time before the return date of the subpoena to consider and resolve whether a claim of executive privilege should be asserted by the President, the question may arise whether the documents may be withheld without the formal assertion of a claim on the basis that additional time is necessary to determine whether a claim should be made.

We conclude that, inherent in the constitutional doctrine of executive privilege is the right to have sufficient time to review subpoenaed documents in order to determine whether an executive privilege claim should be made. If the Executive Branch could be required to respond to a subpoena (either judicial or congressional) without having adequate opportunity to review the demanded documents and determine whether a privilege claim would be necessary in order to protect the constitutional prerogatives of the President, the President's ability effectively to assert a claim of executive privilege would be effectively nullified. Therefore, if the President is to be able to assert executive privilege at all, he must have adequate time within which to make a determination whether or not to assert the privilege. Thus, in the right to withhold documents for a time sufficient to make a determination whether to assert privilege is an element of executive privilege itself, and it is a justifiable basis upon which to withhold documents.

This Office has previously concluded that it would be constitutionally impermissible to prosecute an Executive Branch official for asserting the President's constitutionally based claim of executive privilege. *See "Prosecution for Contempt of Congress of an Executive Branch Official Who Has Asserted a Claim of Executive Privilege,"* 8 Op. O.L.C. 101 (1984). For the reasons articulated in that memorandum, it would be equally impermissible to prosecute an Executive Branch official for withholding subpoenaed documents for a reasonable time sufficient to make a determination whether executive privilege should be asserted.

> Robert B. Shanks
> Deputy Assistant Attorney General
> Office of Legal Counsel

B. Congress's Oversight Interests in Federal Law Enforcement

Perhaps unsurprisingly, Congress takes a vastly divergent view of these issues. Congress often starts with the Supreme Court's explicit endorsement of the concept of parallel criminal and legislative investigations in *Hutcheson v. United States*.[15] There, the Court noted that "surely a congressional committee which is engaged in a legitimate legislative investigation need not grind to a halt whenever responses to its inquiries might potentially be harmful to a witness in some distinct proceeding ... or when crime or wrongdoing is exposed."

The congressional motion for summary judgment excerpted below comes from a dispute between a Republican-led House committee and Obama administration Attorney General Eric Holder related to a number of problematic gun trafficking investigations along the southwest U.S. border commonly referred to as "Operation Fast and Furious."

Committee on Oversight and Government Reform, United States House of Representatives v. Eric H. Holder, Jr — Plaintiff's Motion for Summary Judgment
IN THE UNITED STATES DISTRICT COURT
FORTH DISTRICT OF COLUMBIA

	)
COMMITTEE ON OVERSIGHT AND	)
GOVERNMENT REFORM,	)
UNITED STATES HOUSE OF	)
REPRESENTATIVES,	)
	)
Plaintiff,	)
	)

---

15. 369 U.S. 599, 617 (1962).

	)	Case No. 1:12-cv-01332-ABJ
v.	)	
	)	
ERIC H. HOLDER, JR.,	)	
in his official capacity as Attorney	)	
General of the United States,	)	
	)	
	)	
Defendant.	)	

Plaintiff's Motion for Summary Judgment

Pursuant to Rule 56 of the Federal Rules of Civil Procedure and Local Civil Rule 7, Plaintiff Committee on Oversight and Government Reform of the United States House of Representatives respectfully moves for entry of judgment on Count I of, and the sole remaining count in, the First Amended Complaint (Jan. 15, 2013) (ECF No. 35). With respect to Count I, there is no genuine issue as to any material fact and, for all the reasons set forth in the accompanying Memorandum of Points and Authorities in Support of Plaintiff's Motion for Summary Judgment, the Committee is entitled to judgment as a matter of law. * * *

I. Congressional Oversight Generally.

"[The] power of the Congress to conduct investigations is inherent in the legislative process. That power is broad. It encompasses inquiries concerning the administration of existing laws as well as proposed or possibly needed statutes." *Watkins v. United States*, 354 U.S. 178, 187 (1957). Watkins specifically noted that the first Congresses held "inquiries dealing with suspected corruption or mismanagement of government officials," * * * and stressed that Congress' power to investigate is at its peak when focused on alleged waste, fraud, abuse, or incompetent administration within a government department, * * *

A direct corollary of Congress' constitutionally-mandated oversight and investigative responsibility is the authority to obtain information, including by use of compulsory process.

> [The] power to secure needed information by such means [i.e., compulsory process] has long been treated as an attribute of the power to legislate. It was so regarded in the British Parliament * * *

> We are of [the] opinion that the power of inquiry—with process to enforce it—is an essential and appropriate auxiliary to the legislative function.

> A legislative body cannot legislate wisely or effectively in the absence of information respecting the conditions which the legislation is intended to affect or change; and where the legislative body does not itself possess the requisite information—which not infrequently is true—recourse must be had to others who do possess it. Experience has taught that mere requests for such information often are unavailing, and also that information which is volunteered is not always accurate or complete; so some means of compulsion are essential to obtain what is needed. All this was true before and when the Constitution was framed and adopted. In that period the power of inquiry, with enforcing

process, was regarded and employed as a necessary and appropriate attribute of the power to legislate—indeed, was treated as inhering in it.

McGrain v. Daugherty, 273 U.S. 135, 161, 174–75 (1927); *see also Eastland v. U.S. Servicemen's Fund*, 421 U.S. 491, 504 n.15 (1975) ("[T]he scope of [Congress'] power of inquiry is as penetrating and far-reaching as the potential power to enact and appropriate under the Constitution" (ellipsis and quotation marks omitted).); *id.* at 504 ("Issuance of subpoenas ... has long been held to be a legitimate use by Congress of its power to investigate."); *Barenblatt v. United States*, 360 U.S. 109, 111 (1959) ("The power of inquiry has been employed by Congress throughout our history, over the whole range of the national interests concerning which Congress might legislate or decide upon due investigation not to legislate."). And, when Congress does resort to compulsory process,

> [i]t is unquestionably the duty of all citizens to cooperate with the Congress in its efforts to obtain the facts needed for intelligent legislative action. It is their unremitting obligation to respond to subpoenas, to respect the dignity of the Congress and its committees and to testify fully with respect to matters within the province of proper investigation.

Watkins, 354 U.S. at 187–88.

Pursuant to the Rulemaking Clause, U.S. Const. art. I, § 5, cl. 2 ("Each House may determine the Rules of its Proceedings * * *")—and also by statute, *see* 2 U.S.C. § 190d—the House has delegated this substantial and wide-ranging oversight and investigative authority to its committees. *See* Rule XI.1(b)(1), Rules of the House of Representatives ("Each committee may conduct at any time such investigations and studies at it considers necessary or appropriate in the exercise of its responsibilities under rule X."). The House has delegated particularly broad responsibilities to the Oversight Committee, including authority to conduct oversight regarding "[g]overnment management and accounting measures generally," "[o]verall economy, efficiency, and management of government operations and activities," and "[r]eorganizations in the executive branch of the Government." House Rule X.1(n). In addition, the Oversight Committee is authorized to "*at any time conduct investigations of any matter* without regard to ... this clause conferring jurisdiction over the matter to another standing committee" House Rule X.4(c)(2) (emphasis added).

To carry out these responsibilities, the Committee may issue subpoenas for testimony and documents. *See* House Rule XI.2(m)(1)(B), (3)(A)(i); Rule 12(d), Rules of the Comm. on Oversight & Gov't Reform (vesting chair with authority to "authorize and issue subpoenas ... in the conduct of any investigation or activity ... within the jurisdiction of the committee").

II. Congressional Oversight of the Department of Justice.

In 1789, Congress created the Office of the Attorney General. *See* Judiciary Act of 1789, ch. 20, § 35, 1 Stat. 73, 92–93 (1789). One hundred years later, Congress created DOJ, to which Congress' oversight authority unquestionably extends. *See* Act to Establish the Department of Justice, ch. 150, 16 Stat. 162 (1870). Over the years, Congress has investigated DOJ on many occasions, repeatedly probing its inner workings, organizational structure, management, and administration, as well as its conduct in responding to congressional investigations.

For example, in the 1920s, Congress investigated DOJ's role in the Teapot Dome scandal. The investigation began as a Senate inquiry into leases of government-owned, oil-rich lands in Wyoming, but the focus shifted when investigators discovered that the leases resulted from wrongdoing by high-ranking government officials. *See generally* John C. Grabow, *Congressional Investigations: Law and Practice*, § 2.3 (1988); CONGRESS INVESTIGATES: A DOCUMENTED HISTORY 1792–1974, vol. IV, 6–7 (ARTHUR SCHLESINGER, JR. & ROGER BURNS EDS., 1983). The Senate empowered a select committee to investigate "charges of misfeasance and nonfeasance" at DOJ for its failure to bring criminal prosecutions against various wrongdoers. *McGrain*, 273 U.S. at 151. DOJ initially balked at providing the select committee with internal reports and other investigative documents. *See Investigation of Hon. Harry M. Daugherty, Formerly Att'y Gen. of the U.S.: Hr'gs Before the Select Comm. on Investigation of the Att'y Gen., U.S. Senate*, 68th Cong., vol. I at 1015–16, and vol. II at 1159–60 (1924). Ultimately, however, the select committee gained broad access to DOJ's files, including factual findings and recommendations compiled by DOJ line employees. *See id.*, vol. III at 2389. The Supreme Court expressed no discomfort whatsoever with Congress' investigation:

> [T]he subject to be investigated was the administration of [DOJ] — whether its functions were being properly discharged or were being neglected or misdirected, and particularly whether the Attorney General and his assistants were performing or neglecting their duties in respect of the institution and prosecution of proceedings to punish crimes and enforce appropriate remedies against the wrongdoers.... Plainly the subject was one on which legislation could be had and would be materially aided by the information which the investigation was calculated to elicit. *This becomes manifest when it is reflected that the functions of [DOJ], the powers and duties of the Attorney General, and the duties of his assistants are all subject to regulation by congressional legislation, and that [DOJ] is maintained and its activities are carried on under such appropriations as in the judgment of Congress are needed from year to year.*

McGrain, 273 U.S. at 177–78 (emphasis added).

In 1952, a House subcommittee investigated "the administration of the Department of Justice and the Attorney General of the United States." H. Res. 95, 82d Cong. (1952). The investigation covered, among other things, whether DOJ had attempted improperly to curb a grand jury inquiry into its failure to enforce federal tax fraud laws, and whether DOJ was dilatory in handling certain cases. *See* Investigation of the Dep't of Justice, H. Rep. No. 83-1079, at 26, 54, 69 (1953). The subcommittee reviewed thousands of pages of testimony on a range of allegations of abuses and inefficiencies at DOJ, as well as deliberative materials obtained from the agency, including internal correspondence and memoranda, and transcripts of interdepartmental telephonic communications. *See, e.g., id.* at 22, 35, 61.

In 1982, a Senate committee investigated undercover activities at the Federal Bureau of Investigation ("FBI") and other DOJ component entities. *See* Final Rep. of the [Sen.] Select Comm. to Study Undercover Activities of Components of the Dep't of Justice, S. Rep. No. 97-682 (1982), *available at* https://www.ncjrs.gov/pdffiles1/ Digitization/124269NCJRS.pdf. As part of the investigation, the committee demanded and obtained "almost all of the confidential documents generated during the covert stage of the undercover operation." *Id.* at V. While the select committee allowed DOJ to retain certain documents that the committee determined might compromise ongoing DOJ investigations, it did so only after DOJ provided the committee with a satisfactory log of the documents and a briefing on their contents. *See id.* at V, 479, 483.

And, in 1983, the House investigated DOJ's role in the response of the Environmental Protection Agency ("EPA") to an underlying congressional investigation into EPA's enforcement of the Superfund law. In connection with the underlying investigation, two House committees issued document subpoenas to EPA Administrator Anne Gorsuch Burford, *see* H. Judiciary Comm., Rep. on Investigation of the Role of the Dep't of Justice in the Withholding of EPA Docs., H. Rep. No. 99-435, vol. I at 3–4 (1985). On DOJ's advice, Ms. Burford asserted Executive privilege and withheld responsive documents, whereupon the House held her in contempt. *See id.* at 4. Believing DOJ may have provided improper guidance to Ms. Burford, a House committee sought from DOJ "all documents prepared by or in the possession of [DOJ] in any way relating to the withholding of documents that Congressional committees have subpoenaed from the EPA." *Id.* at 605, 613, 640, 645.

The committee agreed to review certain responsive documents and, once that review was complete, to consider narrowing its request. *See id.* at 605. The documents reviewed included internal records of the offices of the Attorney General, Deputy Attorney General, Solicitor General, Office of Legal Counsel ("OLC"), and Office of Legislative Affairs ("OLA"). See id. Ultimately, the committee demanded and obtained copies of many of the reviewed documents, along with others DOJ had not made available for the committee's review. See id. at 606, 608.

In sum, there is nothing unusual or unprecedented about the Committee's investigation, either of Operation Fast and Furious itself or of DOJ's response thereto. What is remarkable is the lengths to which DOJ has gone to try to thwart a concededly legitimate Committee investigation, and the lengths to which the Attorney General has gone to avoid answering the Committee's also concededly legitimate questions about that obstruction.

* * *

CONCLUSION

For all of the foregoing reasons, this Court should grant the Committee's motion for summary judgment.

Respectfully submitted,

/s/ Kerry W. Kircher
KERRY W. KIRCHER, General Counsel

D.C. Bar No. 386816
WILLIAM PITTARD, Deputy General Counsel
D.C. Bar No. 482949
CHRISTINE DAVENPORT, Sr. Assistant Counsel
TODD B. TATELMAN, Assistant Counsel
MARY BETH WALKER, Assistant Counsel
D.C. Bar No. 501033
ELENI M. ROUMEL, Assistant Counsel

Note and Questions

Who Won the Debate? Did Congress or the Executive have the better of the arguments? If you believe both raise important points, how would you fashion a compromise? In addition, ask yourself whether the judiciary or political processes are better suited to resolve this dispute.

Chapter Four

The Mueller Investigation and Legal Ethics

I. Generally

The conduct of many of the high-profile lawyers in the Mueller investigation raises interesting and significant legal ethics issues. Most prominently, the actions of Michael Cohen, Donald Trump's former lawyer, and Rudy Giuliani, one of President Trump's current lawyers have sparked significant debate in the legal community and in the news media. Was it ethical for Michael Cohen to secretly tape Donald Trump? What are the limits of lawyer-client confidentiality? Is Rudy Giuliani subject to sanction for his media commentary in defense of Donald Trump? What about other lawyer-pundits in the media? These are among the controversial ethics issues for lawyers that arise in connection with the Mueller investigation. This chapter first discusses the ethical issues regarding secret taping, and then considers the ethics issues about public commentary and the media.

The foundation of the lawyer-client relationship is trust, loyalty and a pledge of confidentiality. Even before the early days of lawyer regulation, there was an implicit understanding that lawyers must be loyal to their clients and may not reveal client communications without client consent except in carefully circumscribed instances. It is believed that lawyers will not be able to competently and diligently counsel and otherwise represent a client unless that client can be assured of the lawyer's obligation of confidentiality. Another essential aspect of the lawyer-client relationship is trust and loyalty. The lawyer is not permitted to act contrary to the client's interests except in unusual and narrow circumstances. Thus, there are specific rules prohibiting lawyers from representing a client when there is a personal or professional conflict of interest. These conflicts include those with the lawyer's own interests.

Ethics codes emphasize the notion that lawyers should exhibit the highest standards of conduct in order to instill clients' trust in lawyers and to promote public confidence in the profession. Thus, the issue of secret taping of clients strikes at the core of issues of confidentiality and trust. It is both the secret taping itself and the revelation of the tape's contents that give rise to controversy about the norms and rules of the legal profession.

As is well known, Michael Cohen was the longstanding attorney for then-presidential nominee Donald Trump. In July 2016, Michael Cohen secretly recorded Trump's conversation about former Playboy model Karen McDougal's story of her affair with him and how he planned to get the publisher of the *National Enquirer* to purchase her story to prevent it from becoming public before the 2016 presidential election.[1] Trump's plan worked. The *National Enquirer* purchased McDougal's story in August 2016.[2] Trump was elected President in November 2016.

On April 9, 2018, the Federal Bureau of Investigation (FBI) raided and seized audio tapes from Michael Cohen's office, home, and hotel room.[3] Sometime later, the media reported that Cohen was cooperating with special counsel Robert Mueller's investigation into Russia's interference in the 2016 presidential election and possible coordination between the Russian government and individuals associated with the Trump's presidential campaign.[4] Among the issues under investigation was the payment to the National Enquirer to quash the story that Donald Trump had an affair with Karen McDougal. Trump claimed that he knew nothing about payments to her.

In July 2018, Cohen's lawyer released a copy of the tape that contradicted Trump's public pronouncements of his lack of knowledge of the National Enquirer payment.[5] Cohen said, "'I'm not going to be a punching bag anymore.'"[6] Trump, reacting in characteristic mode, tweeted "Even more inconceivable that a lawyer would tape a client—totally unheard of & perhaps illegal."[7] Trump also tweeted, "What kind of a lawyer would tape a client? So sad! Is this a first, never heard of it before? ... I hear there are other clients and many reporters that are taped—can this be so? Too bad!"[8]

---

1. Chris Cuomo et al., *Exclusive: CNN Obtains Secret Trump-Cohen Tape*, CNN Politics, July 25, 2018, *available at* https://tinyurl.com/ydez25m9; Dylan Matthews, *Michael Cohen's Hush Money Payments to Stormy Daniels and Karen McDougal, Explained: A Timeline of Michael Cohen's Hush Money Payments to Help Trump*, Vox, Aug. 21, 2018, *available at,* https://tinyurl.com/ybaom6q8.

2. Matthews, *supra* note 1.

3. Erica Orden & Kara Scannell, *Feds Have 12 Michael Cohen Audio Recordings*, CNN Politics, July 23, 2018, *available at* https://tinyurl.com/yceobbcv. Another report states that the FBI seized more than 100 tapes from Cohen's office, home, and hotel room. Philip Rucker et al., *'I'm not going to be a punching bag anymore': Inside Michael Cohen's Break with Trump*, Wash.Post, July 25, 2018, *available at* https://tinyurl.com/ydfmebqs. The FBI raid took place on April 9, 2018. Matt Apuzzo, *F.B.I. Raids Office of Trump's Longtime Lawyer Michael Cohen; Trump Calls It 'Disgraceful'*, NY Times, Apr. 9, 2018, *available at* https://tinyurl.com/y8cw7zly.

4. Brad Heath et al., *Cohen Takeaways: As Trump's Former Lawyer Heads to Prison, Political and Legal Implications Grow for White House*, USA Today, Dec. 12, 2018, *available at* https://tinyurl.com/ycyawoyb.

5. Cuomo et al., *supra* note 1; Matt Apuzzo et al., *Michael Cohen Secretly Taped Trump Discussing Payment to Playboy Model*, NY Times, July 20, 2018, *available at* https://tinyurl.com/y7aluhdh.

6. *"I'm not going to be a punching bag anymore:" Inside Michael Cohen's Break with Trump*, Wash. Post, July 25, 2018, *available at* https://tinyurl.com/ydfmebqs.

7. Emily Stewart *Trump Reacts to Michael Cohen's Secret Recording: "Inconceivable,"* Vox, July 21, 2018, *available at* https://tinyurl.com/ycb89k8f.

8. Donald Trump (@realDonaldTrump), Twitter (July 25, 2018 5:34 AM), https://twitter.com/realdonaldtrump/status/1022097879253635072 ("Is this a first, never heard of it before.... I hear there are other clients and many reporters that are taped—can this be so? Too bad").

This was one of hundreds of Cohen's secret recordings of Donald Trump during the course of Cohen's representation.[9]

II. Nixon Recordings and Watergate

The Cohen incident is hardly the first time that a lawyer has engaged in secretly taping of conversations with a client or with others. Famously, President Richard Nixon, himself a lawyer, secretly tape recorded every conversation in the White House Oval Office. Revelation of the existence and content of the tapes eventually led to his resignation. Those tapes were part of the scandal known as "Watergate," that stemmed from the 1972 pre-presidential election break-in of the Democratic National Committee headquarters in the Watergate complex in Washington, D.C.[10] After the break-in, the Washington Post reported links between Nixon's re-election campaign and the burglars.[11] Nixon was re-elected, but in May 1973, Attorney General Elliot Richardson appointed a special prosecutor, Archibald Cox, to investigate the break-in and any links to Nixon's re-election campaign.[12] The prosecutor learned of the existence of Nixon's Oval Office taped discussions and of the efforts of Nixon and others to cover up the links of the Watergate break-in to the reelection campaign.[13] Cox tried to subpoena the tapes, but Nixon directed Cox to be fired.[14] This controversial matter of the tapes went to the United States Supreme Court and it decided that Nixon must release the tapes. Those tapes provided evidence of Nixon's involvement in the Watergate crimes and cover-up.[15] They were the key evidence that led to Nixon's resignation from office under the threat of impeachment.[16]

---

9. Rucker et al., *supra* note 3.

10. *The Complete Watergate Timeline (It Took Longer than You Realize)*, PBS News Hour, (May 30, 2017), *available at* https://tinyurl.com/y9gp67sc.

11. *Id.*

12. *Id.*

13. *Watergate Scandal*, History, *available at* https://tinyurl.com/ybcmco9h.

14. Marjorie Cohn, *The Politics of the Clinton Impeachment and the Death of the Independent Counsel Statute: Toward Depoliticization*, 102 W. Va. L. Rev. 59, 61 (1999).

15. *Watergate Scandal*, *supra* note 13.

16. *Id.* Another infamous instance of tape recording was during the Clinton era. The secret recordings of recordings by Gennifer Flowers of her personal relationship with President Bill Clinton and Linda Tripp's secret recordings of Monica Lewinsky, spurred the investigation that led to President Clinton's impeachment. Linda Tripp secretly recorded her phone conversations with Monica Lewinsky, the White House intern who had an affair with President Bill Clinton. In 1998, Tripp gave the tapes to independent counsel Kenneth Starr, who was investigating Clinton's involvement in a real estate venture, known as Whitewater, in Arkansas. Clinton, testifying before a grand jury denied his relationship with Lewinsky. Then, after Clinton, learned about the tapes that conflicted with his testimony, he admitted the affair. Those tapes gave Starr the evidence necessary to prompt the cooperation of Lewinsky, and Starr then claimed that her testimony would prove that Clinton committed perjury by lying under oath to the grand jury. The House of Representatives impeached Clinton in December 1998, but the Senate acquitted him in February 1999. Brooks Jackson, *Clinton's Three Lies, According to Starr*, CNN.com (Sept. 21, 1998), *available at* https://tinyurl.com/ydzcd5em. Clinton's lawyers

The notorious illegal actions and criminal conviction of lawyers in the Watergate incident spawned a longstanding concentration upon legal ethics in the profession and an overhaul of the ethics rules for lawyers culminating in the Model Rules of Professional Conduct (hereinafter "RPC").[17]As a consequence of Watergate, legal ethics training is required in all accredited law schools and the consistent attention to legal ethics rules, opinions and training is a consequence of the Watergate era.[18]

III. Secret Recordings

Certainly, lawyers are not the only people who engage in secret recordings. Prominently, Donald Trump has been taped by others. Famously, in the *Access Hollywood* tape made while Trump believed the microphone should have been turned off,[19] Trump bragged about kissing women and grabbing their genitals, stating, "when you're a star, they [women] let you do it. You can do anything."[20] Then, Omarosa Manigault Newman, former assistant to Trump as Director of Communications for the White House office of Public Liaison, made secret recordings because without the tapes "no one in America would believe me."[21] Over many years, politicians and public figures have been involved in scandals as a result of leaked recordings.[22] Secret recordings feature prominently in whistleblower and employment discrimination claims, and in cases of domestic violence, elder abuse and misconduct by teachers.[23]

---

argued that Clinton did not commit perjury because he gave literally true answers even if they were misleading. *Id.* Clinton was never criminally prosecuted.

17. Ted Schneyer, *Professionalism as Bar Politics: The Making of the Model Rules of Professional Conduct*, 14.4 L. & Soc. Inquiry 677, 688 (1989).

18. The Model Rules of Professional adopted by the ABA are the basis for the adoption of Rules of Professional Conduct by individual states. Many State provisions vary from the Model Rules. *See* Model Rules of Prof'l Conduct (Am. Bar Ass'n 2016) [hereinafter MRPC], *available at* https://www.americanbar.org/groups/professional_responsibility/publications/model_rules_of_professional_conduct/.

19. Lisa de Moraes, *Donald Trump Blames NBCU Microphone for His Lewd 'Access Hollywood' Boast in New Interview*, Deadline Hollywood (Oct. 27, 2016, 11:13 AM), *available at* https://deadline.com/2016/10/donald-trump-blames-nbcu-microphone-access-hollywood-groping-women-tape-1201843905/.

20. The following is a portion of the transcript of the *Access Hollywood* tape in which Trump is filmed talking with television personality Billy Bush:

> **Trump:** I better use some Tic Tacs just in case I start kissing her. You know, I'm automatically attracted to beautiful — I just start kissing them. It's like a magnet. Just kiss. I don't even wait. And when you're a star, they let you do it. You can do anything.
> **Bush:** Whatever you want.
> **Trump:** Grab 'em by the pussy. You can do anything.

Mark Makela, *Transcript: Donald Trump's Taped Comments About Women*, N.Y. Times (Oct. 8, 2016), *available at* https://www.nytimes.com/2016/10/08/us/donald-trump-tape-transcript.html.

21. Anne Flaherty, *Lordy, They Have Tapes: Secret Tapes in Trump Orbit Not New*, AP News (Aug. 13, 2018), *available at* https://apnews.com/92b8ee71029447e99a35484dc89d9f8b.

22. John Bliss, *The Legal Ethics of Secret Recording*, forthcoming, Geo. J. Legal Ethics, (2019).

23. *Id.* (*citing* John Burchill, *Tale of the Tape: Policing Surreptitious Recordings in the Workplace*, 40 Man. L.J. 247 (2017)).

In this era of iphones and enhanced technology, it is no longer shocking or indeed, surprising, that citizens engage in secret recording.

Is such secret taping legal? Even if legal, is it ethical if done by lawyers? Is a lawyer's secret taping of clients permissible? Did Cohen act ethically? His secret taping has been criticized as contrary to the lawyer's fundamental obligations of loyalty. It is perceived to be deceitful and dishonest.

Ethics rules in all jurisdictions prohibit a lawyer from engaging in conduct involving dishonesty, fraud, deceit or misrepresentation. (RPC 8.4 (c)). At face value, secret taping would seem to violate this fundamental ethical precept. But legal ethics opinions and case law are mixed. There are circumstances under which such taping is or should be permissible and history demonstrates why this should be so.

A. Law Regarding Tape Recording

The first consideration is whether such secret taping is lawful. Nine states prohibit such secrecy and require that all parties must consent to being recorded.[24] In those "all party consent" states, it is therefore illegal if secret taping is carried out by anyone.[25] If illegal, it is also unethical for a lawyer or a person under the lawyer's direction to carry out secret taping.[26] These statutes regulating secret recording are usually referred to eavesdropping or anti-wiretap laws.[27] Federal law prohibits the admissibility of evidence from an illegally taped conversation.[28] Some states also preclude evidence obtained in violation of the statutes that regulate the recording of conversations.[29]

---

24. Matthiesen, Wickert & Lehrer, S.C., *Laws on Recording Conversations in All 50 States* 1, 10/18/18, *available at* https://tinyurl.com/yd9wl7lx.

25. Maryland, where Linda Tripp secretly recorded conversations with Monica Lewinsky, is an all consent state. After Linda Tripp's secret taping of Monica Lewinsky became public, the police sought charges against her. The Maryland prosecutor later dropped the charges. Saundra Torry & Raja Mishra, *Tripp Indicted on Charges of Wiretapping*, Wash. Post, July 31, 1999, at A1.

26. Lawyers may not engage in illegal conduct that adversely reflects on their honesty, trustworthiness or fitness to practice law RPC 8.4(b). A lawyer is responsible for supervision of others in the firm and for their conduct that would be a violation of the Rules of Professional Conduct if engaged in by the lawyer. RPC 5.3.

27. *See, e.g.*, Celia Guzaldo Gamrath, *A Lawyer's Guide to Eavesdropping in Illinois*, 87 Ill. B.J. 362 (1999) (discussing the history of eavesdropping and anti-wiretapping laws in Illinois). Electronic eavesdropping refers to overhearing, recording, or transmitting any part of a private communication without the consent of at least one party to the communication. Wiretapping is using "covert means to intercept, monitor, and record telephone conversations of individuals." *Id.*

28. 18 U.S.C. § 2515 (2018). The federal statute provides:

Whenever any wire or oral communication has been intercepted, no part of the contents of such communication and no evidence derived therefrom may be received in evidence in any trial, hearing, or other proceeding in or before any court, grand jury, department, officer, agency, regulatory body, legislative committee, or other authority of the United States, a State, or a political subdivision thereof if the disclosure of that information would be in violation of this chapter.

Id.

29. *See* Peter Joy, *Special Counsel and Legal Ethics: The Role of Secret Taping*, 57 Duq. U. L. Rev. 252 (2019) *available at* https://ssrn.com/abstract=3402591.

By contrast, forty-one states, the District of Columbia, and federal law permit the taping of conversations if one party to the conversation consents.[30] These jurisdictions are known as "one-party consent" jurisdictions. Thus, anyone in those jurisdictions—non-lawyers and lawyers—may legally and secretly record a conversation with any person or persons. This includes New York where Cohen made the recordings.[31]

Consequently, it is lawful in most states and in federal law for a lawyer to secretly record a conversation with a client, potential witness or other person. The lawyer may use the recording in a proceeding to impeach a witness with a prior inconsistent statement, or have the recording admitted into evidence under applicable rules.[32] If the recording is of a client, there are limited circumstances, described below, where a lawyer may use the recording for self-defense.[33]

B. Ethical Constraints on Lawyer Secret Recordings

While making such recordings is not illegal under the one-party consent rule, the question of whether it is ethical for lawyers to secretly tape record anyone, including clients, is of longstanding controversy. Ethics opinions vary across the country. There is no national consensus.

Ethics codes, including the American Bar Association's (ABA) Model Rules of Professional Conduct, and state equivalents of the ethics rules[34] do not directly address secret taping by lawyers but secret recording of conversations implicates some ethics rules. Model Rule 8.4 that states: "It is professional misconduct for a lawyer to ... (c) engage in conduct involving dishonesty, fraud, deceit or misrepresentation."[35] If secret

---

30. Matthiesen, Wickert & Lehrer, S.C., *supra* note 24.

31. N.Y. Penal Law § 250.00(1); N.Y. Penal Law § 250.05. "It is not unlawful for an individual who is a party to or has consent from a party of an in person or electronic communication to record and or disclose the content of said communication."

32. Impeachment by prior inconsistent statements is governed by Federal Rules of Evidence Hearsay exceptions under the Federal Rules of Evidence that may be admitted into evidence include: a present sense impression, which is a "statement describing or explaining an event or condition made while or immediately after the declarant perceived it[,]" FED. R. EVID. 803(1); an excited utterance, which is a "statement relating to a startling event or condition, made while the declarant was under the stress of excitement that it caused [,]" FED. R. EVID. 803(2); and "[a] statement of the declarant's then-existing state of mind (such as motive, intent, or plan) or emotional, sensory, or physical condition (such as mental feeling, pain, or bodily health)...." FED. R. EVID. 803(3).

33. The "self-defense" exception to confidentiality is MRPC r.1.6 (b)(5) that permits a lawyer to "reveal or use confidential information to the extent that lawyer reasonably believes necessary to establish a claim or defense on behalf of the lawyer in a controversy between the lawyer and client, to establish a defense to a criminal charge or civil claim against the lawyer based upon conduct in which the client was involved, or to respond to allegations in any proceeding concerning the lawyer's representation of the client; N.Y. RULES OF PROF'L CONDUCT r.1.6 (b)(5)(2018) [hereinafter NYRPC] permits a lawyer to "reveal or use confidential information to the extent that lawyer reasonably believes necessary to defend the lawyer or the lawyer's employees and associates against an accusation of wrongful conduct."

34. MODEL RULES OF PROF'L CONDUCT (AM. BAR ASS'N 1983).

35. *Id.* at r. 8.4. The older ABA Model Code of Professional Responsibility, which the Model Rules replaced, had a virtually identical prohibition in DR 1-102. The older ABA Model Code of Professional

taping by a lawyer is inherently deceitful or dishonest, then such conduct would violate Model Rule 8.4(c).

The ABA has long-perceived secret taping by lawyers to be deceitful and therefore violative of ethics rules. In August 1974, the day after President Nixon's resignation, the ABA issued Formal Ethics Opinion 337 stating that the secret taping of conversations by a lawyer was inherently deceitful and therefore prohibited.[36] It acknowledged that secret recording was not a federal crime in a one-party jurisdiction, but determined that then-existing Model Code provision DR 1-102,'s prohibition against conduct involving "dishonesty, fraud, deceit, or misrepresentation" "clearly encompass[ ] the making of recordings without the consent of all parties," and Canon 9's proscription that a lawyer "[s]hould [a]void [e]ven the [a]ppearance of [p]rofessional [i]propriety" would not condone secret taping.[37] The Committee noted a possible exception to this prohibition where, under "extraordinary circumstances" a prosecutor "might ethically make and use secret recordings if acting within strict statutory limitations conforming to constitutional requirements."[38]

A year later, the ABA reconsidered and affirmed its position that secret taping was unethical, with a limited exception for prosecutors. It added that a lawyer in private practice could not ethically direct an investigator to tape record a conversation without the knowledge of the other party.[39]

A number of states that adopted the ABA's position.[40] The rationale of most of those states was a version of "appearance of impropriety" because "attorneys are held to a higher standard" than simply what the law permits, and "secret recording of conversations offends the sense of honor and fair play of most people."[41] From 1978 through 1995, ethics authorities in Alabama, Alaska, Colorado, Hawaii, Iowa, Missouri, and Virginia issued similar advisory ethics opinions.[42]

Responsibility, which the Model Rules replaced, had a virtually identical prohibition in DR 1-102. DR 1-102, which defined professional misconduct, stated in pertinent part: "(A) A lawyer shall not … (4) Engage in conduct involving dishonesty, fraud, deceit, or misrepresentation." MODEL CODE OF PROF'L RESPONSIBILITY DR 1-102(A)(4) (AM. BAR ASS'N 1980). The Model Code also contained a broad provision, Canon 9, that a lawyer "should avoid even the appearance of professional impropriety *Id.* at Canon 9.

36. ABA Comm'n on Ethics & Prof'l Responsibility, Formal Op. 337 (1974).

37. *Id.* Canon 9.

38. *Id.*

39. ABA Comm'n on Ethics & Prof'l Responsibility, Informal Op. 1320 (1975). The Committee noted that this opinion was limited to lawyers in private practice. *Id.* Model Rule 5.3 and the rules of all jurisdictions make clear that the lawyer is ethically responsible for the conduct of nonlawyer assistants and Model Rule 8.4 prohibits sanctions a lawyer from violating the Rules of Professional Conduct "through the acts of another."

40. *See, e.g.*, Carol M. Bast, *Surreptitious Recording by Attorneys: Is It Ethical?*, 39 ST. MARY'S L.J. 661, 665 (2008) ("ABA opinions carry a great deal of weight and a number of states were influenced by Formal Opinion 337.").

41. Tex. Comm'n on Prof'l Ethics, Formal Op. 392 (1978).

42. CHARLES DOYLE, CONG. RESEARCH SERV., R42650, WIRETAPPING, TAPE RECORDERS, AND LEGAL ETHICS: AN OVERVIEW OF QUESTIONS POSED BY ATTORNEY INVOLVEMENT IN SECRETLY RECORDING CONVERSATION 2 n.4 (2018) (identifying the state ethics opinions).

Other states adopted the basic ABA approach to secret recording but expanded the list of exceptions. These include Arizona, Idaho, Kansas, Kentucky, Minnesota, Ohio, South Carolina, and Tennessee. They contained one or more of the following exceptions: permitting recording by law enforcement personnel generally, not just when judicially supervised; or recording by criminal defense counsel; or recording statements that themselves constitute crimes such as bribery, offers or threats; or recording confidential conversations with clients; or recordings made solely for the purpose of creating a memorandum for the files; or recording by a government attorney in connection with a civil matter; or recording under other extraordinary circumstances.[43]

Ethics authorities in other jurisdictions—including the District of Columbia, Mississippi, New Mexico, North Carolina, Oklahoma, Oregon, Utah, and Wisconsin— rejected the ABA approach and held that whether a secret recording violated any ethical rules had to be decided on a case-by-case basis.[44]

The issue percolated for years. In 2001, the ABA revisited its 1974 opinion and reversed itself.[45] The notion that secret recordings were inherently deceitful lost its force. In ABA Formal Opinion 01-422, the Committee on Ethics and Professional Responsibility ("the Committee"), decided that "[a] lawyer who electronically records a conversation without the knowledge of the other party or parties to the conversation does not necessarily violate the Model Rules," provided the lawyer is not violating the law in making the secret recording.[46] ABA 01-422 formally withdrew the 1974 Formal Opinion 337.[47] It noted that its earlier opinion relied on the Code of Professional Responsibility provisions that lawyers "should avoid even the appearance of impropriety," and that provision was omitted from the Model Rules of Professional Conduct.[48]

ABA 01-422 opinion noted two instances in which secret recording could violate an ethics rule. First, and most obviously, a lawyer who secretly records a conversation in an all-party consent state or secretly records a conversation without being a party to the conversation, has "likely has violated Model Rule 8.4(b) or 8.4(c) or both."[49] The Committee noted that it is professional misconduct under Model Rule 8.4(b) to "commit a criminal act that reflects adversely on the lawyer's honesty, trustworthiness or fitness as a lawyer in other respects,"[50] and misconduct under Model Rule 8.4(c) to "engage in conduct involving dishonesty, fraud, deceit or misrepresentation."[51] The Committee also opined that such an illegal secret recording would also violate Model Rule 4.4, which prohibits using "methods of obtaining evidence that violate the legal rights of [a third] person."[52]

---

43. *Id.* at 2.
44. *Id.* at n.12 (*citing* to the ethics opinions).
45. ABA Comm'n on Ethics & Prof'l Responsibility, Formal Op. 01-422 (2001).
46. *Id.*
47. *Id.*
48. *Id.*
49. *Id.*
50. MRPC r. 8.4(b).
51. *Id.* at r. 8.4(c).
52. ABA Formal Op. 01-422.

Second, while the Committee found that secretly recording a conversation may not violate an ethics rule, a lawyer who falsely denies that a conversation is being recorded "would likely violate Model Rule 4.1, which prohibits a lawyer from making a false statement of material fact to a third person."[53]

However, the Committee did not reach consensus on the Michael Cohen issue: whether secret recording of a confidential conversation *with a client* would violate any of the Model Rules.[54] It noted that a recording could capture a client saying something profane or slanderous, and if the recording was disclosed, it could be damaging or embarrassing to the client.[55] The ABA Committee was unanimous in stating "that it is almost always advisable for a lawyer to inform a client that a conversation is being or may be recorded, before recording such a conversation."[56] The Committee also opined that the trust and confidence of the client would likely be undermined if a client discovered that her lawyer had secretly recorded her.[57]

However, the Committee identified two exceptional circumstances that would permit a lawyer to *disclose* confidential client communications, including recordings secretly taped. Those exceptional circumstances that permit disclosure of confidential communications are in the Model Rules. They include a client's "plans or threats by a client to commit a criminal act that the lawyer believes is likely to result in imminent death or substantial bodily harm."[58] The second exceptional circumstance is when a lawyer may use "confidential information necessary to establish a defense by the lawyer to charges based upon conduct in which the client is involved."[59]

States currently remain divided about the ethical propriety of secret taping. Colorado and South Carolina, having considered the ABA Op. 01-422 ethics opinion, rejected the view that secret recording does not necessarily violate an ethics rule.[60] The Colorado Bar Ethics Committee stated: "Because surreptitious recording of con-

---

53. Miss. Bar v. Attorney ST, 621 So. 2d 229, 232–33 (Miss. 1993) (false denial of recording).
54. ABA Formal Op. 01-422.
55. *Id.*
56. ABA Formal Op. 01-422.
57. *Id.*
58. ABA Formal Op. 01-422. The current provision of Model Rule 1.6(b)(1) does not have an "criminal act" requirement. It states that "A lawyer may reveal information relating to the representation of a client to the extent that the lawyer reasonably believes necessary to prevent reasonably certain death or substantial bodily harm." New York's RPC has a provision to permit disclosure of confidential information when the lawyer reasonably believes necessary to prevent the client from committing a crime. NYRPC r. 1.6 (b)(2).
59. ABA Formal Op. 01-422; MRPC r. 1.6 (b) (5) provides: "A lawyer may reveal information relating to the representation of a client to the extent that the lawyer reasonably believes necessary: … (5) to establish a claim or defense on behalf of the lawyer in a controversy between the lawyer and the client, to establish a defense to a criminal charge or civil claim against the lawyer based upon conduct in which the client was involved, or to respond to allegations in any proceeding concerning the lawyer's representation of the client." MODEL RULES Rule 1.6(b)(5). New York's RPC's "self-defense" exception to confidentiality is "to defend the lawyer or the lawyer's employees and associates against an accusation of wrongful conduct." NYRPC rule1.6 (b)(5)(i).
60. DOYLE, *supra* note 42, at 4 (citing the ethics opinions).

versations or statements by an attorney may involve an element of trickery or deceit, it is generally improper for an attorney to engage in surreptitious recording even if the recording is legal under state law."[61] The Colorado Committee, however, adopted the ABA position in the criminal law setting, stating that "an attorney may surreptitiously record, and may direct a third party to surreptitiously record conversations or statements for the purpose of gathering admissible evidence in a criminal matter."[62] The South Carolina Bar Ethics Advisory Committee also decided that "[w]hile representing a client, a lawyer may not surreptitiously record any conversation except for certain law-enforcement related purposes."[63] Several other states — including Arizona, Idaho, Indiana, Iowa, Kansas, and Kentucky — have not revised their earlier opinions. Thus, in those states, lawyers who secretly record conversations are usually acting unethically.[64]

Most other jurisdictions that revisited the issue after 2001 agree with the ABA's position.[65] Like ABA Formal Opinion 01-422, the ethics opinions in these jurisdictions find that under some circumstances, secret taping may still be unethical, such as when the taping is done in violation of the law or when a lawyer falsely denies the taping.[66]

Most ethics opinions do not distinguish between secret recording of clients and other persons. But in states that do consider the issue, jurisdictions are split.[67] Wisconsin and Missouri specifically prohibit secret recordings of clients by reference to distinct fiduciary and other duties owed to a client.[68] Other jurisdictions, such as Ohio, that changed their position after ABA 01-422, found that secret taping that is legal is also usually ethical. It agreed with the ABA Committee that it was advisable for a lawyer to inform a client before recording a conversation. It extended this admonition to recording prospective clients.[69] Texas, by contrast, went further and permitted lawyers to record clients without notice when the recording is "made to further a legitimate purpose of the lawyer or the client."[70]

In New York, the jurisdiction with regulatory power over Michael Cohen's conduct, the Association of the Bar of the City of New York's Professional Ethics Committee promulgated NY City Bar Op 2003-02.[71] It noted that its prior opinion, like the earlier

---

61. Colo. Bar Ass'n Comm'n, Formal Op. 112 (2003).

62. *Id.*

63. *Id.*

64. Doyle, *supra* note 42, at 4.

65. *Id.*

66. *Id.*

67. Mo. Sup. Ct. Advisory Comm., Formal Op. 123 (2006); Neb. Ethics Advisory Op. for Lawyers No. 06-07 (2006); Wis. St. B. Prof'l Ethics Comm., Formal Op. E-94-5 (1994).

68. *Id*; Wis. Op. E-94-5 ("Different standards apply when the other party involved is a client. The fiduciary duties owed by a lawyer to a client and the duty of communication under SCR 20:1.4 dictate that statements made by clients over the telephone not be recorded without advising the client and receiving consent to the recording after consultation").

69. Ohio Sup. Ct., Bd. of Comm'rs on Grievance & Disciple, Op. 2012-1, at 7 (2012). The Board revisited Ohio Sup. Ct., Bd. of Comm'rs on Grievance & Discipline, Op. 97-3 (1997). *Id.*

70. Sup. Ct. of Tex. Prof'l Ethics Comm. Op. No. 575 (2006).

71. N.Y. City B. Ass'n, Formal Op. No. 2003-02 (2004) [hereinafter "2004 NYC Opinion"].

ABA 337, "swept too broadly." However, it differed from the ABA 01-422 calling that opinion an "overcorrection." It opined that while undisclosed taping is improper as a routine practice because it "smacks of trickery," there are circumstances in which it should be permissible: Those are where the lawyer has a "reasonable basis for believing that it advance[s] a generally accepted societal good" and those circumstances are "consistent with the standards of fair play and candor applicable to lawyers."[72] Thus, Michael Cohen could offer the rationale that the taping was permissible because it served the public good in exposing falsehoods and preventing the harmful conduct of a person seeking the public office of the President. Whether such a "public good" rationale would be a viable justification for Cohen is subject to debate.

In addition to the "public good" rationale, there are other reasons why secretly recording clients could be acceptable even though these reasons are not sufficiently acknowledged in ethics opinions. They include advancing the client's interest or advancing the lawyer's interest. For example, some recordings could enhance the client's matter by creating documentation of his statements. The recordings capture verbatim statements. For clients with significant mental or other disabilities, such a recording may help their case. The recording may help to avoid faulty recollection over time or distortion of memory. Although consent should be sought as a general rule, it may be more valuable to record the client secretly to obtain the most candid results. It is better than notetaking if the client's statements are likely to be at issue.[73] The countervailing concern is the fact of such secret recording itself—whether or not it is ultimately disclosed—may be harmful to the client's dignity and autonomy. It still has a "sufficient element of trickery" even if undertaken for a good purpose.

Another rationale for secret recording is to protect the lawyers' interests. The lawyer may be concerned that the client may make false accusations against the lawyer. A classic case is where a criminal defense lawyer represents a client in a multi-defendant drug conspiracy. That lawyer suspects (but does not know) that his client may decide to cooperate with the prosecution and law enforcement by making false claims that the lawyer attempted to assist the client in suborning perjury. That lawyer knows of past instances in that jurisdiction where clients have received generous plea bargains from the prosecution by offering evidence against their lawyer. In such a case, the lawyer may decide to secretly record client conversations. At the point at which accusations are made against the lawyer, Rule 1.6(b)(5) permits the lawyer to disclose the secretly recorded conversation.[74] Similarly, a lawyer who suspects that the client seeks advice as to how to commit a crime may decide to secretly record the client.

---

72. *Id.*

73. John Bliss, *supra*, note 22, at 23 (noting that Cohen initially may have believed that the recordings would ultimately help his client).

74. Rule 1.6(b)(5) *supra* note 34.

That lawyer is permitted to disclose that information when that lawyer believes disclosure is reasonably necessary to prevent the commission of certain crimes.[75]

However, where the lawyer actually *knows* that the client will cooperate with the government against him, a conflict exists, and the lawyer should withdraw from representation.[76] Until the lawyer has such knowledge, she should be permitted to remain in the representation and record the client. A suspicion or belief that the client might cooperate with the authorities and turn against his lawyer generally does not require withdrawal. This may be a controversial proposition. Some argue that a lawyer must withdraw as soon as that lawyer has a suspicion that the client will engage in accusatory criminal accusations against the lawyer.

In any case from the client's perspective, it is difficult to imagine how the lawyer secretly taping their conversations would not undermine trust and confidence in the lawyer, just as the ABA's current ethics opinion predicts.[77] Certainly, Trump's tweets starkly demonstrate that he believed that Cohen had acted improperly by taping their conversations.[78]

Overall, from the public's viewpoint, secret taping of a client by a lawyer reflects negatively on the profession. It may be that Fox News is correct when one of its com-

---

75. Rule 1.6 permits a lawyer to reveal information related to representation of a client to the extent the lawyer reasonably believes necessary:

(1) To prevent reasonably certain death or substantial bodily injury

(2) To prevent the client from committing a crime or fraud that is reasonably certain to result in substantial injury to the financial interests or property of another and in furtherance of which the client has used the lawyer's services:

(3) To prevent, mitigate or rectify substantial injury to the financial interests or property of another that is reasonably certain to result or has resulted from the client's commission of a crime or fraud in furtherance of which the client has used the lawyer's services;

Id. The ethics opinions do not sufficiently distinguish the harm caused by the recording itself as compared with the harm caused by its disclosure. The fact of recording itself is generally a "sufficient lack of candor and a sufficient element of trickery" to render it unethical in most circumstances. NY Op. *supra* note 71. The lawyer's obligation to communicate with a client — to keep the client reasonably informed about the means of representation and to provide reasonable communication so that the client may effectively participate in and make informed decisions MRPC 1.4 — also militates against secret recordings in most situations. But there are circumstances where disclosure of confidential communications is permitted — notably to prevent serious crimes and some frauds. The rationale for such disclosure of client confidences is the recognition of the "overriding value of life and physical integrity" and the necessity to prevent a "real and substantial threat "that another person will suffer harm." MRPC r. 1.6 cmt. 6. In such case, the greater harm to the public caused by the client's outweighs the harm of revelation of client confidential information.

76. RPC 1.7 (a)(2) prohibits a lawyer from representation if "there is a significant risk that the representation ... will be materially limited by ... a personal interest of the lawyer." RPC 1.16 (a)(1) provides that a lawyer shall withdraw from the representation if it will result in a violation of the rules of professional conduct.

77. ABA Comm'n on Ethics & Prof'l Responsibility, Formal Op. 01-422 (2001).

78. Danny Cevallos, *If Trump Lawyer Cohen Recorded Conversations, Is that Ok?*, NBC News, Apr. 16, 2018; Greg Price, *Michael Cohen Recorded Donald Trump for "Insurance" Should President Turn on Him, Legal Expert Says*, Newsweek July 20, 2018; Robert Charles, *Most Americans Agree with Trump, not Cohen — Taping Clients 'Smacks of Trickery'*, Fox News, July 31, 2018 (suggesting that most Americans would be outraged to find that their lawyer had secretly recorded their lawyer-client conversation, as this would be the "antithesis of the revered attorney-client relationship").

mentators said that "most Americans will likely side with President Trump,"[79] that secret taping "smacks of trickery."[80] On the other hand, it is unlikely that Michael Cohen, had he not been disbarred for the conviction of criminal offenses, would have been subject to discipline for the secret taping.[81]

IV. Public Commentary by Lawyers — Media Pundits and Counsel

A. Overview

A recurrent issue now that legal commentators have become a cottage industry is the extent to which lawyers are subject to ethical constraints for their public statements. This includes lawyers who make public commentary as part of their role as counsel and media commentators who do not represent clients. Alan Dershowitz and Jeanine Pirro are among other well-known lawyers whose appear as media commentators and not as client representatives.[82] Perhaps the most noted and infamous is Rudy Giuliani who acted initially as a media consultant, and then as counsel for Donald Trump. The former New York City mayor assumed the position as President Trump's personal lawyer in April 2018, and since that time, he has made numerous appearances on media outlets on behalf of his client. Throughout his arguably tumultuous tenure as the President's personal lawyer, he has made statements that are exaggerations, misleading comments and outright lies. Prior to assuming his role as Trump's personal lawyer, his statements were similarly obfuscations and false ones.

---

79. Charles, *supra* note 78.

80. *Id.*

81. Deanna Paul, *Michael Cohen Secretly Recorded Donald Trump. Does that Make Him a Bad Lawyer?* Wash. Post (July 26, 2018) (suggesting that Cohen would be unlikely to be disbarred for secretly recording the client); Bernie Berk, *Was Michael Cohen's Secret Taping of his Then-Client Donald Trump Improper?*, The Faculty Lounge (July 26, 2018) (concluding that Cohen's recordings were likely improper on the basis of multiple professional duties); Carry Covert, *Can You Record a Client or Fellow Counsel without Consent*, Buff L.J. (November 2018); David L. Hudson Jr., *Is Recording Others Legal, and Is It Ethical?* ABA Journal (January 2019); Andrew Strickler, *Cohen Tapes Show Broken Attorney-Client Relationship*, Law 360 (July 23, 2018) (stressing that there is no "black and white" rule, but that lawyers who secretly record clients disrupt trust in the lawyer-client relationship); "antithesis of the revered attorney-client relationship").

82. Dean Falvy, *Reversal of Reputation: How Dershowitz is Taking Liberties to Defend Trump*, The Verdict, *available at* https://verdict.justia.com/2018/10/15/reversal-of-reputation-how-dershowitz-is-taking-liberties-to-defend-trump; Michael Grynbaum, *The Rise and Fall of Jeanine Pirro on Fox News*, N.Y. Times, Apr. 9, 2019, *available at* https://www.nytimes.com/2019/04/09/business/media/jeanine-pirro-fox-news-trump.html.

Giuliani's media statements and appearances as Trump's counsel have been characterized by retractions[83] and half-truths.[84] He infamously remarked, "truth isn't truth"[85] during a back-and-forth on NBC. When asked whether President Trump told James Comey, the former director of the Federal Bureau of Investigation, that he hoped he could see his way to ending Michael Flynn's case, Giuliani said, "What he said to him was, 'Can you give him a break?" Giuliani later said, "That's crazy. I never said that."[86] Professor Bennett Gershman terms many of Giuliani's statements "bullshit," that is, "False statements made ... with an indifference, even a contempt for the truth."[87] "Salient features of bullshit include misstating, deceiving, misrepresenting, and misleading. What distinguishes 'bullshit' from knowingly making false factual statements is the speaker's indifference to the truth and disregard whether his statement is factually correct."[88] Perhaps many of Giuliani's statements would only be considered half-truths and obfuscations with or without "indifference to the truth." But there are other clear instances of numerous falsehoods, lies and misrepresentations.

Significant noted instances of falsehoods include the statements about the famed June 2016 meeting at Trump Tower. On Meet the Press, Giuliani claimed that when Donald Jr and others met Natalia Veselnitsyaka at that meeting in June 2016, they "didn't know that she was a representative of the Russian government." Emails from Donald Jr. clearly showed that Donald Jr. knew and that Giuliani was aware of that fact.[89] In another significant instance regarding Michael Cohen, Giuliani falsely claimed that the $130,000 reimbursement to Michael Cohen for the "hush money" to adult

---

83. On "Meet the Press," Giuliani admitted that Trump had been involved in discussion to build a Trump Tower Moscow throughout the 2016 campaign. Later the same day, Giuliani said it was a hypothetical and not based on actual conversations he had with the President. Isaac Chotiner, *"Even if He Did Do It, It Wouldn't be a Crime: Rudy Giuliani on President Trump,"* The New Yorker (Jan. 21, 2019), *available at* https://www.newyorker.com/news/q-and-a/even-if-he-did-do-it-it-wouldnt-be-a-crime-rudy-giuliani-donald-trump-robert-mueller-moscow-buzzfeed. As to whether a letter of intent had been created regarding President Trump's desire to build Trump Tower Moscow, Giuliani claimed that while a letter of intent had been created, "no one signed it." President Trump had in fact signed it. Giuliani later said, "I was wrong if I said it." Chris Cillizza, *How Can Rudy Giuliani Possibly Still be Donald Trump's Lawyer?,* CNN (Dec. 19, 2018), *available at* https://www.cnn.com/2018/12/19/politics/rudy-giuliani-donald-trump-letter-of-intent-russia/index.html.

84. On "Fox News Sunday," Giuliani stated that "nothing was denied" to the special counsel from the Trump administration. Trump refused to do an in-person interview with investigators, however, and the Mueller report said his written responses to questions were inadequate. Eugene Kiely, Lori Robertson & Robert Farley, *Giuliani's Obstruction Distortions,* FactCheck.org (Apr. 22, 2019), *available at* https://www.factcheck.org/2019/04/giulianis-obstruction-distortions/.

85. Caroline Kenny, *Rudy Giuliani Says 'Truth Isn't Truth,'* CNN (Aug. 19, 2018), *available at* https://www.cnn.com/2018/08/19/politics/rudy-giuliani-truth-isnt-truth/index.html.

86. Maggie Haberman, *Trump and Comey Had 'No Conversation About Michael Flynn,' Giuliani Says,* N.Y. Times (Aug. 12, 2018), *available at* https://www.nytimes.com/2018/08/12/us/politics/giuliani-trump-comey-flynn.html.

87. Bennett L. Gershman, *Rudolph Giuliani and the Ethics of Bullshit,* 57 Duq. L. Rev. 293 (2019).

88. *Id.*

89. Eugene Kiely, *Giuliani Misleads on the Trump Tower Meeting,* Fact check. Org, August 20, 2018, *available at* https://www.factcheck.org/2018/08/giuliani-misleads-on-trump-tower-meeting/.

film star Stormy Daniels to silence her about her affair with Trump was made by Trump personally and not by the Trump organization or campaign.[90] He also claimed that the payments were drawn from a retainer. These were significant facts in criminal investigations. Neither of the statements was true and the DOJ stated that there was no such retainer.[91] As to the investigation of former Secretary of State Hillary Clinton and the mishandling of classified information, Giuliani claimed, "there is overwhelming evidence" that she "actually obstructed justice." This was false.[92] Reputable media organizations such as Factcheck.org have documented Giuliani's numerous falsehoods.

Additionally, there are repeated instances of Giuliani's apparent intentional misstatements for the purpose of confusion. On Morning Joe, Giuliani created the impression that there was a second meeting at Trump Tower.[93] This was demonstrated to be intentional obfuscation.[94] On other occasions, Meet the Press reported that Giuliani called the New York Times and discussed the timing of Trump's involvement in the Moscow deal as beyond the June 6, 2016, Trump Tower meeting "though the end of 2016." When the dates become troubling because of potential election and criminal law violations, he then retracted it and changed it several times.[95] Meet the Press said that it is "either carelessness or incompetence that causes us to doubt his

---

90. Eugene Kiely & Lori Robertson, *Cohen Plea Deal Exposes Repeated False Claims*, *available at* FACTCHECK.ORG, https://www.factcheck.org/2018/08/cohen-plea-deal-exposes-repeated-false-claims/; August 22, 2018; Alex Shepard, *Rudy Giuliani Just Gave Stormy Daniels Game Away*, The New Republic, May 3, 2018, *available at* https://newrepublic.com/minutes/148223/rudy-giuliani-just-gave-stormy-daniels-game-away.

Glenn Kessler, *Not Just Misleading, Not Just False. A Lie*. WASH. POST, August 22, 2018, *available at* https://www.washingtonpost.com/politics/2018/08/23/not-just-misleading-not-merely-false-lie/?noredirect=on&utm_term=.4b11a408bc80 (Trump's Lie and Giuliani's subsequent lie); *What Giuliani Said About Cohen's Payments to Stormy Daniels*, N.Y. TIMES, May 2, 2018, https://www.nytimes.com/2018/05/02/us/politics/rudy-giuliani-stormy-daniels-transcript.html.

John Kruzel, *Trump's shifting explanations for the Stormy Daniels payment (Updated)*, POLITIFACT, Aug. 23, 2018, *available at* https://www.politifact.com/truth-o-meter/article/2018/aug/23/donald-trumps-shifting-explanations-stormy-daniels/.

91. Kiely & Robertson, *supra* note 90.

92. *Statement from Attorney General Loretta E. Lynch Regarding State Department Email Investigation*, DOJ (Jul. 6, 2016), https://www.justice.gov/opa/pr/statement-attorney-general-loretta-e-lynch-regarding-state-department-email-investigation. There are many other Giuliani statements that are not true. He said that the conviction rate for blacks and whites is the same, that food stamps doubled under President Obama, and that Hillary Clinton is for open borders. He noted widely erroneous data on prostate cancer among other falsehoods. Factcheck.org.

93. CNN, based on Giuliani's statements, reported that there was a second meeting and Giuliani went on Fox News to denounce CNN's account. Giuliani told the Daily Beast that he made up this story to head off a story from Maggie Haberman of the NY Times about Russian offers that were made at the only Trump Tower meeting on June 6. 2016. Giuliani and Jay Sekulow, another Trump lawyers, then defeated the story that they had promoted about the second meeting.

94. *Id.*

95. Amanda Sakuma, *Rudy Giuliani Just Muddied the Waters even more about the 2016 Trump Tower Moscow Taks*, Vox, Jan 22, 2019, *available at* https://www.vox.com/2019/1/20/18190524/giuliani-trump-tower-moscow-2016.

word." Giuliani said, "I'm afraid that on my gravestone it will say 'He lied for Trump.'"[96] In a Chris Cuomo television interview where Cuomo confronted Giuliani with his lies, Giuliani said "I never said 'no collusion,' Chris Cuomo said, "yes you have."[97] There are many other obfuscations, misleading comments and instances of outright falsehoods uttered by Giuliani when he was Trump's lawyer.[98] Giuliani's mental health has been questioned and commentators note that he appears perplexed, befuddled and frustrated.

Giuliani's principal task in the media appears to political rather than legal, to sow confusion and undercut Mueller's investigation. Some observers contend that he has behaved like a fool. He has been described by critics as "Trump's clown,"[99] a "fool for our time,"[100] a "big dumb idiot,"[101] "weird,"[102] "dopey,"[103] and a "bumbling idiot."[104]

The unresolved question: Is Giuliani subject to ethical constraints for his public commentary? He is admitted to practice in New York, yet no disciplinary measures appear to have been instituted against him.[105] To address this question, it is first es-

---

96. Isaac Chotiner, *Even if He Did Do it, It Would Not Be a Crime: Rudy Giuliani on President Trump*, New Yorker, Jan 21, 2019, *available at* https://www.newyorker.com/news/q-and-a/even-if-he-did-do-it-it-wouldnt-be-a-crime-rudy-giuliani-donald-trump-robert-mueller-moscow-buzzfeed.

97. Ian Schwartz, *Giuliani vs. CNN Cuomo: I Never Said There Was No Collusion between People in the Trump Campaign and Russia*, Real Clear Politics, Jan. 17, 2019, *available at* https://www.rea-lclearpolitics.com/video/2019/01/17/giuliani_vs_cnn_cuomo_i_never_said_there_was_no_collusion_between_people_in_trump_campaign_and_russia.html.

98. *All False Statements by Rudy Giuliani*, Politifact, *available at* https://www.politifact.com/personalities/rudy-giuliani/statements/byruling/false/; Factcheck.org, *available at* https ://www.factcheck.org/person/rudy-giuliani/; *supra* notes 90–92.

99. Jeffrey Toobin, *How Rudy Giuliani Turned Into Trump's Clown*, The New Yorker (September 10, 2018), *available at* https://www.newyorker.com/magazine/2018/09/10/how-rudy-giuliani-turned-into-trumps-clown.

100. Dana Milbank, *Rudy Giuliani is the fool for out time*, Wash. Post (December 19, 2018), *available at* https://www.washingtonpost.com/opinions/rudy-giuliani-is-the-fool-for-our-time/2018/12/19/0a9f4a92-03b8-11e9-b5df-5d3874f1ac36_story.html?utm_term=.1beabd87cd28.

101. Rafi Schwartz, *Rudy You Big Dumb Idiot*, Splinter (Dec. 19, 2018), *available at* https://splinternews.com/rudy-you-big-dumb-idiot-1831199867.

102. *Rudy Giuliani's Weird Faces of the Week*, Daily Beast, *available at* https://www.thedailybeast.com/rudy-giulianis-weird-faces-of-the-week.

103. Letter to the Editor, *Giuliani may be "Dopey" but he's no Royal "Fool,"* Wash. Post (December 25, 2018), *available at* https://www.washingtonpost.com/opinions/giuliani-may-be-dopey-but-hes-no-royal-fool/2018/12/25/0fa89626-0541-11e9-958c-0a601226ff6b_story.html?utm_term=.e75fce40fd0d.

104. Jared Yates Sexton, *Is Rudy Giuliani truly a bumbling idiot? Maybe — or he's an effective agent of chaos*, Salon (August 1, 2018), *available at* https://www.salon.com/2018/08/01/is-rudy-giuliani-truly-a-bumbling-idiot-maybe-or-hes-an-effective-agent-of-chaos/.

105. Any person can file a disciplinary complaint against a lawyer and the fact of such filing is not public information. Also, the Departmental Disciplinary Committees (DDC) in New York can institute a *sua sponte* investigation against a lawyer. The existence of such complaints is not public knowledge. Thus, a complaint could have been filed, but this appears to be unlikely because the DDCs do not often wade into the waters of public statements unless they affect an adjudicative proceeding. Richard Supple, Hal Lieberman, and Harvey Prager, New York Attorney Discipline Practice and Procedure 2016.

sential to distinguish between Giuliani' role as a legal commentator and his conduct as Trump's counsel.

B. Legal Commentators

Legal commentators, now ubiquitous on television and social media, are supposed to educate the public and inform viewers about legal issues and the justice system. Despite the near universality of legal commentators, there are no rules that govern them despite many ethics issues that arise: Are they members of the bar or of the press when broadcasting? Do they have an obligation to be evenhanded and present many sides of an issue as neutral observers? Are they permitted to mislead? To offer opinions on guilt or innocence? To have conflicts of interest yet nonetheless appear on television without revealing those conflicts?

Neither the Rules of Professional Conduct nor standards for journalists provide guidance for the conduct and ethical responsibilities for those lawyers. Rather, the regulation of lawyer extrajudicial speech in the Rules of Conduct is confined to lawyers handling a matter whose commentary may be viewed as having an effect upon pending or anticipated matters. RPC 3.6 provides that a lawyer who is participating in the investigation or litigation of a matter "shall not make an extrajudicial statement that a reasonable person would expect to be disseminated by means of public communication if the lawyer knows or reasonably should know that it will have a substantial likelihood of materially prejudicing an adjudicatory proceeding in the matter."[106] And, there are other limits on lawyer speech in a proceeding because the lawyers are officers of the court.[107] The rationale for such government regulation by lawyers' ethics rules is to ensure fair adjudicatory proceedings. There is no such compelling rationale for government limitations on commentator speech. Rather, the First Amendment's metaphor of the "marketplace of ideas" is prominent. The prevailing view is that free speech promotes the search for truth and that lawyer media commentators should be free to express their views without being subject to government regulation.

In this "Age of Legal Commentary," cognizant of these significant First Amendment implications, there are proposals for a voluntary Code of Conduct for legal commentators.[108] The provisions in such a voluntary code would include the duty not to commit acts of deceit, dishonesty, fraud, or misrepresentation, a provision similar to that

---

106. MRPC r. 3.6 (2001) (specifying categories of permissible statements).

107. Other Model Rules include 3.3 (a)(1) ("A lawyer shall not knowingly make a false statement of fact or law to a tribunal"); Rule 3.3(a)(3) ("A lawyer shall not knowingly ... offer evidence that the lawyer knows to be false"); Rule 3.3 (b) ("A lawyer who represents a client in an adjudicative proceeding and who knows that a person intends to engage, is engaging or has engaged in criminal or fraudulent conduct related to the proceeding shall take reasonable remedial measures, including, if necessary, disclosure to the tribunal."); Rule 4.1 (a) ("In the course of representing a client a lawyer shall not knowingly make a false statement of material fact or law to a third person").

108. Erwin Chermerinsky & Laurie Levinson, *The Ethics of Being a Commentator*, 69 So. CAL L REV. 1303 (1996).

contained in the Rules of Professional Conduct. No such code has emerged. To date, the only organization that has given serious consideration to such a voluntary code is the National Association of Criminal Defense Lawyers.[109]

In 2013, the American Bar Association ("ABA) adopted criminal justice ethical standards for legal commentators (the "2013 Standards").[110] These Standards provide ethical guidance to legal commentators by specifying how a commentator can become competent to provide commentary on a given case, what conflicts a commentator should disclose, and what types of comments a commentator should avoid making.[111] Of course, standards are not enforceable ethics rules.

C. Ethics Rules Prohibiting Deceit and Misrepresentation

The ethics rules do, however, sanction some public commentary by lawyers who operate as counsel, as government lawyers, or in other capacities. Rule 8.4(c) of the Model Rules of Professional Conduct, the anti-deceit and misrepresentation provision, provides that "It is professional misconduct for a lawyer to engage in conduct involving dishonesty, fraud, deceit or misrepresentation."[112]

Rule 8.4(c) serves as somewhat of a catch-all provision designed to discipline a range of lawyer misconduct that might otherwise go unpunished. It is broad in scope and its breadth and vagueness may subject the rule to future constitutional challenge. Some scholars argue it to be poor public policy because it chills diligent representation, is inefficient, and creates the danger of disparate application.[113] Others argue that it should be applied to a narrow range of "grave misrepresentations."[114]

---

109. Gerald B. Lefcourt, *Ethics for Legal Commentators*, CHAMPION (Nov. 1997, *available at* https://www.nacdl.org/CHAMPION/PRESPAGE/97nov.htm.

110. Standard 8-24, Standards for Legal Commentators, ABA STANDARDS FOR FAIR TRIAL AND PUBLIC DISCOURSE, (2013);https://www.americanbar.org/groups/criminal_justice/standards/crimjust_standards_fairtrial_blk/.

111. There is a critique that the standards do not provide sufficient guidance. For instance, the Standards do not define "legal commentator," leaving room for interpretation as to what types of attorneys qualify as commentators. Then, they limit the types of statements that qualify as commentary, excluding certain ones that could nevertheless cause harm to individuals, the public, and the legal system. Chermerinsky & Levinson, *supra* note 109.

112. "It is professional misconduct for a lawyer to engage in conduct involving dishonesty, fraud, deceit or misrepresentation." MRPC r. 8.4(c) (2012); Ellen Yaroshefsky, *Regulation of Government Lawyers Beyond the Client Representation Role*, NOTRE DAME J. L. ETHICS & PUB. POL'Y 151 (2019).

113. W. Bradley Wendel, *Government Lawyers in the Trump Administration*, 69 HASTINGS L.J. 275, 282 (2017).

114. *See* David B. Isbell & Lucantonio N. Salvi, *Ethical Responsibility of Lawyers for Deception by Undercover Investigators and Discrimination Testers: An Analysis of the Provisions Prohibiting Misrepresentation Under the* Model Rules of Professional Conduct, 8 GEO. J. LEGAL ETHICS 791 (1995) (arguing that under standard rules of statutory construction, Rule 8.4(c) should be read not as overlapping other rules, but as covering only grave misrepresentations made in a private capacity).

Despite often compelling arguments that Rule 8.4 is unconstitutionally vague and broad, the "common sense" sentiment is the one seemingly adopted by courts.[115] Consequently, especially for cases about conduct within the practice of law, constitutional challenges have had little success.[116] Courts opine that "the traditions of the legal profession" flesh out the rules and provide adequate notice of prohibited conduct to reasonable lawyers.[117] Discipline for Rule 8.4 (c) violations is inconsistent and context dependent.[118]

Certainly, the anti-deceit Rule applies to conduct within the context of client representation, but it has been applied to conduct outside the practice of law.[119] Most famously, in a lawyer disciplinary case against former Vice President Spiro Agnew during the Watergate era, the Maryland Court stated:

> The professional ethical obligations of an attorney, as long as he remains a member of the bar, are not affected by a decision to pursue his livelihood by practicing law, entering the business world, becoming a public servant, or embarking upon any other endeavor. If a lawyer elects to become a businessman, he brings to his merchantry the professional requirements of honesty, uprightness, and fair dealing.[120]

Bar opinions in other jurisdictions have achieved consensus about lawyer discipline outside the practice of law, but the parameters of such sanctionable conduct are not always clear. Lawyers have been sanctioned for conduct in business and other dealings.[121]

---

115. Richard K. Burke, *"Truth in Lawyering": An Essay on Lying and Deceit in the Practice of Law*, 38 ARK. L. REV. 1, 11 (1984). "Fundamental in our legal system are the general obligations of citizens to bear witness to civil and criminal wrongs and to tell the truth in doing so." *Id.* at 4.

116. *See, e.g., In re* Vogel, 382 A.2d 275, 280 (D.C. 1978) ("[C]ourts have recognized that the words in a statute or rule describing prohibited conduct must be general, that the duty of the professional is high, and that the professional is to be charged with understanding the level and content of that duty.").

117. Comm. on Legal Ethics v. Douglas, 370 S.E.2d 325, 328 (W.Va. 1988); *see* W. Bradley Wendel, *Free Speech for Lawyers*, 28 HASTINGS CONST. L.Q., 305, 389 n. 418 (2001).(citing numerous cases where state and federal courts have "accepted the argument that professional norms or traditions are sufficiently clear to provide guidance for lawyers" and make statements such as the "'lore of the profession' must be set forth in disciplinary codes in order to serve as grounds for sanctions").

118. Office of Disciplinary Counsel v. Grigsby, 425 A.2d 730, 733 (Pa. 1981) ("Truth is the cornerstone of the judicial system; a license to practice law requires allegiance and fidelity to truth.... [F]alse swearing and dishonest conduct are the antithesis of these requirements.").

119. Yaroshefsky, *supra* note 112. (cataloging 8.4 (c) disciplinary cases outside the practice of law).

120. Md. State Bar Ass'n, Inc. v. Agnew, 318 A.2d 811, 815 (Md. 1974).

121. Pa. State Bar Op. 94-118 (1994), *available at* http://www.pabar.org/members/catalogs/Ethics%20Opinions/informal/1994-118.pdf (rules apply to the lawyer who worked as an account executive selling securities and financial products to the public); *see also* Iowa Supreme Court Bd. of Prof'l Ethics and Conduct v. Mulford, 625 N.W.2d 672, 679 (Iowa 2001) ("This court's authority to discipline lawyer ... is not suspended merely because the attorney does not hold an active license and is not actively engaged in the practice of law."). Nevada Opinion 45 (2011) allows a lawyer to own and operate

In addition to subjecting businesspeople who are lawyers to the RPCs, the rules apply to lawyers who engage in criminal conduct outside the practice of law as well as to conduct that is deemed so beyond norms of reasonableness that it adversely affects the trustworthiness and integrity of the lawyer. In 2004, a lawyer was sanctioned because he posted a message on an Internet site and falsely claimed to be a teacher who was a local high school counselor and coach.[122] He implied in that message that the teacher had engaged in sexual behavior with students. The court examined the "rational connection" between that lawyer's conduct and whether it "jeopardizes the public's interest in the integrity and trustworthiness of lawyers."[123] The Court found that this conduct that disregarded the rights of the teacher reflected adversely on the trustworthiness and integrity of the lawyer.

A 2003 Colorado Lawyer article notes a "trend around the country" to "expect lawyers to always conform to formal rules of professional conduct, even when they are engaged in 'private' activities separate from lawyers' professional activities."[124] A "trend" may be an overstatement because there are few cases disciplining lawyers for such violations in the last decade.[125]

Such cases serve as a guidepost even though the parameters remain unclear. It is generally understood that lawyers can be disciplined for conduct outside the profession if the conduct "functionally relates" to the practice of law.[126] This, of course, leads to

---

a nonlaw business but all the applicable ethics rules still apply to the lawyer. The Nevada opinion voiced an oft-heard concern that lawyers not use the business as a means of soliciting clients to the law practice. Any referral to the law practice would be considered to be a conflict under rules 1.7 *Conflict of Interest: Current Clients* and 1.8 *Conflict of Interest: Current Clients: Specific Rules*. Nev. Op. 45 (2011), *available at* https://www.nvbar.org/wp-content/uploads/Ethics_Op_45.pdf. *See also* District of Columbia Ethics Op. 336 (2006) (lawyer who acts as guardian for disabled individual must at all times comply with Rule 8.4(c)), *available at* https://www.dcbar.org/bar-resources/legal-ethics/opinions/opinion336.cfm. In Opinion 90-9 (1990), the Ohio Board of Commissioners on Grievances and Discipline found that a lawyer, whether acting as lawyer or realtor, is bound by the applicable disciplinary rules. Ohio Op. 90-9 (1990), *available at* https://www.ohioadvop.org/wp-content/uploads/2017/04/Op-90-009.pdf. It set forth strict restrictions against overlap between the two businesses, particularly in regard to signage, letterhead, and referrals. *Id.*

122. *In re* Conduct of Carpenter, 95 P.3d 203 (Or. 2004).

123. *Id.* at 208.

124. Patrick T. O'Rourke, *Discipline Against Lawyers for Conduct Outside the Practice of Law*, 32 Colo. Law. 75, 75 (2003).

125. In the notorious 1986 case, *In re* Johnson, a lawyer was disciplined in for making false statements in the political campaign against a candidate for county attorney because it was deemed prejudicial to the administration of justice and a violation of DR 1-102 (A)(5). *In re* Johnson, 729 P. 2d 1175, 1182 (Kan. 1986) (DR 1-102 is the precursor to Rule 8.4); Comm. on Prof'l Ethics & Conduct of Iowa State Bar Ass'n v. Mollman, 488 N.W.2d 168 (Iowa 1992) (sanctioning a lawyer for securing admissions to criminal conduct by deceit and misrepresentation from friend who was a former client; even though the lawyer acted as a private citizen and not as an attorney; rejecting lawyer's argument that there is a "zone of privacy" here for "purely personal matters" that remains free from scrutiny from the Disciplinary committee because the victim relied on the lawyer for guidance).

126. Ronald D. Rotunda & John S. Dzienkowski, The Lawyer's Deskbook on Professional Responsibility § 8.4-1(a) (2013).

the question of the meaning of "functionally related," a term rarely used by courts and not sufficiently defined or applied consistently.[127]

Functionally related includes lawyers in government who do not represent clients but work in government agencies. The public has the right to expect those who serve them at the municipal, state or federal level "to act according to general standards of decency, and members of a bar can be assumed to know that certain kinds of conduct, generally condemned by responsible men, will be grounds for disbarment."[128] Thus, D.C. Ethics Opinion 323 specifically addressed the application of Rule 8.4 in the context of government employees.[129] It was careful to note that the scope for discipline under Rule 8.4 was for conduct that indicates that an "attorney lacks the character required for bar membership."[130] The Comments to D.C. Rule 8.4 elaborate that this may include "violence, dishonesty, breach of trust, or serious interference with the administration of justice."[131] The opinion clarified that this does not "encompass all acts of deceit—for example, a lawyer is not to be disciplined professionally for committing adultery, or lying about the lawyer's availability for a social engagement."[132]

The D.C. bar opined that Rule 8.4 is limited in scope to conduct demonstrating "lack of character required for bar membership."[133] This standard is reflected in Rule 8.4 (b) and the history of the anti-deceit rule. Discipline should be limited to significant acts of dishonesty, deceit, and misrepresentation that adversely reflected upon a person's "fitness to practice law."

Giuliani's consistent and intentional dishonesty, including misrepresentations and falsehoods, could readily be deemed to render him unfit to practice law. Rule of Professional Conduct 1.1 requires a lawyer to have the requisite "knowledge, skill, thoroughness and preparation" necessary for the representation. There are significant instances of Giuliani's lack of competence aside from his falsehoods and misrepresentations.[134] But even if Giuliani has not violated Rule 1.1, he could be subject to discipline because his violations of Rule 8.4 (c) render him unfit to practice law. If

---

127. The court in *In re Kline* rejected the argument that 8.4(c) is only for conduct "egregious and flagrantly violative of accepted professional norms that would be recognized by a reasonable attorney practicing in the same situation." *In re Kline*, 311 P.3d 321, 338 (Kan. 2013). The court also rejected the argument that Kansas Rules of Professional Conduct 8.4(c) requires proof that the lawyer acted with "malevolent intent that rises above mistake." *Id.*

128. Sean Keveney, *The Dishonesty Rule: A Proposal for Reform*, 81 Tex. L Rev. 381, 398 (2002), (quoting *In re* Ruffalo, 390 U.S. 544, 555 (1968) (White, J., concurring)). *But see, In re* Conduct of Carpenter, 95 P.3d 203 (Or. 2004) and cases cited therein.

129. D.C. Bar, Ethics Op. 323 (2004), *available at* https://www.dcbar.org/bar-resources/legal-ethics/opinions/opinion323.cfm (discussing misrepresentation by an attorney employed by a government agency as part of official duties).

130. *Id.*

131. *Id.* (*quoting* D.C. Rule 8.4, Comment [1]).

132. *Id.*

133. *Id.*

134. *See e.g., supra*, notes 90–92.

he were representing a client in a private enterprise, he would be subject to discipline for this conduct.

There is a further argument that lawyers in Giuliani's position have a heightened obligation to avoid making false statements by virtue of his public position. Although Giuliani is President Trump's personal lawyer, his position is a unique one in that he represents the highest public figure in the United States. Figuratively, his words command or should command respect and are much more pronounced. He holds the public's trust (or his position should command such trust) and is therefore the quintessential "public citizen,"[135] more duty-bound to exhibit a higher standard of conduct[136] or to at least avoid impropriety, as an extension of the President of the United States. Lawyers are custodians of their profession and of their societies. In light of the spirit of the Model Rules,[137] lawyers in Giuliani's position should, at the very least, be subject to Rule 8.4(c)'s prohibitions if and when those lawyers willfully or intentionally engage in significant acts of dishonesty, deceit, or misrepresentation that undermines a duty of honesty and integrity and is deemed to adversely reflect upon that lawyer's "fitness to practice law."[138]

Lawyer speech—that which is patently false and made by one in Giuliani's position—is deserving of regulation where it reflects adversely upon a lawyer's "fitness to practice law." Such speech does not foster First Amendment protection because there is no constitutional value in false statements of fact.[139] Although there are multiple rationales for the First Amendment's protection of free speech—namely personal autonomy, democratic self-governance, and the marketplace of ideas[140]—it is difficult to place false statements of fact in any one of them.

---

135. The Preamble to the Model Rules states, a lawyer plays an important role as a "public citizen." This view was articulated by Justice Brandeis—that a lawyer is a public citizen whose role is to promote justice, particularly to enhance democracy. WILLIAM H. SIMON, THE PRACTICE OF JUSTICE 130–31 (1998).

136. *See* DAVID LUBAN, LAWYERS AND JUSTICE: AN ETHICAL STUDY (1988); Anthony T. KRONMAN, THE LOST LAWYER (1993); Deborah L. Rhode, *Institutionalizing Ethics*, 44 CASE W. RES. L. REV. 665 (1994); THOMAS L. SHAFFER & ROBERT F. COCHRAN, JR., LAWYERS, CLIENTS, AND MORAL RESPONSIBILITY (1994); Robert W. Gordon, *The Independence of Lawyers*, 68 B.U. L. REV. 1 (1988); RONALD DWORKIN, LAW'S EMPIRE (1988).

137. Kevin Cole & Fred C. Zacharias, *The Agony of Victory and the Ethics of Lawyer Speech*, 69 S. CAL. L. REV. 1627, 1644 (1996) ("If, as a result of misstatements, observers of the newscasts came away with the sense that [lawyers] could not be trusted and that these lawyers were representative of the bar as a whole, then the spirit of the rules [would be] frustrated.").

138. I have previously addressed the application of Rule 8.4 (c) to government lawyers who do not represent clients.

See Yaroshefsky, *supra* note 112. This article was based on a complaint that a number of ethicists, (including me) filed against Trump advisor Kelly Anne Conway who initially was held out to be Trump's "counselor." The authors of the complaint received significant criticism arguing that we had politicized and weaponized the disciplinary process and that discipline for Conway should not be countenanced despite her repeated falsehoods.

139. Keeton v. Hustler Magazine, Inc., 465 U.S. 770 (1984); Herbert v. Lando, 441 U.S. 153, 171 (1979). Facts, not expressions of opinion, which are not subject to objective proof or disproof.

140. Alexander Tsesis, *Free Speech Constitutionalism*, 2015 U. ILL. L. REV. 1015 (2015).

Despite these arguments, the issue of discipline for Giuliani remains contentious and unresolved. Some argue that the disciplinary system should not be utilized to sanction the lawyer for a high-ranking public official. The argument is that the venue for accountability of lawyers like Giuliani is the public arena; that his reputational cost is sufficient sanction, and that paramount First Amendment values should render discipline inappropriate in this instance.

Those who argue against such discipline claim that public ridicule, and not regulation, it is the appropriate sanction. But this argument renders the ethics rules applicable mostly to lawyers with "low-profile" clients. If high profile lawyers and their client can escape discipline because of their position and public commentary, the Rule will have limited applicability with unfair consequences.

A further argument against disciplinary sanctions against Giuliani for Rule 8.4 violations is separation of powers concerns about the executive branch's role. Giuliani occupies a unique position as an extension of the President — on many occasions, his role is that of a spokesperson who effectively delivers information coming from the President to the public. If so, it is necessary to consider whether regulating a lawyer in Giuliani's position would unconstitutionally diminish or take powers away from the President, thereby violating the separation of powers principle. This requires a multifaceted analysis: the results differ depending on whether Giuliani's statements relate to the President's personal matters rather than to his duties as an executive. If they relate to the former, a better case would be made that state disciplinary bodies can and should regulate his conduct. If they relate to the latter, the appropriate analysis would be to decide whether the executive branch has been "infringed" upon.

Personal matters of the President receive different treatment in many ways. Personal matters do not fall within the scope of executive privilege.[141] The 1998 spectacle of the Ken Starr investigation of former President Bill Clinton led to his impeachment by the House of Representatives.[142] Thus, if Giuliani were to speak on strictly personal matters of the President, regulation by a state disciplinary committee would likely not implicate separation of powers concerns. It is apparent, however, that personal matters may also indicate a dereliction of a President's executive duties.[143]

The extent of Giuliani's representation for personal as opposed to governmental matters is unclear and entangled and the debate about whether or not Giuliani should be subject to discipline through the Rules of Professional Conduct will continue.

---

141. *When Can the President Claim Executive Privilege?* Nat'l Const. Ctr. (Mar. 21, 2019), *available at* https://constitutioncenter.org/debate/podcasts/when-can-the-president-claim-executive-privilege.

142. *President Bill Clinton Acquitted on Both Articles of Impeachment*, History (Mar. 7, 2019), *available at* https://www.history.com/this-day-in-history/president-clinton-acquitted.

143. *See, e.g.*, Julia Harte, *Exclusive: Foreign Government Leases at Trump World Tower Stir More Emoluments Concerns*, Reuters (May 2, 2019), *available at* https://www.reuters.com/article/us-usa-trump-emoluments-exclusive/exclusive-foreign-government-leases-at-trump-world-tower-stir-more-emoluments-concerns-idUSKCN1S80PP?utm_source=twitter&utm_medium=Social.

There is unlikely to be resolution of this issue because the disciplinary committees are unlikely to engage it. Political expediency, and not ethics rules, may prevail.

Chapter Five

The Attorney-Client Privilege

I. Generally

The attorney-client privilege is the oldest privilege for confidential communications in the common law. The attorney-client privilege applies when:

> (1) the asserted holder of the privilege is or sought to become a client; (2) the person to whom the communication was made (a) is a member of the bar of a court [and] ... (b) in connection with the communication is acting as a lawyer; (3) the communication relates to a fact of which the attorney was informed (a) by his client (b) without the presence of strangers (for the purpose of securing primarily either (i) an opinion on law or (ii) legal services or (iii) assistance in some legal proceeding, and not (d) for the purpose of committing a crime or tort; and (4) the privilege has been (a) claimed and (b) not waived by the client.

United States v. United Shoe Machinery Corp., 89 F.Supp. 357, 358–59 (D. Mass. 1950). In *Upjohn Co. v. United States*, 449 U.S. 383 (1981), the Supreme Court explained that the purpose of the attorney-client privilege "is to encourage full and frank communication between attorneys and their clients and thereby promote broader public interests in the observance of law and administration of justice." The Court went on to explain that, "the privilege recognizes that sound legal advice or advocacy serves public ends and that such advice or advocacy depends upon the lawyer's being fully informed by the client."

II. Applying the Attorney-Client Privilege

In Chapter Three we considered the attorney-client privilege as it arises in parallel legislative proceedings. With respect to Michael Cohen, former Trump Organization Executive Vice President and Special Counsel to Donald J. Trump, there are also several issues surrounding the attorney-client privilege. First, although Michael Cohen was a licensed attorney during his employment at the Trump Organization, was he acting as an attorney and providing legal advice to Donald J. Trump? Or, was he simply providing business advice? Second, assuming that the attorney-client privilege applied to communications between Michael Cohen and Donald J. Trump, was Donald J. Trump using Cohen's legal advice to commit a crime or fraud which would effectively waive the attorney-client privilege? Third, with respect to the search warrants that were executed at Michael Cohen's home, office, and hotel room, what is the appropriate way to protect the attorney-client privilege (to the extent that it is applicable)?

A. Select Cases

1. Attorney as Business Advisor

In-house counsel sometimes serves dual roles as legal advisor and business consultant. The attorney-client privilege, however, is only triggered by a client's request for legal advice and limited to communications made to attorneys for the purpose of seeking legal advice and its counsel rendering it. As the Second Circuit explained in *In re County of Erie*, 473 F.3d 413 (2d Cir. 2007), "Fundamentally, legal advice involves the interpretation and application of legal principles to guide future conduct or to assess past conduct. It requires a lawyer to rely on legal education and experience to inform judgment. But it is broader, and is not demarcated by a bright line." For Michael Cohen, the question is whether his communications involving the Trump Tower Moscow project and the cover-up involving payments to Stormy Daniels involve legal or business advice.

United States v. Chen
99 F.3D 1495 (9th Cir. 1996)

KLEINFELD, Circuit Judge

* * * Mr. Chen and his wife own Sunrider Corporation and operate TF Chen Products, Inc., a subsidiary of Sunrider. The companies manufacture health food and skin care products and import from Taiwan, Hong Kong, Japan, and other countries. The importation tariffs the companies pay depend on the price they declare they paid for the goods. Undervaluation may result in administrative, civil, and criminal penalties. A statutory procedure allows an importer to mitigate or avoid penalties by filing a disclosure statement before the Customs Service learns of the undervaluation independently. *See* 19 U.S.C. § 1592(c)(4).

Of course an importer also pays taxes on profits. The higher the cost of goods sold, then, other things being equal, the lower the level of income taxes. Thus, an importer saves money on tariffs to the extent the goods are cheap, but pays more in income tax. Conversely, the company saves money on taxes, but pays higher tariffs, to the extent its cost of goods is higher.

The Customs duties on the higher values are much less than the additional taxes which would be due based on the true values. Thus, an importer can come out ahead by overpaying tariffs and underpaying income taxes, by overstating the cost of the goods imported.

Mr. and Mrs. Chen and Sunrider were indicted for conspiracy, tax evasion, and other crimes. The indictment alleged that Mr. and Mrs. Chen imported their inventory and paid tariffs based on the true invoiced price. Then Mr. Chen's sister, Jau Hwa, the comptroller of Sunrider, would prepare entirely fictional invoices on blank forms from Sunrider's Hong Kong affiliate, owned largely by the Chens and operated by Mrs. Chen's brother. The fake invoices purported to charge much higher prices for the goods. The fake invoices were then given to Sunrider's accountants to prepare trial balances, which were themselves given to Sunrider's tax preparers. Thus, tariffs would be paid on the true lower price of the goods, but taxes would be paid as though the goods had cost much more than they really did. Mr. Chen periodically instructed Jau Hwa to wire excess money to the Hong Kong affiliate's bank accounts, to maintain the fiction that Sunrider's payments were based on the fake invoices, not the real ones. Mr. and Mrs. Chen would subsequently recover the excess with the connivance of Mrs. Chen's brother. The government alleges that the Chens skimmed almost $90 million this way.

According to the indictment, the Chens eventually became concerned that IRS and Customs enforcement agents might communicate on their case and discover the difference in the claimed cost of their inventory. To protect themselves, they caused a disclosure to be made to Customs, purporting to acknowledge that they had understated their cost of goods imported. In the disclosure, they stated that the true cost of the goods was what they had reflected in their tax returns. Thus, the original Customs declarations were true, but the correcting disclosure was actually not a disclosure at all, but a fraud, intended to shield their tax evasion scheme. This scheme is entirely theoretical at this point, because nothing has yet been proven.

Mr. Chen's attorneys, Stein, Shostak, Shostak & O'Hara, filed a prior disclosure pursuant to 19 U.S.C. § 1592(c)(4) and section 162.74 of the Customs regulations stating that a review gave rise to the discovery that "certain charges relating to the imported products may not have been properly included in the entered value." A check for over $381,000 was enclosed with the disclosure. The law firm said that more money would be paid as more data were assembled revealing underpayments.

Jau Hwa eventually left Sunrider. She then gave the government materials she had taken from Sunrider's files, and gave a customs agent her account of events on which the indictment is based. The Customs agent filed an affidavit saying that according to Jau Hwa, "Marjorie Shostak [Sunrider's lawyer] proposed that Sunrider should file a disclosure with Customs." Though this affidavit does not say in so many words that Ms. Shostak knew that the disclosure would be false, and intended to hide a tax evasion scheme, the Assistant United States Attorney argued that the differences between the initial and supplemental invoices was "substantial enough to put any reasonable professional on notice that this was, in all likelihood, a fraudulent scheme."

Joseph P. Cox had worked on the Sunrider matter for the Stein, Shostak firm; James D. Wilets was in-house Sunrider counsel. Both were subpoenaed before the Grand Jury. The Chens and Sunrider moved to quash these two subpoenas based on their attorney-client privilege. The government moved for an order allowing the subpoenas, and establishing that Sunrider's communications to the lawyers were not privileged because of the crime-fraud exception. The government included with its cross-motion the affidavits from Agent Diciurcio and from Jau Hwa, disclosing Sunrider's alleged communications with its lawyers.

Sunrider and the Chens opposed the government's cross-motion. Their declarations stated that, upon review of documents the government disclosed, they found that Jau Hwa had stolen a box of documents from Sunrider, including "privileged correspondence between Sunrider's general counsel and outside counsel," and that Jau Hwa had thus revealed attorney-client communications. The declarations and oppositions say that Jau Hwa had demanded millions of dollars as the company became successful, and when Mr. Chen would not pay, she left and started a competing company with another sister, while trying to damage Sunrider and lure away its customers. Papers were submitted to show that there was no tax evasion at all. The defense theory was that Sunrider had a more complex scheme for paying its suppliers than the government understood. The scheme, developed by Ernst & Whinney, provided for purchasing inventory by letters of credit cashed on shipment and a loan agreement for a remaining balance. The tariff underpayment resulted from using only the amount paid on the letter of credit, and leaving out the loan agreement, so there was no intent to evade income tax by overstating cost of goods sold.

Ms. Shostak filed a declaration that her firm was employed to avoid litigation by bringing Sunrider into compliance with the Customs laws, by voluntarily disclosing supplemental payments already reported to the IRS. Ms. Shostak countered the attack on her professional integrity by the Assistant United States Attorney and stated that the accountants "consistently said that the payments to Paget were legitimately a part of the costs of the goods sold for tax purposes." She explained in detail the nature of the transactions and why her firm "saw nothing to suggest that a prior disclosure would further some alleged tax evasion scheme." She stated plainly that neither she nor any attorney to her knowledge had engaged in the conduct alleged by Jau Hwa, done anything to mislead Customs, or had any knowledge of or participation in any fraud on the government. Mr. Wilets and Mr. Cox also filed affidavits explaining what services they had performed on behalf of the Chens and Sunrider, stating that to the best of their knowledge neither they, the accountants, the Ernst & Young Customs group assisting with the prior disclosure, nor anyone else involved, including the Chens, had ever intended to further any tax evasion scheme or known about such a scheme. General counsel for Sunrider, Cynthia Muldrow, filed an affidavit establishing that no one had authorized Jau Hwa to take any documents with her when she left the corporation, or to disclose any attorney-client information to anyone outside Sunrider.

* * * The attorney-client privilege is essential to preservation of liberty against a powerful government. People need lawyers to guide them through thickets of complex government requirements, and, to get useful advice, they have to be able to talk to their lawyers candidly without fear that what they say to their own lawyers will be transmitted to the government. *See United States v. Zolin*, 491 U.S. 554, 562 (1989) ("clients [must] be free to 'make full disclosure to their attorneys' of past wrongdoings ... in order that the client may obtain 'the aid of persons having knowledge of the law and skilled in its practice' "); *Upjohn Co. v. United States*, 449 U.S. 383, 389

(1981) ("assistance can only be safely and readily availed of when free from the consequences or the apprehension of disclosure").

* * * Because of the delicacy and importance of the attorney-client privilege in the counseling relationship, both the district court's task and ours are especially difficult when the United States Attorney insists upon using a person's own lawyer against him.

The government argues without citation that "[w]here attorneys are involved in business decision-making, or, as Cox and Wilets acted here, as spokespersons for a company, they are clearly not acting as 'professional legal advisors.'" The government argues that this proposition takes the lawyers' planning for correcting understated customs declarations out of the privilege.

The lawyers in this case were "spokespersons" only in the sense that, as lawyers, they communicated their clients' positions to the government agencies dealing with their clients. They were not engaged in a public relations business separate from their law firm, as the government's term "spokespersons" may imply. For a lawyer to tell a judge, jury, or administrative agency, his client's position and the basis for it, that is, to be his client's spokesman, is a traditional and central attorney's function as an advocate. The communications between lawyer and client which enable a lawyer to perform this function are privileged. The government's argument implies that when a lawyer speaks on a client's behalf to a jury, the client forfeits his privilege for the attorney-client communications relating to the lawyer's statements on the client's behalf, obviously an untenable proposition.

The government's phrase, "involved in business decision-making," obscures the issue. A client is entitled to hire a lawyer, and have his secrets kept, for legal advice regarding the client's business affairs. This principle has long been the law:

> The principle we take to be this; that so numerous and complex are the laws by which the rights and duties of citizens are governed, so important is it that they should be permitted to avail themselves of the superior skill and learning of those who are sanctioned by the law as its ministers and expounders, both in ascertaining their rights in the country, and maintaining them most safely in the courts, without publishing those facts, which they have a right to keep secret, but which must be disclosed to a legal advisor and advocate, to enable him successfully to perform the duties of his office, that the law has considered it the wisest policy to encourage and sanction this confidence, by requiring that on such facts the mouth of the attorney shall be forever sealed.

Hatton v. Robinson, 31 Mass. (14 Pick) 416, 422 (1833) (Shaw, C.J.), *cited* in 8 JOHN H. WIGMORE, EVIDENCE at 547 (MCNAUGHTON REV. ED. 1961). It is not true, and has not been true since the early nineteenth century, that the confidences of a client are "respected only when given for the purpose of securing aid in litigation." *WIGMORE.* "The attorney-client privilege protects confidential disclosures made by a client to an attorney in order to obtain legal advice, ... as well as an attorney's advice in response to such disclosures." *In re Grand Jury Investigation (Corporation)*, 974 F.2d 1068, 1070 (9th Cir.1992). The attorney-client privilege applies to communications between lawyers and their clients when the lawyers act in a counseling and planning role, as well as when lawyers represent their clients in litigation. Indeed, the axiom that "every man knows the law" presupposes that everyone can find it out by consulting a lawyer, before being hauled into court for violating the law. *WIGMORE.*

That a person is a lawyer does not, ipso facto, make all communications with that person privileged. The privilege applies only when legal advice is sought "from a professional legal advisor in his capacity as such." *WIGMORE.* For example, where a counterfeiter hired a man who was a lawyer to buy printing equipment for him, no privilege could be asserted because the lawyer was merely a "business agent" and not a "legal advisor." *United States v. Huberts*, 637 F.2d 630, 640 (9th Cir.1980). Likewise, lawyer-client communications were not privileged where the "clients did not approach him for legal advice and assistance, but rather with the aim of finding [investment opportunities]." *Liew v. Breen*, 640 F.2d 1046, 1050 (9th Cir.1981). A lawyer's account ledgers revealing a client's financial transactions with third parties, which did not reveal the client's communications with the lawyer, or the lawyer's advice, were not privileged. *In re Fischel*, 557 F.2d 209, 212 (9th Cir.1977).

If a person hires a lawyer for advice, there is a rebuttable presumption that the lawyer is hired "as such" to give "legal advice," whether the subject of the advice is criminal or civil, business, tort, domestic relations, or anything else. But the presumption is rebutted when the facts show that the lawyer was "employed without reference to his knowledge and discretion in the law":

> A lawyer is sometimes employed without reference to his knowledge and discretion in the law—as where he is charged with finding a profitable investment for trust funds. So, too, one not a lawyer is sometimes asked for legal advice—as where a policeman or a clerk of court is consulted. It is not easy to frame a definite test for distinguishing legal from nonlegal advice. Where the general purpose concerns legal rights and obligations, a particular incidental transaction would receive protection, though in itself it were merely commercial in nature—as where the financial condition of a shareholder is discussed in the course of a proceeding to enforce a claim against a corporation. But apart from such cases the most that can be said by way of generalization is that a matter committed to a professional legal adviser is prima facie so committed for the sake of the legal advice which may be more or less desirable for some aspect of the matter, and is therefore within the privilege unless it clearly appears to be lacking in aspects requiring legal advice.

WIGMORE. Calling the lawyer's advice "legal" or "business" advice does not help in reaching a conclusion; it is the conclusion. That the lawyers were "involved in business decision-making," as the government puts it, is irrelevant. What matters is whether the lawyer was employed with or without "reference to his knowledge and discretion in the law," id., to give the advice. In this case, the attorneys were employed for their legal knowledge, to bring their clients into compliance with the law in the least burdensome way possible (so far as the lawyers knew). Their communications with their clients were therefore within the scope of the attorney-client privilege.

2. Crime Fraud Exception to the
Attorney-Client Privilege

It is well-established that communications that would otherwise be protected by the attorney-client privilege are not protected if they relate to client communications in furtherance of contemplated or ongoing criminal or fraudulent conduct. "Whereas confidentiality of communications … facilitates the rendering of sound legal advice, advice in furtherance of a fraudulent or unlawful goal cannot be considered 'sound.' Rather advice in furtherance of such goals is socially perverse, and the client's communications seeking such advice are not worthy of protection." *In re Grand Jury Subpoena Duces Tecum Dated Sept. 15, 1983*, 731 F.2d 1032, 1038 (2d Cir. 1984). For Michael Cohen, the question is whether his communications with Donald J. Trump in connection with hush money payments to conceal Trump's alleged affairs (which ultimately led to Cohen's conviction for campaign finance violations) were in furtherance of criminal or fraudulent conduct.

In re Grand Jury Investigation
445 F.3d 266 (3d Cir. 2006)

SLOVITER, Circuit Judge.

* * * In late 2003, a grand jury began investigating the financial arrangements and business dealings of the individual who we believe *may* be the Primary Target. Some of his business dealings have apparently been carried out by an entity we call, for want of a better designation, the Organization. The grand jury investigation led to inquiry of Jane Doe, the Executive Director of the Organization, who had, and has, intimate knowledge of and access to the papers and other material of both the Primary Target and the Organization. It appears that Jane Doe is also a target of the grand jury investigation. If she was not at the outset, she certainly has become a target in light of the events with which we are concerned. The Organization, through its counsel ("Attorney"), has entered into a joint-defense agreement with Jane Doe and her counsel in response to the investigation.

On April 27, 2004, the Government issued a grand jury subpoena to the Organization. It requested all documents, including email, from January 1, 1996 to the present, concerning, inter alia: the Organization's document retention and destruction policy; the payment of certain expenses, contributions, or donations to the Primary Target; and all grants, contributions, or donations to the Primary Target. * * *

The Government was unsatisfied with the document production, particularly with respect to what it perceived as the Organization's failure to search for and produce email stored on the Organization's computer hard drives. On January 18, 2005, the Government issued a second subpoena to the Organization, requesting essentially the same documents as in its previous subpoena. In a letter dated January 19, 2005, the Government notified Attorney that it wished to have FBI and IRS experts perform a scan of the Organization's computers to recover stored information, including deleted email files.

On February 10, 2005, pursuant to an agreement among the parties, an FBI computer technician went to the Organization's place of business and "imaged" the hard drive on Jane Doe's computer. The Government thus made an exact copy of the contents of the hard drive, including deleted email files. It uncovered numerous stored messages which could be construed to show a conscious effort by the Organization's staff to destroy emails.

Concerned about the potential obstruction of justice by Jane Doe and others at the Organization, the Government issued a subpoena duces tecum to Attorney on March 1, 2005. It sought to compel grand jury testimony regarding his discussions with Jane Doe as to her compliance (or apparent non-compliance) with the prior subpoenas for production of the Organization's email. The Government also sought production of Attorney's notes concerning his conversation with Jane Doe regarding the Organization's compliance with the two grand jury subpoenas and the January 19, 2005, letter. On March 10, 2005, the Government issued a separate subpoena for production of documents to the custodian of records at Attorney's law firm.

The Government, Attorney and Jane Doe then sought to reach an agreement that would limit the scope of Attorney's testimony before the grand jury. The Government proposed that Attorney testify on five subjects: (1) that he represents the Organization in connection with the April 27, 2004, and January 18, 2005, subpoenas; (2) that he received the January 18, 2005, subpoena and January 19 letter from the Government; (3) that he informed Jane Doe by telephone on January 20, 2005, of his receipt of the January 18 subpoena; (4) that he faxed a cover letter to Jane Doe enclosing the cover letter and subpoena from the Government; and (5) that he advised Jane Doe on January 20 regarding how to comply with the subpoena. Jane Doe voiced no objection to subjects (1)–(4), but she challenged number (5), claiming that Attorney's advice regarding compliance with the subpoena is privileged.

On January 4, 2006, the Government filed a motion to enforce the subpoena and to compel Attorney's testimony. Attorney and Jane Doe were permitted to intervene with regard to the motion, and they filed a motion to quash or to modify the subpoena to the extent that it required disclosure of privileged information.

On January 17, 2006, the District Court held a closed-court hearing on the motions. The Government argued that the crime-fraud exception should overcome the claim of privilege. In support of its position, it submitted an ex parte affidavit from an FBI agent with knowledge of the evidence gathered in the investigation. The District Court also heard testimony from Attorney and from Jane Doe's Attorney (hereinafter "Doe's Attorney"). With the Government absent from the courtroom, the two Attorneys testified essentially to their recollection of the conversations with Jane Doe on January 20, 2005, after receipt of the second subpoena and the Government's cover letter.

The dispute before the District Court was limited to whether Attorney should be compelled to reveal the substance of his January 20, 2005, telephone conversation with Jane Doe and to produce his handwritten notes concerning that conversation. On February 1, 2006, the District Court granted the Government's motion to enforce its subpoena. The Court concluded that although Attorney's advice regarding the subpoena is protected by the attorney-client privilege, and his notes are covered by the work-product doctrine, disclosure was appropriate in light of the crime-fraud exception. Based on its review of the Government's ex parte affidavit, the District Court found sufficient evidence that Jane Doe was in the process of committing obstruction of justice at the time of her January 20 conversation with Attorney, and used the information provided by Attorney in furtherance of the crime.

The Government promptly scheduled Attorney's appearance before the grand jury. The District Court denied a stay pending appeal. Jane Doe timely appealed, and this court also denied a stay. On February 7, 2006, Attorney provided the requested documents and testified before the grand jury.

* * * [Jane Doe] argues that the District Court's order enforcing and refusing to quash the subpoena to Attorney undermines the attorney-client privilege because the subpoena seeks to ascertain the contents of her conversation with Attorney on January 20, 2005. Although Jane Doe retained a personal lawyer, her lawyer and Attorney (who represents the Organization) entered into a joint defense agreement, and therefore the attorney-client privilege is applicable. In any event, the Supreme Court has held that communication between a corporation's counsel and the employees of the corporation are covered by the attorney-client privilege. *Upjohn Co. v. United States*, 449 U.S. 383, 397 (1981).

The Court stated that the attorney-client privilege is the "oldest of the privileges for confidential communications known." "[C]ourts long have viewed [the privilege's] central concern as one 'to encourage full and frank communication between attorneys and their clients and thereby promote broader public interests in the observance of law and administration of justice.'" *United States v. Zolin*, 491 U.S. 554, 562 (1989) (quoting *Upjohn*).

Despite the importance of the attorney-client privilege in the administration of justice, the Supreme Court in *Zolin* commented on the costs of the privilege in that it "has the effect of withholding relevant information from the factfinder." Therefore, the privilege can be overridden if the client used the lawyer's services to further a continuing or future crime or fraud. *See In Re Grand Jury Proceedings*, 604 F.2d 798, 802 (3d Cir.1979).

Jane Doe argues that the crime-fraud exception is inapplicable in this case because she did not initiate the communication with Attorney or solicit any advice. She relies on the language in *Doe*, where this court stated, "[o]nly when a client knowingly seeks legal counsel to further a continuing or future crime does the crime-fraud exception apply." *United States v. Doe*, 429 F.3d 450, 454 (3d Cir.2005).

That sentence in the *Doe* opinion reflects the facts in that case, i.e., the client, a law enforcement officer, initiated the communication with the attorney and sought his advice as to how to circumvent the prohibition against investing in a witness's business. Nothing in that opinion, or in any opinion, suggests that the crime-fraud exception applies only if the client initiates the conversation.

To the contrary, the crime-fraud exception is equally applicable in situations where there has been a prior attorney-client relationship and the communication at issue was made in the context of that relationship. There would be no reason to limit the applicability of the crime-fraud exception to client-initiated contact, as the exception's purpose is to further frank and open exchanges between the client and his or her attorney, whether newly retained for purposes of the investigation or otherwise.

The burden to make the necessary showing for the crime-fraud exception falls on the party who seeks application of the exception. In criminal cases, it is the Government that seeks to invoke the crime-fraud exception to counter a defendant's effort to prevent disclosure of certain testimony or documents on the ground of the attorney-client privilege. Therefore, it is the Government that must bear the initial burden. We have described the showing that must be made as follows:

> [T]he government must make a prima facie showing that (1) the client was committing or intending to commit a fraud or crime, and (2) the attorney-client communications were in furtherance of that alleged crime or fraud. A "prima facie showing" requires presentation of "evidence which, if believed by the fact-finder, would be sufficient to support a finding that the elements of the crime-fraud exception were met."

In re Grand Jury Subpoena, 223 F.3d 213, 217 (3d Cir.2000).

In *Clark v. United States*, 289 U.S. 1 (1933), the Supreme Court, in describing the evidentiary standard for the application of the crime-fraud exception, stated:

> There must be a showing of a prima facie case sufficient to satisfy the judge that the light should be let in....
>
> ... To drive the [attorney-client] privilege away, there must be "something to give colour to the charge"; there must be "prima facie evidence that it has some foundation in fact." When that evidence is supplied, the seal of secrecy is broken.

The burden is not a particularly heavy one. As the Court of Appeals for the Seventh Circuit stated, prima facie evidence cannot mean "enough to support a verdict in favor of the person making the claim." *In re Feldberg*, 862 F.2d 622, 624 (7th Cir.1988).

In this case, the District Court found that at the time of Jane Doe's January 20, 2005 conversation with Attorney, Jane Doe was committing the crime of obstruction of justice. The Court's finding that the Government met its burden of presenting evidence demonstrating a reasonable basis to suspect the perpetration of a crime, if based on adequate evidence, satisfies the first prong of the crime-fraud exception.

The District Court based its finding on the evidence before it, which included the ex parte affidavit provided by the Government. The Supreme Court has made clear that the district courts may use ex parte evidence supplied by the Government in order to make the required findings.

In *Zolin*, the IRS sought to use two tape recordings produced in an earlier case to make the required showing that the crime-fraud exception overcame the claimed attorney-client privilege. The Court of Appeals for the Ninth Circuit had opined that the determination of the applicability of the crime-fraud exception must be based on "sources independent of the attorney-client communications recorded on the tapes." In holding that was error, the Supreme Court stated that "a rigid independent evidence requirement does not comport with 'reason and experience,' ... that *in camera* review may be used to determine whether allegedly privileged attorney-client communications fall within the crime-fraud exception," and that the party opposing the privilege "must present evidence sufficient to support a reasonable belief that *in camera* review may yield evidence that establishes the exception's applicability."

In accordance with *Zolin,* the District Court here used the affidavit of the FBI agent to support its finding that at the time of Jane Doe's January 20, 2005 conversation with Attorney, Jane Doe was committing the crime of obstruction of justice by participating in a scheme to delete emails on the computers of the Organization, its officers, and staff. That this was the crime on which the Government hinged its arguments with respect to the crime-fraud exception was made clear in the Assistant U.S. Attorney's arguments before this court.

In conducting our review of the District Court's finding, we too must base our decision on the evidence submitted to the District Court ex parte. We are hampered in articulating the basis for our conclusion by the need to keep the evidentiary support confidential because much of the relevant information that was before the District Court is sealed as it pertains to the ongoing investigation of the grand jury. Moreover, the parties' briefs have been sealed. We are therefore comfortable to discuss only such facts as the Assistant U.S. Attorney disclosed in his argument in open court before us.

Based on our review, we agree that there was sufficient evidence to support the District Court's finding that Jane Doe could be found to have engaged in the ongoing crime of obstruction of justice. That does not mean we believe there is sufficient evidence to support a jury verdict to that effect beyond a reasonable doubt. However, there is enough evidence to meet the first prong of the crime-fraud standard.

* * * This court's precedential opinions have repeatedly set forth the crime-fraud test as requiring that the communication have been "in furtherance" of the crime, not only in *In re Grand Jury Subpoena,* but more recently in *Doe.*

* * * When questioned by this court at the oral argument as to how the Attorney-Jane Doe conversation furthered the crime of obstruction of justice, the Assistant U.S. Attorney used as an example a baseball player who seeks information about a grand jury investigation of the illegal use of steroids. He posited a player who "receive[d] a subpoena that directly asks for documents related to his potential criminal use of illegal drugs. And in the course of that he does, takes certain steps to prevent the documents from being turned over, for example, by destroying them." One may infer from his use of that example that the obstruction of justice that the Government is investigating is the deletion of potentially relevant email files with knowledge of their relevance to the grand jury's investigation.

In this era, when communications between leaders of business organizations are transmitted to their employees by email rather than by phone or mail, examination of those emails is the method most commonly used by government investigators. That is evident to those engaged in the criminal or fraudulent activity that is the subject of the investigation. It should therefore come as no surprise that efforts to forestall such investigations frequently take the form of deletion of past emails. *See, e.g., Arthur Andersen LLP v. United States,* 544 U.S. 696 (2005).

* * * Concededly, there are no opinions of which we are aware that apply the crime-fraud exception in precisely these circumstances. However, we see no reason why it does not apply. The Assistant U.S. Attorney stated, or it can be inferred from his statements at oral argument, that in the course of the communication between Jane Doe and Attorney, Attorney advised Jane Doe of the contents of the most recent subpoena and of the Government's interest in retrieving from Organization's computers emails to or from certain persons, including Jane Doe, who were or are connected with the Organization. Apparently, the ongoing deletion of email included information stored on the hard drive of Jane Doe's own computer. There is no suggestion that Attorney did anything improper in transmitting this communication to Jane Doe and providing legal advice on how to respond. Nor is there any suggestion that Attorney was aware of either past wrongdoing or potential future wrongdoing.

If, with knowledge of the Government's interest in retrieving any remaining emails, Jane Doe continued to receive emails that were arguably responsive to the subpoena and failed to use her position as an executive of the Organization to direct that all email deletions stop immediately, she may be viewed as furthering the obstruction of the grand jury's investigation or the obstruction of justice. Certainly, the temporal proximity of the ongoing deletion of emails after January 20 could be viewed as an additional indication that Jane Doe intended to use the information she gathered from the January 20 communication to further the scheme to obstruct. In any event, if Jane Doe learned of the Government's interest in certain documents from her conversation with Attorney on January 20, 2005 and subsequently acquiesced in the deletion or destruction of those documents, the second prong of the crime-fraud exception would be satisfied.

According to the Assistant U.S. Attorney's statements at the oral argument, Jane Doe's communication with Attorney on January 20 made it clear what the Government wanted and what was called for in response to the subpoenas. As we previously noted, the Government does not bear a heavy burden in showing that Jane Doe misused her communication with Attorney in furtherance of an improper purpose. As one court has observed, "The government does not have to show that the intended crime or fraud was accomplished, only that the lawyer's advice or other services were misused. Typically that can be shown by evidence of some activity following the improper consultation, on the part of either the client or the lawyer, to advance the intended crime or fraud." *In re Public Defender Serv.,* 831 A.2d 890, 910 (D.C. 2003).

* * * The District Court here was required to, and did, closely scrutinize the Government's evidence, and it also received in camera evidence proffered by Attorney and Doe's Attorney regarding the substance of the January 20 communication. Although the District Court was compelled by the secrecy of the grand jury proceeding to redact its substantive analysis from the version of its Opinion that it released to the parties, an unredacted version of its Opinion has been provided to this court. Based on our review of the same evidentiary record and the District Court's thoughtful analysis, we see no abuse of discretion in the District Court's decision to enforce the subpoena to Attorney.

B. Search Warrants for Attorneys

In the past, government investigative techniques such as search warrants and wiretaps were primarily used in street crime. Increasingly, however, the government is employing search warrants in lieu of subpoenas in white collar criminal cases. In white collar criminal cases, the focus of these searches is typically documents. There is, however, a higher threshold to be met to obtain a search warrant than to issue a subpoena. The Warrant Clause in the Fourth Amendment contains four textual requirements for the issuance of a warrant: (1) probable cause; (2) the claim of probable cause must be supported by Oath or affirmation; (3) the place to be searched must be described with particularity; and (4) the thing to be seized must be described with particularity. U.S. Const. amend. IV. The purpose of the particularity requirement is to prevent general wide-ranging searches by requiring a neutral judicial officer to define the scope of the search to the areas and items for which probable cause exists that a crime has been committed. *Stanford v. Texas*, 379 U.S. 476, 481 (1965); *Marron v. United States*, 275 U.S. 192, 196 (1927) ("The requirement that warrants shall particularly describe the things to be seized makes general searches under them impossible and prevents the seizure of one thing under a warrant describing another."). Therefore, the "description must be specific enough to enable the person conducting the search reasonably to identify the things authorized to be seized." *United States v. Smith*, 424 F.3d 992 (9th Cir. 2005).

Thus, to obtain a search warrant for documents, the government must convince a judicial officer that there is probable cause to believe that a crime has been committed, that documents in the subject's possession are evidence of the crime, and that the documents can be located in a particular place such as a home or office.

When the government seeks a search warrant for an attorney, an important first question is whether the government is seeking evidence of a client's crime, the lawyer's crime, or both. When an attorney is the subject of the investigation, it may be necessary to obtain a search warrant for the attorney's premises. There is a serious concern, however, that such a search could potentially uncover materials that are protected by the attorney-client privilege. Thus, the Department of Justice exercises "close control" over this type of search.

1. Department of Justice Policy
(as Outlined in the Justice Manual)
9-13.420 —
Searches of Premises of Subject Attorneys

* * * There are occasions when effective law enforcement may require the issuance of a search warrant for the premises of an attorney who is a subject of an investigation, and who also is or may be engaged in the practice of law on behalf of clients. Because of the potential effects of this type of search on legitimate attorney-client relationships and because of the possibility that, during such a search, the government may encounter material protected by a legitimate claim of privilege, it is important that close control be exercised over this type of search. Therefore, the following guidelines should be followed with respect to such searches:

A. **Alternatives to Search Warrants.** In order to avoid impinging on valid attorney-client relationships, prosecutors are expected to take the least intrusive approach consistent with vigorous and effective law enforcement when evidence is sought from an attorney actively engaged in the practice of law. Consideration should be given to obtaining information from other sources or through the use of a subpoena, unless such efforts could compromise the criminal investigation or prosecution, or could result in the obstruction or destruction of evidence, or would otherwise be ineffective.

> NOTE: Prior approval must be obtained from the Assistant Attorney General for the Criminal Division to issue a subpoena to an attorney relating to the representation of a client. See *JM 9-13.410.*

B. **Authorization by United States Attorney or Assistant Attorney General.** No application for such a search warrant may be made to a court without the express approval of the United States Attorney or pertinent Assistant Attorney General. Ordinarily, authorization of an application for such a search warrant is appropriate when there is a strong need for the information or material and less intrusive means have been considered and rejected.

C. **Prior Consultation.** In addition to obtaining approval from the United States Attorney or the pertinent Assistant Attorney General, and before seeking judicial authorization for the search warrant, the federal prosecutor must consult with the Criminal Division.

> NOTE: Attorneys are encouraged to consult with the Criminal Division as early as possible regarding a possible search of an attorney's office. Telephone No. (202) 305-4023; Fax No. (202) 305-0562.

To facilitate the consultation, the prosecutor should submit the attached form (see *Criminal Resource Manual at 265*) containing relevant information about the proposed search along with a draft copy of the proposed search warrant, affidavit in support thereof, and any special instructions to the searching agents regarding search procedures and procedures to be followed to ensure that the prosecution team is not "tainted" by any privileged material inadvertently seized during the search. This information should be submitted to the Criminal Division through the Office of Enforcement Operations. This procedure does not preclude any United States Attorney or Assistant Attorney General from discussing the matter personally with the Assistant Attorney General of the Criminal Division.

If exigent circumstances prevent such prior consultation, the Criminal Division should be notified of the search as promptly as possible. In all cases, the Criminal Division should be provided as promptly as possible with a copy of the judicially authorized search warrant, search warrant affidavit, and any special instructions to the searching agents.

The Criminal Division is committed to ensuring that consultation regarding attorney search warrant requests will not delay investigations. Timely processing will be assisted if the Criminal Division is provided as much information about the search as early as possible. The Criminal Division should also be informed of any deadlines.

D. **Safeguarding Procedures and Contents of the Affidavit.** Procedures should be designed to ensure that privileged materials are not improperly viewed, seized or retained during the course of the search. While the procedures to be followed should be tailored to the facts of each case and the requirements and judicial preferences and precedents of each district, in all cases a prosecutor must employ adequate precautions to ensure that the materials are reviewed for privilege claims and that any privileged documents are returned to the attorney from whom they were seized.

E. **Conducting the Search.** The search warrant should be drawn as specifically as possible, consistent with the requirements of the investigation, to minimize the need to search and review privileged material to which no exception applies.

While every effort should be made to avoid viewing privileged material, the search may require limited review of arguably privileged material to ascertain whether the material is covered by the warrant. Therefore, to protect the attorney-client privilege and to ensure that the investigation is not compromised by exposure to privileged material relating to the investigation or to defense strategy, a "privilege team" should be designated, consisting of agents and lawyers not involved in the underlying investigation.

Instructions should be given and thoroughly discussed with the privilege team prior to the search. The instructions should set forth procedures designed to minimize the intrusion into privileged material, and should ensure that the privilege team does not disclose any information to the investigation/prosecution team unless and until so instructed by the attorney in charge of the privilege team. Privilege team lawyers should be available either on or off-site, to advise the agents during the course of the search, but should not participate in the search itself.

The affidavit in support of the search warrant may attach any written instructions or, at a minimum, should generally state the government's intention to employ procedures designed to ensure that attorney-client privileges are not violated.

If it is anticipated that computers will be searched or seized, prosecutors are expected to follow the procedures set forth in the current edition of *Searching and Seizing Computers*, published by CCIPS.

F. **Review Procedures.** The following review procedures should be discussed prior to approval of any warrant, consistent with the practice in your district, the circumstances of the investigation and the volume of materials seized.

   • Who will conduct the review, i.e., a privilege team, a judicial officer, or a special master.

   • Whether all documents will be submitted to a judicial officer or special master or only those which a privilege team has determined to be arguably privileged or arguably subject to an exception to the privilege.

   • Whether copies of all seized materials will be provided to the subject attorney (or a legal representative) in order that: a) disruption of the law firm's operation is minimized; and b) the subject is afforded an opportunity to participate in the process of submitting disputed documents to the court by raising specific claims of privilege. To the extent possible, providing copies of seized records is encouraged, where such disclosure will not impede or obstruct the investigation.

   • Whether appropriate arrangements have been made for storage and handling of electronic evidence and procedures developed for searching computer data (i.e., procedures which recognize the universal nature of computer seizure and are designed to avoid review of materials implicating the privilege of innocent clients).

These guidelines are set forth solely for the purpose of internal Department of Justice guidance. They are not intended to, do not, and may not be relied upon to create any rights, substantive or procedural, enforceable at law by any party in any matter, civil or criminal, nor do they place any limitations on otherwise lawful investigative or litigative prerogatives of the Department of Justice.

2. Taint Teams versus Special Masters

The Department of Justice policy on searching attorney offices discusses both the use of privilege teams (also known as filter or taint teams) and special masters to make privilege determinations. The filter team refers to a search procedure in which the team executing the search is divided into two groups: an investigative team and a filter team. The filter team is the group that actually searches the seized material. Although a filter team could also be used to distinguish responsive from nonresponsive documents, in this context the filter team identifies files that contain attorney-client privileged material and passes only the files without privileged information onto the investigative team. This separates the investigative team from privileged information. A special master, on the other hand, is a neutral third party who, in this context, reviews the seized documents to determine if they are protected by the attorney-client privilege. Oftentimes, judges appoint retired or magistrate judges as special masters.

The choice between a filter team and a special master is usually hotly contested between the government and defense counsel. Typically, the government prefers a filter team because they view the filter team as the most time and cost-efficient way to make privilege determinations. Defense counsel typically advocates for the use of a special master due to concerns about the filter team leaking privileged information to the prosecution team and the filter team not fully protecting the attorney-client privilege.

District courts have struggled with whether to permit a taint team or special master to make privilege determinations. Some courts, such as the Sixth Circuit, have acknowledged the risk of leaks:

> [T]aint teams present inevitable, and reasonably foreseeable risks to privilege, for they have been implicated in the past in leaks of confidential information to prosecutors. That is to say, the government taint team may have an interest in preserving privilege, but it also possesses a conflicting interest in pursuing the investigation, and, human nature being what it is, occasionally some taint-team attorneys will make mistakes or violate their ethical obligations. It is thus logical to suppose that taint teams pose a serious risk to holders of the privilege, and this supposition is supported by past experience.

In re Grand Jury Subpoenas, 454 F.3d 511, 522 (6th Cir. 2006).

Other courts have expressed concern regarding the appearance of fairness. In *In re Search Warrant for Law Offices Executed on March 19, 1992*, 153 F.R.D. 55 (S.D.N.Y. 1992), a federal judge made the following observations:

> [T]his court notes that reliance on the implementation of a Chinese Wall, especially in the context of a criminal prosecution, is highly questionable and should be discouraged. The appearance and interests of Justice must be served. It is a great leap of faith to expect that members of the general public would believe that any such Chinese Wall would be impenetrable; this is not withstanding our own trust in the honor of the AUSA. Furthermore, in a case such as this the Chinese Wall attorney to perform the search required the physical assistance of agents, laborers, truckmen and others not bound by ethical considerations which affect a lawyer. Those on the Mongol side of the Wall may well access the same information from other sources, and have difficulty convincing a defendant or the public that the information did not pass over the wall.

The concerns over taint teams seem to be heightened when the government executes a search warrant on the offices of a criminal defense attorney. In those situations, courts in unpublished opinions have explained that Sixth Amendment right to counsel concerns are raised when the government seizes active criminal case files and that the use of a taint team does not provide adequate protection for the Sixth Amendment rights of criminal defendants. *See, e.g., United States v. Kaplan*, No. 02 Cr. 883 (DAB), 2003 WL 22880914, at *11 (S.D.N.Y. Dec. 5, 2003) (appointing a special master and explaining that "a search of the law offices of a criminal defense attorney raises Sixth Amendment concerns not otherwise present in the search of the offices of a civil litigation attorney"); *United States v. Gallego*, No. CR-18-01537-001-TUC-RM (BPV),

2018 WL 4257967 (D. Arizona Sep. 5, 2018) (same); *United States v. Stewart*, No. 02 CR 396 JGK, 2002 WL 1300059 (S.D.N.Y. May 25, 2004) (same). In *United States v. Grant*, No. 04 CR 207BSJ, 2004 WL 1171258 at *3 (D. Arizona Sep. 6, 2004), the court found that because the lawyer was engaged in civil litigation, there was no Sixth Amendment concern or need for a special master.

III. Background Concerning Michael Cohen

Michael Cohen was an employee of the Trump Organization from 2007 until January 2017. He was Executive Vice President and Special Counsel to Donald J. Trump. Cohen was commonly referred to as Donald J. Trump's "fixer" or "pit bull." Cohen explained to ABC News that "if somebody does something Mr. Trump doesn't like, I do everything in my power to resolve it to Mr. Trump's benefit."

A. Cohen's Involvement in Trump Tower Moscow

The Mueller Report details the contacts between Donald J. Trump's presidential campaign and Russia. The earliest contact between Russia and the Trump campaign involved Michael Cohen. In September 2015, Felix Sater contacted Cohen about a Trump Tower project in Moscow. Sater, a New York-based real estate advisor, reached out to Cohen on behalf of I.C. Expert Investment Company, a Russian real-estate development company controlled by Andrei Vladimirovich Rozov. Sater had previously worked with the Trump Organization and advised it on a number of projects. Mueller Report, Vol. I., p. 69. During his previous work with the Trump Organization, Sater had explored the idea of a Trump Tower in Moscow and therefore knew that the Trump Organization had an interest in a deal there. Mueller Report, Vol. I., p. 69. Sater suggested to Rozov that I.C. Expert build a building with residential, commercial, and hotel properties and license the name and brand from the Trump Organization. Mueller Report, Vol. I., p. 69. Cohen negotiated directly with I.C. Expert and its agents and reported on the status of the project to Donald J. Trump and other executives in the Trump Organization. Mueller Report, Vol. I., p. 69. Cohen discussed design elements of the building with Ivanka Trump and he spoke with Donald J. Trump Jr. about his experience in Moscow. Mueller Report, Vol. I., p. 69.

Cohen also discussed the Trump Tower Moscow project with Giorgi Rtskhiladze, a business executive who was involved in a Trump Organization business deal in Batumi, Georgia because Rtskhiladze had pursued business ventures in Moscow. Mueller Report, Vol. I., p. 70. Cohen forwarded a preliminary design study for the project to Rtskhiladze seeking his feedback. Rstskhiladze forwarded Cohen's email to an associate and stated that the "project would receive worldwide attention" if they could organize a meeting in New York with Donald J. Trump and the highest level of the Russian government. Mueller Report, Vol. I., p. 70. Rtskhiladze responded to Cohen and told him that they needed to send a letter to the mayor of Moscow in order to receive his support. Rtskhiladze proposed that the Trump Organization partner with

Global Development Group, LLC, but Cohen declined and continued to work with I.C. Expert. Mueller Report, Vol. I., p. 70.

Donald J. Trump signed a letter of intent (LOI) for Trump Tower Moscow sometime between October 13, 2015, and November 2, 2015. The LOI was intended to facilitate further discussions in an "attempt to enter into a mutually acceptable agreement" concerning the Trump project in Moscow. Mueller Report, Vol. I., p. 71. The LOI contemplated a project that would have commercial, residential, hotel, and office components which should include about 250 luxury residential condominiums and a luxury hotel with at least 150 hotel rooms. The LOI set forth the fee structure that the Trump Organization would receive for the initial groundbreaking, condominium sales, rental and other revenue, and the hotel. Mueller Report, Vol. I., p. 71. On November 3, 2015, Sater emailed Cohen and suggested that the project could help Trump's chances of being elected president. He explained, "Buddy our boy can become President of the USA and we can engineer it. I will get all of Putins team to buy in on this, I will manage this process … Michael, Putin gets on stage with Donald for a ribbon cutting for Trump Moscow, and Donald owns the republican nomination." Mueller Report, Vol. I., p. 71. Sater sent another email to Cohen later that day and stated:

> Donald doesn't stare down, he negotiates and understands the economic is-
> sues and Putin only want to deal with a pragmatic leader, and a successful
> business man is a good candidate for someone who knows how to negotiate.
> "Business, politics, whatever it all is the same for someone who knows how
> to deal." I think I can get Putin to say that at the Trump Moscow press con-
> ference. If he says it we own this election. Americas most difficult adversary
> agreeing that Donald is a good guy to negotiate … We can own this election.
> Michael my next steps are very sensitive with Putins very close people, we
> can pull this off. Michael lets go. 2 boys from Brooklyn getting a USA pres-
> ident elected. This is good really good.

Mueller Report, Vol. I., pp. 71–72. Cohen claims, however, that he did not consider the impact of the Moscow deal on the election and that he does not recall Donald J. Trump discussing that either. Trump did state that the campaign would be a great "infomercial" for Trump-branded properties. Mueller Report, Vol. I., p. 72.

Sater and Cohen believed that they would need Russian government approval to proceed due to the size of the project. Sater began working on setting up the appropriate meetings in the Presidential Administration of Russia. In late December 2015, Cohen was unhappy with Sater because he had not set up meetings with Russian government officials. Cohen said that he would do it himself. On January 11, 2016, Cohen emailed the office of Dmitry Peskov, the Russian government press secretary, indicating that he wanted contact with Sergei Ivanov, Putin's chief of staff. Cohen sent it to the wrong email address. Mueller Report, Vol. I., p. 74. On January 14, 2016, Cohen sent the email again. Cohen initially told the Special Counsel's office and Congress that he did not recall receiving a response and terminated work on the project in January 2016. He later admitted that was false. Mueller Report, Vol. I., p.

75. On January 20, 2016, Cohen received an email from Elena Poliakova, Peskov's personal assistant. Mueller Report, Vol. I., p. 75. After receiving Poliakova's email, Cohen spoke with her on the phone for 20 minutes and requested assistance in moving the Trump Tower Moscow project forward. Cohen did not receive additional follow-up from Poliakova or other representatives of the Russian government. Mueller Report, Vol. I., p. 75.

The day after Cohen spoke with Poliakova, he received a text message from Sater indicating that Putin or someone from his office contacted Sater and asking Cohen to call him back right away. Sater also sent Cohen a draft invitation for Cohen to visit Moscow to discuss the project. Cohen said that he did not travel at that time, however, because he was concerned about a lack of concrete proposals. Through June 2016, Sater repeatedly tried to arrange travel to Russia for Cohen and Donald J. Trump, but Cohen did not follow through with the travel for various reasons. Mueller Report, Vol. I., pp. 76–78. Cohen told the Special Counsel's office that he spoke with Trump about traveling to Russia in late 2015 and in the spring of 2016. Mueller Report, Vol. I., p. 78. As the Mueller Report explains:

> During the summer of 2016, Cohen recalled that candidate Trump publicly claimed that he had nothing to do with Russia and then shortly afterwards privately checked with Cohen about the status of the Trump Tower Moscow project, which Cohen found "interesting." At some point that summer, Cohen recalled having a brief conversation with Trump in which Cohen said the Trump Tower Moscow project was going nowhere because the Russian development company had not secured a piece of property for the project. Trump said that was "too bad," and Cohen did not recall talking with Trump about the project after that. Cohen said that at no time during the campaign did Trump tell him not to pursue the project or that the project should be abandoned.

Mueller Report, Vol. II., pp. 137–38.

In January 2017, Cohen began receiving inquiries from the media concerning the Trump Tower Moscow project. Cohen recalled that he spoke with President-Elect Trump when he started receiving those inquiries. "Cohen was concerned that truthful answers about the Trump Tower Moscow project might not be consistent with the 'message' that the President-Elect had no relationship with Russia." Mueller Report, Vol. II., p. 138. The Mueller Report further explains:

> In an effort to "stay on message," Cohen told a New York Times reporter that the Trump Tower Moscow deal was not feasible and had ended in January 2016. Cohen recalled that this was part of a "script" or talking points he had developed with President-Elect Trump and others to dismiss the idea of a substantial connection between Trump and Russia. Cohen said that he discussed the talking points with Trump but he did not explicitly tell Trump he thought they were untrue because Trump already knew they were untrue. Cohen thought it was important to say the deal was done in January 2016,

rather than acknowledge that talks continued in May and June 2016, because it limited the period when candidate Trump could be alleged to have a relationship with Russia to an early point in the campaign, before Trump had become the party's presumptive nominee …

In early May 2017, Cohen received requests from Congress to provide testimony and documents in connection with congressional investigations of Russian interference in the 2016 election … On May 18, 2017, Cohen met with the President to discuss the request from Congress, and the President instructed Cohen that he should cooperate because there was nothing there.

Cohen eventually entered into a joint defense agreement (JDA) with the President and other individuals who were part of the Russia investigation. In the months leading up to his congressional testimony, Cohen frequently spoke with the President's personal counsel. Cohen said that in those conversations the President's personal counsel would sometimes say that he had just been with the President. Cohen recalled that the President's personal counsel told him the JDA was working well together and assured him that there was nothing there and if they stayed on message the investigations would come to an end soon. At that time, Cohen's legal bills were being paid by the Trump Organization, and Cohen was told not to worry because the investigations would be over by summer or fall of 2017. Cohen said that the President's personal counsel also conveyed that, as part of the JDA, Cohen was protected, which he would not be if he "went rogue." Cohen recalled that the President's personal counsel reminded him that "the President loves you" and told him that if he stayed on message, the President had his back.

In August 2017, Cohen began drafting a statement about Trump Tower Moscow to submit to Congress along with his document production. The final version of the statement contained several false statements about the project. First, although the Trump organization continued to pursue the project until at least June 2016, the statement said, "The proposal was under consideration at the Trump Organization from September 2015 until the end of January 2016. By the end of January 2016, I determined that the proposal was not feasible for a variety of business reasons and should not be pursued further. Based on my business determinations, the Trump Organization abandoned the proposal. Second, although Cohen and candidate Trump had discussed possible travel to Russia by Trump to pursue the venture, the statement said, "Despite overtures by Mr. Sater, I never considered asking Mr. Trump to travel to Russia in connection with this proposal. I told Mr. Sater that Mr. Trump would not travel to Russia unless there was a definitive agreement in place." Third, although Cohen had regularly briefed Trump on the status of the project and had numerous conversations about it, the statement said, "Mr. Trump was never in contact with anyone about this proposal other than me on three occasions, including signing a nonbinding letter of intent in 2015. Fourth, although Cohen's outreach to Peskov in January 2016 had resulted in a lengthy phone call with a representative from the Kremlin, the statement said that Cohen did "not recall any response to my email [to Peskov], nor any other contacts by me with Mr. Peskov or other Russian government officials about the proposal."

Cohen's statement was circulated in advance to, and edited by, members of the JDA …

Cohen said that his "agenda" in submitting the statement to Congress with false representations about the Trump Tower Moscow project was to minimize links between the project and the President, give the false impression that the project had ended before the first presidential primaries, and shut down further inquiry into Trump Tower Moscow, with the aim of limiting the on-going Russia investigations. Cohen said he wanted to protect the President and be loyal to him by not contradicting anything the President had said. Cohen recalled he was concerned that if he told the truth about getting a response from the Kremlin or speaking to candidate Trump about travel to Russia to pursue the project, he would contradict the message that no connection existed between Trump and Russia, and he rationalized his decision to provide false testimony because the deal never happened. He was not concerned that the story would be contradicted by individuals who knew it was false because he was sticking to the party line adhered to by the whole group. Cohen wanted the support of the President and the White House, and he believed that following the party line would help put an end to the Special Counsel and congressional investigations.

Between August 18, 2017, when the statement was in an initial draft stage, and August 28, 2017, when the statement was submitted to Congress, phone records reflect that Cohen spoke with the President's personal counsel almost daily. On August 27, 2017, the day before Cohen submitted the statement to Congress, Cohen and the President's personal counsel had numerous contacts by phone, including calls lasting three, four, six, eleven, and eighteen minutes. Cohen recalled telling the President's personal counsel, who did not have first-hand knowledge of the project, that there was more detail on Trump Tower Moscow that was not in the statement, including that there were more communications with Russia and more communications with candidate Trump than the statement reflected. Cohen stated the President's personal counsel responded that it was not necessary to elaborate or include those details because the project did not progress and that Cohen should keep his statement short and "tight" and the matter would soon come to an end. Cohen recalled that the President's personal counsel said "his client" appreciated Cohen, that Cohen should stay on message and not contradict the President, that there was no need to muddy the water, and that it was time to move on. Cohen said he agreed because it was what he was expected to do. After Cohen later pleaded guilty to making false statements to Congress about the Trump Tower Moscow project, this Office sought to speak with the President's personal counsel about these conversations with Cohen, but counsel declined, citing potential privilege concerns ...

On October 24 and 25, 2017, Cohen testified before Congress and repeated the false statements he had included in his written statement about Trump Tower Moscow. Phone records show that Cohen spoke with the President's personal counsel immediately after his testimony on both days.

Mueller Report, Vol. II., pp. 139–44.

In a footnote concerning the JDA, one of only a handful of times the Mueller Report addresses the attorney-client privilege, the Mueller Report explains:

Cohen told investigators about conversations with the President's personal counsel after waiving any privilege of his own and after this Office advised his counsel not to provide any communications that would be covered by any other privilege, including communications protected by a joint defense or common interest privilege. As a result, most of what Cohen told us about his conversations with the President's personal counsel concerned what Cohen had communicated to the President's personal counsel, and not what was said in response. Cohen described certain statements made by the President's personal counsel, however, that are set forth in this section. Cohen and his counsel were better positioned than this Office to evaluate whether any privilege protected those statements because they had knowledge of the scope of their joint defense agreement and access to privileged communications that may have provided context for evaluating the statements they shared. After interviewing Cohen about these matters, we asked the President's personal counsel if he wished to provide information to us about his conversations with Cohen related to congressional testimony about Trump Tower Moscow. The President's personal counsel declined and, through his own counsel, indicated that he could not disaggregate information he had obtained from Cohen from information he had obtained from other parties in the JDA. In view of the admonition this Office gave to Cohen's counsel to withhold communications that could be covered by the privilege, the President's personal counsel's uncertainty about the provenance of his own knowledge, the burden on a privilege holder to establish the elements to support a claim of privilege, and the substance of the statements themselves, we have included relevant statements Cohen provided in this report. If the statements were to be used in a context beyond this report, further analysis could be warranted.

Mueller Report, Vol. II., pp. 139–140, n. 958.

On November 29, 2018, Cohen pled guilty to a Criminal Information charging him with one count of making false statements to the U.S. Congress during the Russia investigation, in violation of 18 U.S.C. § 1001(a)(2).

Notes & Questions

1. *Business or Legal Advice.* Was Cohen providing business or legal advice regarding Trump Tower Moscow? Would Cohen's discussions with Trump be protected by the attorney-client privilege? With respect to the JDA, if Mueller wanted additional information concerning Cohen's conversations with the President's personal counsel, could he obtain that information based on the crime-fraud exception to the attorney-client privilege?

2. *Congressional Testimony.* Consider the following exchange during Cohen's congressional testimony.

> MR. COHEN: If every time that there was something that seemed amiss that I overheard, I'd spend half of my day looking up to see whether or not I was responsible to tell him on every single thing that's wrong that he's doing. I would probably last there all of 10 seconds.

> MR. CONAWAY: So you're saying then that you weren't really a lawyer in that full sense.

> MR. COHEN: When I was sitting in that room —

> MR. CONAWAY: Yeah.

> MR. COHEN: —at the time? I don't know what I was working on. I did do some legal work, but, no, l was not. There was general counsel; there were 10 other counsels that were there. I was his special counsel. My job was to take care of matters that were of significance and importance to him.

> MR. CONAWAY: So you didn't believe that that phone call was a matter of significance to him from a legal standpoint, based on your training as a lawyer.

> MR. COHEN: I didn't consider it at the time, no.

> MR. CONAWAY: Thank you.

B. Cohen's Involvement in Campaign Finance Violations[1]

According to the Federal Election Campaign Act of 1971, 52 U.S.C. § 30101, individual contributions to a presidential candidate are limited to $2,700 per election and presidential candidates and their committees are prohibited from accepting individual contributions greater than $2,700. According to the Information, in or about August 2015, David Pecker (referred to in the Information as "Chairman-1"), the Chief Executive Officer of American Media Inc. ("AMI") (referred to in the Information as "Corporation-1") offered to assist Michael Cohen and other members of the campaign by dealing with negative stories concerning presidential candidate Donald J. Trump's relationships with women by purchasing the negative stories and then

---

1. *See* Chapter 6 for discussion on campaign finance.

failing to publish them. *Cohen Information* at 12. In June 2016, Karen McDougal (referred to in the Information as "Woman-1"), began attempting to sell her story about an alleged extramarital affair with presidential candidate Donald J. Trump (referred to in the Information as "Individual-1"). *Cohen Information* at 12. McDougal knew that her story would be valuable because of the election. McDougal's attorney contacted the editor-in-chief of the National Enquirer (referred to in the Information as "Magazine-1") and offered to sell the story. *Cohen Information* at 13. Pecker informed Cohen of the story. Cohen urged AMI to purchase the story and promised that AMI would be reimbursed. *Cohen Information* at 13. On or about August 5, 2016, AMI entered into an agreement with McDougal to acquire the rights to her story of her relationship with Donald J. Trump in exchange for $150,000. In the agreement, AMI promised to feature McDougal on two magazine covers and publish over one hundred magazine articles by her. *Cohen Information* at 13. The purpose of the agreement was to suppress the story to keep it from influencing the election. *Cohen Information* at 13.

On or about October 8, 2016, an agent for adult film actress Stephanie Clifford (also known by her stage name "Stormy Daniels" and referred to in the Information as "Woman-2") informed an editor of the National Enquirer that she was willing to confirm that she had allegedly had an affair with presidential candidate Donald J. Trump. *Cohen Information* at 14. Pecker contacted Cohen and put him in touch with Daniels' attorney, Keith Davidson, who was also representing McDougal. Cohen negotiated a $130,000 agreement to purchase Daniels' silence. On October 17, 2016, Davidson emailed Cohen and informed him that if he did not complete the transaction by the end of the day, he would cancel the settlement agreement. *Search Warrant* at 45. On October 26, 2016, Cohen created a shell company called Essential Consultants LLC. Cohen took $131,000 from his fraudulently obtained home equity line of credit and wired it to Essential Consultants. *Cohen Information* at 15. On October 27, 2016, Cohen wired the $130,000 from Essential Consultants to Stephanie Clifford's attorney. Cohen made the payment to influence the outcome of the presidential election. *Cohen Information* at 15–16.

In January 2017, Cohen sought reimbursement from the Trump Organization (referred to in the Information as "the Company") and provided a bank statement that reflected the payment from Essential Consultants to Stephanie Clifford's attorney. He also sought $50,000 for "tech services" and the $35 wire fee. Cohen's total requested reimbursement was $180,035. Cohen *Information* at 16. Executives at the Trump Organization "grossed up" Cohen's requested reimbursement to $360,000 and then added a bonus of $60,000, bringing Cohen's reimbursement total to $420,000 to be paid in monthly installments of $35,000 over twelve months. *Cohen Information* at 16–17. Cohen was to submit monthly invoices to the Trump Organization to obtain his reimbursement. On February 14, 2017, Cohen submitted his first invoice requesting "[p]ursuant to [a] retainer agreement, ... payment for services rendered for the months of January and February, 2017." *Cohen Information* at 17. Cohen continued to submit these invoices throughout 2017 and the Trump Organization accounted for the payments as legal expenses. There was not, however, a retainer agreement between Michael Cohen and the Trump Organization and the invoices were not in connection with legal services provided in 2017. *Cohen Information* at 17.

In January 2018, the media reported Cohen's $130,000 payment to Stephanie Clifford. Although the Special Counsel's office did not investigate Cohen's campaign finance violations, they did find the events to be "potentially relevant to the President's and his personal counsel's interactions with Cohen as a witness who later began to cooperate with the government." Mueller Report, Vol. II., p. 144. As the report explains:

> On February 13, 2018, Cohen released a statement to news organizations that stated, "In a private transaction in 2016, I used my own personal funds to facilitate a payment of $130,000 to [the woman]. Neither the Trump Organization nor the Trump campaign was a party to the transaction with [the woman], and neither reimbursed me for the payment, either directly or indirectly." In congressional testimony on February 27, 2019, Cohen testified that he had discussed what to say about the payment with the President and that the President had directed Cohen to say that the President "was not knowledgeable … of [Cohen's] actions" in making the payment. On February 19, 2018, the day after the New York Times wrote a detailed story attributing the payment to Cohen and describing Cohen as the President's "fixer," Cohen received a text message from the President's personal counsel that stated, "Client says thanks for what you do."

> On April 9, 2018, FBI agents working with the U.S. Attorney's Office for the Southern District of New York executed search warrants on Cohen's home, hotel room, and office. That day, the President spoke to reporters and said that he had "just heard that they broke into the office of one of my personal attorneys—a good man." The President called the searches "a real disgrace" and said, "It's an attack on our country in a true sense. It's an attack on what we all stand for." Cohen said that after the searches he was concerned that he was "an open book," that he did not want issues arising from the payments to women to "come out," and that his false statements to Congress were "a big concern."

Mueller Report, Vol. II., pp. 144–45.

> Beginning on July 20, 2018, the media reported on the existence of a recording Cohen had made of a conversation he had with candidate Trump about a payment made to a second woman who said she had an affair with Trump. On July 21, 2018, the President responded: "Inconceivable that the government would break into a lawyer's office (early in the morning)—almost unheard of. Even more inconceivable that a lawyer would tape a client— totally unheard of and perhaps illegal. The good news is that your favorite President did nothing wrong!" On July 27, 2018, after the media reported that Cohen was willing to inform investigators that Donald Trump Jr. told his father about the June 9, 2016 [Trump tower] meeting to get "dirt" on

Hillary Clinton, the President tweeted: "[S]o the Fake News doesn't waste my times with dumb questions, No, I did NOT know of the meeting with my son, Don jr. Sounds to me like someone is trying to make up stories in order to get himself out of an unrelated jam (Taxi cabs maybe?). He even retained Bill and Crooked Hillary's lawyer. Gee, I wonder if they helped him make the choice!"

On August 21, 2018, Cohen pleaded guilty in the Southern District of New York to eight felony charges, including two counts of campaign-finance violations based on payments he had made during the final weeks of the campaign to women who said they had affairs with the President. During the plea hearing, Cohen stated that he had worked "at the direction of" the candidate in making those payments. The next day, the President contrasted Cohen's cooperation with [Paul] Manafort's refusal to cooperate, tweeting, "I feel very badly for Paul Manafort and his lovely family. 'Justice' took a 12 year old tax case, among other things, applied tremendous pressure on him and, unlike Michael Cohen, he refused to 'break' — make up stories in order to get a 'deal.' Such respect for a brave man!"

Mueller Report, Vol. II., pp. 148–49.

Questions

Are there grounds for piercing the attorney-client privilege between Donald J. Trump and Michael Cohen based on the crime-fraud exception to the attorney-client privilege?

C. Litigation Concerning the Search Warrant of Michael Cohen's Home, Office, and Hotel

On April 9, 2018, the government executed a search warrant on Michael Cohen's home, office, hotel, safety deposit box, and electronic devices. The search warrants identified items related to Michael Cohen's alleged criminal activity involving campaign finance violations (for orchestrating payments to Karen McDougal and Stephanie Clifford in the waning days of the presidential campaign) and potential fraud concerning his taxi medallion business. Each search warrant contains the following provision:

Additionally, because Cohen is an attorney, and claims to serve as a personal attorney for Trump, the review of evidence seized from the Subject Premises and Subject Devices will be conducted pursuant to established screening procedures to ensure that the law enforcement personnel involved in the investigation, including attorneys for the Government, collect evidence in a manner reasonably designed to protect any attorney-client or other applicable privilege. When appropriate, the procedures will include use of a designated "filter team," separate and apart from the investigative team, in order to review potentially privileged communications and determine which communications to release to the investigation and prosecution team.

In the Matter of the Search of Four Premises and Two Electronic Devices, Application for a Search Warrant, No. 18 MAG 2969 at 76 (Apr. 8, 2018).

Following the execution of the search warrants, Michael Cohen filed a motion for a Temporary Restraining Order and a Preliminary Injunction to restrain the government from reviewing the seized items. He sought the following relief:

> (1) have all seized items be made available to Mr. Cohen's counsel to conduct a review of the documents in the first instance and produce to the government all responsive, non-privileged items. The Court could also appoint a Special Master to oversee that review by Mr. Cohen's counsel; (2) keep all documents and information relating to the investigation of Michael D. Cohen under seal, [redacted], all of which were executed on April 9, 2018; and (3) temporarily restrain the government from reviewing any of the seized materials until the Court rules on Mr. Cohen's application, or from publishing the search warrants, search warrant inventory, or this application.

Memorandum of Law in Support of Michael D. Cohen's Order to Show Cause and a Temporary Restraining Order Concerning Warrants Executed on April 9, 2018, No. 18-MJ-03161 at 2–3 (S.D.N.Y. Apr. 13, 2018). Cohen argued that the "search warrants were requested and executed in violation of the guidelines set forth in the USAM, and were wholly unnecessary, given Mr. Cohen's extensive and ongoing cooperation with the government's various investigating agencies." *Id.* at 4. Cohen identified two types of privileged documents that needed protection—those relating to communications between Cohen and his clients and communications between Cohen and his lawyers. Id. Finally, he argued that the seized documents were "uniquely sensitive because they contain documents relating to privileged communications between the President of the United States and his personal lawyer. The retention of such privileged information from the President presents not only routine attorney-client privilege and attorney work product issues, but also creates constitutional concerns regarding officers of the Executive Branch rummaging through the private and privileged papers of the President." *Id.* at 21.

In its opposition motion, the government argued that Cohen is "being investigated for criminal conduct that largely centers on his personal business dealings. Based on information gathered in the investigation to date, the USAO-SDNY and FBI have reason to believe that Cohen has exceedingly few clients and a low volume of potentially privileged communications." *The Government's Opposition to Michael Cohen's Motion for a Temporary Restraining Order*, Michael Cohen v. United States of America, No. 18-MJ-03161 at 2 (S.D.N.Y. Apr. 13, 2018). Specifically, the government stated that they doubted Cohen's claims concerning the amount of privileged documents because "the USAO-SDNY has already obtained search warrants—covert until this point—on multiple different email accounts maintained by Cohen, and has conducted a privilege review of the materials obtained pursuant to those warrants. The results of that review, as reported by the USAO's Filter Team, indicate that Cohen is in fact performing little to no legal work, and that *zero* emails were exchanged with President Trump." *Id.* at 12–13 (emphasis in original). They also noted that Cohen has several business interests and sources of income that do not relate to his work as an attorney and that the government is seeking evidence related to Cohen's business dealings. *Id.* at 4.

The government argued that a special master was not necessary and would cause undue delay. They claimed that they had taken adequate steps to protect the attorney-client privilege and that the use of a filter team was a common procedure. The government noted that the FBI agents who seized materials were filter agents, not members of the investigative team, and that they have been "walled off" from the investigative team. *Id.* at 4. According to the government's motion, "The Filter team is composed of AUSAs who have had, and will have, no involvement in the investigation. The Filter Team is prohibited from disclosing, directly or indirectly, the substance of any material under its review to the Investigative Team, unless and until the Filter Team has determined that the material is not privileged." *Id.* at 5. The government laid out the following procedure for the privilege review:

> To be clear, under no circumstances will a potentially privileged document or a document potentially subject to the crime-fraud exception be provided to or described to the Investigative Team without the consent of the privilege holder or his/her counsel, or the court's approval. If the Filter Team is unable to clarify a document's category, or if there is an exception to the privilege that applies to particular material, such as the crime-fraud exception, or any waiver of the privilege—the Filter Team will (1) confer with counsel for the privilege holder at the appropriate time and before any such material is shared with the Investigative Team and, if no agreement can be reached, submit the material under seal to an appropriate court for a determination as to whether the material is privileged; (2) bring the document to a court for resolution, including by seeking an *ex parte* determination if appropriate; *or* (3) if the document is of obviously minimal probative value, place the document into the "Privileged" category as a means of efficiently completing the review.

Id. at 6.

On April 13, the district court judge held a conference on the issues concerning the use of a special master versus a filter team. At the conference, the judge explained that he needed to know how many legal clients Michael Cohen had so that he could properly determine if the use of a special master would cause undue delay as opposed to the use of a government taint team. Cohen's counsel could not give the court an exact number. Status Hearing, *Cohen v. United States*, No. 18-MJ-03161, Tr. at 23 (S.D.N.Y. Apr. 13, 2018) (hereinafter 4/13 Tr.). Cohen's attorney claimed that it would be difficult to give an exact number because Cohen had an affiliation with another law firm and that he was "on a lot of communications and things with a number of those clients, as I understand it, from that law firm." 4/13 Tr. at 23. The judge also inquired how long it would take to get a special master up to speed. The government explained that selecting the special master and getting her up to speed is not the problem, the problem is that "this is a fast-moving investigation" and the special master's review would take much longer than the taint team. 4/13 Tr. at 24. They discussed the Stewart case and how it took 15 months to get the special master's report. 4/13

Tr. at 25. The government reiterated its belief that only a fraction of the seized documents are likely to be privileged and that the majority of documents could be identified as not privileged by the use of simple search terms and that the process would be greatly aided if Cohen provided the government with a client list. 4/13 Tr. at 26–27. Cohen's lawyers argued that revealing the client's names "would potentially be an ethical breach for us." 4/13 Tr. at 42. The judge asked Cohen's attorneys the basis for their assertion that there are thousands of privileged documents, but his attorney only said that it was an estimate based on conversations amongst defense counsel. 4/13 Tr. at 50. Cohen's attorney also explained, "we don't know exactly how far back in terms of the time period the seized materials go, but just so the Court understands, prior to working for the Trump organization, my understanding is that Mr. Cohen was an attorney for over 20 years before that, with clients, so we believe, we assume that a lot of those communications, that there were privileged communications with clients during that period, and those may well be encompassed in the materials that the government seized, because they seized a lot of stuff." 4/13 Tr. at 57. Cohen's attorney requested additional time to find out the number of clients and their names. The government attorney responded, "Mr. Cohen's counsel says he needs more time, but this is their motion. They made a motion for extraordinary temporary relief asking us not to review lawfully seized materials. As the reason for the immediacy, which is the subject heading in Mr. Harrison's affidavit at page 36, he says, 'the seized materials contain thousands, if not millions of pages of documents that are protected by the attorney-client privilege and/or the attorney work product doctrine.' Now, today he can't tell you how many clients Mr. Cohen has or how many documents are out there." 4/13 Tr. at 60–61. Thus, the government urged the judge to deny Cohen's motion for a temporary restraining order.

The President intervened in the action and, in a letter addressed to the court, argued that the privilege holder should be permitted to review the seized materials before the government. *Letter from Joanna C. Hendon to The Honorable Kimba Wood*, at 2 (April 15, 2018). The President argued that it is unprecedented to use a taint team "where the documents to be reviewed were obtained by the government pursuant to a search of a lawyer's office and the privilege-holder objects to a taint team procedure." *Id.* The President's overarching concern was that that "a taint team member having no first-hand involvement in the underlying representation can only guess as to the nature of the relationships at issue and the circumstances under which particular documents came into being. No one in that position can adequately safeguard the privilege." *Id.* at 3–4.

At a conference on April 16, 2018, the judge denied Cohen's motion for a temporary restraining order as moot, because the government agreed not to review the seized items during the pendency of the proceeding. Status Hearing, *Cohen v. United States*, No. 18-MJ-03161, Tr. at 90–91 (S.D.N.Y. April 16, 2018). On April 26, 2018, the government withdrew its opposition to the appointment of a special master. On April 27, 2018, the court appointed Retired District Judge Barbara Jones as the Special Master. The Special Master's review procedure required the government to provide the parties with copies of all of the items seized on April 9, 2018 on a rolling basis. Upon review, the parties had the opportunity to claim documents as privileged or highly personal. After receiving the privileged and highly personal designations from the parties, the special master then released all of the documents that were not marked as privileged or highly personal to the government. The Special Master then reviewed all of the items designated as privileged or highly personal. If she had questions, she conferred with the parties. As a result of this referral process, the parties withdrew their privileged or highly personal designations from many items. The Special Master completed her review on August 16, 2018 and made final determinations with respect to all designations. She submitted these determinations to the Court in her Final Report. Out of approximately 4 million files seized, the Special Master designated 7,146 items as privileged, 8 partially privileged, and 285 as highly personal. The Special Master also recommended that 57 items that were designated by the parties as privileged be designated as not privileged. The parties did not raise objections concerning these designations with the court. Thus, the Special Master released those items to the government. The Court also reviewed all of the items that the Special Master designated as privileged and agreed with the Special Master's designations. The Court adopted the recommendations in the Special Master's Final Report on August 20, 2018. *Cohen v. United States, Order,* No. 18-MJ-3161 (S.D.N.Y. Aug. 20, 2018).

Questions

If the government had not withdrawn its objection to the appointment of a Special Master, do you think the court would have granted Cohen's motion for a Special Master? Would the use of a filter team have been appropriate here? Why or why not?

Chapter Six

The Value of Information to Election Campaigns

I. Generally

This Chapter considers two issues of election law related to the Trump Campaign's behavior surrounding the 2016 election. First, if Trump Campaign officials agreed to receive damaging information about Secretary Clinton from foreign persons, would the Campaign officials be violating the federal ban on "accept[ing] or receiv[ing]" a "thing of value" from a foreign national? Second, if then-Candidate Trump or his corporation paid hush money to two of Trump's mistresses in an attempt to prevent the public from learning damaging information about the candidate, and failed to report such payments to the FEC, would the hush-money payments be illegal contributions to the Campaign?

Both questions involve the value of information to a political campaign. It is indisputable that damaging information about one's opponent and good publicity (or damage control) about one's own campaign are valuable in a realistic sense, even though it may be difficult to identify the dollar value of such information with any precision. Still, there are reasons not to extend campaign-finance regulations to cover such information. The First Amendment may protect the right to acquire damaging information about a political opponent, regardless of the source; furthermore, treating information as a "thing of value" may unconstitutionally (or at least unwisely) chill individuals from sharing information about political figures. And treating hush-money payments as a political expense would *promote* corruption by encouraging candidates to use campaign funds to pay for personal expenses.

II. The Russian "Contribution" of Opposition Research

Federal campaign-finance law prohibits foreign nationals (excluding permanent-resident aliens) from making contributions to federal candidates, and also prohibits them from making independent expenditures that promote the election or defeat of a federal candidate.[1] Both contributions and expenditures involve giving "money or anything of value … for the purpose of influencing any election for Federal office."[2] It is illegal not only for foreign entities to make contributions or expenditures, but also for others to solicit or receive such foreign contributions or expenditures.[3]

The questions addressed here are whether damaging information on an opposition candidate is a "thing of value" within the meaning of the campaign-finance laws, and, if so, whether it is constitutional to regulate and limit "contributions" of such information to candidates. If opposition research is a "thing of value," then foreign offers to provide such information would violate the law, as would the acceptance of such information by a U.S. campaign. Such an interpretation, however, could also have significant implications domestically. Foreign nationals are banned from making contributions and expenditures; U.S. corporations are banned from making contributions; and U.S. individuals are limited in the amount of contributions they may make to federal candidates. Because contributions and expenditures are defined identically with respect to activity by foreign nationals and U.S. persons, any behavior that qualifies as a contribution when engaged in by a foreign national would also qualify as a contribution when engaged in by an American citizen. Accordingly, if opposition research is a "thing of value," it would be illegal for U.S. persons to provide such information where the value of the information exceeds the applicable contribution limit. As a result, a broad interpretation of "anything of value" (even in the context of foreign contributions) could limit the ability of U.S. persons to give their favored candidates information about the opposition — with grave implications for the First Amendment.

A. Facts

On June 3, 2016, Robert Goldstone, an events promoter, e-mailed Donald Trump Jr. with a tantalizing offer of dirt on Hillary Clinton. Emin Agalarov, a client of Goldstone's, and Emin's father, Aras Agalarov, were offering to provide the Trump Campaign with damaging information about Trump's opponent. Goldstone's e-mail was as follows:

> Good morning
>
> Emin just called and asked me to contact you with something very interesting.
>
> The Crown prosecutor of Russia met with his [Emin's] father Aras this morning and in their meeting offered to provide the Trump campaign with some official documents and information that would incriminate Hillary and her dealings with Russia and would be very useful to your father. This is obviously very high level and sensitive information but is part of Russia and its government's support for Mr. Trump — helped along by Aras and Emin.

---

1. *See* 52 U.S.C. §§ 30121(a)(1)(A), (C).
2. 52 U.S.C. §§ 30101(8)(A)(i); (9)(A)(i).
3. *See* 52 U.S.C. §§ 30121(a)(1)(A), (a)(2).

What do you think is the best way to handle this information and would you be able to speak to Emin about it directly?

I can also send this info to your father via Rhona, but it is ultra sensitive so wanted to send to you first.

Best

Rob Goldstone

Trump, Jr., immediately responded:

Thanks Rob I appreciate that. I am on the road at the moment but perhaps I just speak to Emin first. Seems we have some time and if it's what you say I love it especially later in the summer. Could we do a call first thing next week when I am back?

A meeting was arranged for June 9, 2016, at Trump Jr.'s office in Trump Tower. Trump Jr., campaign chairman Paul Manafort, and advisor Jared Kushner attended. To the Trump Campaign's annoyance, however, the Russians did not have evidence tying Hillary Clinton or her campaign to anything illegal or politically damaging.[4] Rather, the Russians attempted to use the meeting to lobby the Trump Campaign to ease financial sanctions and travel restrictions on Russian officials working in the United States. Trump Jr. told the Russians that his father was still a private citizen and therefore could do nothing about the restrictions. The Trump Campaign never received any of the incriminating information that had been promised in the e-mail.

B. The Legal Controversy

Because no useful information was conveyed to the Trump Campaign, there is no question about anyone's liability for making or receiving a foreign contribution. That is, even if the information that the Russians promised to the Trump Campaign would have been an illegal campaign contribution, the contribution never materialized. Instead, the question raised by the episode is whether Trump Jr. committed a crime by *soliciting* an illegal foreign campaign contribution. The Special Counsel concluded that a prosecution was unwarranted for three reasons. First, it was not clear that the information offered by the Russians would be considered a "thing of value" under the foreign-contribution ban. Second, if the information were a thing of value, it would be difficult to establish how much it was worth—an important question because the violation would be considered a felony only if the value met a threshold amount of $25,000, and the violation would not be criminal at all unless the value of the information was at least $2000.[5] Third, it was not clear that Trump Jr. or anyone else connected with the Trump Campaign acted with the requisite mental state—"knowingly and willfully"[6]—for criminal liability to attach.

---

4. *See* Mueller Report, Vol. I, pp. 110–123.
5. *See* 52 U.S.C. §30109(d)(1).
6. 52 U.S.C. §30109(d)(1)(A)(i).

On the surface, at least, opposition research is a "thing of value" to a campaign. Campaigns pay for opposition research. (In fact, the Clinton Campaign paid for the opposition research in the much-discussed Steele Dossier that contained the initial allegations of connections between Trump and Russia.) And, although Russia did not deliver on its promise of opposition research on Hillary Clinton, it is obvious that opposition research could be quite valuable to a candidate's effort to obtain more votes for himself or herself and to decrease the number of votes for opponents. Indeed, opposition research could be more valuable than other kinds of donations that are indisputably "contributions." As the Mueller Report noted, "[a] foreign entity that engaged in such research and provided resulting information to a campaign could exert a greater effect on an election, and a greater tendency to ingratiate the donor to the candidate, than [it could if it were to provide] a gift of money or tangible things of value."[7]

There is reason to hesitate before interpreting "thing of value" to include information, however. Recall that campaign-finance law not only bans foreign nationals from contributing to U.S. campaigns; it also limits the amount that individual Americans may contribute to campaigns. (The current limit is $2800; the limit in effect in 2016 was $2700.) Accordingly, if providing damaging information about an opponent is a campaign contribution, and if the value of that information exceeds the limit, then Americans, as well as foreigners, could be limited in their ability to share information with their favored candidates. Further, if "anything of value" includes information, the term would have to include far more than opposition research. Polling data and advice about campaign strategy, for example, would be "thing[s] of value"; after all, campaigns regularly pay professionals for both of those, too. Even far more casual information could be considered valuable. Would it be a "contribution" to a candidate if a supporter told a candidate that people in his community are very interested in a particular issue? Or that the supporter saw the opponent commit a particular crime? Taken to that extreme, it seems inevitable that limiting or banning people from providing information to candidates would raise the most serious of First Amendment concerns.

A court might, therefore, strain to interpret the statutory "thing of value" language not to include information — an interpretation that would allow the court to avoid the constitutional question. Alternatively, a court might attempt to distinguish between different kinds of information — between the information that supporters routinely give their favored candidates and information that more closely resembles the kind of campaign intelligence for which campaigns regularly pay researchers, advisors, and consultants. Drawing such a line, however, seems incompatible with constitutional concerns of vagueness — particularly in the First Amendment area.[8] It also oddly protects speech the most when the speech is least valuable.[9] The First Amendment does

---

7. Mueller Report, Vol. I, p. 187.

8. *See, e.g.*, NAACP v. Button, 371 U.S. 415, 432 (1963) ("[S]tandards of permissible statutory vagueness are strict in the area of free expression.").

9. *Cf.* First Nat'l Bank of Boston v. Bellotti, 435 U.S. 765, 790 (1978) ("[T]he fact that advocacy may persuade the electorate is hardly a reason to suppress it....").

not generally permit the government to distinguish between different types of speech based on how professional it appears.[10]

Thus, perhaps a law limiting or banning people from providing information to a candidate would violate the First Amendment—in instances where the First Amendment applies. Under such an interpretation, if the government did try to punish an American from sharing information with a candidate, such a person would be able to challenge the law as applied to his conduct. But the First Amendment may not protect the speech rights of foreigners, and so prohibiting foreign nationals from "contributing" information to U.S. campaigns might not violate the First Amendment.

The Supreme Court has never held that foreign nationals have any First Amendment rights at all, and they certainly do not have any First Amendment right to influence U.S. elections.[11] Although *Citizens United v. FEC* and *First National Bank of Boston v. Bellotti* held that the *corporate* identity of the speaker is generally irrelevant to deciding whether speech deserves constitutional protection,[12] the Court has not applied that reasoning to hold that speech by *foreign* speakers is protected. On that question, then-Judge Kavanaugh, writing for a three-judge district court in *Bluman v. FEC* (a decision summarily affirmed by the Supreme Court), held that the government had a compelling interest in preventing election interference from foreigners:

> It is fundamental to the definition of our national political community that foreign citizens do not have a constitutional right to participate in, and thus may be excluded from, activities of democratic self-government. It follows, therefore, that the United States has a compelling interest for purposes of First Amendment analysis in limiting the participation of foreign citizens in activities of American democratic self-government, and in thereby preventing foreign influence over the U.S. political process.[13]

---

10. *See* Kingsley Int'l Pictures Corp. v. Regents of the University of the State of New York, 360 U.S. 684, 689 (1959) ("[The Constitution] protects expression which is eloquent no less than that which is unconvincing.").

11. The closest case involves the Fourth Amendment. In *United States v. Verdugo-Urquidez*, 494 U.S. 259 (1990), the Court held that the Amendment applied only to those people "who are part of a national community or who have otherwise developed sufficient connection with this country to be considered part of that community." *Id.* at 265. The reasoning of *Verdugo-Urquidez* suggests that foreign nationals (at least those, unlike permanent-resident aliens, lacking a substantial connection to the U.S.) do not have constitutional rights, including the rights to attempt to influence U.S. elections. *But cf.* Boumediene v. Bush, 553 U.S. 723 (2008) (holding that a foreign national could challenge his detention as violating the constitutional guarantee of habeas corpus).

12. Citizens United, Inc. v. FEC, 558 U.S. 310, 365 (2010); *Bellotti*, 435 U.S. at 775–76 (holding that "[t]he proper question ... is not whether corporations 'have' First Amendment rights and, if so, whether they are coextensive with those of natural persons. Instead, the question must be whether [a law] abridges expression that the First Amendment was meant to protect.").

13. Bluman v. FEC, 800 F. Supp. 2d 281, 288 (D.D.C. 2011) (three-judge court), *summarily aff'd* 565 U.S. 1104 (2012). *See also Citizens United*, 558 U.S. at 362 (explicitly not reaching the question whether there is a compelling interest in preventing foreign electoral interference).

Preventing foreigners from communicating information might, however, implicate the rights of Americans to *receive* the information. The Supreme Court precedent on this point is minimal. In *Lamont v. Postmaster General*, the Court held that it was unconstitutional for the postmaster to withhold from U.S. addressees "communist political propaganda" mailed from a foreign country, unless the recipient had indicated his desire to receive it. The Court held that the law abridged the addressee's First Amendment rights, even though refusing to deliver the mail may not have implicated any constitutional rights of the sender.[14]

Might American campaigns have a constitutional right to receive information about opposition candidates, regardless of the source? It is possible, but seems unlikely. *Bluman* held that foreign nationals could be prohibited not only from contributing to campaigns, but also from making expenditures expressly advocating the election or defeat of certain candidates.[15] By holding that foreigners' independent electoral advocacy could be banned, *Bluman* may implicitly have held that there is no First Amendment right of Americans to receive such speech.

Aside from potential First Amendment concerns, a prosecution of Trump Campaign officials for soliciting information from Russia would have been difficult because even if the information was a "thing of value," its value was uncertain. As the Mueller Report noted, the information actually provided was worthless.[16] By itself, that fact does not decide the case; the Trump Campaign still may have solicited an illegal contribution of a "thing of value" even if the information that was delivered actually had no value. In some cases it is possible to assess the value of the information that was solicited — for example, by determining the price that a research firm would have charged to obtain the information that the supplier was offering for free.[17] And if a campaign official solicited information worth $25,000, he is no less guilty of solicitation if the person solicited turns out to be a fraud. Here, however, that was impossible because Trump Jr. did not ask the Russians to obtain information, and did not know what information they were offering. The e-mail to Trump Jr. stated only that the information "would incriminate Hillary and her dealings with Russia and would be very useful to your father." While it is certainly possible that Trump Jr. expected and hoped that the information would be worth a great deal, it would be difficult to say that he solicited something of a value that exceeded the threshold amount.

---

14. *See id.* at 305 ("We conclude that the Act as construed and applied is unconstitutional because it requires an official act (*viz.*, returning the reply card) as a limitation on the unfettered exercise of the addressee's First Amendment rights."). *See also id.* at 308 (Brennan, J., concurring) ("I think the right to receive publications is … a fundamental right. The dissemination of ideas can accomplish nothing if otherwise willing addressees are not free to receive and consider them.").

15. *See Bluman*, 800 F. Supp. 2d at 282–83.

16. *See* Mueller Report, Vol. I, p. 188.

17. In *United States v. Tombrello*, 666 F.2d 485, 489 (11th Cir. 1982), cited by the Mueller Report, the defendant (a robber) was accused of conspiring to transport stolen property worth more than $5000. The robbery was unsuccessful, so the defendant did not transport the requisite amount of stolen property. The court held that there was a conspiracy to do so, however, because the co-conspirators expected to steal more than that amount. *Id.* at 489.

Moreover, the law's scienter requirement posed a substantial obstacle to prosecution. For campaign-finance violations to be criminal, they must be committed "knowingly and willfully," but there is no evidence that Trump Jr. knew that his meeting with the Russians violated the law—if, in fact, it did constitute a violation at all. And given the uncertainty surrounding whether damaging information on an opponent constitutes a "thing of value," it would have been extremely difficult to prove that Trump Jr. was criminally liable.

The messy facts surrounding the June 9 meeting—that the Russians did not actually have dirt on Mrs. Clinton, that there was no evidence that Trump Jr. knew about the campaign-finance restrictions on foreign nationals, and that proving the value of the (nonexistent) information would be difficult—provided ample reasons for the Special Counsel not to prosecute anyone affiliated with the Trump Campaign for soliciting Russian campaign "contributions" in the form of damaging information on Mrs. Clinton.

Nevertheless, the core legal question—whether providing such information amounts to a campaign contribution—remains uncertain. The question is important, for it involves two important values that are in tension with each other. On the one hand, we want candidates to be able to obtain information, and the public interest in obtaining information about candidates for public office is central to the First Amendment. We also want individuals to be free to share information with candidates; in fact, our system of representative government depends on the ability of candidates and voters to share information. On the other hand, our system of self-government may be thought to be undermined if foreign influence undermines the American public's ability to make choices in elections. And if opposition research and other information are immune from campaign-finance laws, contributions could be made well in excess of the current limits, potentially leading to the favoritism and corruption against which contribution limits are designed to protect us.

III. Hush Money as a Campaign Expense

In 2018, Michael Cohen, President Trump's former lawyer, pleaded guilty to several crimes. Two of those crimes were campaign-finance offenses relating to his payment of hush money to two women with whom Trump was alleged to have had affairs. Despite the guilty plea, controversy continues over whether Cohen's conduct actually violated any law. (*See also* Chap. 5, § III.)

The government's theory was that the hush-money payments were designed to influence a federal election, making them "contributions" or "coordinated expenditures" under federal campaign-finance law, and making them subject to limits and reporting requirements.[18] Because the amount of the "contributions" far exceeded the limits, and because there was no reporting of the contributions, the law may have been vi-

---

18. *See* 52 U.S.C. § 30101(8)(A)(i).

olated.[19] Further, if any contributions came from corporations—and at least some of the money appears to have been paid by American Media, Inc., the parent company of the *National Enquirer*—such a contribution would violate the ban on corporate campaign contributions. As to all these issues, the key question is whether the payments should be classified as contributions, which depends on whether they were made "for the purpose of influencing any election for Federal office."[20]

The payments were "for the purpose of influencing an[] election," according to the allegation, because then-Candidate Trump wanted to avoid bad publicity surrounding the alleged mistresses' stories about their relationships with Trump, fearing that the bad publicity would cost him votes. While such a rationale undoubtedly involves, in a literal sense, an attempt to influence an election, there is considerable uncertainty about whether the law should consider these payments to be campaign expenses, instead of personal expenses that Trump faced independent of his status as a candidate.

A. Legal Background

Under campaign-finance law, individuals are limited in the amount they may contribute to federal candidates,[21] and corporations are absolutely prohibited from making contributions.[22] As discussed above in connection with the Russian offers to aid the Trump campaign by providing damaging information about Secretary Clinton, contributions include "anything of value" given "for the purpose of influencing any election for Federal office."[23] Thus, it was illegal for any individual to give the Trump campaign "anything of value" "for the purpose of influencing" the presidential election if the value of the gift exceeded the contribution limit, which was then $2700, and it was illegal for a corporation to give "anything of value" "for the purpose of influencing any election for Federal office," regardless of the value of the gift. It is also illegal to accept an illegal contribution, so both the donor and the recipient of an illegal contribution are potentially liable.[24] Campaign-finance violations are criminal if they are committed "knowingly and willfully."[25]

---

19. Trump's repayment of some of Cohen's expenses raises the possibility that the payments Cohen made were loans. It makes no difference; the law defines "contribution" to include loans. *See id.*

20. *Id.*

21. *See* 52 U.S.C. § 32116(a)(1)(A) (establishing a $2000 limit); 52 U.S.C. § 32116(c)(1)(B) (providing that the limit shall be adjusted for inflation). In 2016 the limit was $2700 per donor, per candidate, per election. The limit is now $2800. *See* 84 Fed. Reg. 2504 (2019); Federal Election Comm'n, *Contribution Limits, at* https://www.fec.gov/help-candidates-and-committees/candidate-taking-receipts/contribution-limits/ (2019). Primary and general elections count as separate elections for purposes of the contribution limits. *See* 52 U.S.C. § 30101(1).

22. *See* 52 U.S.C. § 30118(a).

23. 52 U.S.C. § 30101(8)(A)(i).

24. *See* 52 U.S.C. §§ 30116(f); 30118(a).

25. 52 U.S.C. § 30109(d)(1)(A)(i); *see* Bluman v. FEC, 800 F. Supp. 2d 281, 292 (D.D.C. 2011) (three-judge court) (Kavanaugh, J.); United States v. Danielczyk, 917 F. Supp. 2d 573, 577 (E.D. Va. 2013).

Money raised from contributions may be used to pay campaign expenses but may not be used to pay "personal-use" expenses. Campaign expenses (whether paid with campaign funds or not) must be reported to the Federal Election Commission. Personal-use expenses need not be reported, and are ordinarily paid from a candidate's personal funds.

The difference between campaign expenses and personal expenses is fundamental to maintaining the distinction between campaign-financing and bribery; if a candidate could use campaign funds to pay for vacations and jewelry, then campaign donations would be an easy way to evade bribery laws. It is therefore essential to distinguish between campaign expenses and personal-use expenses.

52 U.S.C. § 30101 —
Definitions

(8)(A) The term "contribution" includes —

(i) any gift, subscription, loan, advance, or deposit of money or anything of value made by any person for the purpose of influencing any election for Federal office * * *.

52 U.S.C. § 32116(a)(7)(B)(i) —
Limitations on contributions and expenditures

[E]xpenditures made by any person in cooperation, consultation, or concert, with, or at the request or suggestion of, a candidate, his authorized political committees, or their agents, shall be considered to be a contribution to such candidate * * *.

52 U.S.C. § 30114 —
Use of contributed amounts for certain purposes

(a) **Permitted uses.** A contribution accepted by a candidate * * * may be used by the candidate * * *—

(1) for otherwise authorized expenditures in connection with the campaign for Federal office of the candidate * * *;

(2) for ordinary and necessary expenses incurred in connection with duties of the individual as a holder of Federal office; * * *

(6) for any other lawful purpose unless prohibited by subsection (b) of this section.

(b) **Prohibited use.**

(1) **In general.** A contribution or donation described in subsection (a) shall not be converted by any person to personal use.

(2) **Conversion.** For the purposes of paragraph (1), a contribution or donation shall be considered to be converted to personal use if the contribution or amount is used to fulfill any commitment, obligation, or expense of a person that would exist irrespective of the candidate's election campaign or individual's duties as a holder of Federal office * * *.

11 C.F.R. § 113.1 —
Definitions

(g) Personal use. Personal use means any use of funds in a campaign account of a present or former candidate to fulfill a commitment, obligation or expense of any person that would exist irrespective of the candidate's campaign or duties as a Federal officeholder. * * *

(6) Third Party Payments. Notwithstanding that the use of funds for a particular expense would be a personal use under this section, payment of that expense by any person other than the candidate or the campaign committee shall be a contribution * * * to the candidate unless the payment would have been made irrespective of the candidacy. Examples of payments considered to be irrespective of the candidacy include, but are not limited to, situations where—

i. The payment is a donation to a legal expense trust fund * * *;

ii. The payment is made from funds that are the candidate's personal funds * * *;

iii. Payments for that expense were made by the person making the payment before the candidate became a candidate. * * *

In sum, campaign funds may not be spent for personal uses, but they may be spent for campaign purposes. Personal uses are those that would exist "irrespective of the candidate's campaign," such as the candidate's mortgage, landscaping, furniture, magazine subscriptions, and general costs of living. The crucial question in evaluating whether a particular payment may be made from campaign funds is thus whether it would have been made "irrespective" of the candidacy.

Expenses that the candidate would have to pay even if he were not running for office are "personal," even if they also help the campaign. Accordingly, candidates may not use campaign funds to pay for stylish clothing or a health-club membership, even if they hope that a good physical appearance will get them more votes. Similarly, legal and travel expenses are campaign expenses only to the extent that they were incurred in connection with the campaign—for example, to ensure compliance with campaign-finance laws or to attend campaign rallies.

B. Facts

In October 2016, two weeks before the presidential election, then-Candidate Donald Trump was facing a scandal relating to his treatment of women. The public had only recently seen the "Access Hollywood" tape, in which Trump spoke in vulgar terms of his liaisons with women. Amid that bad publicity, Trump had to deal with more potentially damaging news. Ten years earlier, Trump appears to have had sexual affairs with two different women: Stephanie Clifford, a pornographic actress who worked under the stage name Stormy Daniels, and Karen McDougal, a former Playboy model. Now both Clifford and McDougal were shopping their stories to the media. (Trump has denied the affairs.) (*See* Chapter 8.)

Michael Cohen, a lawyer who worked for Trump, arranged for payments totaling $280,000 to be made to Clifford and McDougal in exchange for their silence. The $130,000 payment to Clifford appears to have come from Essential Consultants, LLC, a limited-liability company formed very shortly before the payment was made. Cohen initially claimed that he made the payment independently of Trump, although Cohen later changed his story and said that Trump was aware of the payment. Rudolph Giuliani, another of Trump's lawyers, later claimed that Trump had reimbursed Cohen as part of a retainer for Cohen's legal services, without specifically knowing that the money went to Clifford.

The $150,000 payment to McDougal came from American Media, Inc. (AMI), which owns the *National Enquirer*, and was ostensibly for the exclusive rights to McDougal's story. Because AMI's CEO, David Pecker, was a personal friend of Trump's, however, the *Enquirer* had no intention of publishing McDougal's story; the payment was actually part of a plan to ensure that the story would not become public.[26]

After Trump won the election, the story did become public, when both Clifford and McDougal wanted to be released from their non-disclosure agreements. After an investigation, Cohen pleaded guilty in August 2018 to eight charges, including two counts of violating federal campaign-finance laws by arranging the payments "in coordination with, and at the direction of" then-Candidate Trump. AMI reached a non-prosecution agreement with the U.S. Attorney's Office for the Southern District of New York. As part of the agreement, AMI admitted to paying McDougal $150,000 in an attempt to influence the election.

C. The Legal Controversy

If the hush-money payments were "for the purpose of influencing any election for Federal office," they would qualify as contributions, triggering the $2700 limit on individual contributions as well as an obligation on the part of the campaign to report the contribution.[27] Because the "contributions" were in excess of $2700 and were not reported, the law was violated — *if* the hush money was properly regarded as a "contribution."

Even if Trump paid the money himself, there may have been a violation because the payment was not reported. Candidates may personally contribute to their own

---

26. Full analysis is beyond the scope of this Chapter, but it is worth noting that the media exemption, 52 U.S.C. § 30101(9)(B)(i), might permit AMI to make a contribution that would be illegal for non-media corporations to make. That statute exempts "any news story, commentary, or editorial distributed through the facilities of any broadcasting station, newspaper, magazine, or other periodical publication." Thus, had the *Enquirer* published a story favorable to Trump and undermining the credibility of McDougal, the *Enquirer* could not have been punished for an illegal contribution to the Trump Campaign. In the real case, AMI paid the money so that the story would be squelched, rather than published, so the media exemption may not have protected AMI. Still, a media exemption that depends on assessing on the motives for a publisher's decision not to print a story might raise serious First Amendment problems.

27. *See* 52 U.S.C. §§ 30104(a)(3)(A), (b).

campaigns without limit,[28] but even a candidate's own contributions must be reported. And if the money that Cohen paid was a loan, Trump was obligated to report that debt on his financial-disclosure form. He did not report any such debt.

The case for treating the payments as contributions is straightforward. The allegations of affairs were potentially damaging to Trump's image and therefore to his electoral chances. If the payments could ensure that the damaging information would not be released to the public, then Trump would not lose votes from people who would be offended by the alleged affairs, and he would stand a better chance of election. The payments were, then, made for the purpose of influencing the presidential election in a way favorable to Trump.

But that rationale may prove too much. Candidates do a great many things — and incur a great many expenses — to make themselves look more appealing to voters. Yet not all of those expenses are campaign expenses. Expenses for personal uses are not subject to reporting requirements (and may not be paid from campaign funds) even if they are engaged in for the purpose of making the candidate's election more likely. A candidate may not, for example, claim a new suit as a campaign expense, even if he buys the new suit to make a good impression with voters.

So were the payoffs "personal-use" expenses? The timing of the payments is certainly suggestive that influencing the election was a substantial reason for the payments; Cohen and Trump likely would not have spent so much money to conceal allegations of a sexual affair if the allegations would not have posed a threat to Trump's bid for the presidency. After all, he did not make any such hush-money payments in the decade between the alleged affairs and his presidential candidacy. Of course, during that decade the women were not offering to sell their stories to the press, so perhaps the timing is not quite so probative as one might think. The payments were made at the only time when non-payment would have created a risk to Trump's reputation. In any event, it is clear that Trump and his friends had several reasons not to want the allegations to be made public, and surely one important reason was the anticipated effect on the election.

Even so, the payoffs might be personal-use expenses, rather than campaign expenses. Consider the analysis of former FEC Chairman (and current law professor) Bradley Smith:

> [I]magine a wealthy entrepreneur who decides to run for office. * * * The candidate calls in his company attorney: "I want all outstanding lawsuits against our various enterprises settled." His lawyer protests that the suits are without merit — the company should clearly win at trial, and he should protect his reputation of not settling meritless lawsuits. "I agree that these suits lack merit," says our candidate, "but I don't want them as a distraction during the campaign, and I don't want to take the risk that the papers will use them to portray me as a heartless tycoon. Get them settled."

---

28. *See* Buckley v. Valeo, 424 U.S. 1, 51–54 (1976) (*per curiam*).

The settlements in this hypothetical are made "for the purpose of influencing the election," yet they are not "expenditures" under the Federal Election Campaign Act. Indeed, if they were, * * * an unscrupulous but popular businessman could declare his candidacy, gather contributions from the public, use those contributions to settle various preexisting lawsuits, and then withdraw from the race. A nice trick!

But in fact, the contrary rule prevails, because the candidate's obligation to resolve the business's lawsuits exists "irrespective" of the campaign. Similarly, any payments made to women by Mr. Trump or his associates are independent of the campaign.[29]

Are hush-money payments analogous to the lawsuits hypothesized by Professor Smith? Does the hypothetical businessman have more of an "obligation to resolve the business's lawsuits" than Trump had to control the public-relations fallout from his alleged mistresses' stories? Would it have made any difference if the payments were settlements of suits alleging sexual harassment or unpaid child support?

There is not much precedent on point. The only roughly parallel case is the 2011 prosecution of former Senator John Edwards, who had been a candidate for President and a candidate for Vice President. The case involved nearly $1 million paid to Edwards's mistress in an attempt to conceal Edwards's affair from his wife, voters, or both. He was tried for campaign-finance violations on the same theory that applied to Cohen—that the payoffs were illegal campaign contributions. Although the judge in Edwards's case permitted the case to go to the jury, the jury found Edwards not guilty on one count and deadlocked on the other five counts. As a result, the defense could not appeal the judge's ruling on the question whether the payments could legally be considered campaign contributions.[30] Thus, although Cohen's case is not the first of its kind, the sole analogous precedent does not resolve the question whether hush-money payments are personal-use or campaign expenditures, or the question whether a third party who pays those expenses would be making a campaign contribution.

Even if the hush-money payments were "personal-use" expenses, Cohen may still be in legal trouble for making them on Trump's behalf. Recall that FEC regulations make it illegal for a third party to pay a candidate's personal-use expenses, treating such payments as contributions. If Cohen made the payments in consultation with Trump or the Trump Campaign (as he admitted as part of his plea deal), they would

---

29. Bradley A. Smith, *Michael Cohen Pled Guilty to Something That Is Not a Crime*, Nat'l Rev., Dec. 12, 2018, *at* https://www.nationalreview.com/2018/12/michael-cohen-sentencing-campaign-finance-law/.

30. Two former FEC Commissioners (Thomas and Lenhardt) testified in the case that the FEC would not consider Edwards's payments to be campaign expenditures. Two more (Smith and von Spakovsky) have argued that Trump's payments are not campaign expenditures. One (Potter) has argued to the contrary. *See* George T. Conway III, Trevor Potter, & Neal Katyal, *Trump's Claim that He Didn't Violate Campaign Finance Law Is Weak—and Dangerous*, Wash. Post, Dec. 14, 2018, *at* https://www.washingtonpost.com/outlook/2018/12/14/trumps-claim-that-he-didnt-violate-campaign-finance-law-is-weak-dangerous/?noredirect=on&utm_term=.e6763caaf2f7.

be "coordinated expenditures" in excess of the legal limit. If the payments came from a corporation (Essential Consultants, AMI, or both), FEC regulations would have treated the payments as contributions to the campaign, in violation of the ban on corporate contributions, unless they would have been made irrespective of the candidacy. And even if Cohen made the payments himself (as Cohen originally claimed), those same FEC regulations would have treated such third-party payments as contributions to the campaign—in excess of the legal limit—unless the payments would have been made irrespective of the candidacy. (If the payments came from Trump's personal resources, however, they would not be "third-party payments" and therefore would not be problematic.)[31]

How can this be? Aren't "personal-use" expenses by definition those that would exist irrespective of the candidacy? How can a third-party payment for a personal-use expense be a contribution unless it would have been made irrespective of the candidacy, if personal-use expenses by definition are those that would exist irrespective of the candidacy? The answer may lie in a subtle shift of language in the FEC regulation. Notice that the FEC's definition of "personal use" asks whether the "*expense*" "would exist irrespective of the candidate's campaign," whereas the regulation says that third-party payments for personal expenses shall be treated as contributions "unless the *payment* would have been made irrespective of the candidacy."

The small but significant difference in language makes sense when one considers the purpose of the restriction. Personal-use expenses are those debts or obligations that would be incurred irrespective of the candidacy. But if those personal-use expenses would not have been *paid* by a third party were it not for the campaign, then payments that are made during a campaign could count as contributions. For example, a candidate's student-loan payments are personal-use expenses because the candidate would have an obligation to pay them whether or not he was running for office. Because the payments would be for a personal use, it would be illegal to make the payments out of campaign funds.

If a third party made the student-loan payments for the candidate, those payments would be contributions to the candidate's campaign unless that third-party would have made the payment irrespective of the candidacy. For example, if the candidate's employer had been paying the candidate's student loans regularly, the employer could continue to do so without the payments being considered campaign contributions.

The difficulty in the Trump case is that the hush-money payments did not begin until Trump became a candidate. The payments would therefore not be covered by the safe harbor in the FEC regulations for "[p]ayments for [a personal-use] expense [that] were made by the person making the payment before the candidate became a candidate."[32] In other words, the FEC regulation says that third-party payments of personal-use expenses may *continue* while the beneficiary is a candidate, but third-

---

31. *See* 11 C.F.R. § 113.1(g)(6)(ii) (stating that payments from a "candidate's personal funds" shall not be considered to be third-party contributions).

32. 11 C.F.R. § 113.1.

party payments of personal-use expenses may not be begun during the campaign if the payments would not have been made had the beneficiary not run for office. Ultimately, however, the determining factor is not the date on which the payments began, but whether the payments would have been made irrespective of the candidacy.[33]

So would the payments have been made irrespective of Trump's candidacy? We cannot know for sure, but here are some possibilities:

1. If Trump had not become a candidate for president, Clifford and McDougal would not have threatened to tell their stories publicly, and so the payments would not have been made because the expenses would not have been necessary.

2. If Trump had not become a candidate for President, Clifford and McDougal would have threatened to tell their stories publicly and Trump (or his corporation or AMI) would have made the payments to keep the alleged affairs secret from his family.

3. If Trump had not become a candidate for President, Clifford and McDougal would have threatened to tell their stories publicly and Trump (or his corporation or AMI) would have declined to pay hush money. Under this scenario, the money was paid only to help Trump's electoral chances; he was not sufficiently concerned about the impact on his family to justify paying the money for that reason alone.

In scenario 2, the expenditures were made irrespective of the candidacy. In scenario 3, the expenditures were not made irrespective of the candidacy; the candidacy was the key factor causing the expenditures to be made.

In scenario 1 — perhaps the most likely scenario, given that Clifford and McDougal did not seek to publicize their stories until Trump became a presidential candidate — the expenditures were made because of the candidacy, but in a counter-intuitive sense: Clifford and McDougal — not Trump — behaved differently because of the candidacy. In such a situation, it makes little sense to have liability turn on the motivations of people other than the candidate and the third-party donor. Rather, the best approach would appear to be asking whether — if the candidate had not run for office *and* Clifford and McDougal had nonetheless gone to the press with their stories — the third-parties would have made the payments. Such an inquiry would involve the subjective and difficult attempt to determine a counter-factual, but that is inherent in asking whether a person acted a certain way "irrespective of" a given fact.

* * *

There is considerable irony in the claim that the Trump Campaign committed a campaign-finance violation by making, and failing to report, the hush-money payments: Proving a violation requires one to conclude that buying an alleged mistress's

---

33. *Id.* (stating explicitly that its list of permissible third-party payments, including continuing third-party payments of personal-use expenses, are only non-exclusive "[e]xamples of payments considered to be irrespective of the candidacy").

silence is a campaign expense. If buying an alleged mistress's silence is a campaign expense, however, the hush-money payments could be made from campaign funds. Would it not have been an even larger scandal if the Trump Campaign had used campaign funds to pay off Clifford and McDougal?

The better reading of the law is that the payments to Clifford and McDougal were personal-use expenses that could not be paid from campaign funds. The more difficult question is whether a third-party's payment of those personal-use expenses should be treated as a contribution to the campaign. The answer to that should turn on whether the third party would have made the payments if the candidate had not run for office—if the effect on the voters was the *sine qua non* behind the third party's decision to pay.

Chapter Seven

Obstruction of Justice

I. Generally

Obstruction of justice in the federal system encompasses a host of different federal criminal laws that are found in chapter 73 of Title 18 of the United States Code. The statutes cover obstruction involving an assault on a process server (18 U.S.C. § 1501) to obstruction pertaining to retaliating against a federal judge or federal law enforcement officer by false claims or slander of title (18 U.S.C. § 1521). The statutes can be specific to unique circumstances, such as obstructing a federal audit (18 U.S.C. § 1516), yet can also be general obstruction statutes, such as focusing on obstruction to the due administration of justice (18 U.S.C. § 1503). This latter statute originates from a contempt statute (Act of March 2, 1831) which was later split into two offenses: contempt within a courtroom and obstruction outside the courtroom. The generic obstruction statute for conduct outside the courtroom is the current § 1503 statute.

Because obstruction statutes are relatively easy to prove in comparison to technical and evidence filled statutes, it is one of several crimes that have become "shortcuts offenses" in the federal system. *See* Ellen S. Podgor, *White Collar Shortcuts*, 2018 Ill. L. Rev. 925 (2018). As opposed to charging the underlying conduct, which may be difficult for a jury to understand, crimes such as perjury (18 U.S.C. 1621), false statements (18 U.S.C. § 1001), and obstruction of justice have become common tools for prosecutors. One finds the use of these "shortcut offenses" in both plea agreements and charging documents. For example, Michael Cohen's plea with Special Counsel Mueller's Office was to false statements under 18 U.S.C. § 1001 (a)(2) and Richard W. Gates III's plea agreement included making false statements to Special Agents of the Federal Bureau of Investigation in violation of 18 U.S.C. § 1001. Special Counsel Mueller also charged several individuals under obstruction of justice statutes. For example, these charges can be found in the Indictments of Roger Jason Stone, Jr. (the seven counts were for one count of obstruction of an official proceeding, five counts for false statements, and one count of witness tampering) and Konstantin Kilimnick (conspiracy to obstruct justice and obstruction of justice).

The generic obstruction of justice statute, found in 18 U.S.C. § 1503 is often used today, even when the conduct may fit a newer and more specific obstruction statute. For example, the Victim and Witness Protection Act of 1982 added 18 U.S.C. § 1512, that focuses on witness tampering, and 18 U.S.C. § 1513, that focuses on retaliation on a witness, victim, or informant. The Sarbanes Oxley Act of 2002 added two new obstruction statutes: 18 U.S.C. § 1519, focusing on destruction alteration, or falsification of records in federal investigations and bankruptcy, and 18 U.S.C. § 1520, focusing on the destruction of audit records. Supreme Court and lower court decisions have provided the contours of these statutes with their court interpretations.

This chapter in Part II looks at the key statutes used in Volume II of the Mueller Report. Part III of this chapter looks first at key cases that are often used to interpret these statutes and second the analysis used in the Mueller Report to interpret the elements of obstruction of Justice. Part IV looks at each of the twelve points raised in the Mueller Report regarding obstruction of justice. For each of these points, the executive summary from the Mueller Report is provided. In ten of these points, the executive summary is followed by the legal analysis provided in the Mueller Report that relates to the facts provided. Omitted in this discussion is the evidence on each of these points that is provided in detail in the Mueller Report, Vol. II. Also omitted are the extensive footnotes included in the legal analysis provided in the Mueller Report, Vol. II. Finally, in Part V of this chapter is the Executive Summary of the Statutory and Constitutional Defenses. Here again, the detailed analysis of the defenses is omitted. All of the omitted items can be found in the Report located at https://www.justice.gov/storage/report.pdf. Attorney General William Barr's response to the Mueller Report, including his response to Vol II's discussion on obstruction of justice, can be found in Chapter One of this book.

II. Statutory Basis

Volume II of the Mueller Report focuses on three federal obstruction statutes: 18 U.S.C. §§ 1503, 1505, and 1512. The following are the key provisions from these statutes:

§ 1503. Influencing or injuring officer or juror generally

(a) Whoever corruptly, or by threats or force, or by any threatening letter or communication, endeavors to influence, intimidate, or impede any grand or petit juror, or officer in or of any court of the United States, or officer who may be serving at any examination or other proceeding before any United States magistrate judge or other committing magistrate, in the discharge of his duty, or injures any such grand or petit juror in his person or property on account of any verdict or indictment assented to by him, or on account of his being or having been such juror, or injures any such officer, magistrate judge, or other committing magistrate in his person or property on account of the performance of his official duties, or corruptly or by threats or force, or by any threatening letter or communication, influences, obstructs, or impedes, or endeavors to influence, obstruct, or impede, the due administration of justice, shall be punished as provided in subsection (b). If the offense under this section occurs in connection with a trial of a criminal case, and the act in violation of this section involves the threat of physical force or physical force, the maximum term of imprisonment which may be imposed for the offense shall be the higher of that otherwise provided by law or the maximum term that could have been imposed for any offense charged in such case.

(b) The punishment for an offense under this section is—

(1) in the case of a killing, the punishment provided in sections 1111 and 1112;

(2) in the case of an attempted killing, or a case in which the offense was committed against a petit juror and in which a class A or B felony was charged, imprisonment for not more than 20 years, a fine under this title, or both; and

(3) in any other case, imprisonment for not more than 10 years, a fine under this title, or both.

§ 1505. Obstruction of proceedings before departments, agencies, and committees

Whoever, with intent to avoid, evade, prevent, or obstruct compliance, in whole or in part, with any civil investigative demand duly and properly made under the Antitrust Civil Process Act, willfully withholds, misrepresents, removes from any place, conceals, covers up, destroys, mutilates, alters, or by other means falsifies any documentary material, answers to written interrogatories, or oral testimony, which is the subject of such demand; or attempts to do so or solicits another to do so; or

Whoever corruptly, or by threats or force, or by any threatening letter or communication influences, obstructs, or impedes or endeavors to influence, obstruct, or impede the due and proper administration of the law under which any pending proceeding is being had before any department or agency of the United States, or the due and proper exercise of the power of inquiry under which any inquiry or investigation is being had by either House, or any committee of either House or any joint committee of the Congress—

Shall be fined under this title, imprisoned not more than 5 years or, if the offense involves international or domestic terrorism (as defined in section 2331), imprisoned not more than 8 years, or both.

§ 1512. Tampering with a witness, victim, or an informant

* * *

(b) Whoever knowingly uses intimidation, threatens, or corruptly persuades another person, or attempts to do so, or engages in misleading conduct toward another person, with intent to—

    * * *

(3) hinder, delay, or prevent the communication to a law enforcement officer or judge of the United States of information relating to the commission or possible commission of a Federal offense or a violation of conditions of probation supervised release, parole, or release pending judicial proceedings;

shall be fined under this title or imprisoned not more than 20 years, or both.

(c) Whoever corruptly—

(1) alters, destroys, mutilates, or conceals a record, document, or other object, or attempts to do so, with the intent to impair the object's integrity or availability for use in an official proceeding; or

(2) otherwise obstructs, influences, or impedes any official proceeding, or attempts to do so,

shall be fined under this title or imprisoned not more than 20 years, or both.

* * *

(e) In a prosecution for an offense under this section, it is an affirmative defense, as to which the defendant has the burden of proof by a preponderance of the evidence, that the conduct consisted solely of lawful conduct and that the defendant's sole intention was to encourage, induce, or cause the other person to testify truthfully.

(f) For the purposes of this section—

(1) an official proceeding need not be pending or about to be instituted at the time of the offense; and

(2) the testimony, or the record, document, or other object need not be admissible in evidence or free of a claim of privilege.

(g) In a prosecution for an offense under this section, no state of mind need be proved with respect to the circumstance—

(1) that the official proceeding before a judge, court, magistrate judge, grand jury, or government agency is before a judge or court of the United States, a United States magistrate judge, a bankruptcy judge, a Federal grand jury, or a Federal Government agency; or

(2) that the judge is a judge of the United States or that the law enforcement officer is an officer or employee of the Federal Government or a person authorized to act for or on behalf of the Federal Government or serving the Federal Government as an adviser or consultant.

* * *

(k) Whoever conspires to commit any offense under this section shall be subject to the same penalties as those prescribed for the offense the commission of which was the object of the conspiracy.

III. Interpreting the Statutes

A. Select Cases

The Mueller Report provides for three elements for obstruction of justice: "(1) an obstructive act; (2) a nexus between the obstructive act and an official proceeding;

and (3) a corrupt intent." The Report does note some distinctions when examining witness intimidation. It also speaks to the "requirements for attempted offenses and endeavors to obstruct justice." Consider the following three cases that highlight some of the elements needed for an obstruction of justice case.

United States v. Cueto
151 F.3d 620 (7th Cir. 1998)

Circuit Judge Bauer:

After a jury trial, Amiel Cueto was convicted of one count of conspiracy to defraud the United States, in violation of 18 U.S.C. § 371, and three counts of obstruction of justice, in violation of the omnibus clause of 18 U.S.C. § 1503. The district court sentenced Cueto [an attorney] to 87 months imprisonment and imposed monetary penalties. [On appeal he argued unsuccessfully] challenge[d] each conviction for obstruction of justice in violation of the omnibus clause of § 1503 as invalid, arguing that: (1) the omnibus clause of § 1503 is unconstitutionally vague as applied to the conduct charged in the indictment; (2) the omnibus clause of § 1503 does not cover either the filing of court papers or attempts to encourage a state prosecutor to investigate another state official for misconduct; (3) the conduct charged fails to satisfy the nexus requirement as articulated by the Supreme Court in *United States v. Aguilar*, 515 U.S. 593 (1995); and (4) an attempt to persuade a prosecutor to take action against a state officer for misconduct is speech protected by the First Amendment. * * *

The omnibus clause of § 1503 is a catch-all provision that states:

> Whoever ... *corruptly* or by threats or force, or by any threatening letter or communication, influences, obstructs, or impedes or *endeavors* to influence, obstruct or impede, the due administration of law, shall be imprisoned....

18 U.S.C. § 1503 (emphasis added). This clause was intended to ensure that criminals could not circumvent the statute's purpose "by devising novel and creative schemes that would interfere with the administration of justice but would nonetheless fall outside the scope of § 1503's specific prohibitions." * * * "The obstruction of justice statute was drafted with an eye to 'the variety of corrupt methods by which the proper administration of justice may be impeded or thwarted, a variety limited only by the imagination of the criminally inclined.'" * * *

Cueto also contends that the vagueness problems are exacerbated by this court's broad construction of the term "corruptly," arguing that it fails to provide meaningful and adequate notice as to what conduct is proscribed by the statute. The Seventh Circuit has approved a jury instruction which articulates a definition for the term "corruptly," and the district court judge included this definition in its instructions to the jury:

> Corruptly means to act with the purpose of obstructing justice. The United States is not required to prove that the defendant's only or even main purpose was to obstruct the due administration of justice. The government only has to establish that the defendant should have reasonably seen that the natural and probable consequences of his acts was the obstruction of justice. Intent may be inferred from all of the sur-

rounding facts and circumstances. Any act, by any party, whether lawful or unlawful on its face, may violate Section 1503, if performed with a corrupt motive.

* * * The mere fact that a term "covers a broad spectrum of conduct" does not render it vague, and the requirement that a statute must give fair notice as to what conduct is proscribed "cannot be used as a shield by one who is already bent on serious wrongdoing." * * *

There is little case authority directly on point to consider whether an attorney acting in his professional capacity could be criminally liable under the omnibus clause of §1503 for traditional litigation-related conduct that results in an obstruction of justice. "Correct application of Section 1503 thus requires, in a very real sense, that the factfinder discern—by direct evidence or from inference—the motive which led an individual to perform particular actions.... 'Intent may make any otherwise innocent act criminal, if it is a step in a plot.'" * * * Therefore, it is not the means employed by the defendant that are specifically prohibited by the statute; instead, it is the defendant's corrupt endeavor which motivated the action. Otherwise lawful conduct, even acts undertaken by an attorney in the course of representing a client, can transgress §1503 if employed with the corrupt intent to accomplish that which the statute forbids. * * *

We are not persuaded by Cueto's constitutional challenges, and his focus is misplaced. The government's theory of prosecution is predicated on the fact that Cueto held a personal financial interest in protecting the illegal gambling enterprise, which formed the requisite corrupt intent for his conduct to qualify as violations of the statute. * * * Cueto focuses entirely on the legality of his conduct, and not the requisite criminal intent proscribed by §1503. It is undisputed that an attorney may use any *lawful* means to defend his client, and there is no risk of criminal liability if those means employed by the attorney in his endeavors to represent his client remain within the scope of lawful conduct. However, it is the corrupt endeavor to protect the illegal gambling operation and to safeguard his own financial interest, which motivated Cueto's otherwise legal conduct, that separates his conduct from that which is legal.

Even though courts may be hesitant, with good reason and caution, to include traditional litigation-related conduct within the scope of §1503, the omnibus clause has been interpreted broadly in accordance with congressional intent to promote the due administration of justice and to prevent the miscarriage of justice, and an individual's status as an attorney engaged in litigation-related conduct does not provide protection from prosecution for criminal conduct. * * * There is a discernable difference between an honest lawyer who unintentionally submits a false statement to the court and an attorney with specific corrupt intentions who files papers in bad faith knowing that they contain false representations and/or inaccurate facts in an attempt to hinder judicial proceedings. It is true that, to a certain extent, a lawyer's conduct influences judicial proceedings, or at least attempts to affect the outcome of the proceedings. However, that influence stems from a lawyer's attempt to advocate his client's interests *within the scope of the law*. It is the "corrupt endeavor" to influence the due administration of justice that is the heart of the offense, and Cueto's personal financial interest is the heart of his corrupt motive.

* * *

Nothing in the caselaw, fairly read, suggests that lawyers should be plucked gently from the maddening crowd and sheltered from the rigors of 18 U.S.C. § 1503 in the manner urged by appellant and by the amici. Nor is there sufficient public policy justification favoring such a result. To the contrary, the overriding public policy interest is that "[t]he attorney-client relationship cannot … be used to shield or promote illegitimate acts.…" "[A]ttorneys, just like all other persons, … are not above the law and are subject to its full application under appropriate circumstances." * * * Accordingly, we conclude that the omnibus clause of § 1503 may be used to prosecute a lawyer's litigation-related criminality and that neither the omnibus clause of § 1503 nor this court's construction of the term "corruptly" is unconstitutionally vague as applied to the conduct charged in the indictment for which Cueto was convicted.

We now turn to Cueto's argument that his convictions on the obstruction of justice counts were not supported by sufficient evidence. Cueto's task is a formidable one, and an examination of the record illuminates that the evidence presented in this case overwhelmingly supports the jury's verdict. In order to establish a violation of § 1503, the government must demonstrate that: (1) there was a pending judicial proceeding; (2) the defendant knew of the proceeding; (3) he influenced, obstructed, or impeded, or endeavored to influence, obstruct or impede the due administration of justice; and (4) he did so corruptly. * * * There must be a nexus between the defendant's efforts and the judicial proceeding sought to be corruptly influenced. * * * However, a defendant's actions need not be successful in order to be prosecuted under the statute. All that is required is that the defendant has knowledge or notice that his actions are likely to affect the just administration of the subject proceedings. * * *

The charges in Count 2 of the indictment included allegations of a corrupt endeavor to obstruct the due administration of justice in *Venezia* v. *Robinson* by filing pleadings in federal district court and a continued attempt to hinder the proceedings by filing an appeal in this court and a petition for certiorari in the United States Supreme Court. * * * Cueto's actions may qualify as traditional litigation-related conduct in form, but not in substance, and the evidence presented at trial demonstrates that Cueto clearly intended and corruptly endeavored to obstruct the due administration of justice in *Venezia v. Robinson*.

Similar to Count 2, Count 7 includes allegations of preparing and filing and causing defense counsel to prepare and file false pleadings and other court papers; the indictment specifically charged Cueto with encouraging defense counsel in the racketeering case to file false motions and pleadings for the purpose of impeding and obstructing the administration of justice in that case. We have no doubt that Cueto in fact intended to interfere with the investigation, attempted to delay the indictment, and endeavored to obstruct the proceedings in federal district court in connection with the prosecution of Venezia. * * * We simply are not dealing with non-corrupt, legitimate involvement in the preparation of Venezia's (and his co-defendants') defense. Nor are we dealing with inadvertent interference. From the evidence presented at trial, the jury was amply justified in concluding without a doubt that Cueto corruptly endeavored to obstruct the district court's proceedings in the gambling and racketeering prosecution.

In response to his conviction on Count 6, Cueto argues that his conviction should be reversed because the *Aguilar* nexus is absent; he contends that the government presented insufficient evidence to establish the relationship between his attempts to persuade State's Attorney Haida to investigate and indict Robinson and a pending judicial proceeding. Cueto contends that at the time the conduct charged in the indictment occurred, the grand jury had not yet been empaneled and that Venezia had not been indicted in the racketeering case, and therefore the nexus is lacking. His argument, however, mischaracterizes the frame of time at issue in addition to the indictment and the charges therein. "It is well established that investigations undertaken with the intention of presenting evidence before a grand jury are sufficient to constitute 'the due administration of justice' under § 1503." * * *

* * * We refuse to accept the notion that lawyers may do anything, including violating the law, to zealously advocate their clients' interests and then avoid criminal prosecution by claiming that they were "just doing their job." * * * We respect the importance of allowing defense counsel to perform legitimate activities without hindrance and recognize the potential dangers that could arise if prosecutors were permitted to inquire into the motives of criminal defense attorneys ad hoc. * * * His role as a defense attorney did not insulate him from the criminal consequences of his corruptly-motivated actions. Accordingly, we affirm Cueto's convictions on Counts 2, 6, and 7. * * * we affirm the defendant's convictions and the sentence imposed by the district court.

United States v. Aguilar

515 U.S. 593 (1995)

Chief Justice REHNQUIST delivered the opinion of the Court.

A jury convicted United States District Judge Robert Aguilar of one count of illegally disclosing a wiretap in violation of 18 U.S.C. § 2232(c), and of one count of endeavoring to obstruct the due administration of justice in violation of § 1503. A panel of the Court of Appeals for the Ninth Circuit affirmed the conviction under § 2232(c) but reversed the conviction under § 1503. After rehearing en banc, the Court of Appeals reversed both convictions. We granted certiorari to resolve a conflict among the Federal Circuits over whether § 1503 punishes false statements made to potential grand jury witnesses, and to answer the important question whether disclosure of a wiretap after its authorization expires violates § 2232(c). * * *

Many facts remain disputed by the parties. Both parties appear to agree, however, that a motion for postconviction relief filed by one Michael Rudy Tham represents the starting point from which events bearing on this case unfolded. Tham was an officer of the International Brotherhood of Teamsters, and was convicted of embezzling funds from the local affiliate of that organization. In July 1987, he filed a motion under 28 U.S.C. § 2255 to have his conviction set aside. The motion was assigned to

Judge Stanley Weigel. Tham, seeking to enhance the odds that his petition would be granted, asked Edward Solomon and Abraham Chalupowitz, a.k.a. Abe Chapman, to assist him by capitalizing on their respective acquaintances with another judge in the Northern District of California, respondent Aguilar. Respondent knew Chapman as a distant relation by marriage and knew Solomon from law school. Solomon and Chapman met with respondent to discuss Tham's case, as a result of which respondent spoke with Judge Weigel about the matter.

Independent of the embezzlement conviction, the Federal Bureau of Investigation (FBI) identified Tham as a suspect in an investigation of labor racketeering. On April 20, 1987, the FBI applied for authorization to install a wiretap on Tham's business phones. Chapman appeared on the application as a potential interceptee. Chief District Judge Robert Peckham authorized the wiretap. The 30-day wiretap expired by law on May 20, 1987, 18 U.S.C. §2518(5), but Chief Judge Peckham maintained the secrecy of the wiretap under §2518(8)(d) after a showing of good cause. During the course of the racketeering investigation, the FBI learned of the meetings between Chapman and respondent. The FBI informed Chief Judge Peckham, who, concerned with appearances of impropriety, advised respondent in August 1987 that Chapman might be connected with criminal elements because Chapman's name had appeared on a wiretap authorization.

Five months after respondent learned that Chapman had been named in a wiretap authorization, he noticed a man observing his home during a visit by Chapman. He alerted his nephew to this fact and conveyed the message (with an intent that his nephew relay the information to Chapman) that Chapman's phone was being wire-tapped. Respondent apparently believed, in error, both that Chapman's phones were tapped in connection with the initial application and that the initial authorization was still in effect. Chief Judge Peckham had in fact authorized another wiretap on Tham's phones effective from October 1987 through the period in which respondent made the disclosure, but there is no suggestion in the record that the latter had any specific knowledge of this reauthorization.

At this point, respondent's involvement in the two separate Tham matters con-verged. Two months after the disclosure to his nephew, a grand jury began to inves-tigate an alleged conspiracy to influence the outcome of Tham's habeas case. Two FBI agents questioned respondent. During the interview, respondent lied about his participation in the Tham case and his knowledge of the wiretap. The grand jury re-turned an indictment; a jury convicted Aguilar of one count of disclosing a wiretap, 18 U.S.C. §2232(c), and one count of endeavoring to obstruct the due administration of justice, §1503. * * *

Respondent was charged with a violation of the Omnibus Clause, to wit: with "corruptly endeavor[ing] to influence, obstruct, and impede the … grand jury in-vestigation."

The first case from this Court construing the predecessor statute to §1503 was Pettibone v. United States, 148 U.S. 197 (1893). There we held that "a person is not sufficiently charged with obstructing or impeding the due administration of justice in a court unless it appears that he knew or had notice that justice was being administered in such court." * * * The Court reasoned that a person lacking knowledge of a pending proceeding necessarily lacked the evil intent to obstruct. * * * Recent decisions of Courts of Appeals have likewise tended to place metes and bounds on the very broad language of the catchall provision. The action taken by the accused must be with an intent to influence judicial or grand jury proceedings; it is not enough that there be an intent to influence some ancillary proceeding, such as an investigation independent of the court's or grand jury's authority. * * * In other words, the endeavor must have the "'natural and probable effect'" of interfering with the due administration of justice. * * * This is not to say that the defendant's actions need be successful; an "endeavor" suffices. * * * But as in *Pettibone*, if the defendant lacks knowledge that his actions are likely to affect the judicial proceeding, he lacks the requisite intent to obstruct.

* * * We do not believe that uttering false statements to an investigating agent — and that seems to be all that was proved here — who might or might not testify before a grand jury is sufficient to make out a violation of the catchall provision of § 1503.

The Government did not show here that the agents acted as an arm of the grand jury, or indeed that the grand jury had even summoned the testimony of these particular agents. The Government argues that respondent "understood that his false statements would be provided to the grand jury" and that he made the statements with the intent to thwart the grand jury investigation and not just the FBI investigation. * * * The Government supports its argument with a citation to the transcript of the recorded conversation between Aguilar and the FBI agent at the point where Aguilar asks whether he is a target of a grand jury investigation. The agent responded to the question by stating:

> "[T]here is a Grand Jury meeting. Convening I guess that's the correct word. Um some evidence will be heard I'm ... I'm sure on this issue." * * *

Because respondent knew of the pending proceeding, the Government therefore contends that Aguilar's statements are analogous to those made directly to the grand jury itself, in the form of false testimony or false documents.

We think the transcript citation relied upon by the Government would not enable a rational trier of fact to conclude that respondent knew that his false statement would be provided to the grand jury, and that the evidence goes no further than showing that respondent testified falsely to an investigating agent. Such conduct, we believe, falls on the other side of the statutory line from that of one who delivers false documents or testimony to the grand jury itself. Conduct of the latter sort all but assures that the grand jury will consider the material in its deliberations. But what use will be made of false testimony given to an investigating agent who has not been subpoenaed or otherwise directed to appear before the grand jury is far more speculative. We think it cannot be said to have the "natural and probable effect" of interfering with the due administration of justice.

Justice SCALIA criticizes our treatment of the statutory language for reading the word "endeavor" out of it, inasmuch as it excludes defendants who have an evil purpose but use means that would "only unnaturally and improbably be successful." This criticism is unwarranted. Our reading of the statute gives the term "endeavor" a useful function to fulfill: It makes conduct punishable where the defendant acts with an intent to obstruct justice, and in a manner that is likely to obstruct justice, but is foiled in some way. Were a defendant with the requisite intent to lie to a subpoenaed witness who is ultimately not called to testify, or who testifies but does not transmit the defendant's version of the story, the defendant has endeavored to obstruct, but has not actually obstructed, justice. Under our approach, a jury could find such defendant guilty.

Justice SCALIA also apparently believes that any act, done with the intent to "obstruct ... the due administration of justice," is sufficient to impose criminal liability. Under the dissent's theory, a man could be found guilty under § 1503 if he knew of a pending investigation and lied to his wife about his whereabouts at the time of the crime, thinking that an FBI agent might decide to interview her and that she might in turn be influenced in her statement to the agent by her husband's false account of his whereabouts. The intent to obstruct justice is indeed present, but the man's culpability is a good deal less clear from the statute than we usually require in order to impose criminal liability.

II

[The Court then discussed section 2232(c)].

We affirm the decision of the Court of Appeals with respect to respondent's conviction under § 1503 and reverse with respect to respondent's conviction under § 2232(c). We remand for proceedings consistent with this decision. * * *

Justice STEVENS, concurring in part and dissenting in part.

Although I agree with the Court's disposition of the 18 U.S.C. § 1503 issue, and also with its rejection of the First Amendment challenge to respondent's conviction for disclosing a wiretap application under § 2232(c), I believe the Court of Appeals correctly construed § 2232(c) to invalidate respondent's conviction under that statute. * * * I would affirm the decision of the Court of Appeals in its entirety.

Justice SCALIA, with whom Justice KENNEDY and Justice THOMAS join, concurring in part and dissenting in part.

I join all but Part I and the last paragraph of Part II of the Court's opinion. I would reverse the Court of Appeals, and would uphold respondent's conviction, on the count charging violation of 18 U.S.C. § 1503.

I

The "omnibus clause" of § 1503, under which respondent was charged, provides:

"Whoever ... corruptly or by threats or force, or by any threatening letter or communication, influences, obstructs, or impedes, or endeavors to influence, obstruct, or impede, the due administration of justice, shall be fined not more than $5,000 or imprisoned not more than five years, or both."

This makes criminal not just success in corruptly influencing the due administration of justice, but also the "endeavor" to do so. We have given this latter proscription, which respondent was specifically charged with violating, * * *, a generous reading: "The word of the section is 'endeavor,' and by using it the section got rid of the technicalities which might be urged as besetting the word 'attempt,' and it describes *any effort or essay* to accomplish the evil purpose that the section was enacted to prevent." * * * Under this reading of the statute, it is even immaterial whether the endeavor to obstruct pending proceedings is possible of accomplishment. * * *

Even read at its broadest, however, § 1503's prohibition of "endeavors" to impede justice is not without limits. To "endeavor" means to strive or work for a certain end. Webster's New International Dictionary 844 (2d ed. 1950); 1 New Shorter Oxford English Dictionary 816 (1993). Thus, § 1503 reaches only *purposeful* efforts to obstruct the due administration of justice, i.e., acts performed with that very object in mind. * * * This limitation was clearly set forth in our first decision construing § 1503's predecessor statute, Pettibone, which held an indictment insufficient because it had failed to allege the intent to obstruct justice. That opinion rejected the Government's contention that the intent required to violate the statute could be found in "the intent to commit an unlawful act, in the doing of which justice was in fact obstructed"; to justify a conviction, it said, "the specific intent to violate the statute must exist." * * * *Pettibone* did acknowledge, however—and here is the point that is distorted to produce today's opinion—that the specific intent to obstruct justice could be found where the defendant intentionally committed a wrongful act that had obstruction of justice as its "natural and probable consequence." * * *

Today's "nexus" requirement sounds like this, but is in reality quite different. Instead of reaffirming that "natural and probable consequence" is one way of establishing intent, it *substitutes* " ""natural and probable effect" " " *for* intent, requiring that factor even when intent to obstruct justice is otherwise clear. * * * But while it is quite proper to derive an *intent* requirement from § 1503's use of the word "endeavor," it is quite impossible to derive a *"natural and probable consequence"* requirement. One would be "endeavoring" to obstruct justice if he intentionally set out to do it by means that would only unnaturally and improbably be successful. * * *

The Court does not indicate where its "nexus" requirement is to be found in the words of the statute. Instead, it justifies its holding with the assertion that "[w]e have traditionally exercised restraint in assessing the reach of a federal criminal statute, both out of deference to the prerogatives of Congress and out of concern that a fair warning should be given … of what the law intends to do if a certain line is passed." * * * But "exercising restraint *in assessing the reach* of a federal criminal statute" (which is what the rule of lenity requires * * *) is quite different from importing extratextual requirements *in order to limit the reach* of a federal criminal statute, which is what the Court has done here. By limiting § 1503 to acts having the "natural and probable effect" of interfering with the due administration of justice, the Court effectively reads the word "endeavor," * * * out of the omnibus clause, leaving a prohibition of only actual obstruction and competent attempts.

II

The Court apparently adds to its "natural and probable effect" requirement the requirement that the defendant *know* of that natural and probable effect. * * * Separate proof of such knowledge is not, I think, required for the orthodox use of the "natural and probable effect" rule discussed in *Pettibone* * * * Or, as we would put the point in modern times, the jury is entitled to presume that a person intends the natural and probable consequences of his acts.

* * * As I have said, I think an act committed with intent to obstruct is all that matters; and what one can fairly be thought to have intended depends in part upon what one can fairly be thought to have known. The critical point of knowledge at issue, in my view, is not whether "respondent knew that his false statement *would be provided* to the grand jury," * * *, but rather whether respondent knew—or indeed, even erroneously *believed*—that his false statement *might* be provided to the grand jury (which is all the knowledge needed to support the conclusion that the purpose of his lie was to mislead the jury). * * * I find that a rational juror could readily have concluded beyond a reasonable doubt that respondent had corruptly endeavored to impede the due administration of justice, *i.e.,* that he lied to the FBI agents intending to interfere with a grand jury investigation into his misdeeds. * * *

Respondent next contends that because Congress in 1982 enacted a different statute, 18 U.S.C. § 1512, dealing with witness tampering, and simultaneously removed from § 1503 the provisions it had previously contained specifically addressing efforts to influence or injure witnesses, see Victim and Witness Protection Act of 1982, Pub.L. 97-291, 96 Stat. 1249–1250, 1253, his witness-related conduct is no longer punishable under the omnibus clause of § 1503. The 1982 amendment, however, did nothing to alter the omnibus clause, which by its terms encompasses corrupt "endeavors to influence, obstruct, or impede, the due administration of justice." The fact that there is now some overlap between § 1503 and § 1512 is no more intolerable than the fact that there is some overlap between the omnibus clause of § 1503 and the other provisions of § 1503 itself. It hardly leads to the conclusion that § 1503 was, to the extent of the overlap, silently repealed. It is not unusual for a particular act to violate more than one criminal statute,* * * and in such situations the Government may proceed under any statute that applies, * * *

The "nexus" requirement that the Court today engrafts into § 1503 has no basis in the words Congress enacted. I would reverse that part of the Court of Appeals' judgment which set aside respondent's conviction under that statute.

United States v. Shotts

145 F.3d 1289 (11th Cir. 1998)

HILL, Senior Circuit Judge:

Jessee W. Shotts appeals his convictions and sentences on various counts of mail fraud and obstruction of justice. For the following reasons, we affirm in part [obstruction of justice convictions] and reverse in part [mail fraud convictions].

Jessee W. Shotts is a criminal defense attorney in Birmingham, Alabama. In the 1980's, he also ran a bail bond business called J & J Bonding Co. In 1990, the Alabama Supreme Court promulgated a rule that prohibited attorneys from having an interest in a bail bond business. Shotts closed J & J Bonding Co., and a new corporation called JC Bail Bonds, Inc. ("JC") was formed. Shotts' wife, Jerri Grant, was the sole shareholder. Subsequently, she transferred her shares to Donald Long, who later transferred his shares to David Pettus. At no time did Shotts own any stock in JC.

Shotts directed his secretary, Kandy Kennedy, to mail applications and money to various municipalities to obtain licenses for the business. These applications named Long as the owner of the business. Shotts also directed Kennedy to prepare the annual certification, which stated that Long was the owner of the company and that no lawyer had any interest in the company.

The new firm began to operate in the fall of 1990. On three occasions, Shotts took Long to Judge Jack Montgomery's house. Montgomery was a state district court judge in Birmingham. On each occasion, Shotts would go into Judge Montgomery's house alone and return with bonds signed by Montgomery, but otherwise blank. Shotts referred to these pre-approved bonds as "Jack" bonds. They were used as appearance bonds by JC, but without showing JC as the surety. If the defendant did not appear in court as required, JC had no liability on the bond.

In 1992, the Federal Bureau of Investigation (FBI) began an investigation into allegations of corruption on the part of Judge Montgomery and obtained a wiretap of his home phone. In late 1992, the FBI intercepted a phone call from Shotts to Judge Montgomery in which Shotts asked him to sign a bond for a prisoner in another county. When Montgomery responded that he didn't know if he could sign the bond because he had no jurisdiction in that county, Shotts said he "had 5,000 reasons to try." Montgomery then told Shotts to come to his house.

That evening, the FBI executed a search warrant on Judge Montgomery's house. They found $31,000 in the house. The next day, Montgomery resigned from office.

After the search of Montgomery's house, Shotts was called to testify before a grand jury investigating Montgomery. He was asked whether he owned JC Bail Bonds, Inc. He answered that he did not. He was also asked whether he had any interest in or was associated with a bail bond business, but he invoked his Fifth Amendment privilege and refused to answer. * * *

Shotts appeals each of his convictions. He challenges the legal sufficiency of the mail fraud counts and the constitutionality of the obstruction of justice counts. He also contends that the evidence was insufficient to convict him on any of the obstruction of justice counts. * * *

Shotts appeals his conviction on Count 24 of the indictment which charges that he violated 18 U.S.C. § 1512(b)(3). This section makes it a crime to:

> knowingly use[ ] intimidation or physical force, threaten [ ], or corruptly persuade [ ] another person, or attempt to do so … with intent to … hinder, delay or prevent the communication to a law enforcement officer … of information relating to the commission or possible commission of a Federal offense.…

The indictment alleges that Shotts committed the offense by "corruptly persudad[ing] and attempt[ing] to corruptly persuade an employee of his law office to not tell anything to law enforcement agents investigating Jack Montgomery's activities." Shotts asserts that his conviction on this count must be reversed because the "corruptly persuade" language of Section 1512(b) is unconstitutionally vague and overbroad, and also because the government did not prove the charged crime. * * *

Shotts' constitutional attack on Section 1512(b) relies on *United States v. Poindexter,* 951 F.2d 369, 378 (D.C.Cir.1991). Poindexter had been President Reagan's National Security Advisor. He was accused of lying during the course of a congressional investigation of the Iran-Contra affair and charged under 18 U.S.C. § 1505 which prohibits the making of a false statement to the Congress. The District of Columbia Circuit reversed his conviction, holding that the term "corruptly" as used in Section 1505 was unconstitutionally vague as applied to Poindexter's actions. The court reasoned that the term was so imprecise that "men of common intelligence must necessarily guess at its meaning and differ on its application." * * *

Shotts urges us to extend the *Poindexter* view of Section 1505's "corruptly" to Section 1512(b). We have recently declined a similar invitation. * * * We refused, holding that Section 1505 and 1503 are too materially different for the construction of one to guide the construction of the other, and that *Poindexter* is limited to the specific illegal conduct charged in that case. * * * We again decline to extend *Poindexter* to another section of the obstruction-of-justice statutes. We continue to believe that *Poindexter* must be read narrowly, and not as a broad indictment of the use of "corruptly" in the various obstruction-of-justice statutes.

On the contrary, we agree with the Second Circuit that "corrupt" as used in Section of 1512(b) is neither unconstitutionally overbroad or vague. * * * By targeting only such persuasion as is "corrupt," Section 1512(b) clearly limits only constitutionally unprotected speech, and is not, therefore, overbroad. * * * The Second Circuit noted that the same language in Section 1503(a), the omnibus obstruction-of-justice provision, has long been upheld as meaning with an "improper purpose." * * * So defined, "corrupt" is a scienter requirement which provides adequate notice of what conduct is proscribed. * * *

Having upheld Section 1512 against Shotts' constitutional attack, we turn now to Shotts' contention that the government did not present sufficient evidence that he corruptly persuaded his secretary, Kandy Kennedy, not to talk to law enforcement agents investigating Montgomery. The evidence offered by the government in support of this charge was the following testimony by Kennedy:

Q: Were there any conversations in the office about the FBI after Mr. Montgomery's house was searched?

A: Yes.

Q: Was Mr. Shotts present?

A: Yes

Q: Did he say anything about the FBI to you?

A: I asked him about it. I asked him.

Q: What did he say?

A: He said just not say anything and I wasn't going to be bothered.

Shotts asserts that this testimony proves only that Kennedy asked Shotts about talking to the FBI and that he observed that if she did not talk to the FBI, she would not be bothered. He maintains that the testimony is insufficient to prove that he threatened or intimidated her, offered her any inducement, or persuaded her in any way not to talk to the FBI.

The government argues that Shotts' use of the term "bother" could have included the possibility of Kennedy's being prosecuted and jailed for her involvement with the bail bond business. In this context, the government contends that Shotts' comment was an attempt to frighten Kennedy into not talking to the FBI.

The jury was correctly charged that they must find that Shotts acted "knowingly and dishonestly with the specific intent to subvert or undermine the integrity or truth-seeking ability of an investigation by a federal law enforcement officer." The jury heard Kennedy's testimony. While not overwhelming, the jury could reasonably have inferred from this testimony that Shotts was attempting with an improper motive to persuade Kennedy not to talk to the FBI. There was sufficient evidence from which the jury has determined the facts. Therefore, we affirm Shotts' conviction on this count. * * *

Notes & Questions

1. *Elements of the Crime.* Which elements of the crime of obstruction of justice are demonstrated in each of the above cases? Does the conduct used to support an element also fit with another element of obstruction of justice? Does the merging of the evidence to support different elements of the crime make if difficult to separate some of the elements needed for an obstruction of justice conviction?

2. *Materiality.* Is materiality an element of obstruction of justice? Are the "nexus" or "corruptly" elements of the statute sufficient to meet materiality? Consider the discussion of materiality as discussed in one of the concurring opinions in the *en banc* decision reversing the conviction against baseball player Barry Bonds:

United States v. Bonds

784 F.3d 582 (9th Cir. 2015)

PER CURIAM:

During a grand jury proceeding, defendant gave a rambling, non-responsive answer to a simple question. Because there is insufficient evidence that Statement C was material, defendant's conviction for obstruction of justice in violation of 18 U.S.C. § 1503 is not supported by the record. Whatever section 1503's scope may be in other circumstances, defendant's conviction here must be reversed. * * *

KOZINSKI, Circuit Judge, with whom Circuit Judges O'SCANNLAIN, GRABER, CALLAHAN and NGUYEN join, concurring:

Can a single non-responsive answer by a grand jury witness support a conviction for obstruction of justice under 18 U.S.C. § 1503?

Defendant, who was then a professional baseball player, was summoned before a grand jury and questioned for nearly three hours about his suspected use of steroids. He was subsequently charged with four counts of making false statements and one count of obstruction of justice, all based on his grand jury testimony. The jury convicted him on the obstruction count and was otherwise unable to reach a verdict.

The jury instructions identified seven of defendant's statements that the government alleged obstructed justice. The jury, however, found only one statement obstructive. That statement was referred to as Statement C at trial and is italicized in the passage below:

> Q: Did Greg[, your trainer,] ever give you anything that required a syringe to inject yourself with?
>
> A: I've only had one doctor touch me. And that's my only personal doctor. Greg, like I said, we don't get into each others' personal lives. We're friends, but I don't — we don't sit around and talk baseball, because he knows I don't want — don't come to my house talking baseball. If you want to come to my house and talk about fishing, some other stuff, we'll be good friends. You come around talking about baseball, you go on. I don't talk about his business. You know what I mean?
>
> Q: Right.
>
> A: *That's what keeps our friendship. You know, I am sorry, but that — you know, that — I was a celebrity child, not just in baseball by my own instincts. I became a celebrity child with a famous father. I just don't get into other people's business because of my father's situation, you see.*

* * * As should be apparent, section 1503's coverage is vast. By its literal terms, it applies to all stages of the criminal and civil justice process, not just to conduct in the courtroom but also to trial preparation, discovery and pretrial motions. Indeed, it arguably covers conduct taken in anticipation that a civil or criminal case might be filed, such as tax planning, hiding assets or talking to police. And the text of the

omnibus clause, in concert with our definition of corruptly, encompasses any act that a jury might infer was intended to "influence, obstruct, or impede ... the due administration of justice." That's true even if no actual obstruction occurs, because the clause's use of "endeavors" makes "success ... irrelevant." * * *

Stretched to its limits, section 1503 poses a significant hazard for everyone involved in our system of justice, because so much of what the adversary process calls for could be construed as obstruction. Did a tort plaintiff file a complaint seeking damages far in excess of what the jury ultimately awards? That could be viewed as corruptly endeavoring to "influence ... the due administration of justice" by seeking to recover more than the claim deserves. So could any of the following behaviors that make up the bread and butter of litigation: filing an answer that denies liability for conduct that is ultimately adjudged wrongful or malicious; unsuccessfully filing (or opposing) a motion to dismiss or for summary judgment; seeking a continuance in order to inflict delay on the opposing party; frivolously taking an appeal or petitioning for certiorari — the list is endless. Witnesses would be particularly vulnerable because, as the Supreme Court has noted, "[u]nder the pressures and tensions of interrogation, it is not uncommon for the most earnest witnesses to give answers that are not entirely responsive." * * *

Lawyers face the most pervasive threat under such a regime. Zealous advocacy sometimes calls for pushing back against an adversary's just case and casting a despicable client in a favorable light, yet such conduct could be described as "endeavor[ing] to ... impede ... the due administration of justice." Even routine advocacy provides ample occasion for stumbling into the heartland of the omnibus clause's sweeping coverage. Oral arguments provide a ready example. One need not spend much time in one of our courtrooms to hear lawyers dancing around questions from the bench rather than giving pithy, direct answers. There is, for instance, the ever popular "but that is not *this* case" retort to a hypothetical, which could be construed as an effort to divert the court and thereby "influence ... the due administration of justice."

It is true that any such maneuver would violate section 1503 only if it were done "corruptly." But it is equally true that we have given "corruptly" such a broad construction that it does not meaningfully cabin the kind of conduct that is subject to prosecution. As noted, we have held that a defendant acts "corruptly," as that term is used in section 1503, if he does so "with the purpose of obstructing justice." * * * That a jury or a judge might not buy such an argument is neither here nor there; a criminal prosecution, even one that results in an acquittal, is a life-wrenching event. Nor does an acquittal wipe clean the suspicion that a guilty defendant got off on a technicality.

We have no doubt that United States Attorneys and their Assistants would use the power to prosecute for such crimes judiciously, but that is not the point. Making everyone who participates in our justice system a potential criminal defendant for conduct that is nothing more than the ordinary tug and pull of litigation risks chilling zealous advocacy. It also gives prosecutors the immense and unreviewable power to reward friends and punish enemies by prosecuting the latter and giving the former a pass. The perception that prosecutors have such a potent weapon in their arsenal, even if never used, may well dampen the fervor with which lawyers, particularly those representing criminal defendants, will discharge their duties. The amorphous nature of the statute is also at odds with the constitutional requirement that individuals have fair notice as to what conduct may be criminal. * * *

Because the statute sweeps so broadly, due process calls for prudential limitations on the government's power to prosecute under it. Such a limitation already exists in our case law interpreting section 1503: the requirement of materiality. * * * Materiality screens out many of the statute's troubling applications by limiting convictions to those situations where an act "has a natural tendency to influence, or was capable of influencing, the decision of the decisionmaking body." * * * Put another way, the government must prove beyond a reasonable doubt that the charged conduct was capable of influencing a decisionmaking person or entity—for example, by causing it to cease its investigation, pursue different avenues of inquiry or reach a different outcome. * * *

In weighing materiality, we consider "the *intrinsic* capabilities of the ... statement itself," rather than the statement's actual effect on the decisionmaker, * * * and we evaluate the statement in "the context in which [it was] made," * * *.

We start with the self-evident proposition that Statement C, standing alone, did not have the capacity to divert the government from its investigation or influence the grand jury's decision whether to indict anyone. * * * The statement says absolutely nothing pertinent to the subject of the grand jury's investigation. Even when paired with the question that prompted it,

Did Greg ever give you anything that required a syringe to inject yourself with?

Statement C communicates nothing of value or detriment to the investigation. Had the answer been "I'm afraid of needles," it would have been plausible to infer an unspoken denial, with the actual words serving as an explanation or elaboration. But, as given, the answer did not enlighten, obfuscate, confirm or deny anything within the scope of the question posed.

The most one can say about this statement is that it was non-responsive and thereby impeded the investigation to a small degree by wasting the grand jury's time and trying the prosecutors' patience. But real-life witness examinations, unlike those in movies and on television, invariably are littered with non-responsive and irrelevant answers. This happens when the speaker doesn't understand the question, begins to talk before thinking (lawyers do this with surprising frequency), wants to avoid giving a direct answer (ditto), or is temporizing. Courtrooms are pressure-laden environments and a certain number of non-responsive or irrelevant statements can be expected as part of the give-and-take of courtroom discourse. Because *some* non-responsive answers are among the road hazards of witness examination, any one such statement is not, standing alone, "capable of influencing ... the decision of [a] decisionmaking body." * * *

This is true even if, as the government now argues, Statement C is literally false. An irrelevant or wholly non-responsive answer says nothing germane to the subject of the investigation, whether it's true or false. For example, if a witness is asked, "Do you own a gun?" it makes no difference whether he answers "The sky is blue" or "The sky is green." That the second statement is false makes it no more likely to impede the investigation than the first.

Statement C does not, however, stand alone. It was a small portion of a much longer examination, and we must look at the record as a whole to determine whether a rational trier of fact could have found the statement capable of influencing the grand jury's investigation, in light of defendant's entire grand jury testimony. If, for example, a witness engages in a pattern of irrelevant statements, or launches into lengthy disquisitions that are clearly designed to waste time and preclude the questioner from continuing his examination, the jury could find that the witness's behavior was capable of having some sway.

On careful review of the record, we find insufficient evidence to render Statement C material. In conducting this review, we are mindful that we must give the jury the benefit of the doubt and draw all reasonable inferences in favor of its verdict. * * *

The government charged a total of seven statements, only one of which the jury found to be obstructive. Two of these statements (including Statement C) appear to be wholly irrelevant—verbal detours with no bearing on the proceedings. One statement is "I don't know," followed by a brief explanation for the lack of knowledge. The rest are direct answers that the government claimed were false, all concerning whether defendant's trainer had provided or injected him with steroids. In the context of three hours of grand jury testimony, these six additional statements are insufficient to render the otherwise innocuous Statement C material. If this were enough to establish materiality, few witnesses or lawyers would be safe from prosecution.

B. Mueller Report—Legal Framework

The following is part of the legal framework (without citations) provided in the Mueller Report. The full legal framework with citations can be found in Volume II, pp. 9–12.

Mueller Report—
Legal Framework of Obstruction of Justice
* * *

Obstructive act. Obstruction-of-justice law "reaches all corrupt conduct capable of producing an effect that prevents justice from being duly administered, regardless of the means employed." * * * An "effort to influence" a proceeding can qualify as an endeavor to obstruct justice even if the effort was "subtle or circuitous" and "however cleverly or with whatever cloaking of purpose" it was made. * * * The verbs " 'obstruct or impede' are broad" and "can refer to anything that blocks, makes difficult, or hinders." * * *

An improper motive can render an actor's conduct criminal even when the conduct would otherwise be lawful and within the actor's authority. * * *

Nexus to a pending or contemplated official proceeding. Obstruction-of-justice law generally requires a nexus, or connection, to an official proceeding. * * * Section 1503, the nexus must be to pending "judicial or grand jury proceedings." In Section 1505, the nexus can include a connection to a "pending" federal agency proceeding or a congressional inquiry or investigation. Under both statutes, the government must demonstrate "a relationship in time, causation, or logic" between the obstructive act and the proceeding or inquiry to be obstructed. * * *. Section 1512(c) prohibits obstructive efforts aimed at official proceedings including judicial or grand jury proceedings. * * * "For purposes of" Section 1512, "an official proceeding need not be pending or about to be instituted at the time of the offense." * * * Although a proceeding need not already be in progress to trigger liability under Section 1512(c), a nexus to a contemplated proceeding still must be shown. * * * The nexus requirement narrows the scope of obstruction statutes to ensure that individuals have "fair warning" of what the law proscribes. * * *

The nexus showing has subjective and objective components. As an objective matter, a defendant must act "in a manner that is likely to obstruct justice," such that the statute "excludes defendants who have an evil purpose but use means that would only unnaturally and improbably be successful." * * * "[T]he endeavor must have the natural and probable effect of interfering with the due administration of justice." * * * As a subjective matter, the actor must have "contemplated a particular, foreseeable proceeding." * * * A defendant need not directly impede the proceeding. Rather, a nexus exists if "discretionary actions of a third person would be required to obstruct the judicial proceeding if it was foreseeable to the defendant that the third party would act on the [defendant's] communication in such a way as to obstruct the judicial proceeding." * * *

Corruptly. The word "corruptly" provides the intent element for obstruction of justice and means acting "knowingly and dishonestly" or "with an improper motive." * * * The requisite showing is made when a person acted with an intent to obtain an "improper advantage for [him]self or someone else, inconsistent with official duty and the rights of others." BALLENTINE'S LAW DICTIONARY 276 (3d ed. 1969); * * *

Witness tampering. A more specific provision in Section 1512 prohibits tampering with a witness. See 18 U.S.C. § 1512(b)(1), (3) * * * To establish corrupt persuasion, it is sufficient that the defendant asked a potential witness to lie to investigators in contemplation of a likely federal investigation into his conduct. * * * The "persuasion" need not be coercive, intimidating, or explicit; it is sufficient to "urge," "induce,'" "ask[]," "argu[e]," "giv[e] reasons," * * * or "coach[] or remind[ ] witnesses by planting misleading facts," * * * Corrupt persuasion is shown "where a defendant tells a potential witness a false story as if the story were true, intending that the witness believe the story and testify to it." * * * It also covers urging a witness to recall a fact that the witness did not know, even if the fact was actually true. * * * Corrupt persuasion also can be shown in certain circumstances when a person, with an improper motive, urges a witness not to cooperate with law enforcement. * * *

When the charge is acting with the intent to hinder, delay, or prevent the communication of information to law enforcement under Section 1512(b)(3), the "nexus" to a proceeding inquiry articulated in *Aguilar*—that an individual have "knowledge that his actions are likely to affect the judicial proceeding," * * * does not apply because the obstructive act is aimed at the communication of information to investigators, not at impeding an official proceeding.

Acting "knowingly … corruptly" requires proof that the individual was "conscious of wrongdoing." * * * It is an affirmative defense that "the conduct consisted solely of lawful conduct and that the defendant's sole intention was to encourage, induce, or cause the other person to testify truthfully." 18 U.S.C. § 1512(e).

Attempts and endeavors. Section 1512(c)(2) covers both substantive obstruction offenses and attempts to obstruct justice. Under general principles of attempt law, a person is guilty of an attempt when he has the intent to commit a substantive offense and takes an overt act that constitutes a substantial step towards that goal. * * * "[T]he act [must be] substantial, in that it was strongly corroborative of the defendant's criminal purpose." * * * While "mere abstract talk" does not suffice, any "concrete and specific" acts that corroborate the defendant's intent can constitute a "substantial step." * * * Thus, "soliciting an innocent agent to engage in conduct constituting an element of the crime" may qualify as a substantial step. Model Penal Code§ 5.01(2)(g); * * *

The omnibus clause of 18 U.S.C. § 1503 prohibits an "endeavor" to obstruct justice, which sweeps more broadly than Section 1512's attempt provision. * * * "It is well established that a[n] [obstruction-of-justice] offense is complete when one corruptly endeavors to obstruct or impede the due administration of justice; the prosecution need not prove that the due administration of justice was actually obstructed or impeded." * * *

IV. Obstruction Considerations of the Mueller Report

At the beginning of Volume II of the Mueller Report is an Executive Summary that provides a synopsis of the facts covered in the Report. Most of the individual sections of the Report then discuss the evidence in detail and apply that specific evidence to the legal framework. Below is the Executive Summary's statement of the facts (Mueller Report, Vol. II, pp. 3–7), followed by the analysis section from that particular portion of the Report. Part A and L below do not contain an analysis section, so those parts below are limited to the Executive Summary. Since the comprehensive evidence discussion is omitted below, the pages numbers for the full factual scenario, evidence and analysis is provided next to each heading. The analysis section below also provides the applicable page numbers, as the footnotes from these sections are omitted here. All the page numbers refer to Volume II of the Mueller Report.

A. The Campaign's Response to Reports about Russian Support for Trump (pp. 15–23)

Mueller Report— Executive Summary (p. 3)

During the 2016 presidential campaign, questions arose about the Russian government's apparent support for candidate Trump. After WikiLeaks released politically damaging Democratic Party emails that were reported to have been hacked by Russia, Trump publicly expressed skepticism that Russia was responsible for the hacks at the same time that he and other Campaign officials privately sought information, Harm to Ongoing Matter, about any further planned WikiLeaks releases. Trump also denied having any business in or connections to Russia, even though as late as June 2016 the Trump Organization had been pursuing a licensing deal for a skyscraper to be built in Russia called Trump Tower Moscow. After the election, the President expressed concerns to advisors that reports of Russia's election interference might lead the public to question the legitimacy of his election.

B. Conduct Involving FBI Director Comey and Michael Flynn (pp. 24–48)

1. Mueller Report—Executive Summary (p. 3)

In mid-January 2017, incoming National Security Advisor Michael Flynn falsely denied to the Vice President, other administration officials, and FBI agents that he had talked to Russian Ambassador Sergey Kislyak about Russia's response to U.S. sanctions on Russia for its election interference. On January 27, the day after the President was told that Flynn had lied to the Vice President and had made similar statements to the FBI, the President invited FBI Director Comey to a private dinner at the White House and told Comey that he needed loyalty. On February 14, the day after the President requested Flynn's resignation, the President told an outside advisor, "Now that we fired Flynn, the Russia thing is over." The advisor disagreed and said the investigations would continue.

Later that afternoon, the President cleared the Oval Office to have a one-on-one meeting with Comey. Referring to the FBI's investigation of Flynn, the President said, "I hope you can see your way clear to letting this go, to letting Flynn go. He is a good guy. I hope you can let this go." Shortly after requesting Flynn's resignation and speaking privately to Comey, the President sought to have Deputy National Security Advisor K.T. McFarland draft an internal letter stating that the President had not directed Flynn to discuss sanctions with Kislyak. McFarland declined because she did not know whether that was true, and a White House Counsel's Office attorney thought that the request would look like a quid pro quo for an ambassadorship she had been offered.

2. Mueller Report Analysis (pp. 44–48)

In analyzing the President's conduct related to the Flynn investigation, the following evidence is relevant to the elements of obstruction of justice:

a. <u>Obstructive act</u>. According to Comey's account of his February 14, 2017 meeting in the Oval Office, the President told him, "I hope you can see your way clear to letting this go, to letting Flynn go.... I hope you can let this go." In analyzing whether these statements constitute an obstructive act, a threshold question is whether Comey's account of the interaction is accurate, and, if so, whether the President's statements had the tendency to impede the administration of justice by shutting down an inquiry that could result in a grand jury investigation and a criminal charge.

After Comey's account of the President's request to "let[] Flynn go" became public, the President publicly disputed several aspects of the story. The President told the New York Times that he did not "shoo other people out of the room" when he talked to Comey and that he did not remember having a one-on-one conversation with Comey. The President also publicly denied that he had asked Comey to "let[] Flynn go" or otherwise communicated that Comey should drop the investigation of Flynn. In private, the President denied aspects of Comey's account to White House advisors, but acknowledged to Priebus that he brought Flynn up in the meeting with Comey and stated that Flynn was a good guy. Despite those denials, substantial evidence corroborates Comey's account.

First, Comey wrote a detailed memorandum of his encounter with the President on the same day it occurred. Comey also told senior FBI officials about the meeting with the President that day, and their recollections of what Comey told them at the time are consistent with Comey's account.

Second, Comey provided testimony about the President's request that he "let[] Flynn go" under oath in congressional proceedings and in interviews with federal investigators subject to penalties for lying under 18 U.S.C. § 1001. Comey's recollections of the encounter have remained consistent over time.

Third, the objective, corroborated circumstances of how the one-on-one meeting came to occur support Comey's description of the event. Comey recalled that the President cleared the room to speak with Comey alone after a homeland security briefing in the Oval Office, that Kushner and Sessions lingered and had to be shooed out by the President, and that Priebus briefly opened the door during the meeting, prompting the President to wave him away. While the President has publicly denied those details, other Administration officials who were present have confirmed Comey's account of how he ended up in a one-on-one meeting with the President. And the President acknowledged to Priebus and McGahn that he in fact spoke to Comey about Flynn in their one-on-one meeting.

Fourth, the President's decision to clear the room and, in particular, to exclude the Attorney General from the meeting signals that the President wanted to be alone with Comey, which is consistent with the delivery of a message of the type that Comey recalls, rather than a more innocuous conversation that could have occurred in the presence of the Attorney General.

Finally, Comey's reaction to the President's statements is consistent with the President having asked him to "let [ ] Flynn go." Comey met with the FBI leadership team, which agreed to keep the President's statements closely held and not to inform the team working on the Flynn investigation so that they would not be influenced by the President's request. Comey also promptly met with the Attorney General to ask him not to be left alone with the President again, an account verified by Sessions, FBI Chief of Staff James Rybicki, and Jody Hunt, who was then the Attorney General's chief of staff.

A second question is whether the President's statements, which were not phrased as a direct order to Comey could impede or interfere with the FBI's investigation of Flynn. While the President said he "hope[d]" Comey could "let[] Flynn go," rather than affirmatively directing him to do so, the circumstances of the conversation show that the President was asking Comey to close the FBI's investigation into Flynn. First, the President arranged the meeting with Comey so that they would be alone and purposely excluded the Attorney General, which suggests that the President meant to make a request to Comey that he did not want anyone else to hear. Second, because the President is the head of the Executive Branch, when he says that he "hopes" a subordinate will do something, it is reasonable to expect that the subordinate will do what the President wants. Indeed, the President repeated a version of "let this go" three times, and Comey testified that he understood the President's statements as a directive, which is corroborated by the way Comey reacted at the time.

b. Nexus to a proceeding. To establish a nexus to a proceeding, it would be necessary to show that the President could reasonably foresee and actually contemplated that the investigation of Flynn was likely to lead to a grand jury investigation or prosecution.

At the time of the President's one-on-one meeting with Comey, no grand jury subpoenas had been issued as part of the FBI's investigation into Flynn. But Flynn's lies to the FBI violated federal criminal law, Grand Jury, and resulted in Flynn's prosecution for violating 18 U.S.C. § 1001. By the time the president spoke to Comey about Flynn, DOJ officials had informed McGahn, who informed the President, that Flynn's statements to senior White House officials about his contacts with Kislyak were not true and that Flynn had told the same version of events to the FBI. McGahn also informed the President that Flynn's conduct could violate 18 U.S.C. § 1001. After the Vice President and senior White House officials reviewed the underlying information about Flynn's calls on February 1 0, 2017, they believed that Flynn could not have forgotten his conversations with Kislyak and concluded that he had been lying. In addition, the President's instruction to the FBI Director to "let[] Flynn go" suggests his awareness that Flynn could face criminal exposure for his conduct and was at risk of prosecution.

c. Intent. As part of our investigation, we examined whether the President had a personal stake in the outcome of an investigation into Flynn — for example, whether the President was aware of Flynn's communications with Kislyak close in time to when they occurred, such that the President knew that Flynn had lied to senior White House officials and that those lies had been passed on to the public. Some evidence suggests that the President knew about the existence and content of Flynn's calls when they occurred, but the evidence is inconclusive and could not be relied upon to establish the President's knowledge. In advance of Flynn's initial call with Kislyak, the President attended a meeting where the sanctions were discussed and an advisor may have mentioned that Flynn was scheduled to talk to Kislyak. Flynn told McFarland about the substance of his calls with Kislyak and said they may have made a difference in Russia's response, and Flynn recalled talking to Bannon in early January 2017 about how they had successfully "stopped the train on Russia's response" to the sanctions. It would have been reasonable for Flynn to have wanted the President to know of his communications with Kislyak because Kislyak told Flynn his request had been received at the highest levels in Russia and that Russia had chosen not to retaliate in response to the request, and the President was pleased by the Russian response, calling it a "[g]reat move." And the President never said publicly or internally that Flynn had lied to him about the calls with Kislyak.

But McFarland did not recall providing the President-Elect with Flynn's read-out of his calls with Kislyak, and Flynn does not have a specific recollection of telling the President-Elect directly about the calls. Bannon also said he did not recall hearing about the calls from Flynn. And in February 2017, the President asked Flynn what was discussed on the calls and whether he had lied to the Vice President, suggesting that he did not already know. Our investigation accordingly did not produce evidence that established that the President knew about Flynn's discussions of sanctions before the Department of Justice notified the White House of those discussions in late January 2017. The evidence also does not establish that Flynn otherwise possessed information damaging to the President that would give the President a personal incentive to end the FBI's inquiry into Flynn's conduct.

Evidence does establish that the President connected the Flynn investigation to the FBI's broader Russia investigation and that he believed, as he told Christie, that terminating Flynn would end "the whole Russia thing." Flynn's firing occurred at a time when the media and Congress were raising questions about Russia's interference in the election and whether members of the President's campaign had colluded with Russia. Multiple witnesses recalled that the President viewed the Russia investigations as a challenge to the legitimacy of his election. The President paid careful attention to negative coverage of Flynn and reacted with annoyance and anger when the story broke disclosing that Flynn had discussed sanctions with Kislyak. Just hours before meeting one-on-one with Comey, the President told Christie that firing Flynn would put an end to the Russia inquiries. And after Christie pushed back, telling the President that firing Flynn would not end the Russia investigation, the President asked Christie to reach out to Comey and convey that the President liked him and he was part of "the team." That afternoon, the President cleared the room and asked Comey to "let[] Flynn go."

We also sought evidence relevant to assessing whether the President's direction to Comey was motivated by sympathy towards Flynn. In public statements the President repeatedly described Flynn as a good person who had been harmed by the Russia investigation, and the President directed advisors to reach out to Flynn to tell him the President "care[d]" about him and felt bad for him. At the same time, multiple senior advisors, including Bannon, Priebus, and Hicks, said that the President had become unhappy with Flynn well before Flynn was forced to resign and that the President was frequently irritated with Flynn. Priebus said he believed the President's initial reluctance to fire Flynn stemmed not from personal regard, but from concern about the negative press that would be generated by firing the National Security Advisor so early in the Administration. And Priebus indicated that the President's post-firing expressions of support for Flynn were motivated by the President's desire to keep Flynn from saying negative things about him.

The way in which the President communicated the request to Comey also is relevant to understanding the President's intent. When the President first learned about the FBI investigation into Flynn, he told McGahn, Bannon, and Priebus not to discuss the matter with anyone else in the White House. The next day, the President invited Comey for a one-on-one dinner against the advice of an aide who recommended that other White House officials also attend. At the dinner, the President asked Comey for "loyalty" and, at a different point in the conversation, mentioned that Flynn had judgment issues. When the President met with Comey the day after Flynn's termination—shortly after being told by Christie that firing Flynn would not end the Russia investigation—the President cleared the room, even excluding the Attorney General, so that he could again speak to Comey alone. The President's decision to meet one-on-one with Comey contravened the advice of the White House Counsel that the President should not communicate directly with the Department of Justice to avoid any appearance of interfering in law enforcement activities. And the President later denied that he cleared the room and asked Comey to "let[] Flynn go"—a denial that would have been unnecessary if he believed his request was a proper exercise of prosecutorial discretion.

Finally, the President's effort to have McFarland write an internal email denying that the President had directed Flynn to discuss sanctions with Kislyak highlights the President's concern about being associated with Flynn's conduct. The evidence does not establish that the President was trying to have McFarland lie. The President's request, however, was sufficiently irregular that McFarland—who did not know the full extent of Flynn's communications with the President and thus could not make the representation the President wanted felt the need to draft an internal memorandum documenting the President's request, and Eisenberg was concerned that the request would look like a quid pro quo in exchange for an ambassadorship.

C. The President's Reaction to the Continuing Russia Investigation (pp. 48–61)

1. Mueller Report — Executive Summary (pp. 3–4)

In February 2017, Attorney General Jeff Sessions began to assess whether he had to recuse himself from campaign-related investigations because of his role in the Trump Campaign. In early March, the President told White House Counsel Donald McGahn to stop Sessions from recusing. And after Sessions announced his recusal on March 2, the President expressed anger at the decision and told advisors that he should have an Attorney General who would protect him. That weekend, the President took Sessions aside at an event and urged him to "unrecuse." Later in March, Comey publicly disclosed at a congressional hearing that the FBI was investigating "the Russian government's efforts to interfere in the 2016 presidential election," including any links or coordination between the Russian government and the Trump Campaign. In the following days, the President reached out to the Director of National Intelligence and the leaders of the Central Intelligence Agency (CIA) and the National Security Agency (NSA) to ask them what they could do to publicly dispel the suggestion that the President had any connection to the Russian election-interference effort. The President also twice called Comey directly, notwithstanding guidance from McGahn to avoid direct contacts with the Department of Justice. Comey had previously assured the President that the FBI was not investigating him personally, and the President asked Comey to "lift the cloud" of the Russia investigation by saying that publicly.

2. Mueller Report Analysis (pp. 60–61)

In analyzing the President's reaction to Sessions's recusal and the requests he made to Coats, Pompeo, Rogers, and Comey, the following evidence is relevant to the elements of obstruction of justice:

a. Obstructive act. The evidence shows that, after Comey's March 20, 2017 testimony, the President repeatedly reached out to intelligence agency leaders to discuss the FBI's investigation. But witnesses had different recollections of the precise content of those outreaches. Some ODNI officials recalled that Coats told them immediately after the March 22 Oval Office meeting that the President asked Coats to intervene with Comey and "stop" the investigation. But the first-band witnesses to the encounter remember the conversation differently. Pompeo had no memory of the specific meeting, but generally recalled the President urging officials to get the word out that the President had not done anything wrong related to Russia. Coats recalled that the President asked that Coats state publicly that no link existed between the President and Russia, but did not ask him to speak with Comey or to help end the investigation. The other outreaches by the President during this period were similar in nature. The President asked Rogers if he could do anything to refute the stories linking the President to Russia, and the President asked Comey to make a public statement that would "lift the cloud" of the ongoing investigation by making clear that the President was not personally under investigation. These requests, while significant enough that

Rogers thought it important to document the encounter in a written memorandum, were not interpreted by the officials who received them as directives to improperly interfere with the investigation.

b. Nexus to a proceeding. At the time of the President's outreaches to leaders of the intelligence agencies in late March and early April 2017, the FBI's Russia investigation did not yet involve grand jury proceedings. The outreaches, however, came after and were in response to Comey's March 20, 2017 announcement that the FBI, as a part of its counterintelligence mission, was conducting an investigation into Russian interference in the 2016 presidential election. Comey testified that the investigation included any links or coordination with Trump campaign officials and would "include an assessment of whether any crimes were committed."

c. Intent. As described above, the evidence does not establish that the President asked or directed intelligence agency leaders to stop or interfere with the FBI's Russia investigation—and the President affirmatively told Comey that if "some satellite" was involved in Russian election interference "it would be good to find that out." But the President's intent in trying to prevent Sessions's recusal, and in reaching out to Coats, Pompeo, Rogers, and Comey following Comey's public announcement of the FBI's Russia investigation, is nevertheless relevant to understanding what motivated the President's other actions towards the investigation.

The evidence shows that the President was focused on the Russia investigation's implications for his presidency—and, specifically, on dispelling any suggestion that he was under investigation or had links to Russia. In early March, the President attempted to prevent Sessions's recusal, even after being told that Sessions was following DOJ conflict-of-interest rules. After Sessions recused, the White House Counsel's Office tried to cut off further contact with Sessions about the matter, although it is not clear whether that direction was conveyed to the President. The President continued to raise the issue of Sessions's recusal and, when he had the opportunity, he pulled Sessions aside and urged him to unrecuse. The President also told advisors that he wanted an Attorney General who would protect him, the way he perceived Robert Kennedy and Eric Holder to have protected their presidents. The President made statements about being able to direct the course of criminal investigations, saying words to the effect of, "You're telling me that Bobby and Jack didn't talk about investigations? Or Obama didn't tell Eric Holder who to investigate?"

After Comey publicly confirmed the existence of the FBI's Russia investigation on March 20, 2017, the President was "beside himself" and expressed anger that Comey did not issue a statement correcting any misperception that the President himself was under investigation. The President sought to speak with Acting Attorney General Boente directly and told McGahn to contact Boente to request that Comey make a clarifying statement. The President then asked other intelligence community leaders to make public statements to refute the suggestion that the President had links to Russia, but the leaders told him they could not publicly comment on the investigation. On March 30 and April 11, against the advice of White House advisors who had informed him that any direct contact with the FBI could be perceived as improper interference in an ongoing investigation, the President made personal outreaches to Comey asking him to "lift the cloud" of the Russia investigation by making public the fact that the President was not personally under investigation.

Evidence indicates that the President was angered by both the existence of the Russia investigation and the public reporting that he was under investigation, which he knew was not true based on Comey's representations. The President complained to advisors that if people thought Russia helped him with the election, it would detract from what he had accomplished.

Other evidence indicates that the President was concerned about the impact of the Russia investigation on his ability to govern. The President complained that the perception that he was under investigation was hurting his ability to conduct foreign relations, particularly with Russia. The President told Coats he "can't do anything with Russia," he told Rogers that "the thing with the Russians" was interfering with his ability to conduct foreign affairs, and he told Comey that "he was trying to run the country and the cloud of this Russia business was making that difficult."

D. The President's Termination of Comey (pp. 62–77)

1. Mueller Report — Executive Summary (pp. 4)

On May 3, 2017, Comey testified in a congressional hearing, but declined to answer questions about whether the President was personally under investigation. Within days, the President decided to terminate Comey. The President insisted that the termination letter, which was written for public release, state that Comey had informed the President that he was not under investigation. The day of the firing, the White House maintained that Comey's termination resulted from independent recommendations from the Attorney General and Deputy Attorney General that Comey should be discharged for mishandling the Hillary Clinton email investigation. But the President had decided to fire Comey before hearing from the Department of Justice. The day after firing Comey, the President told Russian officials that he had "faced great pressure because of Russia," which had been "taken off" by Comey's firing. The next day, the President acknowledged in a television interview that he was going to fire Comey regardless of the Department of Justice's recommendation and that when he "decided to just do it," he was thinking that "this thing with Trump and Russia is a made-up story." In response to a question about whether he was angry with Comey about the Russia investigation, the President said, "As far as I'm concerned, I want that thing to be absolutely done properly," adding that firing Comey "might even lengthen out the investigation."

2. Mueller Report Analysis (pp. 74–77)

In analyzing the President's decision to fire Comey, the following evidence is relevant to the elements of obstruction of justice:

a. <u>Obstructive act</u>. The act of firing Comey removed the individual overseeing the FBI's Russia investigation. The President knew that Comey was personally involved in the investigation based on Comey's briefing of the Gang of Eight, Comey's March 20, 2017 public testimony about the investigation, and the President's one-on-one conversations with Comey.

Firing Comey would qualify as an obstructive act if it had the natural and probable effect of interfering with or impeding the investigation—for example, if the termination would have the effect of delaying or disrupting the investigation or providing the President with the opportunity to appoint a director who would take a different approach to the investigation that the President perceived as more protective of his personal interests. Relevant circumstances bearing on that issue include whether the President's actions had the potential to discourage a successor director or other law enforcement officials in their conduct of the Russia investigation. The President fired Comey abruptly without offering him an opportunity to resign, banned him from the FBI building, and criticized him publicly, calling him a "showboat" and claiming that the FBI was "in turmoil" under his leadership. And the President followed the termination with public statements that were highly critical of the investigation; for example, three days after firing Comey, the President referred to the investigation as a "witch hunt" and asked, "when does it end?" Those actions had the potential to affect a successor director's conduct of the investigation.

The anticipated effect of removing the FBI director, however, would not necessarily be to prevent or impede the FBI from continuing its investigation. As a general matter, FBI investigations run under the operational direction of FBI personnel levels below the FBI director. Bannon made a similar point when he told the President that he could fire the FBI director, but could not fire the FBI. The White House issued a press statement the day after Comey was fired that said, "The investigation would have always continued, and obviously, the termination of Comey would not have ended it." In addition, in his May 11 interview with Lester Holt, the President stated that he understood when he made the decision to fire Comey that the action might prolong the investigation. And the President chose McCabe to serve as interim director, even though McCabe told the President he had worked "very closely" with Comey and was part of all the decisions made in the Clinton investigation.

b. Nexus to a proceeding. The nexus element would be satisfied by evidence showing that a grand jury proceeding or criminal prosecution arising from an FBI investigation was objectively foreseeable and actually contemplated by the President when he terminated Comey.

Several facts would be relevant to such a showing. At the time the President fired Comey, a grand jury had not begun to hear evidence related to the Russia investigation and no grand jury subpoenas had been issued. On March 20, 2017, however, Comey had announced that the FBI was investigating Russia's interference in the election, including "an assessment of whether any crimes were committed." It was widely known that the FBI, as part of the Russia investigation, was investigating the hacking of the DNC's computers—a clear criminal offense.

In addition, at the time the President fired Comey, evidence indicates the President knew that Flynn was still under criminal investigation and could potentially be pros-

ecuted, despite the President's February 14, 2017 request that Comey "let[] Flynn
go." On March 5, 2017, the White House Counsel's Office was informed that the FBI
was asking for transition-period records relating to Flynn—indicating that the FBI
was still actively investigating him. The same day, the President told advisors he
wanted to call Dana Boente, then the Acting Attorney General for the Russia investigation, to find out whether the White House or the President was being investigated.
On March 31, 2017, the President signaled his awareness that Flynn remained in legal
jeopardy by tweeting that "Mike Flynn should ask for immunity" before he agreed
to provide testimony to the FBI or Congress. And in late March or early April, the
President asked McFarland to pass a message to Flynn telling him that the President
felt bad for him and that he should stay strong, further demonstrating the President's
awareness of Flynn's criminal exposure.

   c. Intent. Substantial evidence indicates that the catalyst for the President's decision
to fire Comey was Comey's unwillingness to publicly state that the President was not
personally under investigation, despite the President's repeated requests that Comey
make such an announcement. In the week leading up to Comey's May 3, 2017 Senate
Judiciary Committee testimony, the President told McGahn that it would be the last
straw if Comey did not set the record straight and publicly announce that the President
was not under investigation. But during his May 3 testimony, Comey refused to
answer questions about whether the President was being investigated. Comey's refusal
angered the President, who criticized Sessions for leaving him isolated and exposed,
saying "You left me on an island." Two days later, the President told advisors he had
decided to fire Comey and dictated a letter to Stephen Miller that began with a reference to the fact that the President was not being investigated: "While I greatly appreciate you informing me that I am not under investigation concerning what I have
often stated is a fabricated story on a Trump-Russia relationship...." The President
later asked Rosenstein to include "Russia" in his memorandum and to say that Comey
had told the President that he was not under investigation. And the President's final
termination letter included a sentence, at the President's insistence and against Mc-
Gahn's advice, stating that Comey had told the President on three separate occasions
that he was not under investigation.

   The President's other stated rationales for why he fired Comey are not similarly
supported by the evidence. The termination letter the President and Stephen Miller
prepared in Bedminster cited Comey's handling of the Clinton email investigation,
and the President told McCabe he fired Comey for that reason. But the facts surrounding Comey's handling of the Clinton email investigation were well known to
the President at the time he assumed office, and the President had made it clear to
both Comey and the President's senior staff in early 2017 that he wanted Comey to
stay on as director. And Rosenstein articulated his criticism of Comey's handling of
the Clinton investigation after the President had already decided to fire Comey. The
President's draft termination letter also stated that morale in the FBI was at an all-
time low and Sanders told the press after Comey's termination that the White House
had heard from "countless" FBI agents who had lost confidence in Comey. But the

evidence does not support those claims. The President told Comey at their January 27 dinner that "the people of the FBI really like [him]," no evidence suggests that the President heard otherwise before deciding to terminate Comey, and Sanders acknowledged to investigators that her comments were not founded on anything.

We also considered why it was important to the President that Comey announce publicly that he was not under investigation. Some evidence indicates that the President believed that the erroneous perception he was under investigation harmed his ability to manage domestic and foreign affairs, particularly in dealings with Russia. The President told Comey that the "cloud" of "this Russia business" was making it difficult to run the country. The President told Sessions and McGahn that foreign leaders had expressed sympathy to him for being under investigation and that the perception he was under investigation was hurting his ability to address foreign relations issues. The President complained to Rogers that "the thing with the Russians [was] messing up" his ability to get things done with Russia, and told Coats, "I can't do anything with Russia, there's things I'd like to do with Russia, with trade, with ISIS, they're all over me with this." The President also may have viewed Comey as insubordinate for his failure to make clear in the May 3 testimony that the President was not under investigation.

Other evidence, however, indicates that the President wanted to protect himself from an investigation into his campaign. The day after learning about the FBI's interview of Flynn, the President had a one-on-one dinner with Comey, against the advice of senior aides, and told Comey he needed Comey's "loyalty." When the President later asked Comey for a second time to make public that he was not under investigation, he brought up loyalty again, saying "Because I have been very loyal to you, very loyal, we had that thing, you know." After the President learned of Sessions's recusal from the Russia investigation, the President was furious and said he wanted an Attorney General who would protect him the way he perceived Robert Kennedy and Eric Holder to have protected their presidents. The President also said he wanted to be able to tell his Attorney General "who to investigate."

In addition, the President had a motive to put the FBI's Russia investigation behind him. The evidence does not establish that the termination of Comey was designed to cover up a conspiracy between the Trump Campaign and Russia: As described in Volume I, the evidence uncovered in the investigation did not establish that the President or those close to him were involved in the charged Russian computer-hacking or active-measure conspiracies, or that the President otherwise had an unlawful relationship with any Russian official. But the evidence does indicate that a thorough FBI investigation would uncover facts about the campaign and the President personally that the President could have understood to be crimes or that would give rise to personal and political concerns. Although the President publicly stated during and after the election that he had no connection to Russia, the Trump Organization, through Michael Cohen, was pursuing the proposed Trump Tower Moscow project through June 2016 and candidate Trump was repeatedly briefed on the progress of those efforts. In addition, some witnesses said that Trump was aware that at a time when public reports stated that Russian intelligence officials were behind the hacks, and that Trump privately sought information about future WikiLeaks releases. More broadly, multiple witnesses described the President's preoccupation with press coverage of the Russia investigation and his persistent concern that it raised questions about the legitimacy of his election.

Finally, the President and White House aides initially advanced a pretextual reason to the press and the public for Comey's termination. In the immediate aftermath of the firing, the President dictated a press statement suggesting that he had acted based on the DOJ recommendations, and White House press officials repeated that story. But the President had decided to fire Comey before the White House solicited those recommendations. Although the President ultimately acknowledged that he was going to fire Comey regardless of the Department of Justice's recommendations, he did so only after DOJ officials made clear to him that they would resist the White House's suggestion that they had prompted the process that led to Comey's termination. The initial reliance on a pretextual justification could support an inference that the President had concerns about providing the real reason for the firing, although the evidence does not resolve whether those concerns were personal, political, or both.

E. The Appointment of a Special Counsel and Efforts to Remove Him (pp. 77–90)

1. Mueller Report — Executive Summary (pp. 4)

On May 17, 2017, the Acting Attorney General for the Russia investigation appointed a Special Counsel to conduct the investigation and related matters. The President reacted to news that a Special Counsel had been appointed by telling advisors that it was "the end of his presidency" and demanding that Sessions resign. Sessions submitted his resignation, but the President ultimately did not accept it. The President told aides that the Special Counsel had conflicts of interest and suggested that the Special Counsel therefore could not serve. The President's advisors told him the asserted conflicts were meritless and had already been considered by the Department of Justice.

On June 14, 2017, the media reported that the Special Counsel's Office was investigating whether the President had obstructed justice. Press reports called this "a major turning point" in the investigation: while Comey had told the President he was not under investigation, following Comey's firing, the President now was under investigation. The President reacted to this news with a series of tweets criticizing the Department of Justice and the Special Counsel's investigation. On June 17, 2017, the President called McGahn at home and directed him to call the Acting Attorney General and say that the Special Counsel had conflicts of interest and must be removed. McGahn did not carry out the direction, however, deciding that he would resign rather than trigger what he regarded as a potential Saturday Night Massacre.

2. Mueller Report Analysis (pp. 87–90)

In analyzing the President's direction to McGahn to have the Special Counsel removed, the following evidence is relevant to the elements of obstruction of justice:

a. <u>Obstructive act</u>. As with the President's firing of Comey, the attempt to remove the Special Counsel would qualify as an obstructive act if it would naturally obstruct the investigation and any grand jury proceedings that might flow from the inquiry. Even if the removal of the lead prosecutor would not prevent the investigation from continuing under a new appointee, a factfinder would need to consider whether the act had the potential to delay further action in the investigation, chill the actions of any replacement Special Counsel, or otherwise impede the investigation.

A threshold question is whether the President in fact directed McGahn to have the Special Counsel removed. After news organizations reported that in June 2017 the President had ordered McGahn to have the Special Counsel removed, the President publicly disputed these accounts, and privately told McGahn that he had simply wanted McGahn to bring conflicts of interest to the Department of Justice's attention. * * * Some of the President's specific language that McGahn recalled from the calls is consistent with that explanation. Substantial evidence, however, supports the conclusion that the President went further and in fact directed McGahn to call Rosenstein to have the Special Counsel removed.

First, McGahn's clear recollection was that the President directed him to tell Rosenstein not only that conflicts existed but also that "Mueller has to go." McGahn is a credible witness with no motive to lie or exaggerate given the position he held in the White House. McGahn spoke with the President twice and understood the directive the same way both times, making it unlikely that he misheard or misinterpreted the President's request. In response to that request, McGahn decided to quit because he did not want to participate in events that he described as akin to the Saturday Night Massacre. He called his lawyer, drove to the White House, packed up his office, prepared to submit a resignation letter with his chief of staff, told Priebus that the President had asked him to "do crazy shit," and informed Priebus and Bannon that he was leaving. Those acts would be a highly unusual reaction to a request to convey information to the Department of Justice.

Second, in the days before the calls to McGahn, the President, through his counsel, had already brought the asserted conflicts to the attention of the Department of Justice. Accordingly, the President had no reason to have McGahn call Rosenstein that weekend to raise conflicts issues that already had been raised.

Third, the President's sense of urgency and repeated requests to McGahn to take immediate action on a weekend — "You gotta do this. You gotta call Rod." — support McGahn's recollection that the President wanted the Department of Justice to take action to remove the Special Counsel. Had the President instead sought only to have the Department of Justice re-examine asserted conflicts to evaluate whether they posed an ethical bar, it would have been unnecessary to set the process in motion on a Saturday and to make repeated calls to McGahn.

Finally, the President had discussed "knocking out Mueller" and raised conflicts of interest in a May 23, 2017 call with McGahn, reflecting that the President connected the conflicts to a plan to remove the Special Counsel. And in the days leading up to June 17, 2017, the President made clear to Priebus and Bannon, who then told Ruddy, that the President was considering terminating the Special Counsel. Also during this time period, the President reached out to Christie to get his thoughts on firing the Special Counsel. This evidence shows that the President was not just seeking an examination of whether conflicts existed but instead was looking to use asserted conflicts as a way to terminate the Special Counsel.

b. Nexus to an official proceeding. To satisfy the proceeding requirement, it would be necessary to establish a nexus between the President's act of seeking to terminate the Special Counsel and a pending or foreseeable grand jury proceeding.

Substantial evidence indicates that by June 17, 2017, the President knew his conduct was under investigation by a federal prosecutor who could present any evidence of federal crimes to a grand jury. On May 23, 2017, McGahn explicitly warned the President that his "biggest exposure" was not his act of firing Comey but his "other contacts" and "calls," and his "ask re: Flynn." By early June, it was widely reported in the media that federal prosecutors had issued grand jury subpoenas in the Flynn inquiry and that the Special Counsel had taken over the Flynn investigation. On June 9, 2017, the Special Counsel's Office informed the White House that investigators would be interviewing intelligence agency officials who allegedly had been asked by the President to push back against the Russia investigation. On June 14, 2017, news outlets began reporting that the President was himself being investigated for obstruction of justice. Based on widespread reporting, the President knew that such an investigation could include his request for Comey's loyalty; his request that Comey "let[] Flynn go"; his outreach to Coats and Rogers; and his termination of Comey and statement to the Russian Foreign Minister that the termination had relieved "great pressure" related to Russia. And on June 16, 2017, the day before he directed McGahn to have the Special Counsel removed, the President publicly acknowledged that his conduct was under investigation by a federal prosecutor, tweeting, "I am being investigated for firing the FBI Director by the man who told me to fire the FBI Director!"

c. Intent. Substantial evidence indicates that the President's attempts to remove the Special Counsel were linked to the Special Counsel's oversight of investigations that involved the President's conduct—and, most immediately, to reports that the President was being investigated for potential obstruction of justice.

Before the President terminated Comey, the President considered it critically important that he was not under investigation and that the public not erroneously think he was being investigated. As described in [the Mueller Report] Volume II, Section II.D, * * * advisors perceived the President, while he was drafting the Comey termination letter, to be concerned more than anything else about getting out that he was not personally under investigation. When the President learned of the appointment of the Special Counsel on May 17, 2017, he expressed further concern about the investigation, saying "[t]his is the end of my Presidency." The President also faulted Sessions for recusing, saying "you were supposed to protect me."

On June 14, 2017, when the Washington Post reported that the Special Counsel was investigating the President for obstruction of justice, the President was facing what he had wanted to avoid: a criminal investigation into his own conduct that was the subject of widespread media attention. The evidence indicates that news of the obstruction investigation prompted the President to call McGahn and seek to have the Special Counsel removed. By mid-June, the Department of Justice had already cleared the Special Counsel's service and the President's advisors had told him that the claimed conflicts of interest were "silly" and did not provide a basis to remove the Special Counsel. On June 13, 2017, the Acting Attorney General testified before Congress that no good cause for removing the Special Counsel existed, and the President dictated a press statement to Sanders saying he had no intention of firing the Special Counsel. But the next day, the media reported that the President was under investigation for obstruction of justice and the Special Counsel was interviewing witnesses about events related to possible obstruction—spurring the President to write critical tweets about the Special Counsel's investigation. The President called McGahn at home that night and then called him on Saturday from Camp David. The evidence accordingly indicates that news that an obstruction investigation had been opened is what led the President to call McGahn to have the Special Counsel terminated.

There also is evidence that the President knew that he should not have made those calls to McGahn. The President made the calls to McGahn after McGahn had specifically told the President that the White House Counsel's Office—and McGahn himself—could not be involved in pressing conflicts claims and that the President should consult with his personal counsel if he wished to raise conflicts. Instead of relying on his personal counsel to submit the conflicts claims, the President sought to use his official powers to remove the Special Counsel. And after the media reported on the President's actions, he denied that he ever ordered McGahn to have the Special Counsel terminated and made repeated efforts to have McGahn deny the story, as discussed in [Mueller Report] Volume II, Section II.I, * * *. Those denials are contrary to the evidence and suggest the President's awareness that the direction to McGahn could be seen as improper.

F. Efforts to Curtail the Special Counsel's Investigation (pp. 90–98)

1. Mueller Report—Executive Summary (p. 5)

Two days after directing McGahn to have the Special Counsel removed, the President made another attempt to affect the course of the Russia investigation. On June 19, 2017, the President met one-on-one in the Oval Office with his former campaign manager Corey Lewandowski, a trusted advisor outside the government, and dictated a message for Lewandowski to deliver to Sessions. The message said that Sessions should publicly announce that, notwithstanding his recusal from the Russia investigation, the investigation was "very unfair" to the President, the President had done nothing wrong, and Sessions planned to meet with the Special Counsel and "let [him] move forward with investigating election meddling for future elections." Lewandowski said he understood what the President wanted Sessions to do.

One month later, in another private meeting with Lewandowski on July 19, 2017, the President asked about the status of his message for Sessions to limit the Special Counsel investigation to future election interference. Lewandowski told the President that the message would be delivered soon. Hours after that meeting, the President publicly criticized Sessions in an interview with the New York Times, and then issued a series of tweets making it clear that Sessions's job was in jeopardy. Lewandowski did not want to deliver the President's message personally, so he asked senior White House official Rick Dearborn to deliver it to Sessions. Dearborn was uncomfortable with the task and did not follow through.

2. Mueller Report Analysis (pp. 97–98)

In analyzing the President's efforts to have Lewandowski deliver a message directing Sessions to publicly announce that the Special Counsel investigation would be confined to future election interference, the following evidence is relevant to the elements of obstruction of justice:

a. Obstructive act. The President's effort to send Sessions a message through Lewandowski would qualify as an obstructive act if it would naturally obstruct the investigation and any grand jury proceedings that might flow from the inquiry.

The President sought to have Sessions announce that the President "shouldn't have a Special Prosecutor/Counsel" and that Sessions was going to "meet with the Special Prosecutor to explain this is very unfair and let the Special Prosecutor move forward with investigating election meddling for future elections so that nothing can happen in future elections." The President wanted Sessions to disregard his recusal from the investigation, which had followed from a formal DOJ ethics review, and have Sessions declare that he knew "for a fact" that "there were no Russians involved with the campaign" because he "was there." The President further directed that Sessions should explain that the President should not be subject to an investigation "because he hasn't done anything wrong." Taken together, the President's directives indicate that Sessions was being instructed to tell the Special Counsel to end the existing investigation into the President and his campaign, with the Special Counsel being permitted to "move forward with investigating election meddling for future elections."

b. Nexus to an official proceeding. As described above, by the time of the President's initial one-on-one meeting with Lewandowski on June 19, 2017, the existence of a grand jury investigation supervised by the Special Counsel was public knowledge. By the time of the President's follow-up meeting with Lewandowski, Grand Jury * * *. To satisfy the nexus requirement, it would be necessary to show that limiting the Special Counsel's investigation would have the natural and probable effect of impeding that grand jury proceeding.

c. <u>Intent</u>. Substantial evidence indicates that the President's effort to have Sessions limit the scope of the Special Counsel's investigation to future election interference was intended to prevent further investigative scrutiny of the President's and his campaign's conduct.

As previously described, * * * the President knew that the Russia investigation was focused in part on his campaign, and he perceived allegations of Russian interference to cast doubt on the legitimacy of his election. The President further knew that the investigation had broadened to include his own conduct and whether he had obstructed justice. Those investigations would not proceed if the Special Counsel's jurisdiction were limited to future election interference only.

The timing and circumstances of the President's actions support the conclusion that he sought that result. The President's initial direction that Sessions should limit the Special Counsel's investigation came just two days after the President had ordered McGahn to have the Special Counsel removed, which itself followed public reports that the President was personally under investigation for obstruction of justice. The sequence of those events raises an inference that after seeking to terminate the Special Counsel, the President sought to exclude his and his campaign's conduct from the investigation's scope. The President raised the matter with Lewandowski again on July 19, 2017, just days after emails and information about the June 9, 2016 meeting between Russians and senior campaign officials had been publicly disclosed, generating substantial media coverage and investigative interest.

The manner in which the President acted provides additional evidence of his intent. Rather than rely on official channels, the President met with Lewandowski alone in the Oval Office. The President selected a loyal "devotee" outside the White House to deliver the message, supporting an inference that he was working outside White House channels, including McGahn, who had previously resisted contacting the Department of Justice about the Special Counsel. The President also did not contact the Acting Attorney General, who had just testified publicly that there was no cause to remove the Special Counsel. Instead, the President tried to use Sessions to restrict and redirect the Special Counsel's investigation when Sessions was recused and could not properly take any action on it.

The July 19, 2017 events provide further evidence of the President's intent. The President followed up with Lewandowski in a separate one-on-one meeting one month after he first dictated the message for Sessions, demonstrating he still sought to pursue the request. And just hours after Lewandowski assured the President that the message would soon be delivered to Sessions, the President gave an unplanned interview to the New York Times in which he publicly attacked Sessions and raised questions about his job security. Four days later, on July 22, 2017, the President directed Priebus to obtain Sessions's resignation. That evidence could raise an inference that the President wanted Sessions to realize that his job might be on the line as he evaluated whether to comply with the President's direction that Sessions publicly announce that, notwithstanding his recusal, he was going to confine the Special Counsel's investigation to future election interference.

G. Efforts to Prevent Public Disclosure of Evidence (pp. 98–107)

1. Mueller Report — Executive Summary (p. 5)

In the summer of 2017, the President learned that media outlets were asking questions about the June 9, 2016 meeting at Trump Tower between senior campaign officials, including Donald Trump Jr., and a Russian lawyer who was said to be offering damaging information about Hillary Clinton as "part of Russia and its government's support for Mr. Trump." On several occasions, the President directed aides not to publicly disclose the emails setting up the June 9 meeting, suggesting that the emails would not leak and that the number of lawyers with access to them should be limited. Before the emails became public, the President edited a press statement for Trump Jr. by deleting a line that acknowledged that the meeting was with "an individual who [Trump Jr.] was told might have information helpful to the campaign" and instead said only that the meeting was about adoptions of Russian children. When the press asked questions about the President's involvement in Trump Jr.'s statement, the President's personal lawyer repeatedly denied the President had played any role.

2. Mueller Report Analysis (pp. 105–107)

In analyzing the President's actions regarding the disclosure of information about the June 9 meeting, the following evidence is relevant to the elements of obstruction of justice:

a. <u>Obstructive act.</u> On at least three occasions between June 29, 2017, and July 9, 2017, the President directed Hicks and others not to publicly disclose information about the June 9, 2016 meeting between senior campaign officials and a Russian attorney. On June 29, Hicks warned the President that the emails setting up the June 9 meeting were "really bad" and the story would be "massive" when it broke, but the President told her and Kushner to "leave it alone." Early on July 8, after Hicks told the President the New York Times was working on a story about the June 9 meeting, the President directed her not to comment, even though Hicks said that the President usually considered not responding to the press to be the ultimate sin. Later that day, the President rejected Trump Jr.'s draft statement that would have acknowledged that the meeting was with "an individual who I was told might have information helpful to the campaign." The President then dictated a statement to Hicks that said the meeting was about Russian adoption (which the President had twice been told was discussed at the meeting). The statement dictated by the President did not mention the offer of derogatory information about Clinton.

Each of these efforts by the President involved his communications team and was directed at the press. They would amount to obstructive acts only if the President, by taking these actions, sought to withhold information from or mislead congressional investigators or the Special Counsel. On May 17, 2017, the President's campaign received a document request from SSCT that clearly covered the June 9 meeting and underlying emails, and those documents also plainly would have been relevant to the Special Counsel's investigation.

But the evidence does not establish that the President took steps to prevent the emails or other information about the June 9 meeting from being provided to Congress or the Special Counsel. The series of discussions in which the President sought to limit access to the emails and prevent their public release occurred in the context of developing a press strategy. The only evidence we have of the President discussing the production of documents to Congress or the Special Counsel is the conversation on June 29, 2017, when Hicks recalled the President acknowledging that Kushner's attorney should provide emails related to the June 9 meeting to whomever he needed to give them to. We do not have evidence of what the President discussed with his own lawyers at that time.

b. <u>Nexus to an official proceeding</u>. As described above, by the time of the President's attempts to prevent the public release of the emails regarding the June 9 meeting, the existence of a grand jury investigation supervised by the Special Counsel was public knowledge, and the President had been told that the emails were responsive to congressional inquiries. To satisfy the nexus requirement, however, it would be necessary to show that preventing the release of the emails to the public would have the natural and probable effect of impeding the grand jury proceeding or congressional inquiries. As noted above, the evidence does not establish that the President sought to prevent disclosure of the emails in those official proceedings.

c. <u>Intent</u>. The evidence establishes the President's substantial involvement in the communications strategy related to information about his campaign's connections to Russia and his desire to minimize public disclosures about those connections. The President became aware of the emails no later than June 29, 2017, when he discussed them with Hicks and Kushner, and he could have been aware of them as early as June 2, 2017, when lawyers for the Trump Organization began interviewing witnesses who participated in the June 9 meeting. The President thereafter repeatedly rejected the advice of Hicks and other staffers to publicly release information about the June 9 meeting. The President expressed concern that multiple people had access to the emails and instructed Hicks that only one lawyer should deal with the matter. And the President dictated a statement to be released by Trump Jr. in response to the first press accounts of the June 9 meeting that said the meeting was about adoption.

But as described above, the evidence does not establish that the President intended to prevent the Special Counsel's Office or Congress from obtaining the emails setting up the June 9 meeting or other information about that meeting. The statement recorded by Corallo—that the emails "will never get out" can be explained as reflecting a belief that the emails would not be made public if the President's press strategy were followed, even if the emails were provided to Congress and the Special Counsel.

H. Further Efforts to Have the Attorney General Take Control of the Investigation (pp. 107–113)

1. Mueller Report — Executive Summary (p. 5)

In early summer 2017, the President called Sessions at home and again asked him to reverse his recusal from the Russia investigation. Sessions did not reverse his recusal. In October 2017, the President met privately with Sessions in the Oval Office and asked him to "take [a] look" at investigating Clinton. In December 2017, shortly after Flynn pleaded guilty pursuant to a cooperation agreement, the President met with Sessions in the Oval Office and suggested, according to notes taken by a senior advisor, that if Sessions unrecused and took back supervision of the Russia investigation, he would be a "hero." The President told Sessions, "I'm not going to do anything or direct you to do anything. I just want to be treated fairly." In response, Sessions volunteered that he had never seen anything "improper" on the campaign and told the President there was a "whole new leadership team" in place. He did not unrecuse.

2. Mueller Report Analysis (pp. 111–113)

In analyzing the President's efforts to have Sessions unrecuse himself and regain control of the Russia investigation, the following considerations and evidence are relevant to the elements of obstruction of justice:

a. <u>Obstructive act</u>. To determine if the President's efforts to have the Attorney General unrecuse could qualify as an obstructive act, it would be necessary to assess evidence on whether those actions would naturally impede the Russia investigation. That inquiry would take into account the supervisory role that the Attorney General, if unrecused, would play in the Russia investigation. It also would have to take into account that the Attorney General's recusal covered other campaign-related matters. The inquiry would not turn on what Attorney General Sessions would actually do if unrecused, but on whether the efforts to reverse his recusal would naturally have had the effect of impeding the Russia investigation.

On multiple occasions in 2017, the President spoke with Sessions about reversing his recusal so that he could take over the Russia investigation and begin an investigation and prosecution of Hillary Clinton. For example, in early summer 2017, Sessions recalled the President asking him to unrecuse, but Sessions did not take it as a directive. When the President raised the issue again in December 2017, the President said, as recorded by Porter, "Not telling you to do anything. . . . I'm not going to get involved. I'm not going to do anything or direct you to do anything. I just want to be treated fairly." The duration of the President's efforts — which spanned from March 2017 to August 2018 — and the fact that the President repeatedly criticized Sessions in public and in private for failing to tell the President that he would have to recuse is relevant to assessing whether the President's efforts to have Sessions unrecuse could qualify as obstructive acts.

b. <u>Nexus to an official proceeding</u>. As described above, by mid-June 2017, the existence of a grand jury investigation supervised by the Special Counsel was public knowledge. In addition, in July 2017, a different grand jury supervised by the Special Counsel was empaneled in the District of Columbia, and the press reported on the existence of this grand jury in early August 2017. Whether the conduct towards the Attorney General would have a foreseeable impact on those proceedings turns on much of the same evidence discussed above with respect to the obstructive-act element.

c. Intent. There is evidence that at least one purpose of the President's conduct toward Sessions was to have Sessions assume control over the Russia investigation and supervise it in a way that would restrict its scope. By the summer of 2017, the President was aware that the Special Counsel was investigating him personally for obstruction of justice. And in the wake of the disclosures of emails about the June 9 meeting between Russians and senior members of the campaign, see Volume II, Section II.G, * * *, it was evident that the investigation into the campaign now included the President's son, son-in-law, and former campaign manager. The President had previously and unsuccessfully sought to have Sessions publicly announce that the Special Counsel investigation would be confined to future election interference. Yet Sessions remained recused. In December 2017, shortly after Flynn pleaded guilty, the President spoke to Sessions in the Oval Office with only Porter present and told Sessions that he would be a hero if he unrecused. Porter linked that request to the President's desire that Sessions take back supervision of the Russia investigation and direct an investigation of Hillary Clinton. The President said in that meeting that he "just want[ed] to be treated fairly," which could reflect his perception that it was unfair that he was being investigated while Hillary Clinton was not. But a principal effect of that act would be to restore supervision of the Russia investigation to the Attorney General—a position that the President frequently suggested should be occupied by someone like Eric Holder and Bobby Kennedy, who the President described as protecting their presidents. A reasonable inference from those statements and the President's actions is that the President believed that an unrecused Attorney General would play a protective role and could shield the President from the ongoing Russia investigation.

I. Efforts to Have McGahn Deny That the President Had Ordered Him to Have the Special Counsel Removed (pp. 113–120)

1. Mueller Report—Executive Summary (pp. 5–6)

In early 2018, the press reported that the President had directed McGahn to have the Special Counsel removed in June 2017 and that McGahn had threatened to resign rather than carry out the order. The President reacted to the news stories by directing White House officials to tell McGahn to dispute the story and create a record stating he had not been ordered to have the Special Counsel removed. McGahn told those officials that the media reports were accurate in stating that the President had directed McGahn to have the Special Counsel removed. The President then met with McGahn in the Oval Office and again pressured him to deny the reports. In the same meeting, the President also asked McGahn why he had told the Special Counsel about the President's effort to remove the Special Counsel and why McGahn took notes of his conversations with the President. McGahn refused to back away from what he remembered happening and perceived the President to be testing his mettle.

2. Mueller Report Analysis (pp. 118–120)

In analyzing the President's efforts to have McGahn deny that he had been ordered to have the Special Counsel removed, the following evidence is relevant to the elements of obstruction of justice:

a. <u>Obstructive act</u>. The President's repeated efforts to get McGahn to create a record denying that the President had directed him to remove the Special Counsel would qualify as an obstructive act if it had the natural tendency to constrain McGahn from testifying truthfully or to undermine his credibility as a potential witness if he testified consistently with his memory, rather than with what the record said.

There is some evidence that at the time the New York Times and Washington Post stories were published in late January 2018, the President believed the stories were wrong and that he had never told McGahn to have Rosenstein remove the Special Counsel. The President correctly understood that McGahn had not told the President directly that he planned to resign. In addition, the President told Priebus and Porter that he had not sought to terminate the Special Counsel, and in the Oval Office meeting with McGahn, the President said, "I never said to fire Mueller. I never said 'fire.'" That evidence could indicate that the President was not attempting to persuade McGahn to change his story but was instead offering his own — but different — recollection of the substance of his June 2017 conversations with McGahn and McGahn's reaction to them.

Other evidence cuts against that understanding of the President's conduct. As previously described, *see* Volume II, Section II.E, * * * substantial evidence supports McGahn's account that the President had directed him to have the Special Counsel removed, including the timing and context of the President's directive; the manner in which McGahn reacted; and the fact that the President had been told the conflicts were insubstantial, were being considered by the Department of Justice, and should be raised with the President's personal counsel rather than brought to McGahn. In addition, the President's subsequent denials that he had told McGahn to have the Special Counsel removed were carefully worded. When first asked about the New York Times story, the President said, "Fake news, folks. Fake news. A typical New York Times fake story." And when the President spoke with McGahn in the Oval Office, he focused on whether he had used the word "fire," saying, "I never said to fire Mueller. I never said 'fire'" and "Did I say the word 'fire'?" The President's assertion in the Oval Office meeting that he had never directed McGahn to have the Special Counsel removed thus runs counter to the evidence.

In addition, even if the President sincerely disagreed with McGahn's memory of the June 17, 2017 events, the evidence indicates that the President knew by the time of the Oval Office meeting that McGahn's account differed and that McGahn was firm in his views. Shortly after the story broke, the President's counsel told McGahn's counsel that the President wanted McGahn to make a statement denying he had been asked to fire the Special Counsel, but McGahn responded through his counsel that that aspect of the story was accurate and he therefore could not comply with the President's request. The President then directed Sanders to tell McGahn to correct the story, but McGahn told her he would not do so because the story was accurate in reporting on the President's order. Consistent with that position, McGahn never issued a correction. More than a week later, the President brought up the issue again with Porter, made comments indicating the President thought McGahn had leaked the story, and directed Porter to have McGahn create a record denying that the President had tried to fire the Special Counsel. At that point, the President said he might "have to get rid of" McGahn if McGahn did not comply. McGahn again refused and told Porter, as he had told Sanders and as his counsel had told the President's counsel, that the President had in fact ordered him to have Rosenstein remove the Special Counsel. That evidence indicates that by the time of the Oval Office meeting the President was aware that McGahn did not think the story was false and did not want to issue a statement or create a written record denying facts that McGahn believed to be true. The President nevertheless persisted and asked McGahn to repudiate facts that McGahn had repeatedly said were accurate.

b. <u>Nexus to an official proceeding</u>. By January 2018, the Special Counsel's use of a grand jury had been further confirmed by the return of several indictments. The President also was aware that the Special Counsel was investigating obstruction-related events because, among other reasons, on January 8, 2018, the Special Counsel's Office provided his counsel with a detailed list of topics for a possible interview with the President. The President knew that McGahn had personal knowledge of many of the events the Special Counsel was investigating and that McGahn had already been interviewed by Special Counsel investigators. And in the Oval Office meeting, the President indicated he knew that McGahn had told the Special Counsel's Office about the President's effort to remove the Special Counsel. The President challenged McGahn for disclosing that information and for taking notes that he viewed as creating unnecessary legal exposure. That evidence indicates the President's awareness that the June 17, 2017 events were relevant to the Special Counsel's investigation and any grand jury investigation that might grow out of it.

To establish a nexus, it would be necessary to show that the President's actions would have the natural tendency to affect such a proceeding or that they would hinder, delay, or prevent the communication of information to investigators. Because McGahn had spoken to Special Counsel investigators before January 2018, the President could not have been seeking to influence his prior statements in those interviews. But because McGahn had repeatedly spoken to investigators and the obstruction inquiry was not complete, it was foreseeable that he would be interviewed again on obstruction-related topics. If the President were focused solely on a press strategy in seeking to have McGahn refute the New York Times article, a nexus to a proceeding or to further investigative interviews would not be shown. But the President's efforts to have McGahn write a letter "for our records" approximately ten days after the stories had come out—well past the typical time to issue a correction for a news story— indicates the President was not focused solely on a press strategy, but instead likely contemplated the ongoing investigation and any proceedings arising from it.

c. Intent. Substantial evidence indicates that in repeatedly urging McGahn to dispute that he was ordered to have the Special Counsel terminated, the President acted for the purpose of influencing McGahn's account in order to deflect or prevent further scrutiny of the President's conduct towards the investigation.

Several facts support that conclusion. The President made repeated attempts to get McGahn to change his story. As described above, by the time of the last attempt, the evidence suggests that the President had been told on multiple occasions that McGahn believed the President had ordered him to have the Special Counsel terminated. McGahn interpreted his encounter with the President in the Oval Office as an attempt to test his mettle and see how committed he was to his memory of what had occurred. The President had already laid the groundwork for pressing McGahn to alter his account by telling Porter that it might be necessary to fire McGahn if he did not deny the story, and Porter relayed that statement to McGahn. Additional evidence of the President's intent may be gleaned from the fact that his counsel was sufficiently alarmed by the prospect of the President's meeting with McGahn that he called McGahn's counsel and said that McGahn could not resign no matter what happened in the Oval Office that day. The President's counsel was well aware of McGahn's resolve not to issue what he believed to be a false account of events despite the President's request. Finally, as noted above, the President brought up the Special Counsel investigation in his Oval Office meeting with McGahn and criticized him for telling this Office about the June 17, 2017 events. The President's statements reflect his understanding—and his displeasure—that those events would be part of an obstruction-of-justice inquiry.

J. The President's Conduct towards Flynn, Manafort, Harm to Ongoing Matter (pp. 120–133)

1. Mueller Report—Executive Summary (p. 6)

After Flynn withdrew from a joint defense agreement with the President and began cooperating with the government, the President's personal counsel left a message for Flynn's attorneys reminding them of the President's warm feelings towards Flynn, which he said "still remains," and asking for a "heads up" if Flynn knew "information that implicates the President." When Flynn's counsel reiterated that Flynn could no longer share information pursuant to a joint defense agreement, the President's personal counsel said he would make sure that the President knew that Flynn's actions reflected "hostility" towards the President. During Manafort's prosecution and when the jury in his criminal trial was deliberating, the President praised Manafort in public, said that Manafort was being treated unfairly, and declined to rule out a pardon. After Manafort was convicted, the President called Manafort "a brave man" for refusing to "break" and said that "flipping" "almost ought to be outlawed." Harm to Ongoing Matter

2. Mueller Report Analysis (pp. 131–133)

In analyzing the President's conduct towards Flynn, Manafort, Harm to Ongoing Matter the following evidence is relevant to the elements of obstruction of justice:

a. Obstructive act. The President's actions towards witnesses in the Special Counsel's investigation would qualify as obstructive if they had the natural tendency to prevent particular witnesses from testifying truthfully, or otherwise would have the probable effect of influencing, delaying, or preventing their testimony to law enforcement.

With regard to Flynn, the President sent private and public messages to Flynn encouraging him to stay strong and conveying that the President still cared about him before he began to cooperate with the government. When Flynn's attorneys withdrew him from a joint defense agreement with the President, signaling that Flynn was potentially cooperating with the government, the President's personal counsel initially reminded Flynn's counsel of the President's warm feelings towards Flynn and said "that still remains." But when Flynn's counsel reiterated that Flynn could no longer share information under a joint defense agreement, the President's personal counsel stated that the decision would be interpreted as reflecting Flynn's hostility towards the President. That sequence of events could have had the potential to affect Flynn's decision to cooperate, as well as the extent of that cooperation. Because of privilege issues, however, we could not determine whether the President was personally involved in or knew about the specific message his counsel delivered to Flynn's counsel.

With respect to Manafort, there is evidence that the President's actions had the potential to influence Manafort's decision whether to cooperate with the government. The President and his personal counsel made repeated statements suggesting that a pardon was a possibility for Manafort, while also making it clear that the President did not want Manafort to "flip" and cooperate with the government. On June 15, 2018, the day the judge presiding over Manafort's D.C. case was considering whether to revoke his bail, the President said that he "felt badly" for Manafort and stated, "I think a lot of it is very unfair." And when asked about a pardon for Manafort, the President said, "I do want to see people treated fairly. That's what it's all about." Later that day, after Manafort's bail was revoked, the President called it a "tough sentence" that was "Very unfair!" Two days later, the President's personal counsel stated that individuals involved in the Special Counsel's investigation could receive a pardon "if in fact the [P]resident and his advisors. come to the conclusion that you have been treated unfairly" — using language that paralleled how the President had already described the treatment of Manafort. Those statements, combined with the President's commendation of Manafort for being a "brave man" who "refused to 'break,'" suggested that a pardon was a more likely possibility if Manafort continued not to cooperate with the government. And while Manafort eventually pleaded guilty pursuant to a cooperation agreement, he was found to have violated the agreement by lying to investigators.

The President's public statements during the Manafort trial, including during jury deliberations, also had the potential to influence the trial jury. On the second day of trial, for example, the President called the prosecution a "terrible situation" and a "hoax" that "continues to stain our country" and referred to Manafort as a "Reagan/ Dole darling" who was "serving solitary confinement" even though he was "convicted of nothing." Those statements were widely picked up by the press. While jurors were instructed not to watch or read news stories about the case and are presumed to follow those instructions, the President's statements during the trial generated substantial media coverage that could have reached jurors if they happened to see the statements or learned about them from others. And the President's statements during jury deliberations that Manafort "happens to be a very good person" and that "it's very sad what they've done to Paul Manafort" had the potential to influence jurors who learned of the statements, which the President made just as jurors were considering whether to convict or acquit Manafort. Harm to Ongoing Matter

   b. <u>Nexus to an official proceeding</u>. The President's actions towards Flynn, Manafort, Harm to Ongoing Matter appear to have been connected to pending or anticipated official proceedings involving each individual. The President's conduct towards Flynn Harm to Ongoing Matter principally occurred when both were under criminal investigation by the Special Counsel's Office and press reports speculated about whether they would cooperate with the Special Counsel's investigation. And the President's conduct towards Manafort was directly connected to the official proceedings involving him. The President made statements about Manafort and the charges against him during Manafort's criminal trial. And the President's comments about the prospect of Manafort "flipping" occurred when it was clear the Special Counsel continued to oversee grand jury proceedings.

   c. <u>Intent</u>. Evidence concerning the President's intent related to Flynn as a potential witness is inconclusive. As previously noted, because of privilege issues we do not have evidence establishing whether the President knew about or was involved in his counsel's communications with Flynn's counsel stating that Flynn's decision to withdraw from the joint defense agreement and cooperate with the government would be viewed as reflecting "hostility" towards the President. And regardless of what the President's personal counsel communicated, the President continued to express sympathy for Flynn after he pleaded guilty pursuant to a cooperation agreement, stating that Flynn had "led a very strong life" and the President "fe[lt] very badly" about what had happened to him.

   Evidence concerning the President's conduct towards Manafort indicates that the President intended to encourage Manafort to not cooperate with the government. Before Manafort was convicted, the President repeatedly stated that Manafort had been treated unfairly. One day after Manafort was convicted on eight felony charges and potentially faced a lengthy prison term, the President said that Manafort was "a brave man" for refusing to "break" and that "flipping" "almost ought to be outlawed." At the same time, although the President had privately told aides he did not like Manafort, he publicly called Manafort "a good man" and said he had a "wonderful family." And when the President was asked whether he was considering a pardon for Manafort, the President did not respond directly and instead said he had "great respect for what [Manafort]'s done, in terms of what he's gone through." The President added that "some of the charges they threw against him, every consultant, every lobbyist in Washington probably does." In light of the President's counsel's previous statements that the investigations "might get cleaned up with some presidential pardons" and that a pardon would be possible if the President "come[s] to the conclusion that you have been treated unfairly," the evidence supports the inference that the President intended Manafort to believe that he could receive a pardon, which would make cooperation with the government as a means of obtaining a lesser sentence unnecessary.

We also examined the evidence of the President's intent in making public statements about Manafort at the beginning of his trial and when the jury was deliberating. Some evidence supports a conclusion that the President intended, at least in part, to influence the jury. The trial generated widespread publicity, and as the jury began to deliberate, commentators suggested that an acquittal would add to pressure to end the Special Counsel's investigation. By publicly stating on the second day of deliberations that Manafort "happens to be a very good person" and that "it's very sad what they've done to Paul Manafort" right after calling the Special Counsel's investigation a "rigged witch hunt," the President's statements could, if they reached jurors, have the natural tendency to engender sympathy for Manafort among jurors, and a factfinder could infer that the President intended that result. But there are alternative explanations for the President's comments, including that he genuinely felt sorry for Manafort or that his goal was not to influence the jury but to influence public opinion. The President's comments also could have been intended to continue sending a message to Manafort that a pardon was possible. As described above, the President made his comments about Manafort being "a very good person" immediately after declining to answer a question about whether he would pardon Manafort. Harm to Ongoing Matter

K. Conduct Involving Michael Cohen (pp. 134–156)

1. Mueller Report — Executive Summary (p. 6)

The President's conduct towards Michael Cohen, a former Trump Organization executive, changed from praise for Cohen when he falsely minimized the President's involvement in the Trump Tower Moscow project, to castigation of Cohen when he became a cooperating witness. From September 2015 to June 2016, Cohen had pursued the Trump Tower Moscow project on behalf of the Trump Organization and had briefed candidate Trump on the project numerous times, including discussing whether Trump should travel to Russia to advance the deal. In 2017, Cohen provided false testimony to Congress about the project, including stating that he had only briefed Trump on the project three times and never discussed travel to Russia with him, in an effort to adhere to a "party line" that Cohen said was developed to minimize the President's connections to Russia. While preparing for his congressional testimony, Cohen had extensive discussions with the President's personal counsel, who, according to Cohen, said that Cohen should "stay on message" and not contradict the President. After the FBI searched Cohen's home and office in April 2018, the President publicly asserted that Cohen would not "flip," contacted him directly to tell him to "stay strong," and privately passed messages of support to him. Cohen also discussed pardons with the President's personal counsel and believed that if he stayed on message he would be taken care of. But after Cohen began cooperating with the government in the summer of 2018, the President publicly criticized him, called him a "rat," and suggested that his family members had committed crimes.

2. Mueller Report Analysis (pp. 153–156)

In analyzing the President's conduct related to Cohen, the following evidence is relevant to the elements of obstruction of justice.

a. <u>Obstructive act</u>. We gathered evidence of the President's conduct related to Cohen on two issues: (i) whether the President or others aided or participated in Cohen's false statements to Congress, and (ii) whether the President took actions that would have the natural tendency to prevent Cohen from providing truthful information to the government.

i. First, with regard to Cohen's false statements to Congress, while there is evidence, described below, that the President knew Cohen provided false testimony to Congress about the Trump Tower Moscow project, the evidence available to us does not establish that the President directed or aided Cohen's false testimony.

Cohen said that his statements to Congress followed a "party line" that developed within the campaign to align with the President's public statements distancing the President from Russia. Cohen also recalled that, in speaking with the President in advance of testifying, he made it clear that he would stay on message—which Cohen believed they both understood would require false testimony. But Cohen said that he and the President did not explicitly discuss whether Cohen's testimony about the Trump Tower Moscow project would be or was false, and the President did not direct him to provide false testimony. Cohen also said he did not tell the President about the specifics of his planned testimony. During the time when his statement to Congress was being drafted and circulated to members of the JDA, Cohen did not speak directly to the President about the statement, but rather communicated with the President's personal counsel as corroborated by phone records showing extensive communications between Cohen and the President's personal counsel before Cohen submitted his statement and when he testified before Congress.

Cohen recalled that in his discussions with the President's personal counsel on August 27, 2017—the day before Cohen's statement was submitted to Congress—Cohen said that there were more communications with Russia and more communications with candidate Trump than the statement reflected. Cohen recalled expressing some concern at that time. According to Cohen, the President's personal counsel—

who did not have first-hand knowledge of the project — responded by saying that there was no need to muddy the water, that it was unnecessary to include those details because the project did not take place, and that Cohen should keep his statement short and tight, not elaborate, stay on message, and not contradict the President. Cohen's recollection of the content of those conversations is consistent with direction about the substance of Cohen's draft statement that appeared to come from members of the JDA. For example, Cohen omitted any reference to his outreach to Russian government officials to set up a meeting between Trump and Putin during the United Nations General Assembly, and Cohen believed it was a decision of the JDA to delete the sentence, "The building project led me to make limited contacts with Russian government officials."

The President's personal counsel declined to provide us with his account of his conversations with Cohen, and there is no evidence available to us that indicates that the President was aware of the information Cohen provided to the President's personal counsel. The President's conversations with his personal counsel were presumptively protected by attorney-client privilege, and we did not seek to obtain the contents of any such communications. The absence of evidence about the President and his counsel's conversations about the drafting of Cohen's statement precludes us from assessing what, if any, role the President played.

ii. Second, we considered whether the President took actions that would have the natural tendency to prevent Cohen from providing truthful information to criminal investigators or to Congress.

Before Cohen began to cooperate with the government, the President publicly and privately urged Cohen to stay on message and not "flip." Cohen recalled the President's personal counsel telling him that he would be protected so long as he did not go "rogue." In the days and weeks that followed the April 2018 searches of Cohen's home and office, the President told reporters that Cohen was a "good man" and said he was "a fine person with a wonderful family … who I have always liked & respected." Privately, the President told Cohen to "hang in there" and "stay strong." People who were close to both Cohen and the President passed messages to Cohen that "the President loves you," "the boss loves you," and "everyone knows the boss has your back." Through the President's personal counsel, the President also had previously told Cohen "thanks for what you do" after Cohen provided information to the media about payments to women that, according to Cohen, both Cohen and the President knew was false. At that time, the Trump Organization continued to pay Cohen's legal fees, which was important to Cohen. Cohen also recalled discussing the possibility of a pardon with the President's personal counsel, who told him to stay on message and everything would be fine. The President indicated in his public statements that a pardon had not been ruled out, and also stated publicly that "[m]ost people will flip if the Government lets them out of trouble" but that he "d[idn't] see Michael doing that."

After it was reported that Cohen intended to cooperate with the government, however, the President accused Cohen of "mak[ing] up stories in order to get himself out of an unrelated jam (Taxi cabs maybe?)," called Cohen a "rat," and on multiple occasions publicly suggested that Cohen's family members had committed crimes. The evidence concerning this sequence of events could support an inference that the President used inducements in the form of positive messages in an effort to get Cohen not to cooperate, and then turned to attacks and intimidation to deter the provision of information or undermine Cohen's credibility once Cohen began cooperating.

b. Nexus to an official proceeding. The President's relevant conduct towards Cohen occurred when the President knew the Special Counsel's Office, Congress, and the U.S. Attorney's Office for the Southern District of New York were investigating Cohen's conduct. The President acknowledged through his public statements and tweets that Cohen potentially could cooperate with the government investigations.

c. Intent. In analyzing the President's intent in his actions towards Cohen as a potential witness, there is evidence that could support the inference that the President intended to discourage Cohen from cooperating with the government because Cohen's information would shed adverse light on the President's campaign-period conduct and statements.

i. Cohen's false congressional testimony about the Trump Tower Moscow project was designed to minimize connections between the President and Russia and to help limit the congressional and DOJ Russia investigations—a goal that was in the President's interest, as reflected by the President's own statements. During and after the campaign, the President made repeated statements that he had "no business" in Russia and said that there were "no deals that could happen in Russia, because we've stayed away." As Cohen knew, and as he recalled communicating to the President during the campaign, Cohen's pursuit of the Trump Tower Moscow project cast doubt on the accuracy or completeness of these statements.

In connection with his guilty plea, Cohen admitted that he had multiple conversations with candidate Trump to give him status updates about the Trump Tower Moscow project, that the conversations continued through at least June 2016, and that he discussed with Trump possible travel to Russia to pursue the project. The conversations were not off-hand, according to Cohen, because the project had the potential to be so lucrative. In addition, text messages to and from Cohen and other records further establish that Cohen's efforts to advance the project did not end in January 2016 and that in May and June 2016, Cohen was considering the timing for possible trips to Russia by him and Trump in connection with the project.

The evidence could support an inference that the President was aware of these facts at the time of Cohen's false statements to Congress. Cohen discussed the project with the President in early 2017 following media inquiries. Cohen recalled that on September 20, 2017, the day after he released to the public his opening remarks to Congress—which said the project "was terminated in January of 2016"—the President's personal counsel told him the President was pleased with what Cohen had said about Trump Tower Moscow. And after Cohen's guilty plea, the President told reporters that he had ultimately decided not to do the project, which supports the inference that he remained aware of his own involvement in the project and the period during the Campaign in which the project was· being pursued.

ii. The President's public remarks following Cohen's guilty plea also suggest that the President may have been concerned about what Cohen told investigators about the Trump Tower Moscow project. At the time the President submitted written answers to questions from this Office about the project and other subjects, the media had reported that Cohen was cooperating with the government but Cohen had not yet pleaded guilty to making false statements to Congress. Accordingly, it was not publicly known what information about the project Cohen had provided to the government. In his written answers, the President did not provide details about the timing and substance of his discussions with Cohen about the project and gave no indication that he had decided to no longer pursue the project. Yet after Cohen pleaded guilty, the President publicly stated that he had personally made the decision to abandon the project. The President then declined to clarify the seeming discrepancy to our Office or answer additional questions. The content and timing of the President's provision of information about his knowledge and actions regarding the Trump Tower Moscow project is evidence that the President may have been concerned about the information that Cohen could provide as a witness.

iii. The President's concern about Cohen cooperating may have been directed at the Southern District of New York investigation into other aspects of the President's dealings with Cohen rather than an investigation of Trump Tower Moscow. There also is some evidence that the President's concern about Cohen cooperating was based on the President's stated belief that Cohen would provide false testimony against the President in an attempt to obtain a lesser sentence for his unrelated criminal conduct. The President tweeted that Manafort, unlike Cohen, refused to "break" and "make up stories in order to get a 'deal.'" And after Cohen pleaded guilty to making false statements to Congress, the President said, "what [Cohen]'s trying to do is get a reduced sentence. So he's lying about a project that everybody knew about." But the President also appeared to defend the underlying conduct, saying, "Even if [Cohen] was right, it doesn't matter because I was allowed to do whatever I wanted during the campaign." As described above, there is evidence that the President knew that Cohen had made false statements about the Trump Tower Moscow project and that Cohen did so to protect the President and minimize the President's connections to Russia during the campaign.

iv. Finally, the President's statements insinuating that members of Cohen's family committed crimes after Cohen began cooperating with the government could be viewed as an effort to retaliate against Cohen and chill further testimony adverse to the President by Cohen or others. It is possible that the President believes, as reflected in his tweets, that Cohen "ma[d]e[] up stories" in order to get a deal for himself and "get his wife and father-in-law ... off Scott Free." It also is possible that the President's mention of Cohen's wife and father-in-law were not intended to affect Cohen as a witness but rather were part of a public-relations strategy aimed at discrediting Cohen and deflecting attention away from the President on Cohen-related matters. But the President's suggestion that Cohen's family members committed crimes happened more than once, including just before Cohen was sentenced (at the same time as the President stated that Cohen "should, in my opinion, serve a full and complete sentence") and again just before Cohen was scheduled to testify before Congress. The timing of the statements supports an inference that they were intended at least in part to discourage Cohen from further cooperation.

L. Overarching Factual Issues (pp. 156–158)

1. Mueller Report — Executive Summary (p. 7)

We did not make a traditional prosecution decision about these facts, but the evidence we obtained supports several general statements about the President's conduct.

Several features of the conduct we investigated distinguish it from typical obstruction-of-justice cases. First, the investigation concerned the President, and some of his actions, such as firing the FBI director, involved facially lawful acts within his Article II authority, which raises constitutional issues discussed below. At the same time, the President's position as the head of the Executive Branch provided him with unique and powerful means of influencing official proceedings, subordinate officers, and potential witnesses — all of which is relevant to a potential obstruction-of-justice analysis. Second, unlike cases in which a subject engages in obstruction of justice to cover up a crime, the evidence we obtained did not establish that the President was involved in an underlying crime related to Russian election interference. Although the obstruction statutes do not require proof of such a crime, the absence of that evidence affects the analysis of the President's intent and requires consideration of other possible motives for his conduct. Third, many of the President's acts directed at witnesses, including discouragement of cooperation with the government and suggestions of possible future pardons, took place in public view. That circumstance is unusual, but no principle of law excludes public acts from the reach of the obstruction laws. If the likely effect of public acts is to influence witnesses or alter their testimony, the harm to the justice system's integrity is the same.

Although the series of events we investigated involved discrete acts, the overall pattern of the President's conduct towards the investigations can shed light on the nature of the President's acts and the inferences that can be drawn about his intent. In particular, the actions we investigated can be divided into two phases, reflecting a possible shift in the President's motives. The first phase covered the period from the President's first interactions with Comey through the President's firing of Comey. During that time, the President had been repeatedly told he was not personally under investigation. Soon after the firing of Comey and the appointment of the Special Counsel, however, the President became aware that his own conduct was being investigated in an obstruction-of-justice inquiry. At that point, the President engaged in a second phase of conduct, involving public attacks on the investigation, non-public efforts to control it, and efforts in both public and private to encourage witnesses not to cooperate with the investigation. Judgments about the nature of the President's motives during each phase would be informed by the totality of the evidence.

2. Mueller Report Analysis (pp. 156–158)

Although this report does not contain a traditional prosecution decision or declination decision, the evidence supports several general conclusions relevant to analysis of the facts concerning the President's course of conduct.

1. Three features of this case render it atypical compared to the heartland obstruction-of-justice prosecutions brought by the Department of Justice.

First, the conduct involved actions by the President. Some of the conduct did not implicate the President's constitutional authority and raises garden-variety obstruction-of-justice issues. Other events we investigated, however, drew upon the President's Article II authority, which raised constitutional issues that we address in Volume II, Section III.B, * * *. A factual analysis of that conduct would have to take into account both that the President's acts were facially lawful and that his position as head of the Executive Branch provides him with unique and powerful means of influencing official proceedings, subordinate officers, and potential witnesses.

Second, many obstruction cases involve the attempted or actual cover-up of an underlying crime. Personal criminal conduct can furnish strong evidence that the individual had an improper obstructive purpose, see, e.g., United States v. Willoughby, 860 F.2d 15, 24 (2d Cir. 1988), or that he contemplated an effect on an official proceeding, see, e.g., United States v. Binday, 804 F.3d 558, 591 (2d Cir. 2015). But proof of such a crime is not an element of an obstruction offense. See United States v. Greer, 872 F.3d 790, 798 (6th Cir. 2017) (stating, in applying the obstruction sentencing guideline, that "obstruction of a criminal investigation is punishable even if the prosecution is ultimately unsuccessful or even if the investigation ultimately reveals no underlying crime"). Obstruction of justice can be motivated by a desire to protect non-criminal personal interests, to protect against investigations where underlying criminal liability falls into a gray area, or to avoid personal embarrassment. The injury to the integrity of the justice system is the same regardless of whether a person committed an underlying wrong.

In this investigation, the evidence does not establish that the President was involved in an underlying crime related to Russian election interference. But the evidence does point to a range of other possible personal motives animating the President's conduct. These include concerns that continued investigation would call into question the legitimacy of his election and potential uncertainty about whether certain events — such as advance notice of WikiLeaks's release of hacked information or the June 9, 2016 meeting between senior campaign officials and Russians — could be seen as criminal activity by the President, his campaign, or his family.

Third, many of the President's acts directed at witnesses, including discouragement of cooperation with the government and suggestions of possible future pardons, occurred in public view. While it may be more difficult to establish that public-facing acts were motivated by a corrupt intent, the President's power to influence actions, persons, and events is enhanced by his unique ability to attract attention through use of mass communications. And no principle of law excludes public acts from the scope of obstruction statutes. If the likely effect of the acts is to intimidate witnesses or alter their testimony, the justice system's integrity is equally threatened.

2. Although the events we investigated involved discrete acts—e.g., the President's statement to Comey about the Flynn investigation, his termination of Comey, and his efforts to remove the Special Counsel—it is important to view the President's pattern of conduct as a whole. That pattern sheds light on the nature of the President's acts and the inferences that can be drawn about his intent.

a. Our investigation found multiple acts by the President that were capable of exerting undue influence over law enforcement investigations, including the Russian-interference and obstruction investigations. The incidents were often carried out through one-on-one meetings in which the President sought to use his official power outside of usual channels. These actions ranged from efforts to remove the Special Counsel and to reverse the effect of the Attorney General's recusal; to the attempted use of official power to limit the scope of the investigation; to direct and indirect contacts with witnesses with the potential to influence their testimony. Viewing the acts collectively can help to illuminate their significance. For example, the President's direction to McGahn to have the Special Counsel removed was followed almost immediately by his direction to Lewandowski to tell the Attorney General to limit the scope of the Russia investigation to prospective election-interference only—a temporal connection that suggests that both acts were taken with a related purpose with respect to the investigation.

The President's efforts to influence the investigation were mostly unsuccessful, but that is largely because the persons who surrounded the President declined to carry out orders or accede to his requests. Comey did not end the investigation of Flynn, which ultimately resulted in Flynn's prosecution and conviction for lying to the FBI. McGahn did not tell the Acting Attorney General that the Special Counsel must be removed, but was instead prepared to resign over the President's order. Lewandowski and Dearborn did not deliver the President's message to Sessions that he should confine the Russia investigation to future election meddling only. And McGahn refused to recede from his recollections about events surrounding the President's direction to have the Special Counsel removed, despite the President's multiple demands that he do so. Consistent with that pattern, the evidence we obtained would not support potential obstruction charges against the President's aides and associates beyond those already filed.

b. In considering the full scope of the conduct we investigated, the President 's actions can be divided into two distinct phases reflecting a possible shift in the President's motives. In the first phase, before the President fired Comey, the President had been assured that the FBI had not opened an investigation of him personally. The President deemed it critically important to make public that he was not under investigation, and he included that information in his termination letter to Comey after other efforts to have that information disclosed were unsuccessful.

Soon after he fired Comey, however, the President became aware that investigators were conducting an obstruction-of-justice inquiry into his own conduct. That awareness marked a significant change in the President's conduct and the start of a second phase of action. The President launched public attacks on the investigation and individuals involved in it who could possess evidence adverse to the President, while in private, the President engaged in a series of targeted efforts to control the investigation. For instance, the President attempted to remove the Special Counsel; he sought to have Attorney General Sessions unrecuse himself and limit the investigation; he sought to prevent public disclosure of information about the June 9, 2016 meeting between Russians and campaign officials; and he used public forums to attack potential witnesses who might offer adverse information and to praise witnesses who declined to cooperate with the government. Judgments about the nature of the President's motives during each phase would be informed by the totality of the evidence.

Note

Throughout the Mueller Report there are passages that have been redacted with a designation of "Grand Jury." Rule 6(e) of the Federal Rules of Criminal Procedure provides the secrecy mandates prohibiting participants in the grand jury process from disclosing "a matter occurring before the grand jury." A witness, however, who testifies before the grand jury is not bound by the secrecy rule. Rule 6 also provides exceptions to the secrecy rule and the method for obtaining judicial permission for disclosure of grand jury material. Grand jury leaks have been raised in several cases, requiring courts to examine whether there has been a violation of the grand jury secrecy requirements. *See In re Sealed Case No. 99-3091* (Office of Independent Counsel Contempt Proceeding, 192 F.3d 995 (D.C. Cir. 1999)) (reversing contempt proceedings against the Office of Independent Counsel related to claims of a grand jury leak during the investigation of former President William J. Clinton).

V. Defenses

The Mueller Report presents a detailed analysis of the statutory and constitutional defenses (pp. 159–181). In the executive summary those statutory and constitutional defenses are summarized as follows:

Mueller Report — Executive Summary
Statutory and Constitutional Defenses (pp. 7–8)

The President's counsel raised statutory and constitutional defenses to a possible obstruction-of-justice analysis of the conduct we investigated. We concluded that none of those legal defenses provided a basis for declining to investigate the facts.

Statutory defenses. Consistent with precedent and the Department of Justice's general approach to interpreting obstruction statutes, we concluded that several statutes could apply here. *See* 18 U.S.C. §§ 1503, 1505, 1512(b)(3), 1512(c)(2). Section 1512(c)(2) is an omnibus obstruction-of-justice provision that covers a range of obstructive acts directed at pending or contemplated official proceedings. No principle of statutory construction justifies narrowing the provision to cover only conduct that impairs the integrity or availability of evidence. Sections 1503 and 1505 also offer broad protection against obstructive acts directed at pending grand jury, judicial, administrative, and congressional proceedings, and they are supplemented by a provision in Section 1512(b) aimed specifically at conduct intended to prevent or hinder the communication to law enforcement of information related to a federal crime.

Constitutional defenses. As for constitutional defenses arising from the President's status as the head of the Executive Branch, we recognized that the Department of Justice and the courts have not. definitively resolved these issues. We therefore examined those issues through the framework established by Supreme Court precedent governing separation-of-powers issues. The Department of Justice and the President's personal counsel have recognized that the President is subject to statutes that prohibit obstruction of justice by bribing a witness or suborning perjury because that conduct does not implicate his constitutional authority. With respect to whether the President can be found to have obstructed justice by exercising his powers under Article II of the Constitution, we concluded that Congress has authority to prohibit a President's corrupt use of his authority in order to protect the integrity of the administration of justice.

Under applicable Supreme Court precedent, the Constitution does not categorically and permanently immunize a President for obstructing justice through the use of his Article II powers. The separation-of-powers doctrine authorizes Congress to protect official proceedings, including those of courts and grand juries, from corrupt, obstructive acts regardless of their source. We also concluded that any inroad on presidential authority that would occur from prohibiting corrupt acts does not undermine the President's ability to fulfill his constitutional mission. The term "corruptly" sets a demanding standard. It requires a concrete showing that a person acted with an intent to obtain an improper advantage for him self or someone else, inconsistent with official duty and the rights of others. A preclusion of "corrupt" official action does not diminish the President's ability to exercise Article II powers. For example, the proper supervision of criminal law does not demand freedom for the President to act with a corrupt intention of shielding himself from criminal punishment, avoiding financial liability, or preventing personal embarrassment. To the contrary, a statute that prohibits official action undertaken for such corrupt purposes furthers, rather than hinders, the impartial and evenhanded administration of the law. It also aligns with the President's constitutional duty to faithfully execute the laws. Finally, we concluded that in the rare case in which a criminal investigation of the President's conduct is justified, inquiries to determine whether the President acted for a corrupt motive should not impermissibly chill his performance of his constitutionally assigned duties. The conclusion that Congress may apply the obstruction laws to the President's corrupt exercise of the powers of office accords with our constitutional system of checks and balances and the principle that no person is above the law.

Questions

Looking at each of the points raised in Volume II of the Mueller Report, which, if any, of the items discussed in this Report provide sufficient evidence of obstruction of justice? What if any defenses can be raised to claims of obstruction of justice, and would they be likely to be successful if in a court of law?

Chapter Eight

Sexual Misconduct, Defamation, and the President

I. Introduction

The subject of the President's sexual misconduct appears only obliquely in the Mueller Report. The order appointing the Special Counsel authorized him to investigate "the Russian government's efforts to interfere in the 2016 presidential election," including any links or coordination between the Russian government and individuals associated with the Trump Campaign (Volume I), and including "whether the President had obstructed justice in connection with Russia-related investigations" also covering "potentially obstructive acts related to the Special Counsel's investigation itself" (Mueller Report, Volume II). In Volume I, the President's possible sexual misconduct arises as background in two instances. First, the Report includes a discussion of then-F.B.I. Director James Comey's briefing President-Elect Trump concerning the Steele dossier's "allegation that the Russians had compromising tapes of the President involving conduct when he was a private citizen during a 2013 trip to Moscow for the Miss Universe Pageant." (Mueller Report, Vol. I at 27–28 n. 112), known in some circles as the Moscow "pee-tape." Second, Volume I of the Mueller Report refers to the Hollywood Access video in which, as the Report describes it, "Candidate Trump can be heard off camera making graphic statements about women," and less than an hour after which, "WikiLeaks released the first set of emails stolen by the GRU"— GRU is Main Intelligence Directorate of the General Staff of the Russian Army— "from the account of Clinton Campaign chairman John Podesta." (Mueller Report, Vol. I at 58). Much of this discussion is redacted as "Harm to Ongoing Matter." In Volume II, the Mueller Report addresses possible obstruction related to alleged campaign finance violations of the "hush-money" payments to women in consensual sexual relationships with the President [See *supra* Chapter Seven].

However, beyond the Mueller Report—and sometimes confusingly conflated with it—are allegations against the President involving sexual misconduct which could constitute criminal acts and could result in civil lawsuits, including lawsuits for defamation. This Chapter considers issues relating to those civil lawsuits. After a brief introduction to the types of civil lawsuits and the issue of statutes of limitations, Part II considers the hurdle of Presidential immunity to civil lawsuits, first relating to lawsuits in federal court and the landmark case of *Clinton v. Jones* (1997) which also arose from allegations of sexual misconduct, and then relating to civil lawsuits in state court, including the pending litigation in New York state courts in *Zervos v. Trump*. In Part III, this Chapter explores the doctrine of defamation, which is at issue in *Zervos v. Trump* and other cases involving Trump, and which Trump has suggested is too restrictive. Finally, Part IV considers civil lawsuits naming Trump as a defendant alleging unwanted sexual advances.

Approximately twenty women have accused now-President Trump of some type of sexual misconduct. This Chapter considers these allegations and so the material can be sensitive in the description of the allegations as well as the manner in which the allegations are treated in the litigation.

Of the more than twenty women, for many reasons, only a few have chosen to pursue legal remedies. One reason is the paucity of causes of action. Federal statutes can provide relief for sexual harassment as a form of sex discrimination, under Title VII, Title IX, and the Fair Housing Act, covering some employment, educational, and housing situations. A more generalized civil remedy against gender-based violence was part of the Violence Against Women Act (VAWA), but the United States Supreme Court held that the civil remedy exceeded Congressional power under either the Commerce Clause or the Fourteenth Amendment in *United States v. Morrison*, 529 U.S. 598 (2000). A very few states and localities have passed laws providing a cause of action for gender-based violence, but absent a statutory right, the most obvious claim for relief for unwanted sexual conduct would be a tort such as assault or battery or possibly other torts such as infliction of emotional distress or false imprisonment. There are well-known difficulties of proof for claims of sexual misconduct, especially if there are no witnesses or if an affirmative defense of consent is raised. A related cause of action may arise if there are statements or publications about the alleged misconduct giving rise to claims of defamation, libel or slander. These claims also involve problems of proof because the statement must be proven false.

Additionally, there are procedural obstacles to lawsuits that would be raised in a motion to dismiss. Assuming jurisdiction over the parties, one of the primary obstacles is the statute of limitations, a recurring issue in the cases discussed in this Chapter.

Generally, claims for torts have a relatively short statute of limitations. In New York, the statute of limitations is exceedingly short for intentional torts such as assault, battery, libel, and slander: only one year from the act. N.Y. CPLR § 215(3). In California, claims for assault and battery must be made within two years, but claims for false imprisonment and libel or slander must be made within one year; however, a 2019 amendment raised the limit to ten years for sexual assault. Cal. Stat. §§ 335.1; 340; 340.16. In Florida, the statute of limitations is four years from the time of the act for intentional torts including assault, battery, and false imprisonment, although it is only two years for libel and slander. Fla. Stat. §§ 95.11(3)(0); 95.11 (4)(g). And in Arkansas, the statute of limitations for intentional torts is generally three years, although for assault, battery, false imprisonment, and slander, it is only one year. Ark. Stat. §§ 16-56-105; 16-56-104.

In addition to bringing a timely claim within the statute of limitations, if the defendant happens to be the President of the United States, the defendant can raise a claim of presidential immunity for the period during which he is President. In short, the President's argument is a practical one, that if he has to defend such suits, this would be too distracting from his constitutional duties as President under Article II.

II. Presidential Immunity from Civil Suit

A. Immunity in Federal Courts: The Case of Bill Clinton

President Bill Clinton made such an argument in defense of a civil suit filed by Paula Corbin Jones in May 1994, just a few days before the statute of limitations expired. Ms. Jones filed the complaint in federal court, primarily based on acts in Arkansas in 1991 when Bill Clinton was Governor, alleging that he alone and in conspiracy with other state actors deprived her of equal protection on the basis of gender and due process under the Fourteenth Amendment. The complaint also included a state tort claim of infliction of emotional distress. Jones's complaint also included a count of defamation based on statements made by Clinton and the other defendant in 1994, after Clinton became President.

The United States Supreme Court unanimously rejected the President's claim for immunity.

Clinton v. Jones
520 U.S. 681 (1997)

Justice Stevens delivered the opinion of the Court.

This case raises a constitutional and a prudential question concerning the Office of the President of the United States. Respondent, a private citizen, seeks to recover damages from the current occupant of that office based on actions allegedly taken before his term began. The President submits that in all but the most exceptional cases the Constitution requires federal courts to defer such litigation until his term ends and that, in any event, respect for the office warrants such a stay. Despite the force of the arguments supporting the President's submissions, we conclude that they must be rejected.

Petitioner, William Jefferson Clinton, was elected to the Presidency in 1992, and re-elected in 1996. His term of office expires on January 20, 2001. In 1991 he was the Governor of the State of Arkansas. Respondent, Paula Corbin Jones, is a resident of California. In 1991 she lived in Arkansas, and was an employee of the Arkansas Industrial Development Commission.

On May 6, 1994, she commenced this action in the United States District Court for the Eastern District of Arkansas by filing a complaint naming petitioner and

Danny Ferguson, a former Arkansas State Police officer, as defendants. * * * As the case comes to us, we are required to assume the truth of the detailed—but as yet untested—factual allegations in the complaint.

Those allegations principally describe events that are said to have occurred on the afternoon of May 8, 1991, during an official conference held at the Excelsior Hotel in Little Rock, Arkansas. The Governor delivered a speech at the conference; respondent—working as a state employee—staffed the registration desk. She alleges that Ferguson persuaded her to leave her desk and to visit the Governor in a business suite at the hotel, where he made "abhorrent" sexual advances that she vehemently rejected. She further claims that her superiors at work subsequently dealt with her in a hostile and rude manner, and changed her duties to punish her for rejecting those advances. Finally, she alleges that after petitioner was elected President, Ferguson defamed her by making a statement to a reporter that implied she had accepted petitioner's alleged overtures, and that various persons authorized to speak for the President publicly branded her a liar by denying that the incident had occurred.

Respondent seeks actual damages of $75,000, and punitive damages of $100,000. Her complaint contains four counts. * * * Inasmuch as the legal sufficiency of the claims has not yet been challenged, we assume, without deciding, that each of the four counts states a cause of action as a matter of law. With the exception of the last charge [of defamation] which arguably may involve conduct within the outer perimeter of the President's official responsibilities, it is perfectly clear that the alleged misconduct of petitioner was unrelated to any of his official duties as President of the United States and, indeed, occurred before he was elected to that office.

* * * [procedural history omitted]

While our decision to grant the petition [for certiorari] expressed no judgment concerning the merits of the case, it does reflect our appraisal of its importance. * * * [We] identify two important constitutional issues not encompassed within the questions presented by the petition for certiorari that we need not address today.

First, because the claim of immunity is asserted in a federal court and relies heavily on the doctrine of separation of powers that restrains each of the three branches of the Federal Government from encroaching on the domain of the other two, *see, e.g., Buckley v. Valeo*, 424 U.S. 1, 122 (1976), it is not necessary to consider or decide whether a comparable claim might succeed in a state tribunal. If this case were being heard in a state forum, instead of advancing a separation of powers argument, petitioner would presumably rely on federalism and comity concerns, as well as the interest in protecting federal officials from possible local prejudice that underlies the authority to remove certain cases brought against federal officers from a state to a federal court, *see* 28 U.S.C. § 1442(a); *Mesa v. California*, 489 U.S. 121, 125–126 (1989). Whether those concerns would present a more compelling case for immunity is a question that is not before us.

Second, our decision rejecting the immunity claim and allowing the case to proceed does not require us to confront the question whether a court may compel the attendance of the President at any specific time or place. We assume that the testimony of the President, both for discovery and for use at trial, may be taken at the White House at a time that will accommodate his busy schedule, and that, if a trial is held, there would be no necessity for the President to attend in person, though he could elect to do so.

Petitioner's principal submission—that "in all but the most exceptional cases," the Constitution affords the President temporary immunity from civil damages litigation arising out of events that occurred before he took office—cannot be sustained on the basis of precedent.

Only three sitting Presidents have been defendants in civil litigation involving their actions prior to taking office. Complaints against Theodore Roosevelt and Harry Truman had been dismissed before they took office; the dismissals were affirmed after their respective inaugurations. Two companion cases arising out of an automobile accident were filed against John F. Kennedy in 1960 during the Presidential campaign. After taking office, he unsuccessfully argued that his status as Commander in Chief gave him a right to a stay under the Soldiers' and Sailors' Civil Relief Act of 1940, 50 U. S. C. App. §§ 501–525. The motion for a stay was denied by the District Court, and the matter was settled out of court. Thus, none of those cases sheds any light on the constitutional issue before us.

The principal rationale for affording certain public servants immunity from suits for money damages arising out of their official acts is inapplicable to unofficial conduct. In cases involving prosecutors, legislators, and judges we have repeatedly explained that the immunity serves the public interest in enabling such officials to perform their designated functions effectively without fear that a particular decision may give rise to personal liability. * * * *

That rationale provided the principal basis for our holding that a former President of the United States was "entitled to absolute immunity from damages liability predicated on his official acts," *Nixon v. Fitzgerald*, 457 U.S. 731, 749(1982). Our central concern was to avoid rendering the President "unduly cautious in the discharge of his official duties."

This reasoning provides no support for an immunity for unofficial conduct. As we explained in *Fitzgerald*, "the sphere of protected action must be related closely to the immunity's justifying purposes." * * *

Petitioner's effort to construct an immunity from suit for unofficial acts grounded purely in the identity of his office is unsupported by precedent.

We are also unpersuaded by the evidence from the historical record to which petitioner has called our attention. He points to a comment by Thomas Jefferson protesting the subpoena duces tecum Chief Justice Marshall directed to him in the Burr trial, a statement in the diaries kept by Senator William Maclay of the first Senate debates, in which then Vice President John Adams and Senator Oliver Ellsworth are recorded as having said that "the President personally [is] not ... subject to any process whatever," lest it be "put ... in the power of a common Justice to exercise any Authority over him and Stop the Whole Machine of Government," and to a quotation from

Justice Story's Commentaries on the Constitution. None of these sources sheds much light on the question at hand.

Respondent, in turn, has called our attention to conflicting historical evidence. Speaking in favor of the Constitution's adoption at the Pennsylvania Convention, James Wilson—who had participated in the Philadelphia Convention at which the document was drafted—explained that, although the President "is placed [on] high," "not a single privilege is annexed to his character; far from being above the laws, he is amenable to them in his private character as a citizen, and in his public character by impeachment." 2 J. Elliot, Debates on the Federal Constitution 480 (2d ed. 1863) (emphasis omitted). This description is consistent with both the doctrine of presidential immunity as set forth in Fitzgerald, and rejection of the immunity claim in this case. With respect to acts taken in his "public character"—that is official acts—the President may be disciplined principally by impeachment, not by private lawsuits for damages. But he is otherwise subject to the laws for his purely private acts.

In the end, as applied to the particular question before us, we reach the same conclusion about these historical materials that Justice Jackson described when confronted with an issue concerning the dimensions of the President's power. "Just what our forefathers did envision, or would have envisioned had they foreseen modern conditions, must be divined from materials almost as enigmatic as the dreams Joseph was called upon to interpret for Pharoah. A century and a half of partisan debate and scholarly speculation yields no net result but only supplies more or less apt quotations from respected sources on each side.... They largely cancel each other." *Youngstown Sheet & Tube Co. v. Sawyer*, 343 U.S. 579, 634–635 (1952) (concurring opinion).

Petitioner's strongest argument supporting his immunity claim is based on the text and structure of the Constitution. He does not contend that the occupant of the Office of the President is "above the law," in the sense that his conduct is entirely immune from judicial scrutiny. The President argues merely for a postponement of the judicial proceedings that will determine whether he violated any law. His argument is grounded in the character of the office that was created by Article II of the Constitution, and relies on separation of powers principles that have structured our constitutional arrangement since the founding.

As a starting premise, petitioner contends that he occupies a unique office with powers and responsibilities so vast and important that the public interest demands that he devote his undivided time and attention to his public duties. He submits that—given the nature of the office—the doctrine of separation of powers places limits on the authority of the Federal Judiciary to interfere with the Executive Branch that would be transgressed by allowing this action to proceed.

We have no dispute with the initial premise of the argument. Former presidents, from George Washington to George Bush, have consistently endorsed petitioner's characterization of the office. After serving his term, Lyndon Johnson observed: "Of all the 1,886 nights I was President, there were not many when I got to sleep before 1 or 2 a.m., and there were few mornings when I didn't wake up by 6 or 6:30." In

1967, the Twenty fifth Amendment to the Constitution was adopted to ensure continuity in the performance of the powers and duties of the office; one of the sponsors of that Amendment stressed the importance of providing that "at all times" there be a President "who has complete control and will be able to perform" those duties. As Justice Jackson has pointed out, the Presidency concentrates executive authority "in a single head in whose choice the whole Nation has a part, making him the focus of public hopes and expectations. In drama, magnitude and finality his decisions so far overshadow any others that almost alone he fills the public eye and ear." *Youngstown Sheet & Tube Co. v. Sawyer*, 343 U. S., at 653 (Jackson, J., concurring). We have, in short, long recognized the "unique position in the constitutional scheme" that this office occupies. Thus, while we suspect that even in our modern era there remains some truth to Chief Justice Marshall's suggestion that the duties of the Presidency are not entirely "unremitting," *United States v. Burr*, 25 F. Cas. 30, 34 (CC Va. 1807), we accept the initial premise of the Executive's argument.

It does not follow, however, that separation of powers principles would be violated by allowing this action to proceed. The doctrine of separation of powers is concerned with the allocation of official power among the three co equal branches of our Government. The Framers "built into the tripartite Federal Government ... a self executing safeguard against the encroachment or aggrandizement of one branch at the expense of the other." *Buckley v. Valeo*, 424 U. S. at 122. [n.30] * * *

But in this case there is no suggestion that the Federal Judiciary is being asked to perform any function that might in some way be described as "executive." Respondent is merely asking the courts to exercise their core Article III jurisdiction to decide cases and controversies. Whatever the outcome of this case, there is no possibility that the decision will curtail the scope of the official powers of the Executive Branch. The litigation of questions that relate entirely to the unofficial conduct of the individual who happens to be the President poses no perceptible risk of misallocation of either judicial power or executive power.

Rather than arguing that the decision of the case will produce either an aggrandizement of judicial power or a narrowing of executive power, petitioner contends that—as a by product of an otherwise traditional exercise of judicial power—burdens will be placed on the President that will hamper the performance of his official duties. We have recognized that "[e]ven when a branch does not arrogate power to itself ... the separation of powers doctrine requires that a branch not impair another in the performance of its constitutional duties." As a factual matter, petitioner contends that this particular case—as well as the potential additional litigation that an affirmance of the Court of Appeals judgment might spawn—may impose an unacceptable burden on the President's time and energy, and thereby impair the effective performance of his office.

Petitioner's predictive judgment finds little support in either history or the relatively narrow compass of the issues raised in this particular case. As we have already noted, in the more than 200 year history of the Republic, only three sitting Presidents have been subjected to suits for their private actions. If the past is any indicator, it seems unlikely that a deluge of such litigation will ever engulf the Presidency. As for the case at hand, if properly managed by the District Court, it appears to us highly unlikely to occupy any substantial amount of petitioner's time.

Of greater significance, petitioner errs by presuming that interactions between the Judicial Branch and the Executive, even quite burdensome interactions, necessarily rise to the level of constitutionally forbidden impairment of the Executive's ability to perform its constitutionally mandated functions. * * * As Madison explained, separation of powers does not mean that the branches "ought to have no *partial agency* in, or no *controul* over the acts of each other." The fact that a federal court's exercise of its traditional Article III jurisdiction may significantly burden the time and attention of the Chief Executive is not sufficient to establish a violation of the Constitution. Two long settled propositions, first announced by Chief Justice Marshall, support that conclusion.

First, we have long held that when the President takes official action, the Court has the authority to determine whether he has acted within the law. Perhaps the most dramatic example of such a case is our holding that President Truman exceeded his constitutional authority when he issued an order directing the Secretary of Commerce to take possession of and operate most of the Nation's steel mills in order to avert a national catastrophe. *Youngstown Sheet & Tube Co. v. Sawyer*, 343 U.S. 579 (1952). Despite the serious impact of that decision on the ability of the Executive Branch to accomplish its assigned mission, and the substantial time that the President must necessarily have devoted to the matter as a result of judicial involvement, we exercised our Article III jurisdiction to decide whether his official conduct conformed to the law. Our holding was an application of the principle established in *Marbury v. Madison*, 1 Cranch 137 (1803), that "[i]t is emphatically the province and duty of the judicial department to say what the law is."

Second, it is also settled that the President is subject to judicial process in appropriate circumstances. Although Thomas Jefferson apparently thought otherwise, Chief Justice Marshall, when presiding in the treason trial of Aaron Burr, ruled that a subpoena duces tecum could be directed to the President. *United States v. Burr*, 25 F. Cas. 30 (No. 14,692d) (CC Va. 1807). We unequivocally and emphatically endorsed Marshall's position when we held that President Nixon was obligated to comply with a subpoena commanding him to produce certain tape recordings of his conversations with his aides. *United States v. Nixon*, 418 U.S. 683 (1974). As we explained, "neither the doctrine of separation of powers, nor the need for confidentiality of high level communications, without more, can sustain an absolute, unqualified Presidential privilege of immunity from judicial process under all circumstances."

Sitting Presidents have responded to court orders to provide testimony and other information with sufficient frequency that such interactions between the Judicial and Executive Branches can scarcely be thought a novelty. President Monroe responded to written interrogatories, President Nixon—as noted above—produced tapes in response to a subpoena duces tecum, President Ford complied with an order to give a deposition in a criminal trial, and President Clinton has twice given videotaped testimony in criminal proceedings. Moreover, sitting Presidents have also voluntarily complied with judicial requests for testimony. President Grant gave a lengthy deposition in a criminal case under such circumstances and President Carter similarly gave videotaped testimony for use at a criminal trial.

In sum, "[i]t is settled law that the separation of powers doctrine does not bar every exercise of jurisdiction over the President of the United States." If the Judiciary may severely burden the Executive Branch by reviewing the legality of the President's official conduct, and if it may direct appropriate process to the President himself, it must follow that the federal courts have power to determine the legality of his unofficial conduct. The burden on the President's time and energy that is a mere by product of such review surely cannot be considered as onerous as the direct burden imposed by judicial review and the occasional invalidation of his official actions. We therefore hold that the doctrine of separation of powers does not require federal courts to stay all private actions against the President until he leaves office.

The reasons for rejecting such a categorical rule apply as well to a rule that would require a stay "in all but the most exceptional cases." Brief for Petitioner i. Indeed, if the Framers of the Constitution had thought it necessary to protect the President from the burdens of private litigation, we think it far more likely that they would have adopted a categorical rule than a rule that required the President to litigate the question whether a specific case belonged in the "exceptional case" subcategory. In all events, the question whether a specific case should receive exceptional treatment is more appropriately the subject of the exercise of judicial discretion than an interpretation of the Constitution. * * *

[W]e are persuaded that it was an abuse of discretion for the District Court to defer the trial until after the President leaves office. Such a lengthy and categorical stay takes no account whatever of the respondent's interest in bringing the case to trial. The complaint was filed within the statutory limitations period—albeit near the end of that period—and delaying trial would increase the danger of prejudice resulting from the loss of evidence, including the inability of witnesses to recall specific facts, or the possible death of a party.

The decision to postpone the trial was, furthermore, premature. The proponent of a stay bears the burden of establishing its need. In this case, at the stage at which the District Court made its ruling, there was no way to assess whether a stay of trial after the completion of discovery would be warranted. Other than the fact that a trial may consume some of the President's time and attention, there is nothing in the record to enable a judge to assess the potential harm that may ensue from scheduling the trial promptly after discovery is concluded. We think the District Court may have given undue weight to the concern that a trial might generate unrelated civil actions that could conceivably hamper the President in conducting the duties of his office. If and when that should occur, the court's discretion would permit it to manage those actions in such fashion (including deferral of trial) that interference with the President's duties would not occur. But no such impingement upon the President's conduct of his office was shown here.

We add a final comment on two matters that are discussed at length in the briefs: the risk that our decision will generate a large volume of politically motivated harassing and frivolous litigation, and the danger that national security concerns might prevent the President from explaining a legitimate need for a continuance.

We are not persuaded that either of these risks is serious. Most frivolous and vexatious litigation is terminated at the pleading stage or on summary judgment, with little if any personal involvement by the defendant. *See* Fed. Rules Civ. Proc. 12, 56. Moreover, the availability of sanctions provides a significant deterrent to litigation directed at the President in his unofficial capacity for purposes of political gain or harassment. History indicates that the likelihood that a significant number of such cases will be filed is remote. Although scheduling problems may arise, there is no reason to assume that the District Courts will be either unable to accommodate the President's needs or unfaithful to the tradition—especially in matters involving national security—of giving "the utmost deference to Presidential responsibilities." Several Presidents, including petitioner, have given testimony without jeopardizing the Nation's security. In short, we have confidence in the ability of our federal judges to deal with both of these concerns.

If Congress deems it appropriate to afford the President stronger protection, it may respond with appropriate legislation. As petitioner notes in his brief, Congress has enacted more than one statute providing for the deferral of civil litigation to accommodate important public interests. *See, e.g.,* 11 U.S.C. §362 (litigation against debtor stayed upon filing of bankruptcy petition); Soldiers' and Sailors' Civil Relief Act of 1940, 50 U. S. C. App. §§501–525 (provisions governing, inter alia, tolling or stay of civil claims by or against military personnel during course of active duty). If the Constitution embodied the rule that the President advocates, Congress, of course, could not repeal it. But our holding today raises no barrier to a statutory response to these concerns.

The Federal District Court has jurisdiction to decide this case. Like every other citizen who properly invokes that jurisdiction, respondent has a right to an orderly disposition of her claims. Accordingly, the judgment of the Court of Appeals is affirmed. *It is so ordered.*

Note

Subsequent events validated the critique that the unanimous Court's opinion was naïve. In April 1999, United States District Judge Susan Weber Wright issued an opinion considering whether Bill Clinton should be sanctioned for civil contempt, describing the dramatic developments.

Jones v. Clinton
36 F. Supp. 2d 1118 (E.D. Ark. 1999)

What began as a civil lawsuit against the President of the United States for alleged sexual harassment eventually resulted in an impeachment trial of the President in the United States Senate on two Articles of Impeachment for his actions during the course of this lawsuit and a related criminal investigation being conducted by the Office of the Independent Counsel ("OIC"). ***

Following remand of the case to this Court, the President, joined by Ferguson, filed a motion for judgment on the pleadings pursuant to Fed.R.Civ.P. 12(c). By Memorandum Opinion and Order dated August 22, 1997, this Court granted in part and denied in part the President's motion. The Court dismissed plaintiff's defamation claim against the President, dismissed her due process claim for deprivation of a property interest in her State employment, and dismissed her due process claims for deprivation of a liberty interest based on false imprisonment and injury to reputation, but concluded the remaining claims in plaintiff's complaint stated viable causes of action. The Court thereupon issued a Scheduling Order setting forth a deadline of January 30, 1998, for the completion of discovery and the filing of motions.

Discovery in this case proved to be contentious and time-consuming. During the course of discovery, over 50 motions were filed, the Court entered some 30 Orders, and telephone conferences were held on an almost weekly basis to address various disputes and resolve motions. In addition, the Court traveled to Washington, D.C. at the request of the President to preside over his civil deposition on January 17, 1998. It was at a hearing on January 12, 1998, to address issues surrounding the President's deposition and at the deposition itself that the Court first learned of Monica Lewinsky, a former White House intern and employee, and her alleged involvement in this case.

At his deposition, the President was questioned extensively about his relationship with Ms. Lewinsky, this Court having previously ruled on December 11, 1997, that plaintiff was "entitled to information regarding any individuals with whom the President had sexual relations or proposed or sought to have sexual relations and who were during the relevant time frame [of May 8, 1986, up to the present] state or federal employees." Based on that ruling, this Court overruled objections during the deposition from the President's attorney, Robert S. Bennett, that questions concerning Ms. Lewinsky were inappropriate areas of inquiry and required that such questions be answered by the President. Having been so ordered, the President testified in response to questioning from plaintiff's counsel and his own attorney that he had no recollection of having ever been alone with Ms. Lewinsky and he denied that he had engaged in an "extramarital sexual affair," in "sexual relations," or in a "sexual relationship" with Ms. Lewinsky. An affidavit submitted by Ms. Lewinsky in support of her motion to quash a subpoena for her testimony and made a part of the record of the President's deposition likewise denied that she and the President had engaged in a sexual relationship. When asked by Mr. Bennett whether Ms. Lewinsky's affidavit denying a sexual relationship with the President was a "true and accurate statement," the President answered, "That is absolutely true."

The President's denial of a sexual relationship with Ms. Lewinsky at his deposition was consistent with his answer of "None" in response to plaintiff's Interrogatory No. 10, which requested the name of each and every federal employee with whom he had sexual relations when he was President of the United States. This interrogatory was answered on December 23, 1997, after this Court had entered its December 11th Order ruling on plaintiff's motion to compel responses to her second set of interrogatories and finding that plaintiff was entitled to such information.

One day prior to the President's deposition, and unknown to this Court, the Special Division of the United States Court of Appeals for the District of Columbia Circuit granted a request from Attorney General Janet Reno to expand the jurisdiction of Independent Counsel Kenneth W. Starr and entered an Order authorizing the Independent Counsel "to investigate ... whether Monica Lewinsky or others suborned perjury, obstructed justice, intimidated witnesses, or otherwise violated federal law other than a Class B or C misdemeanor or infraction in dealing with witnesses, potential witnesses, attorneys, or others concerning the civil case *Jones v. Clinton*." A short time later, the President's relationship with Ms. Lewinsky and OIC's investigation of that relationship broke in the national media.

On the afternoon of January 28, 1998, with less than 48 hours remaining in the period for conducting discovery, OIC filed with this Court a motion for limited intervention and stay of discovery in this civil case. * * * In essence, the Court concluded that the parties could continue with discovery in the short time that remained of those matters not involving Ms. Lewinsky, but that any discovery that did involve Ms. Lewinsky would not be allowed to go forward and, further, that any evidence concerning Ms. Lewinsky would be excluded from the trial of this matter.

Following the completion of discovery, the President and Ferguson each filed a motion for summary judgment pursuant to Fed. R.Civ.P. 56. By Memorandum Opinion and Order dated April 1, 1998, this Court granted the President's and Ferguson's motions for summary judgment and entered judgment dismissing this case. The Court concluded that there were no genuine issues for trial in this case and that defendants were entitled to judgment as a matter of law with respect to plaintiff's claims that she was subjected to *quid pro quo* and hostile work environment sexual harassment, that the defendants conspired to deprive her of her civil rights, and that she suffered emotional distress so severe in nature that no reasonable person could be expected to endure it. The plaintiff appealed. Meanwhile, OIC's investigation of the President continued.

On August 17, 1998, the President appeared before a grand jury in Washington, D.C., as part of OIC's criminal investigation and testified about his relationship with Ms. Lewinsky and his actions during this civil lawsuit. That evening, the President discussed the matter in a televised address to the Nation. In his address, the President stated that although his answers at his January 17th deposition were "legally accurate," he did not volunteer information and that he did indeed have a relationship with Ms. Lewinsky that was inappropriate and wrong. The President acknowledged misleading people, in part because the questions posed to him "were being asked in a politically inspired lawsuit which has since been dismissed," and because he "had real and serious concerns about an Independent Counsel investigation that began with private business dealings 20 years ago...." *Id.* It was during the President's televised address that the Court first learned the President may be in contempt.

On September 9, 1998, the Independent Counsel, having concluded there was substantial and credible information that the President committed acts that may constitute grounds for impeachment, submitted his findings from his investigation of the Lewinsky matter to the United States House of Representatives pursuant to 28 U.S.C. § 595(c). The House of Representatives thereupon commenced impeachment proceedings, ultimately passing two Articles of Impeachment against the President, one alleging perjury in his August 17th testimony before the grand jury and the other alleging obstruction of justice in this civil case. The matter then proceeded to trial in the United States Senate.

On November 13, 1998, while the impeachment proceedings were taking place in the House of Representatives, the plaintiff reached an out-of-court settlement for $850,000.00 and withdrew her appeal of this Court's April 1st decision granting summary judgment to defendants. Thereafter, on February 12, 1999, the Senate acquitted the President of both Articles of Impeachment.

Following the acquittal of the President, this Court held a telephone conference on February 16, 1999, to address the remaining issues before this Court, including the issue of attorney's fees and the issue of whether the President should be subject to contempt proceedings. * * * As the Court explained to the parties, however, it is now time to address the issue of the President's contempt as all other proceedings that heretofore have precluded this Court from addressing the issue have concluded. * * *

B. Immunity in State Court: Donald J. Trump

Lawsuits against President Trump filed in federal court, such as *Clifford v. Trump* and *Johnson v. Trump*, discussed in part III below are subject to the rule of *Clinton v. Jones*: there is no presidential immunity. But does the same rule apply to litigation in state courts? The Court in *Clinton v. Jones* specifically stated it did not consider the issue of state courts, but it is exactly this issue that is before the New York courts. The New York courts to consider the issue have held that the rule of *Clinton v. Jones* extends to state courts. The appellate division, consisting of five judges, divided 3–2 on the issue.

Zervos v. Trump

171 A.D.3d 110, 94 N.Y.S.3d 75 (2019)

Renwick, J.P., joined by Webber, Kern, JJ.

This case raises a constitutional issue of first impression: whether the Supremacy Clause of the United States Constitution requires a state court to defer litigation of a defamation action against a sitting President until his terms end.

Two decades ago, in *Clinton v Jones* (1997), the United States Supreme Court rejected the then-sitting President's attempt to shield himself from alleged unofficial misconduct by relying upon the constitutional protection of the Presidency. Specifically, the Supreme Court found that the Separation of Powers doctrine of the United

States Constitution did not afford President Clinton temporary immunity from civil damages litigation, in federal court, arising out of events that occurred before he took office. The Court determined that a federal court's exercise of its constitutional authority to decide cases and controversies did not encroach upon the exercise of the executive powers of the President.

More than 20 years later, the current sitting President attempts to shield himself from consequences for his alleged unofficial misconduct by relying upon the constitutional protection of the Presidency. We reject defendant President Trump's argument that the Supremacy Clause of the United States Constitution prevents a New York State court—and every other state court in the country—from exercising its authority under its state constitution. Instead, we find that the Supremacy Clause was never intended to deprive a state court of its authority to decide cases and controversies under the state's constitution.

* * *

Factual and Procedural Background

This defamation lawsuit was commenced by Summer Zervos, a former contestant on the "Apprentice," a reality show starring defendant Donald Trump. Plaintiff alleges that in 2016, when defendant was a Presidential candidate, he wrongly smeared her by claiming that her allegations of sexual misconduct against him were lies.

Specifically, on October 14, 2016, plaintiff held a press conference to recount two separate incidents in which defendant had made unwanted sexual advances towards her. The first incident allegedly occurred when she met with defendant at his New York office in 2007, where he kissed her on the lips upon her arrival, and after stating that he would love to have her work for him, kissed her on the lips again as she was about to leave. The kisses made her feel "very nervous and embarrassed" and "upset."

The second encounter occurred soon thereafter. Ms. Zervos went to meet defendant for dinner at a restaurant in the Beverly Hills Hotel. Instead, she was escorted to his bungalow, where he kissed her "open mouthed," "grabbed her shoulder, again kissing her very aggressively, and placed his hand on her breast." After she pulled back and walked away, defendant took her hand, led her into the bedroom, and when she walked out, turned her around and suggested that they "lay down and watch some telly telly." He embraced her, and after she pushed him away, he "began to press his genitals against her, trying to kiss her again." She "attempt[ed] to make it clear that [she] was not interested" and insisted that she had come to have dinner. They had dinner, which ended abruptly when defendant stated that he needed to go to bed. Later that week, plaintiff, who was seeking a position in the Trump Organization, was offered a job at half the salary that she had been seeking. Plaintiff called defendant and told him that she "was upset, because it felt like she was being penalized for not sleeping with him." Plaintiff concluded her press statement by stating that after hearing the released audiotape and defendant's denials during the debate, "I felt that I had to speak out about your behavior. You do not have the right to treat women as sexual objects just because you are a star."

The audiotape referred to by plaintiff had been released a week earlier. On October 7, 2016, during the 2016 United States presidential election, the Washington Post published a video and accompanying article about then-presidential candidate Donald Trump and television host Billy Bush having an extremely lewd conversation about women in 2005. Trump and Bush were in a bus on their way to film an episode of Access Hollywood. In the video, defendant described his attempt to seduce a married woman and indicated he might start kissing a woman that he and Bush were about to meet. He added, "I don't even wait. And when you're a star, they let you do it. You can do anything. Grab them by the pussy. You can do anything."

Several hours after plaintiff's press conference, defendant posted on his campaign the following statement: "To be clear, I never met her at a hotel or greeted her inappropriately a decade ago. That is not who I am as a person, and it is not how I've conducted my life." Between October 14, 2016 and October 22, 2016, defendant, on Twitter, at campaign rallies, and at a presidential debate, made additional statements in response to plaintiff's allegations and other women's claims of sexual misconduct, including, "These allegations are 100% false.... They are made up, they never happened.... It's not hard to find a small handful of people willing to make false smears for personal fame, who knows maybe for financial reasons, political purposes"; "Nothing ever happened with any of these women. Totally made up nonsense to steal the election"; these were "false allegations and outright lies, in an effort to elect Hillary Clinton President.... False stories, all made-up.... All big lies"; the reports were "totally false," he "didn't know any of these women," and "didn't see these women"; and "Every woman lied when they came forward to hurt my campaign, total fabrication. The events never happened. Never. All of these liars will be sued after the election is over." He also re-tweeted statements by others, including one that had a picture of plaintiff and stated, "This is all yet another hoax."

On January 17, 2017, plaintiff commenced this action against defendant who in November 2016 had been elected President of the United States. Plaintiff alleged that the above statements by defendant were false and defamatory, and that defendant made them "knowing they were false and/or with reckless disregard for their truth or falsity." Plaintiff alleged that the statements about her were "defamatory per se," because "they would tend (and did) injure [her] trade, occupation or business," that "[b]eing branded a liar who came forward only for fame or at the manipulation of the Clinton campaign has been painful and demoralizing," and that as a direct result of those statements, she has suffered "both emotionally and financially." She also alleged that defendant's statements "have been deeply detrimental to [her] reputation, honor and dignity." The complaint seeks an order directing defendant to retract any and all defamatory statements and/or apologize for such statements, as well as an order directing defendant to pay compensatory and punitive damages.

Defendant moved to dismiss the complaint pursuant to CPLR 3211(a) on the basis that the state court had no jurisdiction to entertain a suit against a sitting President. Alternatively, defendant sought a stay, pursuant to CPLR 2201, that would remain in effect for the duration of his presidency. First, defendant argued that, as implied by the United States Supreme Court in *Clinton v Jones* (520 US 681 [1997], *supra*), the Supremacy Clause of the United States Constitution prevents a state court from hearing an action, whatever its merit or lack thereof, against a sitting President, because a state court may not exercise "direct control" over or interfere with the President, and that the action should be dismissed without prejudice to plaintiff's refiling after defendant leaves office, or stayed until such time.

Second, defendant argued that the complaint should be dismissed on the merits because plaintiff, who resides and was allegedly injured in California, cannot state a single cause of action for defamation under California law, because the statements at issue "were made during a national political campaign that involved heated public debate in political forums," and that "[s]tatements made in that context are properly viewed by courts as part of the expected fiery rhetoric, hyperbole, and opinion that is squarely protected by the First Amendment."

Defendant further argued that his denials of plaintiff's "accusations cannot constitute defamation as a matter of law," because plaintiff cannot show that each of the purportedly defamatory statements was "of and concerning" her because they make no mention of her, and that plaintiff's complaint fails to adequately plead damages.

* * *

This appeal ensued. We now affirm for the reasons explained below.

Discussion

We first address the threshold question of whether the Supremacy Clause prevents a New York court from exercising jurisdiction over defendant in this defamation lawsuit.

Defendant essentially argues that the motion court erred in failing to dismiss or stay the action under the Supremacy Clause because the clause makes federal law the "supreme law" of the land, and the Clause is violated when a state court exercises "direct control" over a sitting President, who has principal responsibility to ensure that federal laws are faithfully executed. Defendant submits that such forbidden direct control necessarily occurs where a state court hears an action like this one, that would inevitably involve a court issuing, among others, scheduling and discovery orders that would require a response from the President, such as the production of documents and an appearance at a deposition. As explained below, defendant's arguments fail and he must necessarily revert to the policy arguments made by then-President Clinton and rejected by the United States Supreme Court.

The Supremacy Clause provides, "Th[e] Constitution, and the Laws of the United States which shall be made in Pursuance thereof; and all Treaties made, or which shall be made, under the Authority of the United States, shall be the supreme Law of the Land; and the Judges in every State shall be bound thereby, any Thing in the Constitution or Laws of any State to the Contrary notwithstanding" (US Const, art VI, cl 2).

* * *

Defendant's reading of the Supremacy Clause—that it bars a state court from exercising jurisdiction over him because he is the "ultimate repository of the Executive Branch's powers and is required by the Constitution to be always in function'"—finds no support in the constitutional text or case law. Defendant's interpretation conflicts with the fundamental principle that the United States has a "government of laws and not of men" (*Cooper v Aaron*, 358 US 1, 23 [1958] [internal quotation marks omitted]). Despite the suggestion in his brief that he is the "embodi[ment of] the Executive Branch," and though he is tasked with significant responsibilities, the President is still a person, and he is not above the law. Supremacy Clause jurisprudence makes clear that an affirmative act is required to divest a state court of jurisdiction and defendant is not exempt from state court jurisdiction solely because of his identity as commander-in-chief (*see Clinton v Jones*, 520 US at 695 ["(I)mmunities are grounded in nature of the function performed, not the identity of the actor who performed it"] [internal quotation marks omitted]). Therefore, the Supremacy Clause does not provide blanket immunity to the President from having to defend against a civil damages action against him in state court.

Defendant has not demonstrated entitlement to immunity from a state court civil damages lawsuit where his acts are purely unofficial. Analysis of defendant's presidential immunity argument is informed by *Nixon v Fitzgerald* (457 US 731 [1982]) * * * * Judicial recognition of the President's immunity from civil suit for his official acts protects the nation from a presidential decision based on potential civil liability, which could be significantly different from the decision that is best for the country.

In *Clinton v Jones*, the Supreme Court was presented with the opportunity to expand upon the doctrine of presidential immunity as set forth in *Nixon v Fitzgerald*. The Supreme Court, however, rejected the invitation to extend the reasoning of *Nixon v Fitzgerald* to cases in which a sitting President is sued for civil damages that occurred before he took office. * * * *

In short, the Supreme Court's decision in *Clinton v Jones* clearly and unequivocally demonstrates that the Presidency and the President are indeed separable. Hence, the Court in *Clinton v Jones* effectively recognized that the President is presumptively subject to civil liability for conduct that had taken place in his private capacity. The Supreme Court, however, held that within the exercise of its judicial discretion and power, rather than a constitutionally mandated rule of presidential immunity, a federal court may determine that such presumption has been overcome when the President establishes unusual circumstances that outweigh a plaintiff's legal remedy for constitutionally protected rights.

To be sure, because *Clinton v Jones* did not involve a state court action, the Supreme Court declined to resolve whether the President may claim immunity from suit in state court. Instead, it presumed that if the case was being heard in state court, the President would rely on federalism and comity concerns, "as well as the interest in protecting federal officials from possible local prejudice." In a footnote, the Court also stated:

"Because the Supremacy Clause makes federal law the Supreme Law of the Land,' Art. VI, cl. 2, any direct control by a state court over the President, who has principal responsibility to ensure that those laws are faithfully executed,' Art. II, § 3, may implicate concerns that are quite different from the interbranch separation-of-powers questions addressed here."

This observation by the Court provides the primary fuel for defendant's arguments and the dissent's conclusion that defendant is immune from suit in state court because a state court "is not part of the Constitution's tripartite system of governance and so has none of the powers of a federal court." However, the cases cited in the footnote above suggest only that the Supreme Court was concerned with a state's exercise of control over the President in a way that would interfere with his execution of federal law, *Hancock v Train*, 426 US 167 (1976) (holding that the State of Kentucky could not force federal facilities in the State to obtain state permits to operate); *Mayo v United States*, 319 US 441 (1943) (holding that a Florida state official could not order the cessation of a federal fertilizer distribution program). * * * *

Indeed, aside from the forum, plaintiff's case is materially indistinguishable from *Clinton v Jones*. Plaintiff's state law claims against defendant are based purely on his pre-presidential unofficial conduct. By holding that the President can be sued for civil damages based on his purely unofficial acts, *Clinton v Jones* implicitly rejected the notion that because the President is "always in function," he cannot be subjected to state court litigation ("Petitioner's effort to construct an immunity from suit for unofficial acts grounded purely in the identity of his office is unsupported by precedent"). The Supreme Court also considered that "[i]f Congress deems it appropriate to afford the President stronger protection, it may respond with appropriate legislation," *cf.* Brett M. Kavanaugh, *Separation of Powers During the Forty-Fourth Presidency and Beyond*, 93 MINN. L. REV. 1454, 1460–1461 (2009) ("(I)t would be appropriate for Congress to enact a statute providing that any personal civil suits against presidents ... be deferred while the President is in office. The result the Supreme Court reached in (*Clinton v*) *Jones*.... may well have been entirely correct ... But the Court in (*Clinton v*) *Jones* stated that Congress is free to provide a temporary deferral of civil suits while the President is in office").

Congress has not passed any law immunizing the President from state court damages lawsuits since *Clinton v Jones* was decided. Therefore, because *Clinton v Jones* held that a federal court has jurisdiction over the kind of claim plaintiff now asserts and because there is no federal law limiting a state court from entertaining similar claims, it follows that state courts have concurrent jurisdiction with federal courts over actions against the President based on his purely unofficial acts.

Contrary to defendant's contention, *Clinton v Jones* did not suggest that its reasoning would not apply to state court actions. It merely identified a potential constitutional concern. Notwithstanding that concern, this Court should not be deterred from holding that a state court can exercise jurisdiction over the President as a defendant in a civil lawsuit.

Likewise, defendant's contention that the President is always in function and thus not separable from the office of the Presidency does not make him immune from state civil litigation simply because a court has the power to hold a party in contempt. Defendant's contention and dissent's reasoning rest primarily on a hypothetical concern about a state court's authority to hold the President in contempt and concomitantly impose imprisonment. That is not, however, the question before this Court. The issue before this Court is whether a state court has jurisdiction over the President, not whether it can hold him in contempt. We should not "make mere hypothetical adjudications, where there is no presently justiciable controversy" regarding contempt and "where the existence of a controversy is dependent upon the happening of future events."

Defendant's concerns, adopted by the dissent, regarding contempt are also unsupported. In fact, as a practical matter, courts rarely hold litigants in contempt and the requirements for a finding of contempt are quite onerous. Furthermore, regarding penalties for refusal to comply with discovery demands and notices, CPLR 3126 provides a broad range of sanctions tailored to protect the parties, but which fall short of a finding of contempt. To the extent that the President must be involved in discovery, the court can minimize the impact on his ability to carry out his official duties by issuing protective orders to prevent abuse. Should the trial court find it necessary to require the President to testify, it could allow him to do so by videotape, as has been the custom in recent proceedings involving sitting Presidents.

Ultimately, contrary to defendant and dissent's suggestion, state courts are fully aware that they should not compel the President to take acts or refrain from taking acts in his official capacity or otherwise prevent him from executing the responsibilities of the Presidency. It is likely that holding the President in contempt would be the kind of impermissible "direct control" contemplated by *Clinton v Jones* and violative of the Supremacy Clause.

However, defendant does not appeal from a contempt order and plaintiff does not argue that defendant should be held in contempt. In fact, in *Clinton v Jones*, the Supreme Court held that it did not have to rule on the constitutionality of ordering a President to appear at a particular time and place because it assumed, as we must do here, that reasonable accommodations would be made with respect to the President's schedule, and thus the particular issue of whether any hypothetical order would be so onerous as to interfere with the President's official duties was not relevant to the appeal. We follow the prudent course charted by the *Clinton v Jones* Court.

Accordingly, where, as here, purely unofficial pre-Presidential conduct is at issue, we find, consistent with *Clinton v Jones*, that a court does not impede the President's execution of his official duties by the mere exercise of jurisdiction over him.

Since the Supremacy Clause does not deprive a state court of its power and authority to decide this case, we must examine defendant's alternative grounds for the dismissal of the action * * *.

Mazzarelli, J., joined by Tom, J., dissenting in part.

In *Clinton v. Jones,* the United States Supreme Court held that separation of powers concerns did not preclude a federal lawsuit against a sitting President of the United States based on unofficial acts allegedly committed by him before he assumed office. The Court expressly cautioned in that decision that different concerns, including the Supremacy Clause of the United States Constitution, might influence the result if such a case were brought against the President in state court. However, the Court did not rule that such a suit could or could not proceed. This matter gives us an opportunity to squarely address the question.

* * * Where I depart from the majority is in its conclusion to the question outlined above. As explained below, subjecting the President to a state trial court's jurisdiction imposes upon him a degree of control by the State of New York that interferes with his ability to carry out his constitutional duty of executing the laws of the United States. Since the Supremacy Clause guarantees that any effort by the individual states to annul, minimize, or otherwise interfere with those laws will be struck down, it follows that any effort by a state court to control the President must likewise fail.

As a preliminary matter, I do not accept plaintiff's contention that because defendant did not invoke the Supremacy Clause in unrelated actions in which he or an affiliated entity was sued in the court of a different state for activities not related to his official duties, he cannot invoke it here. Plaintiff has offered no support for the notion that the President can waive the operation of the Supremacy Clause, which is an important underpinning of the Constitution's federalist system.

* * * This, of course, is not a separation of powers case. Indeed, plaintiff fails to address the key hypothetical question posed in footnote 13 of *Clinton,* which is whether there is a corollary notion that a state court, which is not part of the Constitution's tripartite system of governance and so has none of the powers of a federal court, has leeway to "direct appropriate process to the President himself ... [and] determine the legality of his unofficial conduct." In exclusively relying on the logic of *Clinton v. Jones,* which did not analyze the issue, she offers no independent reason why the Supremacy Clause does not prevent the New York state courts from having jurisdiction over her action. I believe that it is her burden to do so, and that she has failed to carry it.

* * * As defendant correctly notes, "the President alone is vested with the entire executive authority, and is therefore uniquely required under the Constitution to be always in function, [such that] he is inseparable from the office he holds." This notion that the President occupies a unique place in the Constitutional structure was endorsed by the *Clinton* Court, which accepted as true the observations of former Presidents from the beginning of the Republic to the modern era as to the sheer magnitude and incessant press of the job. The Court additionally pointed to the 25th Amendment to the Constitution, which was adopted to ensure that there was never a moment when the nation was not without a President who is up to the task of discharging that office's responsibilities. The question then becomes whether this all-consuming

nature of the Presidency creates a constitutional barrier to defendant's susceptibility to suit in state court.

I believe that it does. * * * Besides the court's ability to issue a decree by which a defendant must abide (here, if plaintiff prevails, to award a money judgment and order defendant to retract his statements and offer an apology), the court holds the power to direct him to respond to discovery demands, to sit for a deposition, and to appear before it. This power includes formidable enforcement mechanisms, including the ability to hold parties in criminal contempt, and, as a last resort, to imprison them. I recognize that this is a highly unlikely event in this case, as the motion court made clear that it would accommodate the singular nature of defendant's job. However, while the court's need to order the President of the United States before it so he can answer to contempt charges is hypothetical, the even remote possibility of such an event elevates an arm of the state over the federal government to a degree that the Supremacy Clause cannot abide. While I have no reason to doubt that the court would demonstrate extraordinary deference to defendant and no reason to believe that defendant would not cooperate in the litigation, there is no way to be absolutely certain that the court would not at some point have to take steps to protect its own legitimacy.

* * * [T]he majority minimizes the possibility that the court would have to exercise its contempt power, and is not at all concerned about this sword of Damocles hanging over the President's head. It is instead content to allow the litigation to proceed until such time as a constitutional crisis is at hand. In my view, this is too narrow an approach. It is not the act of holding the President in contempt that would trigger a Supremacy Clause violation, but the very power to do so once personal jurisdiction is conferred over the President. It is at that point that the court unquestionably has "direct control" over the President, that is, the immediate and ever-present power to issue an order *requiring* him to take some action, as mundane as directing him to produce discovery or as consequential as mandating his appearance in court on a date certain. For this reason, the majority's suggestion that the court could employ "reasonable accommodations" designed to alleviate the burden on the President is irrelevant. That there is any burden to be managed is the problem. Furthermore, the *Clinton* Court's discussion of how the litigation involving President Clinton could be managed so as to accommodate his schedule came after it had already determined that he was amenable to suit in federal court, and also after it noted that the analysis might be very different in state court.

* * * Because of the concerns addressed above, the President should not be forced to defend this lawsuit while he is in office. Therefore, in my view the action should be stayed until such time as defendant no longer occupies the office of President of the United States * * * *.

Notes and Questions

1. *Immunity.* Do you think *Clinton v. Jones* was correctly decided? Should it be applicable to state courts? If you were a member of Congress, would you support

a statute that immunized presidents from civil lawsuits during the pendency of their terms?

2. *Contempt.* How persuasive are the arguments regarding contempt? The majority in *Zervos* states that contempt is unusual but recall that President Clinton was ultimately held in contempt in *Jones v. Clinton*, the district court opinion excerpted above. Further, given President Trump's actions during the Mueller investigation, such as the refusal to testify or be interviewed in person, is there a greater possibility of contempt? Even if this is true, how should this be viewed?

3. *Other Factors.* Before becoming President, Donald J. Trump was very litigious, including in state courts, see James Zinn, Plaintiff in Chief: A Portrait of Donald Trump in 3500 Lawsuits (2019). Should this be relevant?

III. Defamation

As the facts recounted by the New York appellate division opinion above relate, Summer Zervos brought an action against Donald Trump for defamation—based upon his statements she was not telling the truth in 2016 in her statements describing unwanted sexual advances—rather than a claim for assault or battery for the 2007 sexual advances themselves, which would clearly be barred by the statute of limitations. The appellate division majority found that there was a claim for defamation; the dissenting judges agreed with this conclusion.

Generally speaking, the elements of a defamation claim are:

- a false statement made by defendant
- about the plaintiff (and that is understood to be about the plaintiff)
- published to a third party
- causes damage to the plaintiff

In libel, the statement is written; in slander the statement is oral. Additionally, this common law tort doctrine is shaped by the First Amendment. If the plaintiff is a public figure or government official, or if the matter is one of "public concern," the plaintiff must prove "actual malice": the defendant must have known that the statement is false or have made the statement with reckless disregard of the statement's truth or falsity.

In analyzing whether the claim for defamation by Summer Zervos survived the motion to dismiss, the New York appellate court first found that that the law of California and New York had no discernible differences regarding the tort, so there was no need to make a "choice of law" finding. The court stated:

> In determining whether a "reasonable" reader would consider that defendant's statements that plaintiff lied about their encounters connotes fact or non-actionable opinion, there are three relevant factors to be considered holistically: (1) whether the statements have a "precise meaning" that is "readily understood"; (2) whether the statements can be proven true or false; and

(3) whether either the context in which the statements were made or the "broader social context and surrounding circumstances [were] such as to signal … readers or listeners that what [was] being read or heard [was] likely to be opinion, not fact."

Here, defendant's denial of plaintiff's allegations of sexual misconduct is susceptible of being proven true or false, since he either did or did not engage in the alleged behavior. To be sure, a denial, which is a statement of purported fact and not mere opinion, does not always provide a basis for a defamation claim, even though it implicitly claims that the alleging party is not telling the truth. However, a denial, coupled with the claim that the accuser is or will be proven a liar, impugns a person's character as dishonest or immoral and typically crosses the line from nonactionable general denial to a specific factual statement about another that is reasonably susceptible of defamatory meaning.

The use of the term liar could be perceived in some cases as no more than rhetorical hyperbole that is a nonactionable personal opinion. However, that is not the case here, where, again, defendant used the term in connection with his specific denial of factual allegations against him, which was necessarily a statement by him of his knowledge of the purported facts. Further, although defendant's statement that plaintiff was motivated by financial gain was not accompanied with recitation of the "facts" upon which it was based, and although it did not plainly imply that it was based on undisclosed facts, the statement could be viewed by a reasonable reader as containing the implication that defendant knows certain facts, unknown to his audience, concerning organized political efforts to destroy his campaign, which supports his opinion. Given that, the complaint at the very least includes allegations of "mixed opinion" that are actionable.

Defendant further argues that the statements, are nonactionable given the political context in which he made them. We recognize that in light of the hotly contested 2016 campaign, not to mention the fora in which the statements were made (defendant's Internet posting, campaign literature, rallies, and debates), the average reader would largely expect to hear the vigorous expressions of personal opinion, rather than rigorous and comprehensive presentation of factual matter. However, defendant's flat-out denial of a provable, specific allegation against him concerning his own conduct, accompanied by a claim that the accuser was lying, could not be viewed even in that context as a rhetorical statement of pure opinion or as "vague, subjective, and lacking in precise meaning." Nor is there any support for defendant's claim that such statements when made in the context of a heated political campaign are protected political speech. Indeed, claims for defamation may arise out of acrimonious political battles.

Defendant's argument that some of the alleged defamatory statements are not "of and concerning plaintiff" is also without merit. Even where statements alleged by plaintiff do not refer to her by name, most of the challenged statements could reasonably be considered of and concerning her. Defendant began making the challenged statements immediately after plaintiff gave her press conference and they were all made within eight days thereafter. The "allegations" that defendant's statements attack as false and politically motivated and the "events" the statements claim "never happened" are easily understood as relating to plaintiff's accusations, as well as the accusations by other women who had come forward by that time.

The court distinguished another defamation case in New York filed against Trump as a defendant, as well as Trump's former campaign manager, Corey Lewandowski, and the campaign organization. In *Jacobus v. Trump*, 55 Misc. 3d 470, 51 N.Y.S. 330 (2017), a judge found that the statements did not constitute defamation and the appellate division affirmed. The plaintiff, Cheryl Jacobus, a "frequent commentator on television news channels" offering "political opinion and analysis from the Republican perspective," had appeared on television on a CNN cable television show to discuss Trump's threat to boycott one of the Republican presidential primary debates unless FOX removed Megyn Kelly as a moderator, and later to discuss the Trump campaign's funding sources.

As the trial judge related, Trump posted the following on Twitter: "Great job on @donlemon tonight @kayleighmcenany @cherijacobus begged us for a job. We said no and she went hostile. A real dummy! @CNN." A few days later, Trump posted the following tweet about plaintiff: "Really dumb @CheriJacobus. Begged my people for a job. Turned her down twice and she went hostile. Major loser, zero credibility!" The trial judge also noted that some of "Trump's numerous Twitter followers responded to his tweets by attacking plaintiff with demeaning, sometimes sexually charged, comments and graphics, including insults aimed at her professional conduct, experience, qualifications, and her purported rejection by Trump. Also tweeted was an image of plaintiff with a grossly disfigured face, and a depiction of her in a gas chamber with Trump standing nearby ready to push a button marked 'Gas.'"

The trial judge in *Jacobus v. Trump* found that Trump's statements were not defamation:

> Trump's characterization of plaintiff as having "begged" for a job is reasonably viewed as a loose, figurative, and hyperbolic reference to plaintiff's a state of mind and is therefore, not susceptible of objective verification. To the extent that the word "begged" can be proven to be a false representation of plaintiff's interest in the position, the defensive tone of the tweet, having followed plaintiff's negative commentary about Trump, signals to readers that plaintiff and Trump were engaged in a petty quarrel. Lewandowski's comments, overall, are speculative and vague, and defendants' implication that plaintiff was retaliating against them for turning her down, notwithstanding the unmistakable reference to her professional integrity, is clearly a matter of speculation and opinion.

Moreover, the immediate context of defendants' statements is the familiar back and forth between a political commentator and the subject of her criticism, and the larger context is the Republican presidential primary and Trump's regular use of Twitter to circulate his positions and skewer his opponents and others who criticize him, including journalists and media organizations whose coverage he finds objectionable. (*See e.g.* Jasmine C. Lee & Kevin Quealy, *The 289 People Places and Things Donald Trump Has Insulted on Twitter: A Complete List*, The Upshot, N.Y. Times [digital ed], Dec. 6, 2016, http://www.nytimes.com/interactive/2016/01/28/upshot/donald-trump-twitter-insults.html [accessed Jan. 8, 2017]). His tweets about his critics, necessarily restricted to 140 characters or less, are rife with vague and simplistic insults such as "loser" or "total loser" or "totally biased loser," "dummy" or "dope" or "dumb," "zero/no credibility," "crazy" or "wacko," and "disaster," all deflecting serious consideration.

And yet, the context of a national presidential primary and a candidate's strategic and almost exclusive use of Twitter to advance his views arguably distinguish this case from those where heated rhetoric, with or without the use of social media, was held to constitute communications that cannot be taken seriously. (*See e.g.* Gerald F. Seib, *The Method in Donald Trump's Maddening Communications Habits,* Wall St. J., Jan. 2, 2017, http://www.wsj.com/articles/the-method-in-donald-trumps-maddeningcommunications-habits-1483377825 (there "seem to be specific objectives behind many of Mr. Trump's seemingly scattershot missives and comments," and that while there is "danger" in leaving world unsure which messages to take literally, it is "also likely Mr. Trump knows exactly what he is doing"); David Danford, *Why Donald Trump's Constant Twitter Battle with the Media Is a Brilliant Strategy,* The Federalist, Dec. 7, 2016, http://thefederalist.com/2016/12/07/donald-trumps-constant-twitterbattle-mediabrilliant-strategy/ ("Trump's seemingly off-the-cuff and thoughtless tweets are no small part of this fascinating display of political skill.") These circumstances raise some concern that some may avoid liability by conveying positions in small Twitter parcels, as opposed to by doing so in a more formal and presumably actionable manner, bringing to mind the acknowledgment of the Court of Appeals that "[t]he publisher of a libel may not, of course, escape liability by veiling a calumny under artful or ambiguous phrases...."

Nevertheless, consistent with the foregoing precedent and with the spirit of the First Amendment, and considering the statements as a whole (imprecise and hyperbolic political dispute *cum* schoolyard squabble), I find that it is fairly concluded that a reasonable reader would recognize defendants' statements as opinion, even if some of the statements, viewed in isolation, could be found to convey facts. Moreover, that others may infer a defamatory meaning from the statements does not render the inference reasonable under these circumstances.

Thus, although the intemperate tweets are clearly intended to belittle and demean plaintiff, any reasonable reading of them makes it "impossible to conclude that [what defendants said or implied] ... could subject ... [plaintiff] to contempt or aversion, induce any unsavory opinion of [her] or reflect adversely upon [her] work," or otherwise damage her reputation as a partisan political consultant and commentator. Indeed, to some, truth itself has been lost in the cacophony of online and Twitter verbiage to such a degree that it seems to roll off the national consciousness like water off a duck's back. (*see e.g.* farhad manjoo, *how the internet is loosening our Grip on the Truth,* N.Y. Times, Dec. 2, 2016, http://www.nytimes.com/2016/11/03/technology/how-the-internet-is-loosening-our-grip-on-the-truth.html [accessed Jan. 8, 2017] [because there is more media from which to choose, people tend to focus on information that fits their personal opinions or narrative whether or not factually accurate]).

Jacobus v. Trump, 55 Misc. 3d 470, 51 N.Y.S. 330 (2017).

Similarly, in *Clifford v. Trump*, 339 F. Supp.3d 915 (C.D. Cal. 2018), a federal district judge dismissed the complaint by Stephanie Clifford, also known as Stormy Daniels, for defamation. The lawsuit does not arise from Clifford's statements about her sexual encounter with Donald Trump, but rather her statements about being threatened should she come forward with her allegations, including a man who approached her in Las Vegas in 2011 and told her, "Leave Trump alone. Forget the story."

The district judge in *Clifford v. Trump* explained:

After Mr. Trump was elected President of the United States on November 8, 2016, Ms. Clifford worked with a sketch artist to render a sketch of the person who had purportedly threatened her in 2011. Ms. Clifford released the sketch publicly on April 17, 2018.

The next day, on April 18, 2018, Mr. Trump, from his personal Twitter account (@RealDonaldTrump), posted a purportedly false statement regarding Ms. Clifford, the sketch, and Ms. Clifford's account of the threatening incident that took place in 2011. Mr. Trump's tweet read as follows: "A sketch years later about a nonexistent man. A total con job, playing the Fake News Media for Fools (but they know it)!" Mr. Trump posted this tweet in response to another tweet posted by an account named DeplorablyScottish (@ShennaFoxMusic), which showed side-by-side images of the sketch released by Ms. Clifford and a picture of Ms. Clifford and her husband.

Based on this tweet, Ms. Clifford brings the instant lawsuit against Mr. Trump for defamation. She argues that Mr. Trump's tweet attacks the veracity of her account of the threatening incident that took place in 2011. She also contends that Mr. Trump's tweet suggests that she is falsely accusing an individual of committing a crime against her. According to Plaintiff, "Mr. Trump meant to convey that Ms. Clifford is a liar, someone who should not be trusted, that her claims about the threatening encounter are false, and that she was falsely accusing the individual depicted in the sketch of committing a crime, where no crime had been committed." As a result, she contends that Mr. Trump's tweet was false and defamatory, and that the tweet was defamation *per se* because it charged her with committing a serious crime.

The district judge found that Trump's tweet was not a statement, but a non-actionable opinion: "the tweet in question constitutes 'rhetorical hyperbole' normally associated with politics and public discourse in the United States. The First Amendment protects this type of rhetorical statement."

The district judge in *Clifford v. Trump* also noted that the tweet involved a matter of public concern "including purported acts committed by the now President of the United States," and further reasoned:

> In filings before this Court, Ms. Clifford has challenged the legitimacy of Mr. Trump's victory in the 2016 Presidential election. Mr. Trump's tweet served as a public rejoinder to allegations made by Plaintiff. If this Court were to prevent Mr. Trump from engaging in this type of "rhetorical hyperbole" against a political adversary, it would significantly hamper the office of the President. Any strongly-worded response by a president to another politician or public figure could constitute an action for defamation. This would deprive this country of the "discourse" common to the political process. In short, should Plaintiff publicly voice her opinions about Mr. Trump, Mr. Trump is entitled to publicly voice non-actionable opinions about Plaintiff. To allow Plaintiff to proceed with her defamation action would, in effect, permit Plaintiff to make public allegations against the President without giving him the opportunity to respond. Such a holding would violate the First Amendment.

> Mr. Trump also made a one-off rhetorical comment, not a sustained attack on the veracity of Plaintiff's claims. * * *

Clifford v. Trump, 339 F. Supp.3d 915 (C.D. Cal. 2018).

Thus, Trump has been able to prevail on the merits in at least two of the complaints filed by women against him for defamation. Yet Trump has argued that defamation laws need to be altered so that it is *easier for plaintiffs* to prevail. For example, in a February 2016 campaign rally, he stated: "I'm going to open up our libel laws so when they write purposely negative and horrible and false articles, we can sue them and win lots of money. We're going to open up those libel laws. So when the *New York Times* writes a hit piece which is a total disgrace or when the Washington Post, which is there for other reasons, writes a hit piece, we can sue them and win money instead of having no chance of winning because they're totally protected." Hadas Gold, *Donald Trump: We're going to 'open up' libel laws,* Politico (Feb. 26, 2016), http://www.politico.com/blogs/on-media/2016/02/donald-trump-libel-laws-219866. This stance is made more understandable by Trump's lack of success as a plaintiff in defamation cases. According to an article in the ABA's newsletter *Communications Lawyer* in 2016, Trump was a "libel bully," who was (with his companies) "involved in a mind-boggling 4,000 lawsuits over the last 30 years," and who "sent countless threatening cease-and-desist letters to journalists and critics," although he and his companies "have never won a single speech-related case filed in a public court." Susan Seager, *Donald J. Trump is a Libel Bully but also a Libel Loser*, 32:3 COMMUNICATIONS LAWYER 1 (Fall 2016). The article, which caused a bit of controversy itself when there were reported efforts by the ABA to temper the contents, discussed seven cases, including lawsuits against an architecture critic who called Trump's planned tower "aesthetically lousy," an author whose book argued Trump was not a billionaire, a former Trump university student who posted on internet message boards and wrote to the Better Business Bureau that the university engaged in fraudulent business practices, a contestant in the Miss USA pageant for posting on Facebook that she had learned the contest was predetermined, and the programming chief of Univision Networks, who posted on Instagram a photo of Trump side-by-side with a photo of Dylann Roof (the white supremacists since convicted of the AEME church shooting in Charleston, South Carolina) with the caption "Sin commentaries/No Comments." Moreover, Trump has often threatened to sue for defamation without doing so. In the 2016 election campaign, Trump vowed to sue all of the women—at least ten, including Summer Zervos—who had come forward accusing him of inappropriate touching: "Every woman lied when they came forward to hurt my campaign," continuing that it was "Total fabrication. The events never happened. Never. All of these liars will be sued after the election is over." CNN Politics (October 26, 2016) (https://www.cnn.com/2016/10/22/politics/trump-says-hell-sue-sexual-misconduct-accusers/index.html).

Perhaps coincidentally, an argument that defamation doctrine should be changed to be more generous towards plaintiffs was recently made by Justice Clarence Thomas in a concurring opinion from a denial of certiorari in *McKee v. Cosby*, 139 S.Ct. 675 (2019) (Thomas, J., concurring). The case arose when the plaintiff, Katharine McKee, sued actor and comedian Bill Cosby for defamation based on publication of a letter impugning her truthfulness after she had publicly accused him of raping her decades earlier. The First Circuit, affirming the district judge, found that the statements involved a matter of public concern— "the web of sexual assault allegations implicating Cosby, an internationally renowned comedian commonly referred to as 'America's Dad,' constitutes a public controversy—and that her argument that it was a private dispute is belied by 'the context in which McKee decided to reveal her rape to the press in December 2014, following decades of silence,' given that she 'came forward after more than twenty other women had levelled highly publicized sexual assault accusations against Cosby, who in response allegedly hired a team of lawyers and investigators 'to discredit them, to intimidate them, and to intimidate any future would-be accusers.'" *McKee v. Cosby*, 874 F.3d 54 (1st Cir. 2017). Thus, the court found that McKee as plaintiff bore the burden of proving that "Cosby made such statements with either "knowledge" that they were false or "reckless disregard" for their truth or falsity," under *New York Times v. Sullivan*, 376 U.S. 254 (1964), a burden which her complaint's allegations, even taken as true, did not satisfy.

In concurring with the denial of certiorari to the First Circuit, Justice Thomas wrote:

New York Times [*v. Sullivan*] and the Court's decisions extending it were policy-driven decisions masquerading as constitutional law. Instead of simply
applying the First Amendment as it was understood by the people who ratified
it, the Court fashioned its own "'federal rule[s]'" by balancing the "competing
values at stake in defamation suits."

We should not continue to reflexively apply this policy-driven approach to
the Constitution. Instead, we should carefully examine the original meaning
of the First and Fourteenth Amendments. If the Constitution does not require
public figures to satisfy an actual-malice standard in state-law defamation
suits, then neither should we.

McKee v. Cosby, 139 S. Ct. at 676. In his rather extensive opinion, Thomas discussed
the history of common law libel and argued that the First Amendment was not intended to displace it. Instead, he contended that the Court's decisions "displacing
state defamation law" need to be reconsidered: "We did not begin meddling in this
area until 1964, nearly 175 years after the First Amendment was ratified. The States
are perfectly capable of striking an acceptable balance between encouraging robust
public discourse and providing a meaningful remedy for reputational harm. We
should reconsider our jurisprudence in this area." 139 S.Ct. at 682.

Notes and Questions

1. *Reputation.* It is widely acknowledged that Donald Trump's general truthfulness
   is questionable, *see e.g.*, Fact Checker, *President Trump has made 10,796 false or
   misleading claims over 869 days*, WASHINGTON POST (June 10, 2019); Julia Man-
   chester, *Poll: Just 13 percent of Americans consider Trump honest and trustworthy*,
   THE HILL (May 17, 2018); Chris Cillizza, *People don't think Donald Trump is
   honest or trustworthy. And they never really have.*, CNN (September 11, 2018)
   ("less than one in three people in the new CNN-SSRS poll believe that President
   Donald Trump is honest and trustworthy"). How does a defendant's reputation
   for untruthfulness assist or hinder a plaintiff's claim for defamation? Note that
   in *Clifford v. Trump*, defendant Trump claimed his tweet was "hyperbole," a claim
   the court accepted.

2. *Justice Thomas*—**McKee v. Cosby.** Justice Thomas's opinion in *McKee v. Cosby*
   attracted considerable attention. Perhaps because a concurring opinion to a denial
   of certiorari is quite rare and serves no obvious purpose, commentators speculated
   about the rationale for writing such an opinion. Some commentators noted that
   the opinion was consistent with Thomas's emphasis on originalism and his willingness to depart from *stare decisis*, and many also noted that Thomas's opinion
   echoed Trump's own views on reforming libel laws. Justice Thomas, and his wife
   Ginni Thomas, are reported to be close with President Trump. *See e.g.*, Maggie
   Haberman and Annie Karni, *Trump Meets With Hard-Right Group Led by Ginni
   Thomas*, NEW YORK TIMES (Jan. 26, 2019) (in an "unusual" White House meeting,
   which "came about after the Thomases had dinner with the president and the
   first lady, Melania Trump," a group led by Ginni Thomas, "denounced transgender

people and women serving in the military" and criticized appointments to Administration posts).

However, other commentators speculated that Thomas's opinion in *McKee v. Cosby*, a case ultimately involving sexual misconduct by Bill Cosby, might spring from Thomas's own experiences. As one journalist wrote:

> Suppose I were to speculate that Thomas has a specific interest in protecting the private lives of public figures because of his own very public debacle in 1991, when he was accused of sexual harassment by a former employee, Anita Hill. In the era of #metoo, many people have sought to revisit these claims or even mount efforts to impeach Justice Thomas himself.
>
> I don't know whether this highly personal motivation is behind Thomas's opinion. But it's a valid question to ask, since it is germane to the reasoning of a Supreme Court justice in a high-profile case.
>
> Yet if *Times v. Sullivan* were overturned, such speculation could be impossible. Which maybe is what Thomas really wants. If I'm still allowed to say that.

Jay Michelson, *If You Don't Value* New York Times v. Sullivan, *You'd Better Start, Because Clarence Thomas Is Gunning for It*, DAILY BEAST (February 19, 2019), https://www.thedailybeast.com/if-you-dont-value-times-v-sullivan-youd-better-start-because-clarence-thomas-is-gunning-for-it.

IV. Complaints against Trump for Unwanted Sexual Conduct

The final section of this Chapter considers two claims against Trump filed in federal court.

First, Alva Johnson, a former Donald Trump campaign worker filed a complaint in the Middle District of Florida. She alleged battery based on sexual assault: during a meet-and-greet event prior to a campaign rally in Tampa, Florida in August 2016, "Trump forcibly kissed Ms. Johnson in the presence of several of her colleagues and others. The forced and unwanted kiss was deeply offensive to Ms. Johnson." Her complaint also alleged violations of the Equal Pay Act, 29 U.S.C. § 216(b), on the basis of gender, and racial discrimination under 42 U.S.C. § 1981, due to unequal pay on the basis of race. In support of Count I alleging battery, the complaint included allegations made by other women of forcible kissing and unwanted sexual contact. The defendants Donald Trump and the Campaign moved to dismiss and to strike the allegations concerning other sexual misconduct.

Johnson v. Trump for President, Inc., and Donald Trump

___ 2019 WL 2492122 (M.D. Fl. June 14, 2019)

ORDER

William F. Jung, United States District Judge

This matter comes to the Court on a Motion to Strike Portions of Plaintiff's Complaint from Defendant Donald J. Trump ("Trump") and Donald J. Trump for President, Inc. ("DJTPI"), and a Motion to Dismiss Plaintiff's Complaint from DJTPI. Plaintiff has filed oppositions in response to both motions, to which Defendants have replied. The Court heard argument from all counsel on June 5, 2019.

Plaintiff's three-count Complaint alleges battery by Defendant Trump in Count I. Plaintiff also seeks recovery against DJTPI for wage-based gender discrimination in violation of the Equal Pay Act (Count II) and race discrimination under 42 U.S.C. § 1981 (Count III).

As currently stated, the Complaint presents a political lawsuit, not a tort and wages lawsuit. Plaintiff will receive a fair day in court, but the Court will try a tort and wages dispute — not a political one. If Plaintiff wishes to make a political statement or bring a claim for political purposes, this is not the forum.

The Court dismisses the Complaint without prejudice. Plaintiff may file an amended complaint within thirty days consistent with this order. In reciting the facts as alleged, the Court considers well-pled facts as true for both a motion to dismiss and a motion to strike.

AS TO COUNT ONE: Plaintiff was a campaign worker for DJTPI during Defendant Trump's presidential election. Count I alleges that at an August 24, 2016 election rally for Defendant Trump in Tampa, Defendant Trump grabbed Plaintiff by the hand, held her hand, and then kissed her without her consent. Plaintiff further alleges that she turned her head to avoid the kiss, and Defendant kissed her on the side of her mouth. She felt humiliated by this contact and, shortly thereafter, she was disappointed because her coworkers were aware of the incident and were joking about it.

On October 7, 2016, a recording became public in which Defendant Trump stated in part, "You know I'm automatically attracted to beautiful — I just start kissing them. It's like a magnet. Just kiss. I don't even wait." Plaintiff heard the statement, which contained highly lascivious portions. On October 14, 2016, Plaintiff moved out of her housing with the campaign and, two days later, emailed the head of human resources for the campaign to let her know that Plaintiff was leaving the campaign. Plaintiff alleges she has suffered damages by the battery, and she seeks money damages for her injury.

Though this simple battery appears to have lasted perhaps 10–15 seconds, Plaintiff has spent 29 pages and 115 paragraphs in the Complaint setting it forth. Many of these allegations describe 19 unrelated incidents involving women upon whom Defendant Trump allegedly committed nonconsensual acts, over the past four decades with differing circumstances.

These 19 separate incidents, all of which Plaintiff seeks to prove through discovery and use at trial, vary in terms of age and circumstance. Most of the incidents do not resemble the present allegation; some do. For example, Plaintiff hopes to prove and introduce at trial evidence that Defendant Trump "was like an octopus" when groping one woman on a commercial flight in the early 1980s, or that 15 years before the instant claim he entered a dressing room where beauty contestants were unclothed. These allegations, salacious and in florid language, appear to come from media reports. Indeed, in attempting to set forth a cause of action for simple battery, the Complaint cites approximately 40 different media reports or newspaper articles.

A court may strike from a pleading "any redundant, immaterial, impertinent, or scandalous matter." Fed. R. Civ. P. 12(f). Courts have "broad discretion" in this determination. The motion's purpose is "to clean up the pleadings, streamline litigation, and avoid unnecessary forays into immaterial matters."

Even if the above allegations do not constitute a "scandalous matter," they are nonetheless immaterial and impertinent to Plaintiff's simple battery claim. Plaintiff argues that evidence of such prior incidents will be admissible under Rule 404(b) of the Federal Rules of Evidence to prove Defendant Trump's motive, intent, knowledge, and absence of mistake for the battery. In other words, these prior incidents would establish Defendant's actionable state of mind because he committed such acts in the past.

To find as Plaintiff urges would ignore the first line of that rule, which states: "**Prohibited Uses.** Evidence of a crime, wrong, or other act is not admissible to prove a person's character in order to show that on a particular occasion the person acted in accordance with the character." Fed. R. Evid. 404(b) (emphasis in original). Defendants rightly suggest that this claim of 404(b) admissibility runs afoul of the basic admonition:

> In order … to admit evidence under Rule 404(b), a court must be able to articulate a way in which the tendered evidence logically tends to establish or refute a material fact in issue, and that chain of logic must include no link involving an inference that a bad person is disposed to do bad acts.

Plaintiff counters that whether this evidence is admissible at trial is a matter for a motion in limine or for summary judgment. But Plaintiff does not cite to any persuasive authority that has allowed potential Rule 404(b) material to be pled in the Complaint, and the cases that Plaintiff does rely on for 404(b) admissibility are distinguishable.

Plaintiff next argues that the prior incidents are offered to establish habit and would therefore be admissible under Rule 406 of the Federal Rules of Evidence. Although the Eleventh Circuit has noted "[t]he difficulty in distinguishing inadmissible character evidence from admissible habit evidence," Plaintiff's allegations plainly do not constitute proper proof of habit; they are, again, proof of character or propensity. In essence, Plaintiff seeks to prove that Defendant acted in conformity with an alleged character and propensity to commit nonconsensual acts on August 24, 2016 at the Tampa rally. Rule 404(a) of the Federal Rules of Evidence bars such evidence.

To paraphrase Dean McCormick [McCORMICK ON EVIDENCE] character and habit are "close akin." Character is a generalized description of one's disposition with respect to a general trait; habit, on the other hand, is more specific and describes one's regular and repeated response to a recurring event. This might include descending a particular stairway two stairs at a time, giving the hand signal for a left turn, alighting from railway cars while they are moving, or, * * * * a regular practice of drinking at work. This habitual action might become semi-autonomous. * * * * In other words, a habit is a behavior repeated so often as to become a reflex.

Judge Weinstein characterizes habit as more than a tendency to act in a given manner; it is a degree of uniform response that requires semi-automatic conduct. 2 WEINSTEIN'S FEDERAL EVIDENCE at 406-3 and n.5 (2d ed. 2019). Weinstein further observes that "prior criminal acts do not constitute admissible evidence of a 'habit' to commit those acts." Indeed, the acts alleged here (including some from the early 1980s and 1990s and dissimilar to the alleged kiss) no more establish habit than did the four prior convictions for public intoxication spanning a 3.5-year period in *Reyes v. Missouri Pac. R.R. Co.*, 589 F.2d 791 (5th Cir. 1979).

Plaintiff wishes to prove that over the past 35-plus years Defendant acted inappropriately with other women in a wide variety of circumstances. In fact, Plaintiff alleges that only one of the 19 prior incidents happened during the presidential campaign. At least as alleged here, an individual's decision to make a romantic advance when that individual determines an opportunity has presented itself is not such a regular, unthinking response. And even if such an action is in line with the individual's character, evidence of that character is inadmissible.

Plaintiff's allegations, accepted as true at this stage in litigation, do not establish admissible evidence of Defendant Trump's habit to commit battery against women. It is instead character evidence unsaved by Rule 406 of the Federal Rules of Evidence. As that rule's advisory committee notes state: "Much evidence is excluded simply because of failure to achieve the status of habit.... [E]vidence of other assaults is inadmissible to prove the instant one in a civil assault action." (citing Annot., 66 A.L.R. 2d 806). This is unchanged by Plaintiff's argument that such evidence is necessary because Defendants have proffered that the witnesses will favor Defendant Trump. The Federal Rules of Evidence must still apply.

Plaintiff also argues that the 19 other incidents, or at least a portion of them, are relevant to Plaintiff's punitive damages claim. Although Plaintiff has stated a claim for unconsented contact, this simple battery does not, as alleged, equate to the malicious conduct sufficient to support punitive damages. For example, the conduct alleged would be insufficient to support a sexual harassment or hostile work environment claim under Title VII of the Civil Rights Act of 1964, 42 U.S.C. § 2000. Plaintiff's lawyer acknowledged this at the hearing. It would be incongruous to find that, at least as alleged here, conduct which fails to state a claim for sexual harassment would be so outrageous and oppressive to entitle the victim to punitive damages in tort. Perhaps some behavior of Defendant Trump vis-à-vis Plaintiff will be established during discovery that would support punitive damages for this battery, but none is currently pled.

Furthermore, apart from the evidence's questionable admissibility and obfuscation of the instant cause of action (or, put differently, its immateriality under Rule 12(f)), setting the many allegations forth in this manner is contrary to Rule 8(a) of the Federal Rules of Civil Procedure and, at best, constitutes surplusage. Indeed, Plaintiff has brought a lengthy philippic, not a "short and plain statement of the grounds … [and] claim showing that the pleader is entitled to relief." Fed. R. Civ. P. 8(a). All of the 19 prior instances against individuals other than Plaintiff are stricken from the Complaint, and Plaintiff may not reallege them in an amended complaint.

AS TO COUNTS TWO AND THREE:

Plaintiff brings Count II against DJTPI under the Fair Labor Standards Act, 29 U.S.C. § 206, *et seq.* ("FLSA"), as amended by the Equal Pay Act of 1963. Plaintiff alleges that she was paid less than similarly situated male colleagues because of her gender. *See Steger v. Gen. Elec. Co.*, 318 F.3d 1066, 1077–78 (11th Cir. 2003) (citation omitted) ("An employee demonstrates a prima facie case of an Equal Pay Act violation by showing that the employer paid employees of opposite genders different wages for equal work for jobs which require 'equal skill, effort, and responsibility, and which are performed under similar working conditions.'"). Plaintiff also seeks a court-produced notice to potential co-plaintiffs, to solicit joinder and a collective action as contemplated by 29 U.S.C. § 216(b). Plaintiff requests declaratory and injunctive relief in addition to money damages. Count III is against DJTPI for wage-based race discrimination under 42 U.S.C. § 1981.

DJTPI moves to dismiss Counts II and III. To survive a motion to dismiss under Rule 12(b)(6) of the Federal Rules of Civil Procedure, a plaintiff must plead sufficient facts to state a claim that is "plausible on its face." *Ashcroft v. Iqbal*, 556 U.S. 662, 678 (2009). Courts should limit their "consideration to the well-pleaded factual allegations, documents central to or referenced in the complaint, and matters judicially noticed.

For Count II, DJTPI correctly argues that Plaintiff's allegations fail to establish FLSA coverage under either an "enterprise" or "individual" coverage theory. It is, first of all, unclear whether enterprise coverage can apply to a political campaign. 29 U.S.C. § 203(r)(1) (defining "enterprise" as "the related activities performed … by any person or persons for a common *business* purpose"). * * * *

Secondly, while Plaintiff does plead some facts that are relevant to the question of individual coverage, she does not plead with sufficient specificity to establish such coverage. It is not enough for Plaintiff as an employee to use the instrumentalities of interstate commerce; she must *regularly* use them. For example, while organizing the travel of recreational vehicles and purchasing out-of-state supplies for the campaign may be relevant, so too is the frequency and scope of this work. Moreover, any interstate nexus as it relates to conducting outreach, opening volunteer offices, and organizing rallies is not clear from the face of the Complaint.

Ultimately, how and why the FLSA applies to DJTPI is a predicate for an Equal Pay Act claim and should be clearly stated. Plaintiff must set this forth in factual detail in an amended complaint, whether she seeks coverage through an enterprise or individual theory, or both.

With respect to the § 1981 claim, Plaintiff must prove that DJTPI engaged in "purposeful discrimination." As such, a showing of disparate impact through a neutral practice alone is insufficient. At this stage, Plaintiff's allegations must "support a reasonable expectation that discovery would reveal evidence that [DJTPI] acted with racially-discriminatory animus." While disparity in wages can serve as evidence of purposeful discrimination, Plaintiff must nonetheless allege that Defendant DJTPI acted with such intent.

Although the Court need not presently resolve the issue, DJTPI also argues that Plaintiff's "comparators" for Counts II and III are insufficient both in detail and in job duty comparison. * * *

Lastly, DJTPI argues that the Complaint does not identify or sufficiently describe the purported collective members for Count II, and that no collective action may proceed without greater specificity. The Court prefers that the parties litigate the bona fides of the asserted collective action at the certification stage. However, should Plaintiff amend Count II of her Complaint, she would be well-advised to provide more detail concerning potential collective joiners in addition to the wage comparators.

Accordingly, it is **ORDERED**:

The Court grants Defendants' motions. The Complaint is dismissed without prejudice. Plaintiff may file an amended complaint within thirty days. Plaintiff should allege a simple battery in ten or fewer pages, including relevant factual allegations. Plaintiff should omit all reference to other incidents beyond her own alleged battery and omit any quotes from the press or media reports in her complaint.

The employment discrimination claims in Counts II and III, including relevant factual allegations, may not exceed fifteen pages in total. * * *

———————

Second is the complaint filed by Jane Doe—or actually more than one complaint—in *Doe v. Trump and Epstein*, Southern District of New York. The first complaint was filed June 20, 2016, and voluntarily dismissed on September 16, 2016. The second complaint, with the same allegations, was filed two weeks later, on September 30, 2016, and dismissed on November 4, 2016, a few days before the 2016 election.

The complaint is harrowing in its detail, but in essence, it alleges that in 1994, the plaintiff, 13 years old, was "enticed by promises of money and a modeling career to attend a series of parties" at the New York City residence of Jeffrey Epstein. It avers that Trump forcibly raped her, including violently striking her, and threatened her if she revealed the incident. It also avers that Epstein thereafter brutally raped her and likewise threatened her and her family. The complaint seeks a tolling of the statute of limitations based on the continuing threats.

The complaint also includes a count for defamation, based on Trump's statements reacting to a complaint filed pro se in California federal court in April 2016 including substantially the same allegations. The complaint avers that Trump provided a statement that read "The allegations are not only categorically false, but disgusting at the highest level and clearly framed to solicit media attention or, perhaps, are simply politically motivated. There is absolutely no merit to these allegations. Period." As the complaint represents, this statement was published in the media, including American Media, Inc. (A.M.I.) and its subsidiary, Radar Online, see *Trump Sued By Teen 'Sex Slave' For Alleged 'Rape' — Donald Blasts 'Disgusting' Suit,* Radar (April 26, 2016), https://radaronline.com/exclusives/2016/04/donald-trump-sued-sexual-abuse-jeffrey-epstein-claims/.

Jeffrey Epstein, the other defendant in the lawsuit, is a controversial figure. He was charged with sex acts with underage girls and did spend some time in a Florida jail in 2008. But this state sentence was pursuant to a plea deal including a grant of federal immunity to himself and "any potential co-conspirators" arranged by federal prosecutors, including the then-United States Attorney for the Southern District of Florida, Alexander Acosta, who became the Secretary of Labor in Donald Trump's administration. There has been much recent litigation and many media reports surrounding the plea deal and its consequences. One particularly important case started as a defamation suit by Virginia Roberts Giuffre, who as a sixteen-year-old was working at Trump's Florida resort, Mar-a-Lago, against Ghislane Maxwell. As recounted by the district judge:

> In early 2011 Giuffre, in an interview with journalist Sharon Churcher which was published in two British tabloids, described Maxwell's alleged role as someone who recruited or facilitated the recruitment of young females for sexual activity with Jeffrey Epstein that she, Giuffre, had been interviewed by the Federal Bureau of Investigation in 2011, and that she had discussed Maxwell's involvement in the described sexual abuse. Maxwell issued a statement denying this account on March 9, 2011.

> On January 1, 2015, Giuffre moved to join two alleged victims of Epstein who had initiated an action under the Crime Victims' Rights Act against the United States, purporting to challenge Epstein's plea agreement. Giuffre's joinder motion included numerous details about Giuffre's sexual abuse and listed the perpetrators of her abuse. Giuffre repeatedly named Maxwell in the Joinder Motion as being personally involved in the sexual abuse and sex trafficking scheme created by Epstein.

> On January 3, 2015, Maxwell again issued a statement, responding to the allegations made in connection with Giuffre's Joinder Motion. Maxwell stated that Giuffre's allegations "against Ghislaine Maxwell are untrue" and that Giuffre's "claims are obvious lies."

> Giuffre filed her complaint in this action on September 21, 2015 setting forth her claim of defamation by Maxwell arising out of the Maxwell January 3 Statement. Giuffre alleged she was the "victim of sexual trafficking and abuse while she was a minor child" and that Maxwell "facilitated" Giuffre's sexual abuse and "wrongfully" subjected Giuffre to "public ridicule, contempt and

disgrace" by denying Giuffre's allegations. Giuffre further alleged that over the course of a decade she had been sexually abused at "numerous locations" around the world with prominent and politically powerful men.

Vigorous litigation was undertaken by the parties, as demonstrated by the 950 docket entries as of August 27, 2018, including a motion to dismiss the Complaint which was denied by opinion of February 29, 2016. The primary issue presented was the truth or falsity of the January 3 statement issued by Maxwell, which in turn challenged all the previous statements made to the press by Giuffre and in Giuffre's Joinder Motion. This resulted, understandably, in a lengthy and tumultuous discovery process resulting in 18 hearings and 15 decisions.

Giuffre v. Maxwell, 325 F. Supp. 3d 428, 433–34 (S.D.N.Y. 2018), *vacated and remanded sub nom. Brown v. Maxwell*, No. 16-3945-CV, 2019 WL 2814839 (2d Cir. July 3, 2019).

The tumultuous discovery process included protective orders sealing the case material. The two women—Giuffre and Maxwell—eventually settled the defamation claim in May 2017 under undisclosed terms. However, a reporter and the Miami Herald filed a motion to intervene seeking to unseal the case materials. While the district judge denied the motion to unseal, the Second Circuit reversed in its opinion in *Brown v. Maxwell*, 2019 WL 2814839, on July 3, 2019. The court held that with respect to documents submitted to the court for its consideration in a summary judgment motion, it is well-settled that such materials "are—as a matter of law—judicial documents to which a strong presumption of access attaches, under both the common law and the First Amendment," and after reviewing the materials found that "there is no countervailing privacy interest sufficient to justify their continued sealing," and should be unsealed. As to the other materials submitted to the court, which are discovery materials related to motions to compel testimony, to quash trial subpoenae, and to exclude certain deposition testimony, the court held that these too bear a presumption of disclosure, although under a somewhat lower presumption than that applied to summary judgment materials. The court found the district court abused its discretion in not conducting an individualized review of each document and remanded to the district judge to conduct such a review of "the thousands of pages at issue. Interestingly, the court stated:

We conclude with a note of caution to the public regarding the reliability of court filings such as those unsealed today.

Materials submitted by parties to a court should be understood for what they are. They do not reflect the court's own findings. Rather, they are prepared by parties seeking to advance their own interests in an adversarial process. Although affidavits and depositions are offered "under penalty of perjury," it is in fact exceedingly rare for anyone to be prosecuted for perjury in a civil proceeding. Similarly, pleadings, complaints, and briefs—while supposedly based on underlying evidentiary material—can be misleading. Such documents sometimes draw dubious inferences from already questionable material or present ambiguous material as definitive.

Brown v. Maxwell, 2019 WL 2814839.

The court added that court filings could be "particularly susceptible to fraud," because under the applicable New York law of defamation, there is "absolute immunity from liability" for oral or written statements made "in connection with a proceeding before a court." Thus, the court urged "the media to exercise restraint in covering potentially defamatory allegations" and cautioned "the public to read such accounts with discernment." *Brown v. Maxwell*, No. 16-3945-CV, 2019 WL 2814839, at *9 (2d Cir. July 3, 2019)

On July 5, 2019, Jeffrey Epstein was arrested returning to the country. The indictment accused him of counts of sex trafficking conspiracy and sex trafficking related to sexual interactions with minor girls at his "mansion in New York" and his "estate in Palm Beach, Florida." The indictment is available here: https://int.nyt.com/data/documenthelper/1362-epstein-indictment/01e39b8c091cbeac3797/optimized/full.pdf. The indictment references Minor Victim 1, 2, and 3, and Employee 1, 2, and 3, but does not specifically identify other people.

A day after the Second Circuit released about 2,000 pages of documents in *Brown v. Maxwell*, Jeffrey Epstein was found dead in his solitary cell in a federal detention facility in New York where he was being held without bail, an "apparent suicide." *Jeffrey Epstein Dead in Suicide at Jail, Spurring Inquiries*, New York Times (August 10, 2019), https://www.nytimes.com/2019/08/10/nyregion/jeffrey-epstein-suicide.html.

Notes and Questions

1. *Scope of Discovery.* If you represented either Alva Johnson or Donald Trump, how would you argue that there should or should not be discovery about other women who say that they had been subjected to similar conduct by Donald Trump? Is this different from how you would argue, under the Federal Rules of Evidence Judge Jung discusses, whether or not such evidence would be admissible? Consider Federal Rule of Evidence 215 entitled "Similar Acts in Civil Cases Involving Sexual Assault or Child Molestation," which provides that a judge *may* admit evidence that the party committed any other sexual assault (emphasis added). Recall that the district judge in *Clinton v. Jones* allowed extensive discovery, including questions about any woman with whom Bill Clinton may have had been sexually involved. Does that hurt or help the argument for either Johnson or Trump?

2. *Scope of Special Counsel.* As the Mueller Report made clear, it did not investigate allegations of sexual misconduct by Trump and this was a subject outside its charge. Given all the allegations, including those of Jane Doe, would you argue that a Special Counsel should be appointed to investigate sexual misconduct by the President? Would this be limited to acts after he became President? Would it include statements made by the President? If you were writing the charge to Special Counsel, how would you phrase it? If you worked in the office of such a Special Counsel, what three questions would you want answered and why?